Ivan William Taylor

System Dynamics

Also of Interest

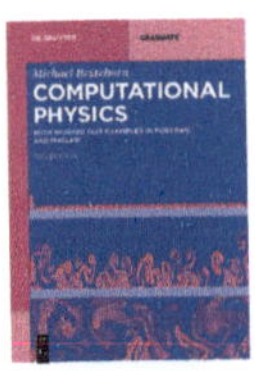

Computational Physics.
With Worked Out Examples in FORTRAN® and MATLAB®
Michael Bestehorn, 2nd edition, 2023
ISBN 978-3-11-078236-3, e-ISBN (PDF) 978-3-11-078252-3,
e-ISBN (EPUB) 978-3-11-078266-0

Environmental Data Analysis.
Methods and Applications
Zhihua Zhang, 2nd edition, 2023
ISBN 978-3-11-101254-4, e-ISBN (PDF) 978-3-11-101268-1,
e-ISBN (EPUB) 978-3-11-101291-9

MATLAB® Programming.
Mathematical Problem Solutions
Dingyü Xue, 2020
ISBN 978-3-11-066356-3, e-ISBN (PDF) 978-3-11-066695-3,
e-ISBN (EPUB) 978-3-11-066370-9

Calculus Problem Solutions with MATLAB®
Dingyü Xue, 2020
ISBN 978-3-11-066362-4, e-ISBN (PDF) 978-3-11-066697-7,
e-ISBN (EPUB) 978-3-11-066375-4

Computational Methods for Data Analysis
Yeliz Karaca, Carlo Cattani, 2019
ISBN 978-3-11-049635-2, e-ISBN (PDF) 978-3-11-049636-9,
e-ISBN (EPUB) 978-3-11-049360-3

Ivan William Taylor

System Dynamics

Modelling and Simulation with Excel

DE GRUYTER

Author
Ivan William Taylor, PhD
Policy Dynamics Inc.
8 Heather Place,
New Hamburg, Ontario
Canada N3A 2G5
ivan@policydynamics.ca

ISBN 978-3-11-154085-6
ISBN 978-3-11-154138-9 (PDF)
ISBN 978-3-11-154225-6 (EPUB)

Library of Congress Control Number: 2026932253

Bibliographic information published by the Deutsche Nationalbibliothek
The Deutsche Nationalbibliothek lists this publication in the Deutsche Nationalbibliografie;
detailed bibliographic data are available on the internet at http://dnb.dnb.de.

De Gruyter and Walter de Gruyter GmbH are part of De Gruyter Brill.
www.degruyterbrill.com

Questions about General Product Safety Regulation:
productsafety@degruyterbrill.com

Cover illustration: Petrovich9/iStock/Getty Images Plus
Printing: CPI books GmbH, Leck

Contents

Introduction to Part 1: **Building System Dynamics Models in Excel**

This book teaches you how to build system dynamics models using Excel. We begin with the basics, including how things increase or decrease over time (stocks and flows), feedback loops, and the concepts of exponential growth and decline. You'll learn by doing, starting with simple models and gradually adding complexity.

Each chapter builds on the last, using real examples and hands-on Excel exercises. You don't need any prior experience. Follow along, and you'll pick up the skills as you go.

The focus here is practical. We're not just explaining theory; we're giving you tools to build and test models in Excel, a programme you probably already know. Whether a student, researcher or working professional, these skills will help you analyse systems and make better decisions using real data.

Here's what you'll learn:

- Chapter 2: Build your first system dynamics model in Excel
- Chapter 3: Understand how things grow and shrink over time
- Chapter 4: Work with changing rates using a goal-gap model
- Chapter 5: Make predictions with your model
- Chapter 6: Match your model's results to real-world data
- Chapter 7: Use lookup tables to add flexibility to your models
- Chapter 8: Model delays in a system

By the end of Part 1, you can build and analyse system dynamics models in Excel. That sets you up for Part 2, where you'll see how these techniques were applied to real-world problems. The working models developed for this book are available at https://github.com/ivanwtaylor/Excel-Book.

https://doi.org/10.1515/9783111541389-001

Chapter 1
Introduction

1.1 Learning Objectives

- Summarize the origins and milestones of system dynamics (SD) (Forrester, Meadows, society formation, Senge, and Sterman).
- Define systems, feedback, stocks, flows, and non-linear behaviour.
- Differentiate between reinforcing and balancing feedback and explain the practical implications of each.
- Explain why time delays matter and identify typical sources of delay in policy and operations.
- Distinguish qualitative (causal loop diagrams, CLDs) from quantitative (stock and flow diagrams, SFDs) models; distinguish exploratory versus calibrated quantitative models.
- Articulate where system dynamics adds value across sectors and for scenario/sensitivity analysis.
- State when Excel is sufficient versus when to use specialized SD tools, and map SD variables to rows/columns in Excel.
- Describe Euler integration at a high level and why the time step size (e.g. powers of two) affects accuracy.

1.2 A Quick History of System Dynamics

Before building models in Excel, it is helpful to understand the origins of system dynamics and its significance. The story starts in the 1950s at MIT. Professor Jay W. Forrester developed system dynamics to understand how systems behave over time, especially those involving feedback loops and time delays.

Forrester published *Industrial Dynamics* in 1961 [1], demonstrating how this approach could be applied to understand complex business and industrial systems. But he didn't stop there. He expanded his work to broader issues in the late 1960s and early 1970s, using system dynamics to explore urban development [2] and global sustainability [3].

Then came *The Limits to Growth*, written by Donella Meadows and her colleagues in 1972 [4]. This book applied Forrester's ideas to the entire planet, examining how unlimited growth could strain Earth's finite resources. It sparked global conversations about sustainability that continue to this day.

In 1983, the System Dynamics Society was established to bring together researchers, educators, and practitioners [5]. That same year, the first annual System Dynamics

https://doi.org/10.1515/9783111541389-002

Conference was held, providing the community with a regular forum to share ideas and advance the field [6].

As the field grew, so did the tools. Software like Vensim [7], Stella [8], and Powersim [9] made building and running models easier by eliminating the need for programming, helping more people explore system dynamics.

In the 1990s, Peter Senge helped bring system dynamics to a broader audience with his book *The Fifth Discipline*, which focussed on systems thinking in organizations [10]. Around the same time, John Sterman published *Business Dynamics* in 2000, a textbook that has become a go-to resource for learning the fundamentals of system dynamics [11]. Sterman's teaching at MIT has trained a new generation of systems thinkers and modellers.

Figure 1.1 gives you a visual timeline of these key books.

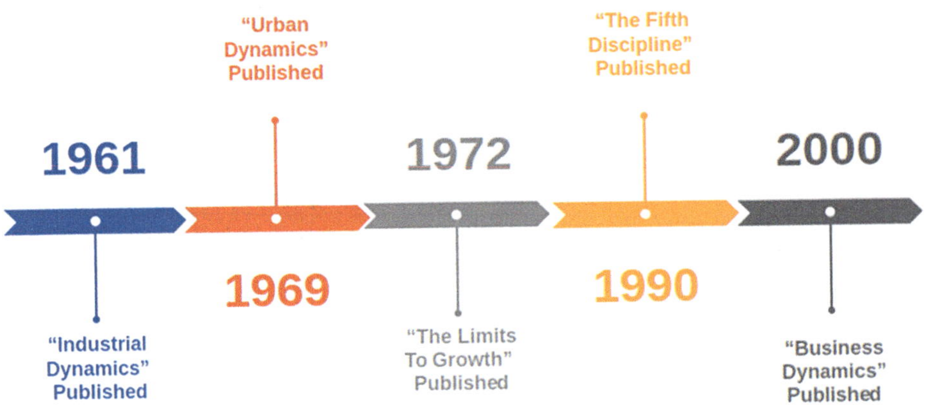

Fig. 1.1: Evolution of system dynamics.

1.3 What Do We Mean by "System Dynamics?"

Before jumping into modelling, let's break down what *system dynamics* means.

First, a *system* is simply a collection of interconnected components that work together to achieve a specific goal. You'll find systems everywhere (e.g. natural ecosystems, businesses, economies, supply chains, and traffic patterns). What makes something a system is how the parts interact, not just the parts themselves. Every system has its structure, patterns of behaviour, and relationships between its components.

The *dynamics* part refers to how the system changes over time. What happens when something is added, removed, delayed, or sped up? How do the parts react to one another as conditions shift? In many systems, outputs loop back and influence future inputs. This is *feedback*.

This is where system dynamics stands out. Unlike other modelling approaches that focus on linear cause-and-effect relationships, system dynamics focusses on feedback loops and time delays, which often lead to surprising ways that actions ripple through a system. Sometimes, a small change has a significant impact, while a major move might barely make a difference. That's the kind of non-linear behaviour that system dynamics helps us understand.

Two key ideas (stocks and flows) are at the core of this approach. We use these to track how things change over time:

- *Stocks* are the stuff that accumulates in a system. Think of the amount of water in a reservoir, money in a bank account, or people in a population.
- *Flows* are the rates at which that stuff changes, what's coming in and going out. For example, rainfall adds water to the reservoir (an inflow), and water flowing out through a dam reduces the water level (an outflow).

Figure 1.2 illustrates a basic example: a reservoir that collects water from rivers and directs it into downstream channels. It's simple, but it illustrates the core idea: stocks go up or down based on flows, and that interaction drives system behaviour over time.

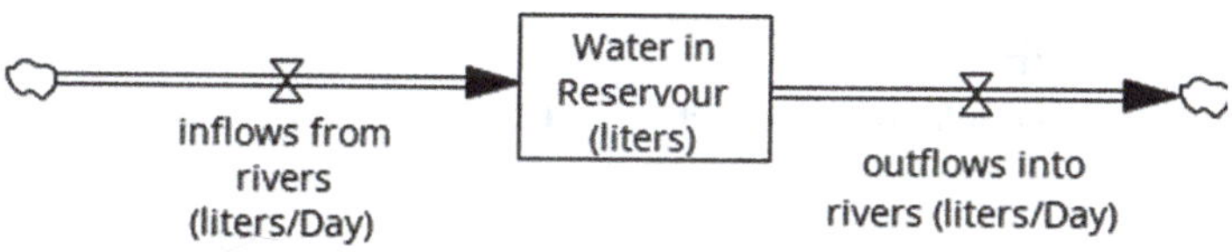

Fig. 1.2: Stock and flow diagram.

Understanding stocks and flows is the first step towards seeing how systems behave and how to change that behaviour smartly. Once you start thinking this way, you'll see these patterns everywhere.

1.3.1 Seeing the World in Loops

One of the big ideas behind system dynamics is thinking in terms of *feedback*. Instead of viewing cause and effect as a straight line, we consider it a loop where the effect becomes a cause of further change. That is, where changes in one part of a system eventually affect that same part again. These *feedback loops* are what give systems their dynamic, often unpredictable behaviour.

There are two types of feedback loops: *reinforcing* and *balancing*.

Reinforcing loops push things in the same direction, creating growth (or decline) that feeds on itself. A classic example is population growth. As the population grows, more births occur, which in turn increase the population even further. That leads to more births, and so on. Unless something slows it down, this loop can lead to exponential growth. It's a self-reinforcing cycle.

Balancing loops, on the other hand, work like brakes. They try to maintain stability by pushing back when things go too far. Consider a thermostat in your home. The heater kicks in when the temperature drops below the set level, warming things up. Once the room hits the target temperature, the heater turns off. This back-and-forth keeps the room from getting too cold or hot. This is a perfect example of a balancing loop.

By identifying these loops that either drive growth or maintain stability, we can better predict how systems behave. More importantly, we can design more innovative interventions that work *with* these natural patterns rather than against them.

Figure 1.3 illustrates two simple loops: one reinforcing loop between population and births, and one balancing loop that controls temperature by utilizing the gap between the current and desired levels. These are basic examples, but they lay the groundwork for understanding much more complex systems later.

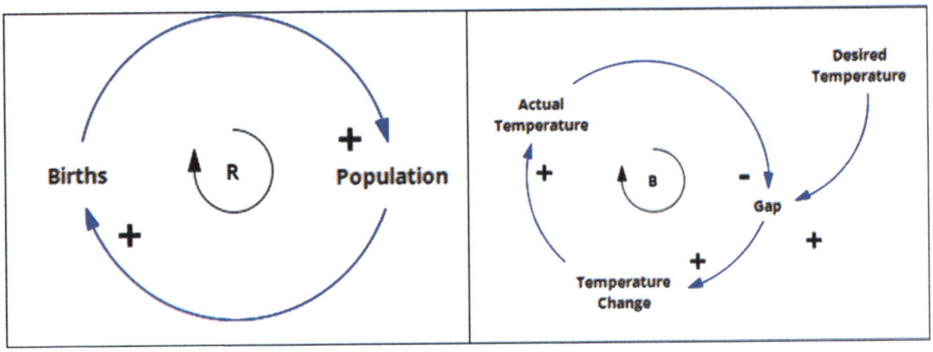

Fig. 1.3: Example: Reinforcing and balancing feedback loops.

1.3.2 Why Delays Matter

Another key component of system dynamics is the consideration of *time delays*. These happen when there's a gap between doing something and seeing the result. And they're everywhere in real-life systems.

Delays often throw people off. You take action, but nothing changes immediately, so it's easy to think it didn't work or that something else is happening. This can lead to bad decisions or overreactions because you're not yet seeing the whole picture.

Take policymaking, for example. Let's say a new education policy is rolled out. You won't see better test scores the next day. First, the curriculum must be updated, teachers need time to adjust, and students must go through the system before any real impact can be made. That process can take years (see Fig. 1.4). But just because you don't see results right away doesn't mean the policy isn't working; it just means you have to wait.

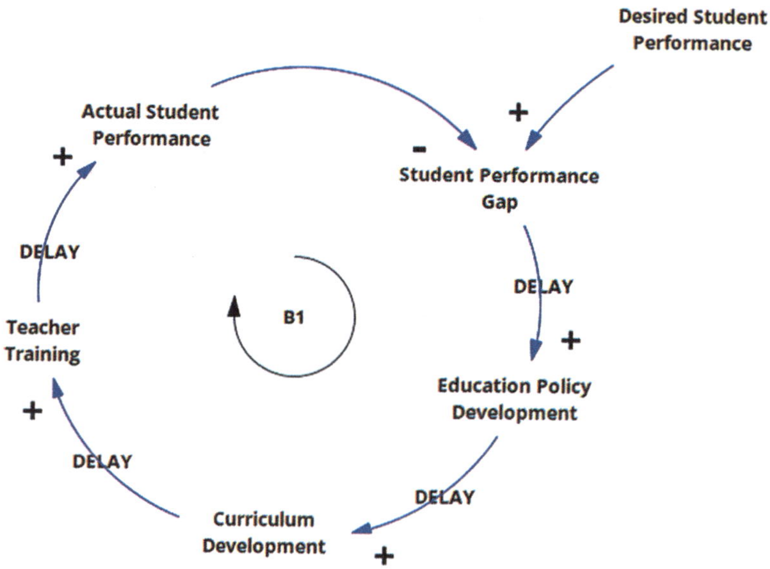

Fig. 1.4: Time delays in the development and implementation of education policy.

Understanding time delays helps us manage expectations and avoid jumping to conclusions. It also allows us to design better strategies that consider when change will happen, not just when we want it to.

1.3.3 Two Ways to Model: Qualitative and Quantitative

System dynamics can be approached in two ways (*qualitatively* and *quantitatively),* and both have their place depending on what you're trying to do.

Qualitative models, on the one hand, use Causal Loop Diagram (CLDs). These diagrams help you map out how different system parts are connected. Each arrow shows a cause-and-effect relationship, either positive (both variables move in the same direction) or negative (they move in opposite directions). By examining how everything is interconnected, you can identify feedback loops and comprehend how the system functions. CLDs are an excellent tool for thinking through a system before crunching numbers.

Quantitative models, on the other hand, use Stock and Flow Diagram (SFDs). These define all the variables, including the equations and parameter values. Quantitative models come in two flavours: *exploratory* and *calibrated.*

– Exploratory models are structured thought experiments. You start with your mental model of how a system works, write it out with equations, and see what happens. These models help you test your assumptions and see where they lead.

Since everything's defined explicitly, anyone else can examine your model, examine your beliefs, and run their tests.
- Calibrated models are more grounded. Here, you collect real-world data – usually historical time series – and fine-tune your model to fit it. The goal is to demonstrate that your model can replicate the patterns we've observed. Calibration enables you to estimate parameter values when data is limited or noisy, thereby making your model more realistic and accurate. Calibration gives us confidence that our model can be used for projecting future behaviour.

In this book, we'll focus on *quantitative* system dynamics models – both exploratory and calibrated – and show you how to build them in Excel [12]. We'll start with simple models in the early chapters and then gradually work up to more complex ones through real-world case studies. Whether you're testing ideas or building data-backed simulations, Excel allows you to do both.

1.4 Why System Dynamics Matters (and Where It's Used)

System dynamics isn't just for academic exercises. It's used in various fields to make sense of complex problems. It is so powerful because it helps you see the *big picture* – not just the individual parts, but also how they interact, often in ways that aren't obvious at first.

One of the primary uses of system dynamics is to predict how systems behave over time. By running *scenario analyses*, you can test different assumptions and explore how various conditions might impact the outcome. This kind of thinking is beneficial for long-term planning and strategic decision-making. It helps organizations anticipate problems before they occur, determine which strategies are most likely to be effective, and assess the resilience of their plans and strategies.

Sensitivity analysis is another valuable tool in this space that identifies the variables with the most significant impact on the system [13]. That way, you can focus your attention (and your resources) where they'll make the most difference.

System dynamics is also widely used for policy analysis and design. Governments use it to evaluate the impact of changes in healthcare [14], the environment [15], and economic policy [16]. For example, in healthcare, models can help optimize hospital staffing, reduce patient wait times, and improve overall care [17]. In public health, it's used to simulate the spread of diseases and to determine which control strategies might be most effective [18].

In environmental planning, system dynamics models help assess the impact of climate change [19] and guide the development of sustainable practices, such as more effective management of water, energy, or land use [20].

It plays a significant role in improving supply chains, forecasting demand, managing inventory, and avoiding bottlenecks in business and management. Companies also use it to better understand how employee behaviour and management decisions affect performance [21]. Marketing teams use it to track consumer behaviour and plan campaigns more strategically.

System dynamics is also valuable for engineering and infrastructure projects. Urban planners use it to simulate cities' growth and determine future transportation or housing needs [22]. Transportation systems utilize it to reduce traffic congestion, enhance public transit, and lower emissions.

Even in education, system dynamics has value. It's used to model how changes in education policy might affect outcomes years down the line, helping policymakers make more intelligent decisions about where and how to invest [23].

Figure 1.5 provides a snapshot of the widespread application of system dynamics, based on a Google Scholar search of keywords across these fields.

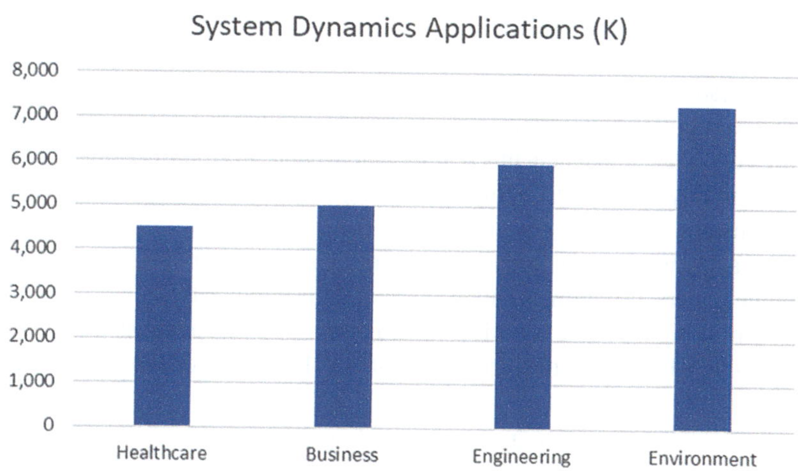

Fig. 1.5: Application areas of system dynamics.

Of course, system dynamics isn't perfect. Like any tool, it comes with its own set of challenges. One big hurdle is obtaining accurate data, especially when validating a model. Sometimes, the data doesn't exist, is incomplete, or is messy. Another challenge is managing complexity. As your model grows, it can become increasingly complex to follow and even more challenging to explain. If it's too complicated, people might not trust it, or worse, they might ignore it entirely.

That's why communication is key. Even the best model won't have much impact if you can't clearly explain what it shows or why it matters. Making the results easy to understand and relevant to your audience is just as crucial as getting the math right.

One of the strengths of system dynamics is that it works well even when you don't have tons of data. It helps you think through how a system works, what's causing what, where the delays are, and how different parts of the system push against or reinforce each other. It's great for understanding *why* things happen, not just *what's* happening.

That said, combining system dynamics with data science offers significant value. Data science involves analysing large datasets to identify patterns and trends. When you combine the two, you get the best of both worlds: the deep structural insight from system dynamics and the detailed evidence from data science.

System dynamics offers a comprehensive view of how everything fits together, while data science helps refine the model and supports it with real-world data. Together, they make a powerful team for better, evidence-based decision-making. You get models that are both conceptually solid and grounded in actual data.

1.5 Tools of the Trade: System Dynamics Software (and Why Excel Still Matters)

To build and run system dynamics models, you typically need specialized software. These tools help you simulate how systems behave over time, and most come with user-friendly interfaces that make modelling much more manageable, even for beginners.

The most commonly used tools include Stella [8], AnyLogic [24], Powersim [9], Vensim [7], and Insight Maker [25]. While it's difficult to determine precisely how many people use each one, Fig. 1.6 shows the frequency with which they've been mentioned in academic papers, providing a rough sense of their popularity.

Stella is known for being super intuitive. Its drag-and-drop setup makes it easy to build models visually, which is particularly beneficial for beginners or those teaching

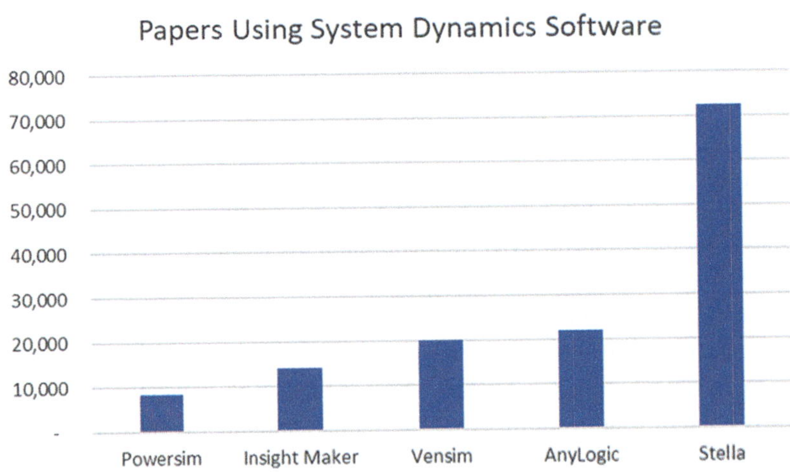

Fig. 1.6: Studies using system dynamics software.

system dynamics. You can create causal loop diagrams and stock-and-flow models without writing any code. It's widely used in schools, universities, and businesses for planning and forecasting.

AnyLogic stands out for its flexibility. It's the only one that lets you combine system dynamics with other modelling approaches, such as discrete-event simulation and agent-based modelling, within a single model. It even supports 2D and 3D visualizations, which helps when you show your model to people who aren't into technical details. AnyLogic is widely used in the healthcare, logistics, manufacturing, and transportation industries.

Vensim is a favourite for large, data-heavy models. It can handle complex systems, run sensitivity analyses, and perform optimization tasks. Vensim is often used in academic research, policy work, and large-scale industrial modelling. In this book, we will use Vensim to build the stock-and-flow diagrams for our models.

Insight Maker is entirely cloud-based, so you can access it from anywhere and easily collaborate with others. It features a simple, intuitive interface that works well for both beginners and experienced modellers. One of its key features is the ability to share models online, making it an ideal tool for teaching, research, and group projects. It's often used in ecology, economics, and organizational behaviour.

Powersim is designed for real-time simulation and works well with other software and databases. It's helpful for decision support in fast-paced environments, such as logistics, energy, or manufacturing, where up-to-date data is needed to guide your next move.

Each tool has its strengths:
- Stella is great for learning and visual modelling.
- AnyLogic is all about flexibility and combining methods.
- Vensim is perfect for detailed, analytical work.
- Insight Maker is great for collaboration and accessibility.
- Powersim excels at real-time, data-driven decisions.

So, where does Excel fit into all of this?

Surprisingly, Excel is a fantastic companion tool for system dynamics. While it's not a dedicated modelling platform, it's beneficial for managing data, doing fundamental analysis, visualizing results, and sharing your work, especially with people who don't use specialized software. Plus, almost everyone already has access to it. Microsoft Office has over a billion licenses, making Excel one of the most widely available applications [26].

Excel's strengths are in its simplicity and flexibility. You can use it to:
- Handle large datasets
- Run basic simulations
- Estimate parameters
- Create clean, easy-to-understand visuals
- Share results with decision-makers

It also integrates well with other tools, so you can use Excel for prep work or reporting alongside your leading modelling software. And for smaller or more focussed models, you can build the whole thing right in Excel.

Table 1.1 compares features across these tools, including Excel. The bottom line? While specialized software is essential for more advanced work, Excel remains a robust and accessible option, particularly for communicating results. Combining Excel with tools like Vensim or Stella gives you the best of both worlds: easy-to-use analysis with deep modelling capabilities when you need them.

Tab. 1.1: Comparison of system dynamics software versus Excel.

Feature	Special purpose software	Excel
Primary use case	Advanced system dynamics modelling, simulation, and analysis	General spreadsheet tasks, basic modelling with limitations
User interface	Specialized graphical interfaces with drag-and-drop functionality; supports causal loop and stock-flow diagramming	Spreadsheet grid interface with cells for data entry and formulas
Modelling capabilities	Advanced capabilities, including system dynamics, agent-based modelling, and discrete event simulation (e.g. AnyLogic supports multi-method modelling)	Essential mathematical and logical functions; limited to cell-based computations
Target users	System dynamics professionals, researchers, educators, and students specializing in modelling and simulation	General business users, analysts, students, and professionals who need data organization and calculations
Data integration	Can integrate with databases, real-time data sources, and other software platforms (varies by software)	Can import/export data in various formats; limited real-time data integration.
Cost	Varies by software: ranges from free (e.g. Insight Maker) to costly commercial licenses (e.g. AnyLogic, Stella).	Typically, some components of the Microsoft Office Suite require a purchase or subscription.
Simulation capabilities	Advanced simulation features, including scenario analysis, optimization, and real-time simulation (e.g. Powersim's real-time integration capabilities).	Limited simulation capabilities; can perform iterative calculations using macros and add-ins
Learning curve	Moderate to steep, depending on the software's complexity and the user's prior experience with modelling	Generally low to moderate; widely used with abundant learning resources available
Support and community	Active professional communities, official support channels, and user forums (vary by software)	Extensive global user community with numerous online tutorials, forums, and documentation

Tab. 1.1 (continued)

Feature	Special purpose software	Excel
Educational use	Widely used in academia for teaching system dynamics concepts (e.g. Stella's visual approach is beneficial for learning)	It is commonly used in education to teach data management, fundamental analysis, and introductory modelling
Integration with other tools	Can integrate with programming languages (e.g. AnyLogic with Java), databases, and other modelling tools for extended functionality	Integrates well with other Microsoft Office applications and supports add-ins for extended features
Estimated users	Smaller, specialized user base focussed on system dynamics and simulation modelling	Vast global user base across various industries and domains

1.6 Getting Started with Excel for System Dynamics

At its core, quantitative system dynamics is about understanding how things change over time. Under the hood, it solves many interconnected equations, specifically first-order differential equations [27]. That might sound intimidating, but you don't need to be a math whiz to use these ideas. Thanks to modern tools (like Excel), we can simulate how systems behave without diving deep into the math.

The key building blocks of system dynamics are *stocks* and *flows;* think of them as containers (stocks) connected by pipes (flows). You control how much "stuff" moves between the containers using valves. Barry Richmond, the creator of Stella, put it perfectly: "You've got to get the plumbing right [27]." And that's really what system dynamics is: getting the flow of things through a system set up in a way that reflects how the real world works.

Figure 1.7 shows a simple population model. You've got a stock of population, with births flowing in and deaths flowing out. It's a great place to start because it introduces all the core ideas without getting too complicated.

In the first chapters of this book, we'll build this population model in Excel to teach you the basics step by step. Then, starting in Chapter 9, we'll apply everything you've learned to more complex, real-world case studies.

Looking at Fig. 1.8, you'll see how the model plays out over time using Vensim. It shows population changes in yearly steps. Births are in one column, deaths in another, and population in the fourth column. For example, in year 1, the population is the previous year's population plus births minus deaths, giving us 1,006.11. Notice that it's not a round number. System dynamics treats these variables as continuous so that you can think of the birth and death rates as probabilities rather than whole numbers representing people. Over time, that gives us an average outcome, which might be a fraction.

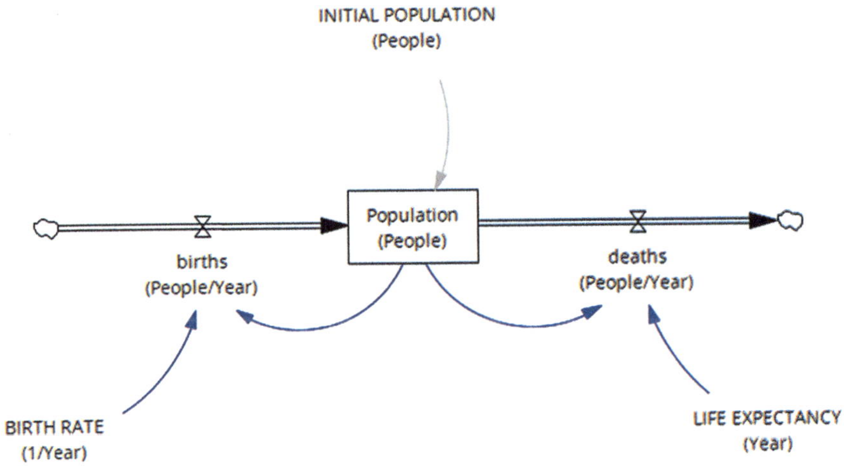

Fig. 1.7: A simple population model.

Time (year)	births : current	deaths : current	Population : current
0	20	13.8889	1000
1	20.1222	13.9738	1006.11
2	20.2452	14.0592	1012.26
3	20.3689	14.1451	1018.45
4	20.4934	14.2315	1024.67
5	20.6186	14.3185	1030.93
6	20.7446	14.406	1037.23
7	20.8714	14.494	1043.57
8	20.9989	14.5826	1049.95
9	21.1273	14.6717	1056.36
10	21.2564	14.7614	1062.82

Fig. 1.8: A display of the tabular results with a time step of 1 year.

If we ran a simulation using whole numbers, we'd need to run it many times to get an average. System dynamics skips all that by working with expected values directly, which is why you'll see decimals even when you're modelling people.

That 1-year time step makes sense for a quick look, but it's an approximation. System dynamics employs Euler integration, which approximates values by incrementing time in small steps. The smaller the step, the better the estimate.

Figure 1.9 illustrates what happens when the time step is reduced to 0.125 years (one-eighth of a year). The model walks through time more carefully, updating the stock in smaller increments. That gives us a slightly more accurate population estimate, 1,006.13 instead of 1,006.11. There is a slight difference, but in more complex models, using smaller time steps can make a significant impact.

Time (year)	births : current	deaths : current	Population : current
0	20	13.8889	1000
0.125	20.0153	13.8995	1000.76
0.25	20.0306	13.9101	1001.53
0.375	20.0459	13.9207	1002.29
0.5	20.0612	13.9314	1003.06
0.625	20.0765	13.942	1003.83
0.75	20.0918	13.9527	1004.59
0.875	20.1072	13.9633	1005.36
1	20.1225	13.974	1006.13

Fig. 1.9: A display of the tabular results with a time step of 0.125 years.

One quick technical tip: it's good practice to use time steps that are negative powers of 2 (like 1, 0.5, 0.25, and 0.125). Why? Computers work in binary, so these values help ensure time calculations line up neatly and reduce rounding errors. You don't need to understand the science behind it entirely, but it's helpful to know that it keeps things running smoothly.

Even though these examples were built in Vensim, you'll see that the same structure works beautifully in Excel. Each variable in a system dynamics model fits naturally into an Excel spreadsheet; specifically, variables are placed in columns, and time steps are arranged in rows. It's a perfect match.

1.7 Wrapping Up

In this chapter, we covered a lot of ground. You got a quick tour of the history of system dynamics, saw how it's applied across different fields, explored the role of software tools (including Excel), and learned how feedback loops, time delays, and non-linear behaviour shape the systems around us.

We also introduced a big idea: Excel isn't just a spreadsheet tool; it's a practical and flexible platform for building and exploring system dynamics models. Combining it with data science insights enables you to test assumptions, make more informed decisions, and gain a deeper understanding of complex systems.

Starting in Chapter 2, we'll shift from theory to practice. You'll walk through building your first model in Excel using the population example we just discussed. From there, we'll expand your skills:

- Chapter 3 dives into exponential growth and decay, showing how simple feedback loops can drive significant changes.
- Chapter 4 discusses a critical concept that we will utilize in the following chapters: the goal-gap model.
- Chapter 5 teaches you how to make forecasts from your models and explore future outcomes.

- Chapter 6 covers how to fit your model to the real world, reflecting historical data.
- Chapter 7 introduces *lookup functions,* a handy way to model changing relationships in system dynamics.
- Chapter 8 focusses on *delays,* one of the trickiest (but most important) parts of modelling realistic systems. We'll also discuss building clean interfaces so you can present your model results clearly, even to someone who doesn't want to see the technical details.

Then, the real fun begins. In the book's second half, you'll work through a series of case studies that grow in complexity, showing how Excel-based system dynamics can be used to tackle real challenges in fields like business, health, education, and sustainability.

By the end of this book, you won't just know how to build models; you'll have the confidence to use system dynamics in your work, using Excel to bring systems thinking to life. Let's get started.

1.8 Discussion Questions

- Which milestone accelerated SD adoption the most, and why? (Forrester vs. Meadows vs. Senge/Sterman).
- Provide a real-world process from your domain and classify at least two loops as reinforcing or balancing. What policy risks follow from misclassification?
- Identify two delays in an education, health, or supply-chain process. How can delays distort decision-making if ignored?
- When is an exploratory model more appropriate than a calibrated model, and vice versa? Provide one example of each.
- For a public-sector use case, which matters more initially: structural insight or data fidelity? Defend your trade-off.
- For which stakeholder audiences is Excel the most suitable delivery vehicle, and when should you escalate to Vensim/Stella/AnyLogic?
- What governance or communication failure most often undermines otherwise sound models? How would you mitigate it?
- How does time step selection alter the perceived performance of a system dynamics model? Illustrate.

1.9 Exercises

1.9.1 SD history timeline

Task. In six to eight bullets, create a timeline of SD milestones (1961 → 1972 → 1983 → 1990s → 2000). Deliverable. One slide or a short paragraph with citations to primary sources in the chapter.

1.9.2 Identify stocks, flows, and loop types.

Task. Pick a familiar process (e.g. clinic visits, order fulfilment, or student enrolment). List:

Two stocks, two flows; one reinforcing loop, one balancing loop; one plausible delay.

Deliverable. Six to ten lines; label each item.

1.9.3 Excel model scaffold

In Excel, set up a population scaffold for 20 years with columns: *time, population, birth rate, death rate, births, and deaths*. Use initial population = 1,000; birth rate = 0.02/year; death rate = 0.01/year; time step dt = 1 year. Implement Euler update: population $(t + \mathrm{dt})$ = population (t) + (births − deaths) * dt, with births = birth rate * population (t) and deaths = death rate * population (t). Duplicate the sheet and rerun with dt = 0.5. Compare the final population in year 1 across both.

Deliverable. Two short screenshots (or the file) plus a one-sentence comparison on time-step sensitivity.

1.9.4 Tooling decision quick take

Given three scenarios: (A) executive briefing with limited tooling on client machines, (B) research replication with unit checking, and (C) hybrid discrete-event and SD simulation, recommend Excel or a specialized tool and justify in two sentences each.

Deliverable. ≤9 sentences total.

1.9.5 Communicate model insights

Draft a 120- to 150-word briefing that explains to a non-technical stakeholder what the population scaffold can and cannot tell them this early (structure insight, delays, approximate integration, need for calibration later). Deliverable. One paragraph in plain language aimed at a manager.

Chapter 2
Your First System Dynamics Model in Excel

2.1 Learning Objectives

- Configure a stock-flow model in any system dynamics tool by setting the time base, units conventions, and an appropriate integration method (e.g. explicit Euler).
- Design a generic stock-flow structure with clear initial conditions and parameter declarations using consistent naming standards.
- Formulate governing equations for inflows/outflows; perform units checks; interpret baseline run outputs.
- Explain the explicit Euler update and assess time-step (dt) sensitivity for numerical accuracy.
- Implement the model in a spreadsheet (e.g. Excel) with simulation columns (time, stocks, and flows), a parameters block, and replicated Euler logic.
- Prevent and correct spreadsheet errors using anchored references and formula auditing.
- Validate cross-platform parity (modelling tool ↔ spreadsheet) at defined checkpoints; reconcile any discrepancies systematically.

2.2 Getting Started – Vensim First, Then Excel

System dynamics isn't that hard. Honestly, it's pretty straightforward. The problem is that it's often taught in a way that makes it feel way more complicated than it needs to be.

You can build models using any tool once you know how system dynamics works. I'll show you how to do it in Excel in this book. However, I first started using Vensim Personal Learning Edition Plus [28] because it's inexpensive (or free), easy to use, and features a visual interface that simplifies understanding what's happening. It is surprisingly simple to build a model in Vensim and then convert it into Excel. I always double-check that the Excel version gives the same results as the Vensim one to ensure everything translates correctly. Once it matches, I can move forward with the Excel version and leave Vensim behind for that model.

Starting with Vensim is smart because its visual interface helps you *see* the stocks and flows. You don't get that when you're working in Excel – you've got to picture it in your head. Having a diagram of the model helps when setting it up in Excel.

https://doi.org/10.1515/9783111541389-003

In this chapter, I'll walk you through the basics of building a simple system dynamics model using Vensim. That said, I'm assuming you already know your way around the Vensim interface. If not, no worries – Craig Kirkwood has a solid tutorial on his website [30], and there are plenty of video tutorials available as well, such as this introductory video from Vensim [31] and this excellent series by James Houghton [32]. A quick search will yield even more results.

After we build the model in Vensim, I'll show you how to re-create it in Excel. I'll assume you already know your way around the basics of Excel [33], Libre Calc [34], or Google Sheets [35]. And don't worry – we'll only use the simple stuff in Excel. That's all you need to build most system dynamics models.

2.3 Building a Model in Vensim (Step-by-Step)

Let's build a basic system dynamics model in Vensim. I'm keeping it simple, but don't let that fool you – the same process applies whether the model is small or huge.

Step 1: Save the Model
Before anything else, save your model. I named mine "population" and saved it in a folder called "Chapter 2." This is also a good time to get into the habit of working in short bursts. Every three minutes: do a units check, run the model, and save it. It'll save you headaches later.

Step 2: Set the Time Units

Go to the model settings and change the time units. Vensim defaults to “month,” but for this model, I’m switching it to “year” (see Fig. 2.1). For now, leave the time step at 1.

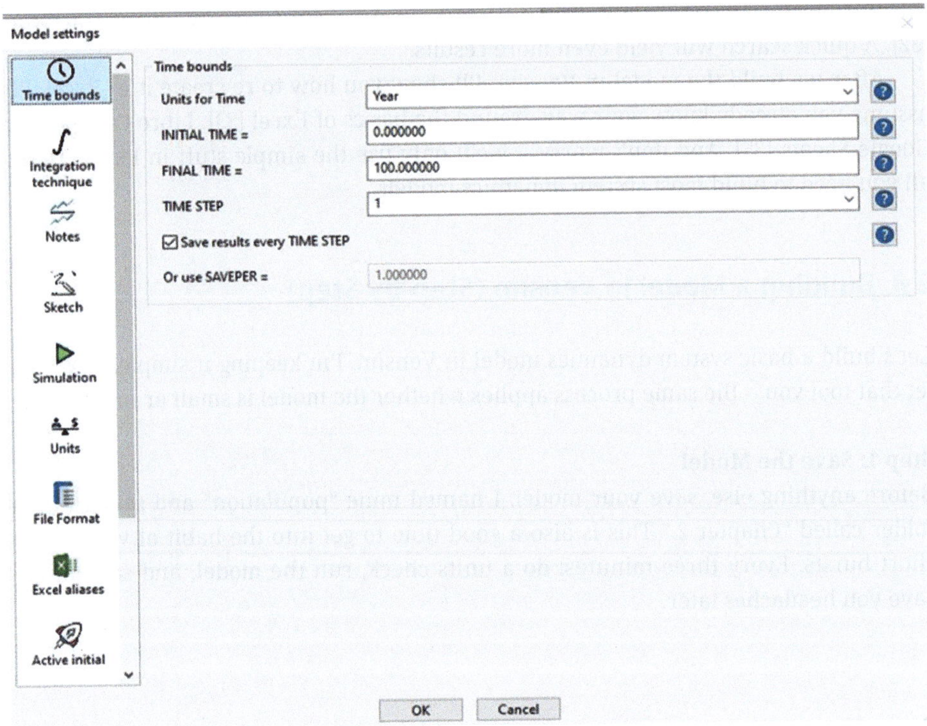

Fig. 2.1: The Vensim settings screen allows changing the time unit to “year.”

Step 3: Show Units on the Sketch

Still in the settings menu, look to the left-hand panel. Under sketch settings, enable the option to display units directly on the model diagram (see Fig. 2.2). This will make your model easier to read and debug later.

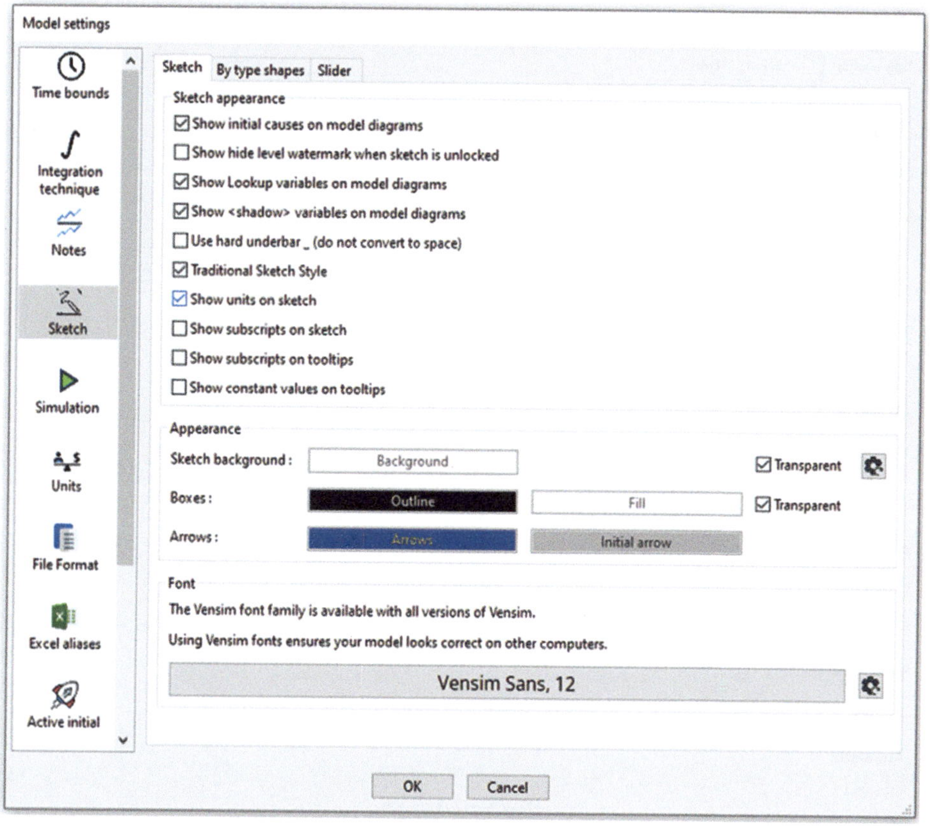

Fig. 2.2: Enabling unit display on the Vensim sketch.

Step 4: Check the Integration Method

While you're still here, click on integration technique. By default, it's set to Euler, which is perfect – we'll use the same method in Excel (see Fig. 2.3).

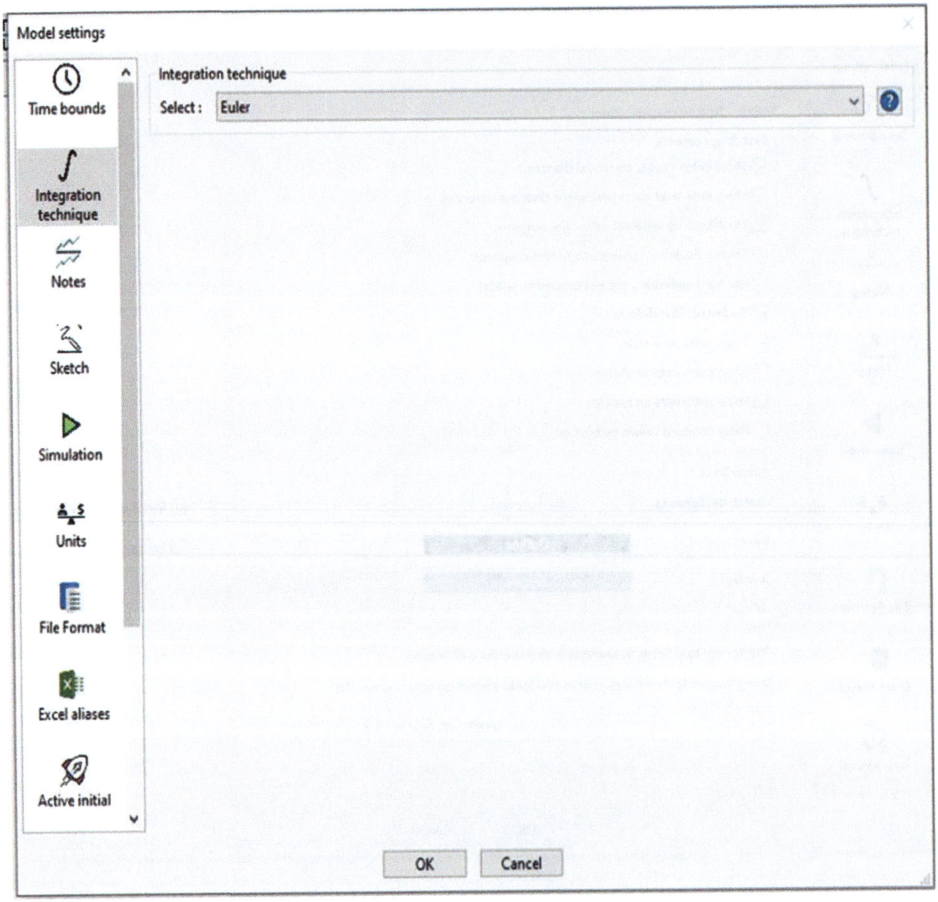

Fig. 2.3: Confirm that Euler integration is selected in the settings.

Step 5: Create the Stock and Flows

Now, let's build the structure. This model is about the population. It has one stock: "population." It has two flows: an inflow called "births" and an outflow called "deaths." I capitalize stock names (with the first letter of each word capitalized) and use lowercase for calculated (endogenous) variables – it helps when translating to Excel (see Fig. 2.4).

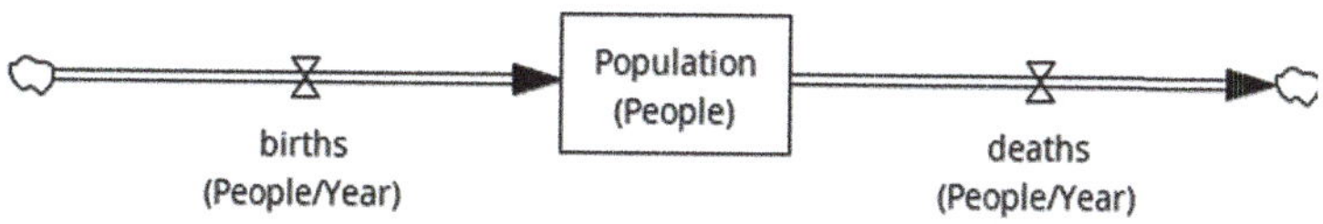

Fig. 2.4: The population stock, along with its inflow and outflow, shown in the Vensim interface.

Step 6: Add Constants

Next, add the constants (also called parameters). I put constants in all caps to make them stand out. For this model, we'll use:

- Initial population
- Birth rate
- Life expectancy

These will feed into the model's equations (see Fig. 2.5).

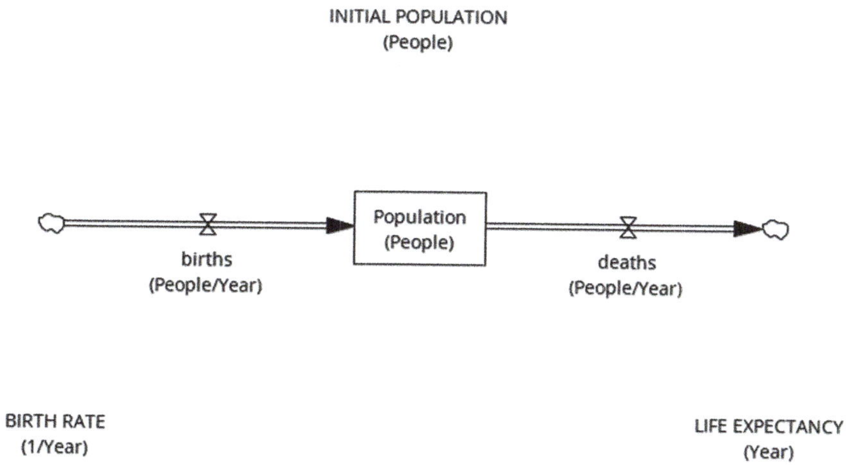

Fig. 2.5: Adding constants to the population model.

Step 7: Connect the Variables

Now wire everything together:

- The initial population connects to the population stock.
- Population connects to births (the more people, the more births) – a reinforcing loop.
- Population also connects to deaths (the more people, the more deaths) – a balancing loop.
- Birth rate connects to births.
- Life expectancy is connected to deaths (see Fig. 2.6).

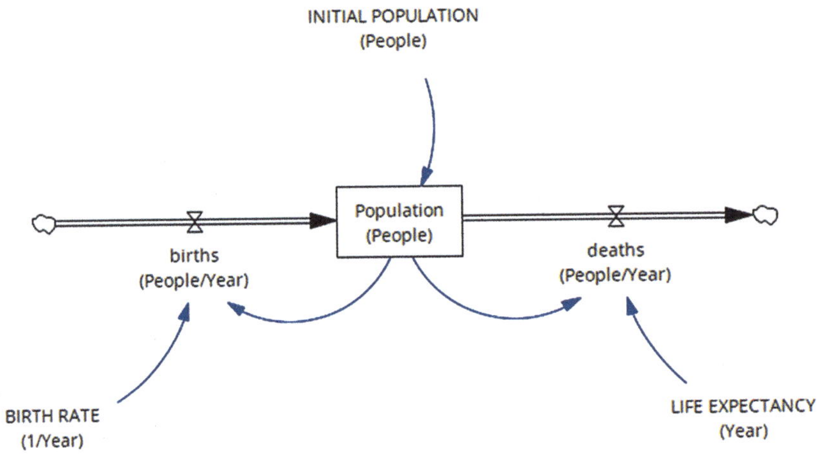

Fig. 2.6: The complete stock-and-flow structure for the population model.

Step 8: Enter Constant Values
Time to plug in the numbers:

- Initial population = 1,000 (units: people)
- Birth rate = 0.02 (units: people/people/year or just 1/year)
- Life expectancy = 72 (units: year)

See how that looks in the equation editor (Fig. 2.7).

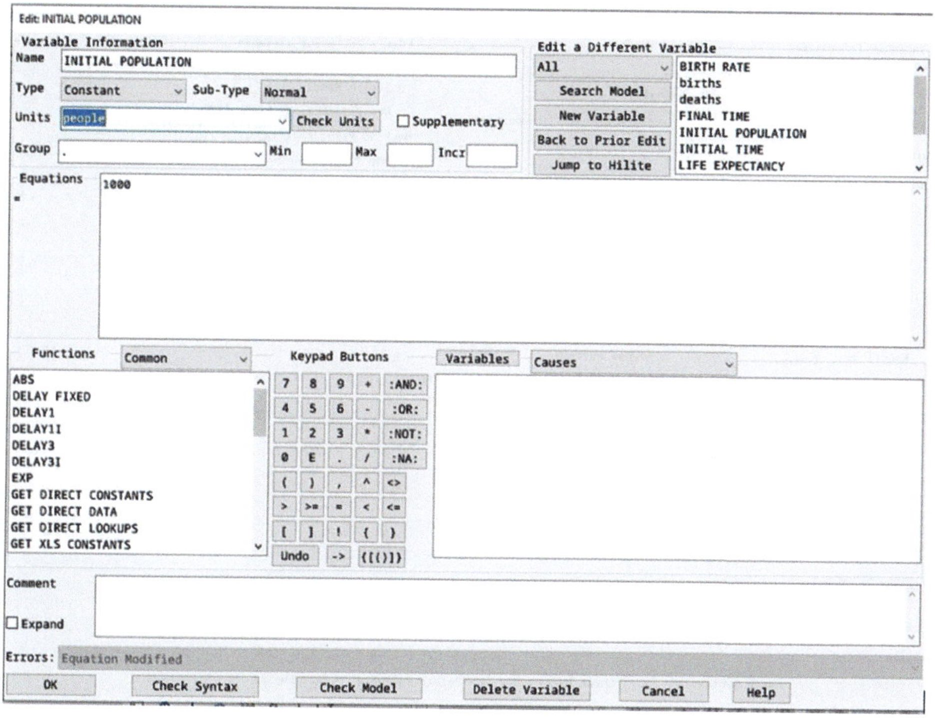

Fig. 2.7: Entering values for constants in Vensim.

Step 9: Write Equations for Flows and Stock

Here's how the logic breaks down:

- The population stock is initially valued at the initial population (units: people).
- Births = population * birth rate (units: people/year).
- Deaths = population/life expectancy (units: people/year).

You can enter those in the equation boxes (see Fig. 2.8).

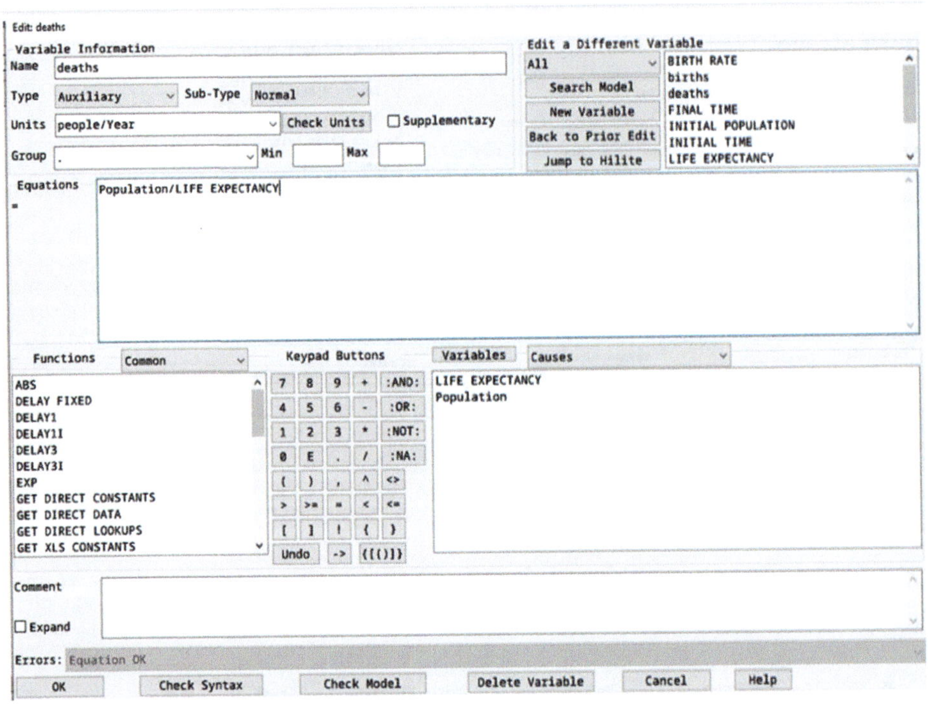

Fig. 2.8: The Vensim screen for the deaths flow.

Step 10: Review the Population Stock Equation
Click on the population stock. You'll see Vensim autofilled the equation as births-deaths. (see Fig. 2.9).

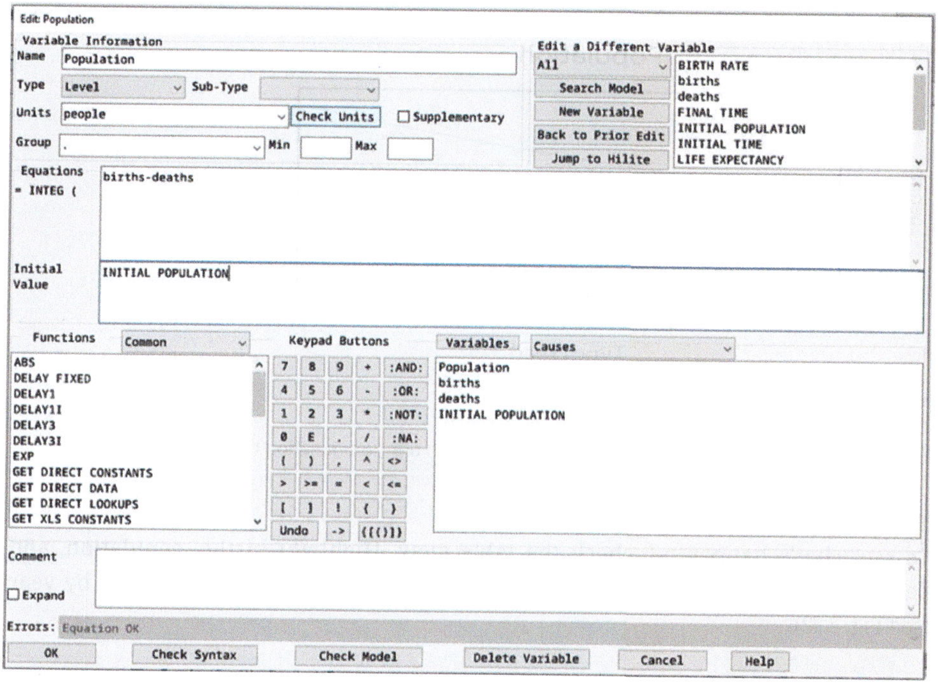

Fig. 2.9: The Vensim screen for the population stock.

Step 11: Check the Units
Now hit the units check. If everything is good, Vensim will let you know. If not, tweak until it is (see Fig. 2.10).

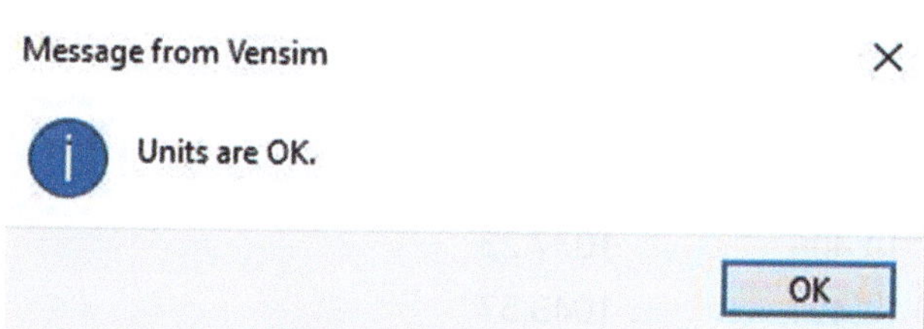

Fig. 2.10: A successful units check in Vensim.

Step 12: Run the Model and View the Graph

Go ahead and run the model. You should see the population growing exponentially over time. The inflow (births) is larger than the outflow (deaths), so the population curve will rise (see Fig. 2.11).

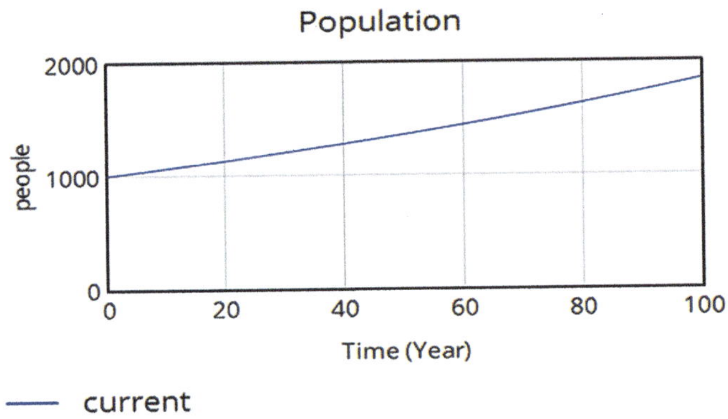

Fig. 2.11: The graph shows exponential population growth after a simulation run.

Step 13: View the Table Output

To see what's happening, check the table view. Highlight births, population, and deaths, then hit the table button. You'll get a step-by-step breakdown year by year (see Fig. 2.12).

Table | Selected Variables

File View Window

Time (Year)	births : current	deaths : current	›pulation : curre
0	20	13.8889	1000
1	20.1222	13.9738	1006.11
2	20.2452	14.0592	1012.26
3	20.3689	14.1451	1018.45
4	20.4934	14.2315	1024.67
5	20.6186	14.3185	1030.93
6	20.7446	14.406	1037.23
7	20.8714	14.494	1043.57
8	20.9989	14.5826	1049.95

Fig. 2.12: Tabular results of the simulation with a 1-year time step.

Notice:
- Year 0: population = 1,000, births = 20, deaths ≈ 13.89
- Year 1: population = 1,006.11
- Year 2: population = 1,012.26

You can see the Euler integration: year 1 population = year 0 population + year 0 births − year 0 deaths. That is, 1,000 + 20 − 13.89 = 1,006.11.

Year 2 population = year 1 population + year 1 births − year 1 deaths. That is, 1,006.11 + 20.1222 − 13.9738 = 1,012.26.

Step 14: Change the Time Step
Try changing the time step to 0.125. This makes the simulation more precise. When using a smaller time step, Vensim recalculates more frequently:
That is:

$$\text{Stock}(t) = \text{Stock}\,(t - \text{dt}) + (\text{inflow} - \text{outflow}) \times \text{dt}$$

In our terminology, dt refers to the time step, also known as delta time.

To be clear, consider another run of the model with a time step of 0.125. Here is the tabular output (see Fig. 2.13).

Table | Selected Variables

File View Window

Time (Year)	births : current	deaths : current	›pulation : curre
0	20	13.8889	1000
0.125	20.0153	13.8995	1000.76
0.25	20.0306	13.9101	1001.53
0.375	20.0459	13.9207	1002.29
0.5	20.0612	13.9314	1003.06
0.625	20.0765	13.942	1003.83
0.75	20.0918	13.9527	1004.59
0.875	20.1072	13.9633	1005.36
1	20.1225	13.974	1006.13

Fig. 2.13: Tabular results with a time step of 0.125 years.

Bonus Tip: Build in Short Bursts

A quick best practice before we move on: work in 3-minute chunks. After every 3 minutes:

- Check your units
- Run the model
- Think: *Does this output make sense?*
- If so, save the model.

This rhythm helps catch mistakes early and trains your intuition over time.

2.4 Converting the Model to Excel (Step-by-Step)

Let's convert our Vensim population model to Excel. Once you understand the process, it's simple.

Step 1: Set Up Your Columns
Start by putting "Time" in column A. Each endogenous variable (such as births, population, and deaths) has its own column. I like to place inflows on the left of the stock and outflows on the right – it keeps things tidy.
So:

- Column B: "births (people/year)"
- Column C: "population (people)"
- Column D: "deaths (people/year)"

Include the units in the column titles. You can copy and paste the variable names and units straight from the Vensim equation editor into row 1 (see Fig. 2.14).

	A	B	C	D
1	Time	births (people/ year)	Population (people)	deaths (people/ year)
2				
3				
4				
5				
6				
7				
8				
9				
10				

Fig. 2.14: Setting up the endogenous variable columns in Excel.

Step 2: Add the Parameter Table

To the right of your variables (start in column E), create a spot for constants. It's useful for calibration later.

- Cell E1: parameters
- F1: values
- G1: units

Then fill out the following:

- E2: initial population | F2: 1,000 | G2: people
- E3: birth rate | F3: 0.02 | G3: people/people/year
- E4: life expectancy | F4: 72 | G4: year
- E5: start year | F5: 0 | G5: year
- E6: time step | F6: 0.125 | G6: year (see Fig. 2.15)

	A	B	C	D	E	F	G
1	Time	births (people/ year)	Population (people)	deaths (people/ year)	PARAMETER	VALUES	UNITS
2					INITIAL POPULATION	1,000	people
3					BIRTH RATE	0.02	1/Year
4					LIFE EXPECTANCY	72	Year
5					START TIME	0	Year
6					TIME STEP	0.125	Year
7							
8							

Fig. 2.15: Parameter section of the Excel model.

Step 3: Set the Initial Time
In cell A2, enter the starting year using: = F5 (see Fig. 2.16).

	A	B	C	D	E	F	G
1	Time	births (people/ year)	Population (people)	deaths (people/ year)	PARAMETER	VALUES	UNITS
2	=F5				INITIAL POPULATION	1,000	people
3					BIRTH RATE	0.02	1/Year
4					LIFE EXPECTANCY	72	Year
5					START TIME	0	Year
6					TIME STEP	0.125	Year
7							

Fig. 2.16: Setting initial time from parameters.

Step 4: Set the Initial population
In cell C2, reference the initial population value: = F2 (see Fig. 2.17).

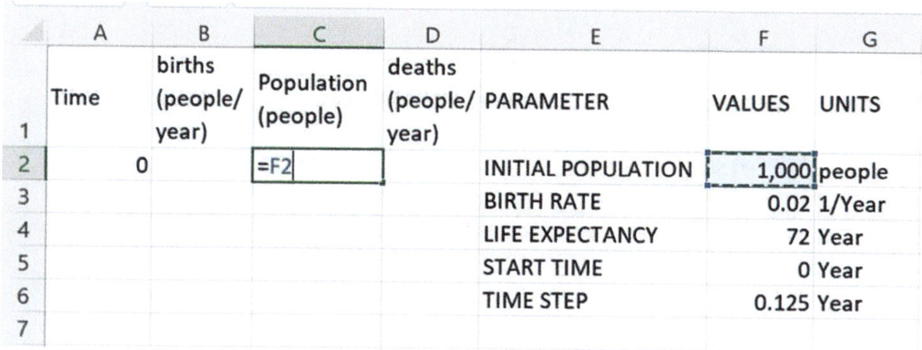

	A	B	C	D	E	F	G
1	Time	births (people/ year)	Population (people)	deaths (people/ year)	PARAMETER	VALUES	UNITS
2	0		=F2		INITIAL POPULATION	1,000	people
3					BIRTH RATE	0.02	1/Year
4					LIFE EXPECTANCY	72	Year
5					START TIME	0	Year
6					TIME STEP	0.125	Year
7							

Fig. 2.17: Setting the initial population value.

Step 5: Calculate Births

In cell B2, use: = C2 * F3

But wait – we need to anchor F3 (the birth rate) so it doesn't shift when copied. Change it to: F$3 (see Figs. 2.18 and 2.19).

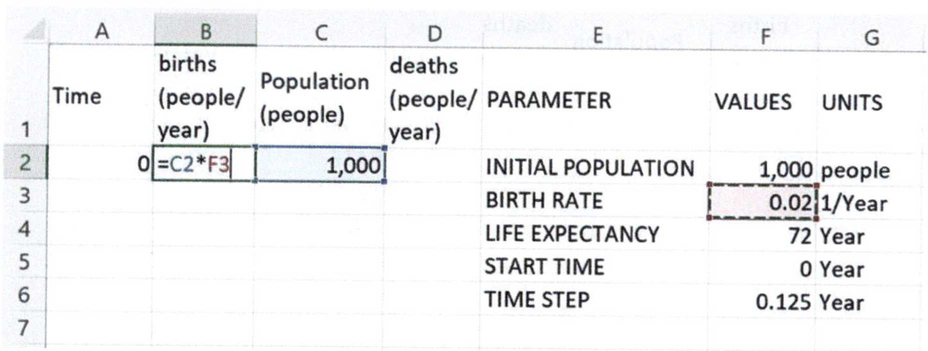

	A	B	C	D	E	F	G
1	Time	births (people/ year)	Population (people)	deaths (people/ year)	PARAMETER	VALUES	UNITS
2	0	=C2*F3	1,000		INITIAL POPULATION	1,000	people
3					BIRTH RATE	0.02	1/Year
4					LIFE EXPECTANCY	72	Year
5					START TIME	0	Year
6					TIME STEP	0.125	Year
7							

Fig. 2.18: Births formula in Excel.

	A	B	C	D	E	F	G
1	Time	births (people/ year)	Population (people)	deaths (people/ year)	PARAMETER	VALUES	UNITS
2	0	=C2*F$3	1,000		INITIAL POPULATION	1,000	people
3					BIRTH RATE	0.02	1/Year
4					LIFE EXPECTANCY	72	Year
5					START TIME	0	Year
6					TIME STEP	0.125	Year
7							

Fig. 2.19: Anchoring the birth rate parameter.

Step 6: Calculate Deaths

In cell D2, enter: = C2/F$4. Again, anchor the life expectancy cell (see Fig. 2.20).

	A	B	C	D	E	F	G
1	Time	births (people/ year)	Population (people)	deaths (people/ year)	PARAMETER	VALUES	UNITS
2	0	20	1,000	=C2/F$4	INITIAL POPULATION	1,000	people
3					BIRTH RATE	0.02	1/Year
4					LIFE EXPECTANCY	72	Year
5					START TIME	0	Year
6					TIME STEP	0.125	Year
7							

Fig. 2.20: Death formula with proper anchoring.

Step 7: Calculate Time for Next Step

In cell A3, calculate the next time step: = A2 + F$6. Don't forget to anchor the time step (see Fig. 2.21).

	A	B	C	D	E	F	G
1	Time	births (people/ year)	Population (people)	deaths (people/ year)	PARAMETER	VALUES	UNITS
2	0	20	1,000	13.8889	INITIAL POPULATION	1,000	people
3	=A2+F$6				BIRTH RATE	0.02	1/Year
4					LIFE EXPECTANCY	72	Year
5					START TIME	0	Year
6					TIME STEP	0.125	Year
7							

Fig. 2.21: Time equation with an anchored time step.

Step 8: Euler Integration for Population

Now apply the Euler formula. In cell C3 = C2 + (B2–D2) * F6 (see Fig. 2.22).

	A	B	C	D	E	F	G
1	Time	births (people/ year)	Population (people)	deaths (people/ year)	PARAMETER	VALUES	UNITS
2	0	20	1,000	13.8889	INITIAL POPULATION	1,000	people
3	0.125		=C2+(B2-D2)*F6		BIRTH RATE	0.02	1/Year
4					LIFE EXPECTANCY	72	Year
5					START TIME	0	Year
6					TIME STEP	0.125	Year
7							

Fig. 2.22: Population stock calculation using Euler's method.

Step 9: Fill in Births and Deaths for Next Step

Copy cell B2 into B3, which will automatically update to use C3 in the calculation (see Fig. 2.23).

	A	B	C	D	E	F	G
1	Time	births (people/ year)	Population (people)	deaths (people/ year)	PARAMETER	VALUES	UNITS
2	0	20	1,000	13.8889	INITIAL POPULATION	1,000	people
3	0.125	20.0153	1000.7639		BIRTH RATE	0.02	1/Year
4					LIFE EXPECTANCY	72	Year
5					START TIME	0	Year
6					TIME STEP	0.125	Year

Fig. 2.23: Calculation of the births for the next time step.

Then copy D2 into D3 (see Fig. 2.24).

	A	B	C	D	E	F	G
1	Time	births (people/ year)	Population (people)	deaths (people/ year)	PARAMETER	VALUES	UNITS
2	0	20	1,000	13.8889	INITIAL POPULATION	1,000	people
3	0.125	20.0153	1000.7639	13.8995	BIRTH RATE	0.02	1/Year
4					LIFE EXPECTANCY	72	Year
5					START TIME	0	Year
6					TIME STEP	0.125	Year

Fig. 2.24: Calculating deaths for the next time step.

Step 10: Fill in the Table

Now copy cells A3 to D3, then paste them down the rows. This gives you the full simulation over time (see Fig. 2.25).

	A	B	C	D	E	F	G
1	Time	births (people/ year)	Population (people)	deaths (people/ year)	PARAMETER	VALUES	UNITS
2	0	20	1,000	13.8889	INITIAL POPULATION	1,000	people
3	0.125	20.0153	1000.7639	13.8995	BIRTH RATE	0.02	1/Year
4	0.250	20.0153	1000.7639	13.8995	LIFE EXPECTANCY	72	Year
5	0.375	20.0153	1000.7639	13.8995	START TIME	0	Year
6	0.500	20.0153	1000.7639	13.8995	TIME STEP	0.125	Year
7	0.625	20.0153	1000.7639	13.8995			
8	0.750	20.0153	1000.7639	13.8995			
9	0.875	20.0153	1000.7639	13.8995			
10	1.000	20.0153	1000.7639	13.8995			
11	1.125	20.0153	1000.7639	13.8995			
12	1.250	20.0153	1000.7639	13.8995			
13	1.375	20.0153	1000.7639	13.8995			
14	1.500	20.0153	1000.7639	13.8995			
15	1.625	20.0153	1000.7639	13.8995			
16	1.750	20.0153	1000.7639	13.8995			

Fig. 2.25: Extending the model by copying down formulas.

Step 11: Debug the Model

Uh-oh. You might notice that births, deaths, and the population don't change after the first step. It's time to debug.

Click on B3 and check the formula in the "fx" bar. You can see something like = C3 * F$3. This formula appears to be correct (see Fig. 2.26).

B3 fx =C3*F$3

	A	B	C	D	E	F	G
1	Time	births (people/ year)	Population (people)	deaths (people/ year)	PARAMETER	VALUES	UNITS
2	0	20	1,000	13.8889	INITIAL POPULATION	1,000	people
3	0.125	20.0153	1000.7639	13.8995	BIRTH RATE	0.02	1/Year
4	0.250	20.0153	1000.7639	13.8995	LIFE EXPECTANCY	72	Year
5	0.375	20.0153	1000.7639	13.8995	START TIME	0	Year
6	0.500	20.0153	1000.7639	13.8995	TIME STEP	0.125	Year

Fig. 2.26: Diagnosing and fixing the anchoring bug (step 1).

Click on C3 and check the formula in the "fx" bar. You can see something like: = C2 + (B2–D2) * F6 (see Fig. 2.27).

The issue? F6 (the time step) isn't anchored. Everything referenced in column F needs to be anchored. When Excel copies that formula, it shifts to F7, which is empty, thereby multiplying everything by zero (see Figs. 2.27 and 2.28).

Fix it by anchoring (see Fig. 2.29).

Then copy that fixed formula down column C (see Fig. 2.30).

C3 | fx | =C2+(B2-D2)*F6

	A	B	C	D	E	F	G
1	Time	births (people/ year)	Population (people)	deaths (people/ year)	PARAMETER	VALUES	UNITS
2	0	20	1,000	13.8889	INITIAL POPULATION	1,000	people
3	0.125	20.0153	1000.7639	13.8995	BIRTH RATE	0.02	1/Year
4	0.250	20.0153	1000.7639	13.8995	LIFE EXPECTANCY	72	Year
5	0.375	20.0153	1000.7639	13.8995	START TIME	0	Year
6	0.500	20.0153	1000.7639	13.8995	TIME STEP	0.125	Year
7	0.625	20.0153	1000.7639	13.8995			

Fig. 2.27: Diagnosing and fixing the anchoring bug (step 2).

C4 | fx | =C3+(B3-D3)*F7

	A	B	C	D	E	F	G
1	Time	births (people/ year)	Population (people)	deaths (people/ year)	PARAMETER	VALUES	UNITS
2	0	20	1,000	13.8889	INITIAL POPULATION	1,000	people
3	0.125	20.0153	1000.7639	13.8995	BIRTH RATE	0.02	1/Year
4	0.250	20.0153	1000.7639	13.8995	LIFE EXPECTANCY	72	Year
5	0.375	20.0153	1000.7639	13.8995	START TIME	0	Year
6	0.500	20.0153	1000.7639	13.8995	TIME STEP	0.125	Year
7	0.625	20.0153	1000.7639	13.8995			

Fig. 2.28: Diagnosing and fixing the anchoring bug (step 3).

SUM | =C2+(B2-D2)*F$6

	A	B	C	D	E	F	G
1	Time	births (people/ year)	Population (people)	deaths (people/ year)	PARAMETER	VALUES	UNITS
2	0	20	1,000	13.8889	INITIAL POPULATION	1,000	people
3	0.125	20.0153	D2)*F$6	13.8995	BIRTH RATE	0.02	1/Year
4	0.250	20.0153	1000.7639	13.8995	LIFE EXPECTANCY	72	Year
5	0.375	20.0153	1000.7639	13.8995	START TIME	0	Year
6	0.500	20.0153	1000.7639	13.8995	TIME STEP	0.125	Year
7	0.625	20.0153	1000.7639	13.8995			

Fig. 2.29: Diagnosing and fixing the anchoring bug (step 4).

	A	B	C	D	E	F	G
1	Time	births (people/ year)	Population (people)	deaths (people/ year)	PARAMETER	VALUES	UNITS
2	0	20	1,000	13.8889	INITIAL POPULATION	1,000	people
3	0.125	20.0153	1000.7639	13.8995	BIRTH RATE	0.02	1/Year
4	0.250	20.0153	1000.7639	13.8995	LIFE EXPECTANCY	72	Year
5	0.375	20.0153	1000.7639	13.8995	START TIME	0	Year
6	0.500	20.0153	1000.7639	13.8995	TIME STEP	0.125	Year
7	0.625	20.0153	1000.7639	13.8995			
8	0.750	20.0153	1000.7639	13.8995			
9	0.875	20.0153	1000.7639	13.8995			
10	1.000	20.0153	1000.7639	13.8995			
11	1.125	20.0153	1000.7639	13.8995			
12	1.250	20.0153	1000.7639	13.8995			
13	1.375	20.0153	1000.7639	13.8995			
14	1.500	20.0153	1000.7639	13.8995			
15	1.625	20.0153	1000.7639	13.8995			
16	1.750	20.0153	1000.7639	13.8995			

Fig. 2.30: Diagnosing and fixing the anchoring bug (step 5).

Step 12: Confirm Model Is Working

Your population, births, and deaths values should change correctly over time (see Fig. 2.31). One of the most common Excel modelling errors? Forgetting to anchor constants. Keep an eye on that.

	A	B	C	D	E	F	G
1	Time	births (people/ year)	Population (people)	deaths (people/ year)	PARAMETER	VALUES	UNITS
2	0	20	1,000	13.8889	INITIAL POPULATION	1,000	people
3	0.125	20.0153	1000.7639	13.8995	BIRTH RATE	0.02	1/Year
4	0.250	20.0306	1001.5284	13.9101	LIFE EXPECTANCY	72	Year
5	0.375	20.0459	1002.2934	13.9207	START TIME	0	Year
6	0.500	20.0612	1003.0591	13.9314	TIME STEP	0.125	Year
7	0.625	20.0765	1003.8253	13.942			
8	0.750	20.0918	1004.5921	13.9527			
9	0.875	20.1072	1005.3595	13.9633			
10	1.000	20.1225	1006.1275	13.974			
11	1.125	20.1379	1006.896	13.9847			
12	1.250	20.1533	1007.6652	13.9954			
13	1.375	20.1687	1008.4349	14.006			
14	1.500	20.1841	1009.2053	14.0167			
15	1.625	20.1995	1009.9762	14.0274			
16	1.750	20.215	1010.7477	14.0382			

Fig. 2.31: Final working version of the Excel model.

2.5 Comparing the Vensim and Excel Results

Let's ensure our Excel model aligns with the Vensim results.

At time 0.5, Vensim gives:

- Births: 20.0612
- Deaths: 13.9314
- Population: 1,003.06 (see Fig. 2.32)

Excel gives:

- Births: 20.0612
- Deaths: 13.9314
- Population: 1,003.0591 (see Fig. 2.31 again)

That's a match!

Table | Selected Variables

File View Window

Time (Year)	births : current	deaths : current	pulation : curre
0	20	13.8889	1000
0.125	20.0153	13.8995	1000.76
0.25	20.0306	13.9101	1001.53
0.375	20.0459	13.9207	1002.29
0.5	20.0612	13.9314	1003.06
0.625	20.0765	13.942	1003.83
0.75	20.0918	13.9527	1004.59
0.875	20.1072	13.9633	1005.36
1	20.1225	13.974	1006.13

Fig. 2.32: Vensim results at time 0.5.

Now let's check at time 100.

Vensim:

- Births: 36.841
- Deaths: 25.584
- Population: 1,842.05 (see Fig. 2.33)

Table | Selected Variables

File View Window

Time (Year)	births : current	deaths : current	pulation : curre
99.125	36.6446	25.4476	1832.23
99.25	36.6725	25.467	1833.63
99.375	36.7006	25.4865	1835.03
99.5	36.7286	25.506	1836.43
99.625	36.7567	25.5255	1837.83
99.75	36.7847	25.545	1839.24
99.875	36.8128	25.5645	1840.64
100	36.841	25.584	1842.05

Fig. 2.33: Vensim model after 100 years.

Excel:
- Same numbers! (see Fig. 2.34)

	A	B	C	D
1	Time	births (people/ year)	Population (people)	deaths (people/ year)
794	99.000	36.6166	1830.8293	25.4282
795	99.125	36.6446	1832.2279	25.4476
796	99.250	36.6725	1833.6275	25.467
797	99.375	36.7006	1835.0282	25.4865
798	99.500	36.7286	1836.4299	25.506
799	99.625	36.7567	1837.8328	25.5255
800	99.750	36.7847	1839.2367	25.545
801	99.875	36.8128	1840.6416	25.5645
802	100.000	36.841	1842.0477	25.584

Fig. 2.34: Excel model after 100 years.

2.6 Bonus: Add a Graph

Use Excel's built-in charting to plot population over time. You'll see a nice upward curve (see Fig. 2.35).

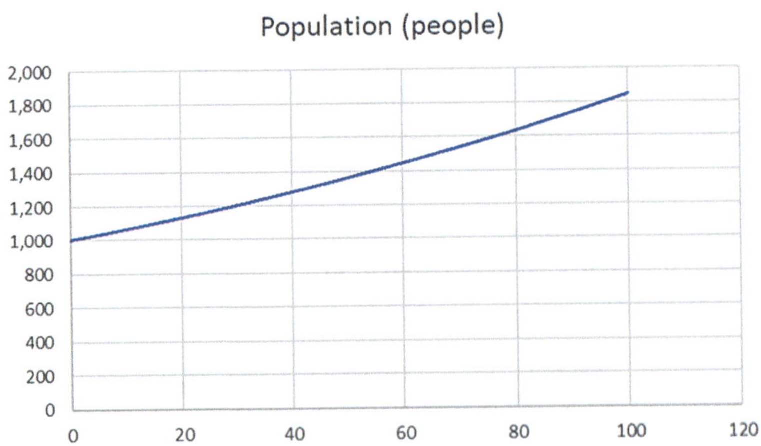

Fig. 2.35: Graph of population over time from the Excel model.

2.7 Wrapping Up

That's all there is to system dynamics in Excel.

- You define a stock
- Set an initial value
- Define flows in and out
- Use Euler integration to step through time

Euler's method is just arithmetic. No magic. It's powerful, and with this structure, you can build and analyse many more models in Excel.

In the next chapter, we'll explore exponential growth and decline.

2.8 Discussion Questions

- Why start in Vensim and then migrate to Excel for delivery? What risks are mitigated by this workflow?
- What specific unit inconsistencies could this model expose, and how would you locate and resolve them systematically?
- Where does dt materially change early-period dynamics, and how would you justify your chosen time step to a stakeholder?
- This chapter suggests using naming conventions (e.g. capitalizing constants). How do such conventions reduce translation errors when moving to Excel?
- In Excel, which classes of errors are most likely? Give two detection tactics.
- When the Vensim and Excel outputs diverge, what is your triage sequence to isolate the fault?

2.9 Exercises

2.9.1 Configure and run the Vensim model
Task. Create the population model with "year" as the time unit, Euler integration, and units on the sketch. Add population (stock), births, deaths (flows), and constants (initial population = 1,000; birth rate = 0.02; and life expectancy = 72). Run and capture the graph.
Deliverable. Screenshot of settings. Stock/flow diagram and graph.

2.9.2 Table verification and time step sensitivity
Task. Produce the tabular output (population, births, and deaths) and verify that the population at year 1 = 1,006.11 with a time step of 1. Rerun with time step = 0.125, explain the difference using Euler's update.
Deliverable. Two short tables or screenshots; two to three sentences on the time-step effect.

2.9.3 Rebuild in Excel
Task. In Excel, create columns (time, births, population, and deaths) and a parameters block (initial population, birth rate, life expectancy, start year, and time step). Implement formulas, including Euler integration.
Deliverable. Spreadsheet file or screenshots of the header row, parameters, and first 10 rows.

2.9.4 Debugging anchored references
Task. Intentionally remove the dollar sign in F$6 within C3 and copy it down. Observe failures and then fix by restoring anchoring.
Deliverable. One-paragraph root-cause note and corrected sheet.

2.9.5 Cross-platform verification
Task. Compare Excel and Vensim outputs using a time step of 0.0625 at times 0.5 and 100. Document whether births, deaths, and population match.
Deliverable. Four to six lines with numeric comparisons.

2.9.6 Communicate insights with a chart
Task. Insert an Excel scatter graph of population vs. time and add a two-sentence takeaway for non-technical stakeholders.
Deliverable. Chart and takeaway blurb.

Chapter 3
Understanding Exponential Growth and Decline

3.1 Learning Objectives

- Characterize exponential dynamics where the rate of change is proportional to the current level, and estimate net growth rates from component drivers.
- Use an analytical solution to compute levels and doubling/halving times.
- Compare Euler integration with analytic results; quantify the discretization error; and select the time step via convergence testing.
- Diagnose reinforcing feedback (virtuous/vicious cycles) and apply doubling-time reasoning to communicate risk and urgency.
- Identify equilibrium (steady state) conditions.
- Model exponential decay and explain asymptotic behaviour.
- Implement and interpret logistic (capacity-limited) growth, recognizing S-curve phases.
- Communicate when linear extrapolation is unsafe in exponential or capacity-constrained regimes and propose defensible alternatives.

3.2 Introduction

In Chapter 2, we built our first system dynamics model in Vensim and translated it into Excel, creating a population model where births and deaths drive changes over time. Through this exercise, we observed how population dynamics emerge from simple stock-and-flow relationships and verified that our Excel implementation produced results identical to those from Vensim.

This chapter examines the fundamental mathematical behaviour underlying our model: exponential growth and exponential decline. These patterns frequently appear in real-world systems, such as the spread of diseases, financial investments, resource depletion, and the adoption of new technologies.

Our population model showed that the population grows exponentially when the birth rate exceeds the death rate. Conversely, if the death rate dominates, the population declines exponentially. But why does this happen? And how can we predict and control such behaviours?

To answer these questions, this chapter will explore the mathematical foundations of exponential growth and decline, their application to our population model, the implementation of exponential equations in Excel, and the role of feedback loops in reinforcing or balancing exponential trends.

https://doi.org/10.1515/9783111541389-004

By the end of this chapter, you'll not only understand exponential change but also see how it shapes the dynamics of systems you model in Excel. Mastering this concept is crucial in developing more sophisticated system dynamics models.

3.3 Exponential Growth

Chapter 2 constructed the population model around a population stock with two key flows: births = population * birth rate and deaths = population/life expectancy (see Fig. 3.1).

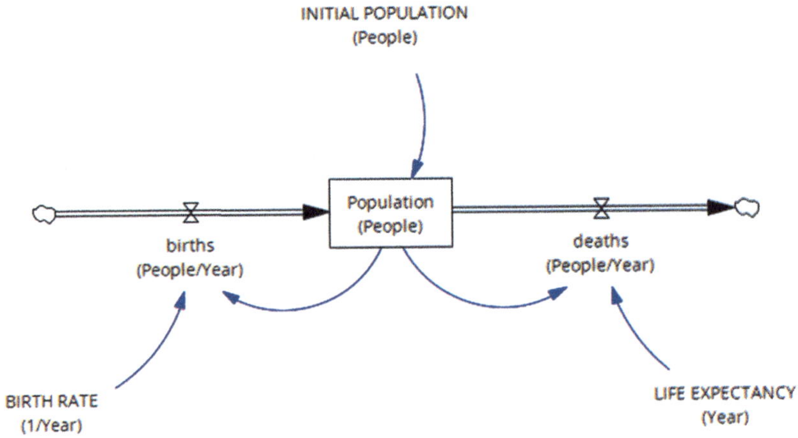

Fig. 3.1: The population model structure in Vensim.

This structure created a simple yet powerful feedback system in which births contributed to population growth, while deaths led to population decline. We observed growth when we ran the model because the births exceeded the deaths (see Figs. 3.2 and 3.3).

	A	B	C	D	E	F	G
1	Time	births (people/ year)	Population (people)	deaths (people/ year)	PARAMETER	VALUES	UNITS
2	0	20	1,000	13.8889	INITIAL POPULATION	1,000	people
3	0.125	20.0153	1000.7639	13.8995	BIRTH RATE	0.02	1/Year
4	0.250	20.0306	1001.5284	13.9101	LIFE EXPECTANCY	72	Year
5	0.375	20.0459	1002.2934	13.9207	START TIME	0	Year
6	0.500	20.0612	1003.0591	13.9314	TIME STEP	0.125	Year
7	0.625	20.0765	1003.8253	13.942			
8	0.750	20.0918	1004.5921	13.9527			
9	0.875	20.1072	1005.3595	13.9633			
10	1.000	20.1225	1006.1275	13.974			
11	1.125	20.1379	1006.896	13.9847			
12	1.250	20.1533	1007.6652	13.9954			
13	1.375	20.1687	1008.4349	14.006			
14	1.500	20.1841	1009.2053	14.0167			
15	1.625	20.1995	1009.9762	14.0274			
16	1.750	20.215	1010.7477	14.0382			

Fig. 3.2: Population model results.

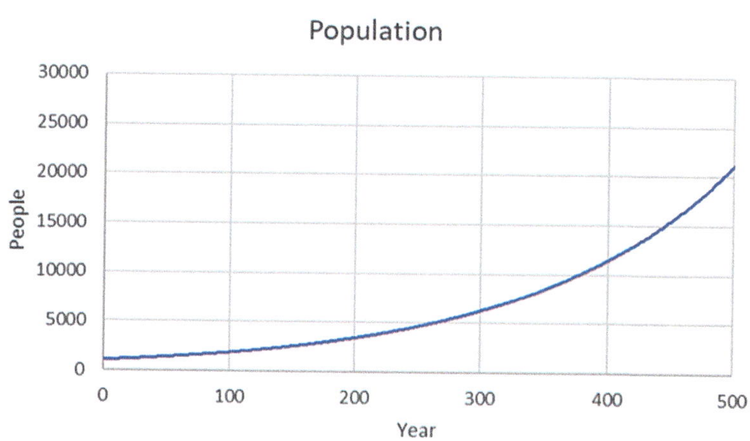

Fig. 3.3: Graphical results from the population model.

Why does this happen?

The behaviour of our population model is governed by a fundamental principle of dynamic systems: exponential change. This occurs when the rate of change of a quantity is proportional to its current size. In our case, the birth rate exceeds 1/life expectancy, and the population grows exponentially.

We will simplify this model using a growth rate rather than a birth rate and a life expectancy. We will calculate the growth rate as follows: birth rate–1/life expectancy = 0.02–1/72 = 0.02–0.01389 = 0.00611 people/people/year. Figure 3.4 shows the revised population model in Vensim, and Fig. 3.5 shows the revised model in Excel. Notice that the population values in Figs. 3.2 and 3.5 are the same.

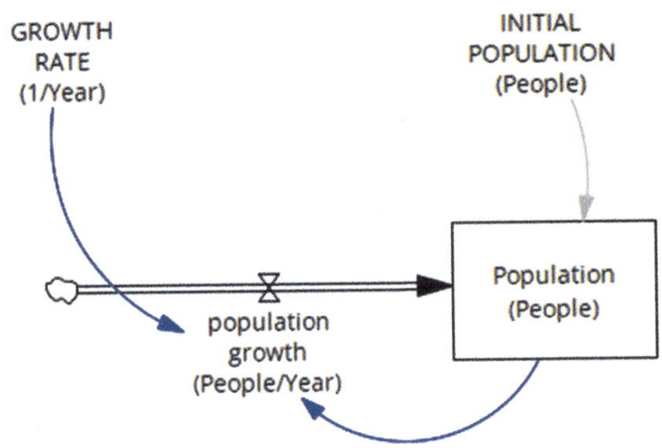

Fig. 3.4: Revised population model in Vensim.

	A	B	C	D	E	F
1	Time (Year)	growth (people/ Year)	Population (people)	PARAMETERS	VALUES	UNITS
2	0	6.1111	1,000	START TIME	0	Year
3	0.125	6.1158	1,000.7639	TIME STEP	0.125	Year
4	0.25	6.1205	1,001.5284	INITIAL POPULATION	1,000	People
5	0.375	6.1251	1,002.2934	GROWTH RATE	0.00611	1/Year
6	0.5	6.1298	1,003.0591			
7	0.625	6.1345	1,003.8253			
8	0.75	6.1392	1,004.5921			
9	0.875	6.1439	1,005.3595			
10	1	6.1486	1,006.1275			
11	1.125	6.1533	1,006.8960			
12	1.25	6.1580	1,007.6652			
13	1.375	6.1627	1,008.4349			
14	1.5	6.1674	1,009.2053			
15	1.625	6.1721	1,009.9762			
16	1.75	6.1768	1,010.7477			

Fig. 3.5: Revised model in Excel.

Exponential growth occurs because more people are added to the population each year than in the previous year (see Fig. 3.6). This growth equals the population growth rate, expressed as people/year, added annually to the existing population. Therefore, the population continues to grow every year, and so does the rate of growth.

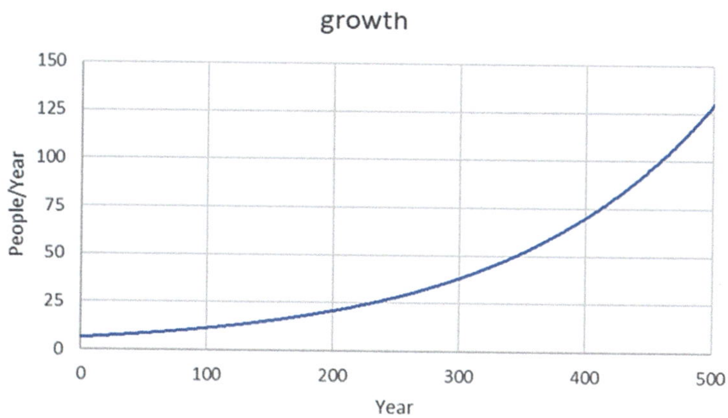

Fig. 3.6: Graphical results of growth in the population model.

Why do we call it exponential?

In Chapter 1, I stated that system dynamics models are essentially solutions to a series of differential equations, which are solved using numerical methods. In Chapter 2, I explained that the numerical method used was called Euler integration. I also mentioned that the Euler integration method is approximate, and the smaller the time step, the more accurate the approximation.

Finding exact solutions to a series of differential equations can be challenging and requires considerable mathematical skill. However, for this population model, we can find the exact value, which is equal to the initial population multiplied by EXP (time * growth rate) people (see Fig. 3.7, where the exact values are shown in column G). The Excel function EXP represents the exponential function, calculated using the number *e*, also known as Euler's number, which equals approximately 2.71828. The EXP function takes *e* to the power of the number in the brackets. For example, EXP (0.00611) = *e* ^ 0.00611 = 2.71828 ^ 0.00611 = 1.0061298. If we multiply 1.0061298 by the initial population of 1,000 people, we get the exact population at year 1: 1,000 * 1.0061298 = 1,006.1298 people, as shown in cell G10. Notice that the values in columns C and G are slightly different.

Recall that I said in Chapter 2 that it is good practice to use time steps that are negative powers of 2. Figure 3.8 shows that when we take a tiny time step, in this case 2 ^ −8 = 1/2 ^ 8 = 0.003906, we get approximate values that match the exact values for the population to four decimal places.

SUM | fx =E$4*EXP(E$5*A2)

	A	B	C	D	E	F	G
1	Time (Year)	growth (people/ Year)	Population Approx. (people)	PARAMETERS	VALUES	UNITS	Population Exact (people)
2	0	6.1111	1,000	START TIME	0	Year	=E$4*EXP(E$5*A2)
3	0.125	6.1158	1,000.7639	TIME STEP	0.125	Year	1,000.7642
4	0.25	6.1205	1,001.5284	INITIAL POPULATION	1,000	People	1,001.5289
5	0.375	6.1251	1,002.2934	GROWTH RATE	0.00611	1/Year	1,002.2943
6	0.5	6.1298	1,003.0591				1,003.0602
7	0.625	6.1345	1,003.8253				1,003.8267
8	0.75	6.1392	1,004.5921				1,004.5939
9	0.875	6.1439	1,005.3595				1,005.3615
10	1	6.1486	1,006.1275				1,006.1298
11	1.125	6.1533	1,006.8960				1,006.8987
12	1.25	6.1580	1,007.6652				1,007.6681
13	1.375	6.1627	1,008.4349				1,008.4382
14	1.5	6.1674	1,009.2053				1,009.2088
15	1.625	6.1721	1,009.9762				1,009.9800
16	1.75	6.1768	1,010.7477				1,010.7518

Fig. 3.7: Comparison of the approximate solution and the exact solution.

E3 | fx =1/2^8

	A	B	C	D	E	F	G
1	Time (Year)	growth (people/ Year)	Population Approx. (people)	PARAMETERS	VALUES	UNITS	Population Exact (people)
2	0	6.1111	1,000	START TIME	0	Year	1,000
3	0.003906	6.1113	1,000.0239	TIME STEP	0.003906	Year	1,000.0239
4	0.007813	6.1114	1,000.0477	INITIAL POPULATION	1,000	People	1,000.0477
5	0.011719	6.1115	1,000.0716	GROWTH RATE	0.00611	1/Year	1,000.0716
6	0.015625	6.1117	1,000.0955				1,000.0955
7	0.019531	6.1118	1,000.1194				1,000.1194
8	0.023438	6.1120	1,000.1432				1,000.1432
9	0.027344	6.1121	1,000.1671				1,000.1671
10	0.03125	6.1123	1,000.1910				1,000.1910
11	0.035156	6.1124	1,000.2149				1,000.2149
12	0.039063	6.1126	1,000.2387				1,000.2387
13	0.042969	6.1127	1,000.2626				1,000.2626
14	0.046875	6.1129	1,000.2865				1,000.2865
15	0.050781	6.1130	1,000.3104				1,000.3104

Fig. 3.8: Comparison of the approximate and exact values with a tiny time step.

3.4 Reinforcing Loops

In Chapter 1, we discussed reinforcing feedback loops. In these loops, if a value increases, the change ripples through the system, returning to its original value and causing a further increase, which is sometimes referred to as a virtuous cycle. You may also know the term "vicious cycle," in which a decrease in value ripples through the system, returning to its original value and causing a further reduction.

Interestingly, although most people understand that vicious cycles are undesirable, they may not realize that virtuous cycles are equally undesirable. Therefore, if unchecked, reinforcing loops can lead to explosive growth if the initial value is positive or to disastrous crashes if it is negative.

Exponential growth is often misunderstood because it starts deceptively slow before accelerating dramatically. A classic illustration of this concept is the well-known lily pond story. Imagine a pond that begins at time zero with a single lily, but the number of lilies doubles daily. At first, the growth seems insignificant. On day 1, the lily is barely noticeable, and even after several days, it covers only a tiny portion of the pond. Let's assume the pond is half-covered on the 10th day. How long will it take for the whole pond to be covered with lilies?

Let's build a model of this. Figure 3.9 shows the Vensim model, and Fig. 3.10 shows the Excel model. The stock of lilies has an initial value of 1 and an approximate growth rate of 1. We have a 100 m^2 pond and a lily that covers 0.05 m^2. The formula for the fraction of the pond covered by lilies = (lilies * lily size)/pond size, or in Excel = C2 * F$6/F$7. Notice that at time 10, the fraction of the pond area covered by lilies is 0.5.

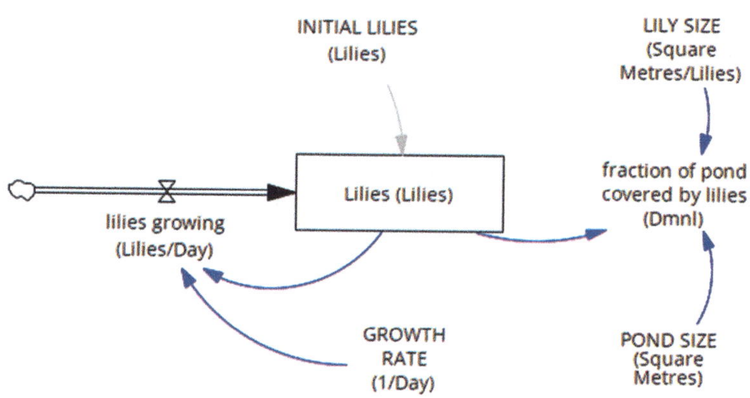

Fig. 3.9: Vensim model of the lily pond.

SUM | fx =C2*F$6/F$7

	A	B	C	D	E	F	G
1	Time (Day)	growth of lilies (Lilies/Day)	Lilies (Lilies)	fraction of pond area covered by lilies (Dmnl)	PARAMETERS	VALUE	UNITS
2	0	1.0000	1.0000	=C2*F$6/F$7	START TIME	0	DAY
3	1	2.0000	2.0000	0.0010	TIME STEP	1	DAY
4	2	4.0000	4.0000	0.0020	INITIAL LILIES	1	LILIES
5	3	8.0000	8.0000	0.0039	GROWTH RATE	1.00	1/DAY
6	4	16.0000	16.0000	0.0078	LILIE AREA	0.05	M^2
7	5	32.0000	32.0000	0.0156	POND AREA	100	M^2
8	6	64.0000	64.0000	0.0313			
9	7	128.0000	128.0000	0.0625			
10	8	256.0000	256.0000	0.1250			
11	9	512.0000	512.0000	0.2500			
12	10	1024.0000	1024.0000	0.5000			

Fig. 3.10: Excel model of the lily pond.

When you hear this story, you may think covering the pond will take 10 more days. However, upon examining the Excel results, you can likely infer that the pond will be covered by day 11, as we will add another 1,024 lilies to the stock. Since 1,024 lilies cover half the pond, another 1,024 lilies on day 11 will cover the whole pond.

This raises another point I need to clarify regarding exponential growth. You may have heard of "The Rule of 72," often associated with the doubling time. The doubling time is the time it takes the population to double with exponential growth.

Using our Excel model, let's revisit the lily story (see Fig. 3.11). This time, we will show a time step of 0.125. Notice that in this case, the Excel model estimates the num-

	A	B	C	D	E	F	G
1	Time (Day)	growth of lilies (Lilies/Day)	Lilies (Lilies)	fraction of pond area covered by lilies (Dmnl)	PARAMETERS	VALUE	UNITS
2	0	1.0000	1.0000	0.0005	START TIME	0	DAY
3	0.125	1.1250	1.1250	0.0005	TIME STEP	0.125	DAY
4	0.25	1.2656	1.2656	0.0006	INITIAL LILIES	1	LILIES
5	0.375	1.4238	1.4238	0.0007	GROWTH RATE	1.00	1/DAY
6	0.5	1.6018	1.6018	0.0008	LILIE AREA	0.05	M^2
7	0.625	1.8020	1.8020	0.0009	POND AREA	100	M^2
8	0.75	2.0273	2.0273	0.0010			
9	0.875	2.2807	2.2807	0.0011			
10	1	2.5658	2.5658	0.0013			
11	1.125	2.8865	2.8865	0.0014			
12	1.25	3.2473	3.2473	0.0016			

Fig. 3.11: Excel model of the lily pond, using a time step of 0.125.

ber of lilies on day 1 to be 2.5658, which provides a better approximation of the lilies if we had actual exponential growth of 1 lily per day. However, this is significantly greater than 2, as shown in Fig. 3.10, where it was equal to 2. So, the doubling time is closer to 0.75 days, as shown in Fig. 3.11, where the value for Lilies at 0.75 days is 2.0273.

The Rule of 72 states that the doubling time is 72/(growth rate * 100). So, if I ignore my advice about time-step values and use a time step of 0.072, Fig. 3.12 shows the number of lilies at time 0.72 is 2.0042, which is a good approximation to double the initial value. Please note that the Rule of 72 is an approximation. Calculating the exact doubling time is a more mathematically challenging task.

	A	B	C	D	E	F	G
1	Time (Day)	growth of lilies (Lilies/Day)	Lilies (Lilies)	fraction of pond area covered by lilies (Dmnl)	PARAMETERS	VALUE	UNITS
2	0	1.0000	1.0000	0.0005	START TIME	0	DAY
3	0.072	1.0720	1.0720	0.0005	TIME STEP	0.072	DAY
4	0.144	1.1492	1.1492	0.0006	INITIAL LILIES	1	LILIES
5	0.216	1.2319	1.2319	0.0006	GROWTH RATE	1.00	1/DAY
6	0.288	1.3206	1.3206	0.0006	LILIE AREA	0.05	M^2
7	0.36	1.4157	1.4157	0.0007	POND AREA	100	M^2
8	0.432	1.5176	1.5176	0.0007			
9	0.504	1.6269	1.6269	0.0008			
10	0.576	1.7440	1.7440	0.0009			
11	0.648	1.8696	1.8696	0.0009			
12	0.72	2.0042	2.0042	0.0010			

Fig. 3.12: Excel model of the lily pond, using a time step of 0.072.

The world's population has grown exponentially over the centuries (see Fig. 3.13). There was little growth from year 0 to 1500, from 232 million to 503 million. Then, after 1800, the world population exploded from 1 billion to 8 billion in 2022 [36].

Now, let's consider a financial situation, such as debt. Figure 3.14 shows the US debt from 1789 to 2024. We can see that the debt was relatively small in 1789, at $71 million, and didn't increase significantly until 1900, when it reached $2,137 million. However, after 1950, US debt increased from $257 billion to over $35 trillion by 2024 [37].

The conclusion you should draw from this discussion is that you shouldn't think of reinforcing loops as good things in most situations. Unchecked exponential growth is an explosive disaster. Therefore, when building models, ensure they include compensating balancing loops to control the reinforcing loops.

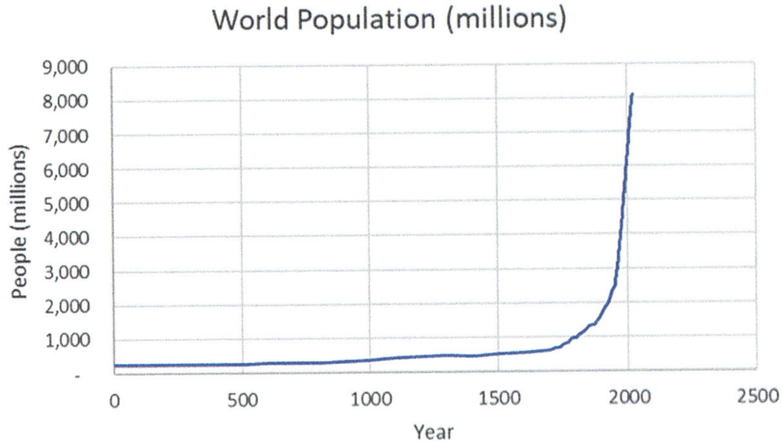

Fig. 3.13: Explosive population growth in the world as a virtuous cycle.

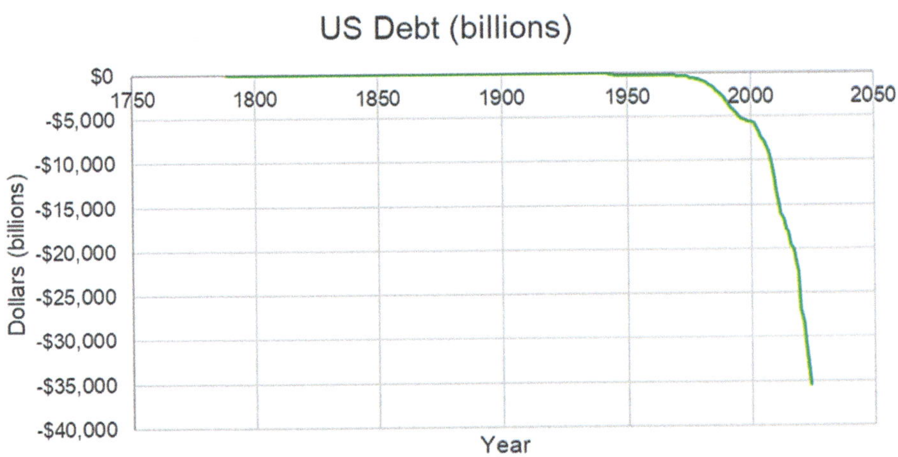

Fig. 3.14: Explosive US debt as a vicious cycle.

3.5 Equilibrium

In our population model, equilibrium occurs when the birth rate converges to 1/life expectancy. So, with a birth rate of 0.02, at a rate of people/people/year, we would have equilibrium if the life expectancy were 1/0.02 = 50 years. Or if we had a life expectancy of 72 years, we would reach equilibrium when the birth rate was 1/72 = 0.0138889 people/people/year. With these values, the births inflow (population * birth rate people/year) would equal the deaths outflow (population/life expectancy people/year).

When you think about the differences between the inflows and the outflows, you can build your intuition about system dynamics models. Some people consider it good practice to start their analysis of a model with parameter values that keep the system in equilibrium. Then apply parameter changes to see how the model reacts. For example, policymakers may introduce improved health care that increases life expectancy, potentially pushing the system out of equilibrium.

3.6 Exponential Decline

In some countries, the birth rate is below 1/life expectancy. In this case, the population suffers an exponential decline.

If the birth rate is 0.01 people/people/year, and the life expectancy is 72 years, the growth rate = birth rate–1/life expectancy = 0.01–1/72 = 0.01–0.0138889 = –0.0038889 people/people/year. Since we have a negative growth rate, we can consider this a decline rate.

Figure 3.15 shows the Vensim model, and Fig. 3.16 shows the Excel version of the model along with the exact solution of the differential equation. Figure 3.17 shows the results of the population decline model.

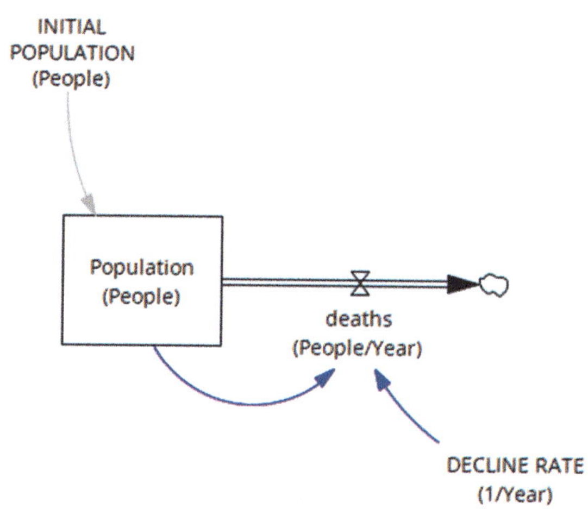

Fig. 3.15: Vensim model of population decline.

	A	B	C	D	E	F	G
1	Time (Year)	Population Approx. (people)	decline (people/ Year)	PARAMETER	VALUES	UNITS	Population Exact (people)
2	0	1000.0000	3.88889	INITIAL TIME	0	Year	1000.0000
3	0.125	999.5139	3.88700	TIME STEP	0.125	Year	999.5140
4	0.25	999.0280	3.88511	INITIAL VALUE	1000.0	People	999.0283
5	0.375	998.5424	3.88322	DECLINE RATE	0.0038889	1/Year	998.5427
6	0.5	998.0570	3.88133				998.0574
7	0.625	997.5718	3.87945				997.5724
8	0.75	997.0869	3.87756				997.0876
9	0.875	996.6022	3.87568				996.6030
10	1	996.1177	3.87379				996.1187
11	1.125	995.6335	3.87191				995.6346
12	1.25	995.1495	3.87003				995.1507

Fig. 3.16: Excel model of population decline.

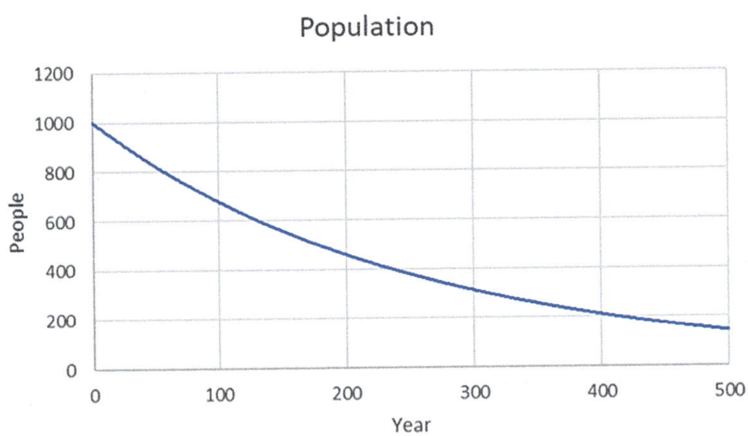

Fig. 3.17: Results of the population decline model.

So, what is happening here?

We see this gradual decline because every year's decline is less than the previous year's. The decline is the decline rate multiplied by the population per year, which is subtracted from the earlier population. Therefore, because the population is decreasing each year, the decline is less pronounced (see Fig. 3.18).

The exact formula for the exponential decline is initial population * EXP (time * (−decline rate)). so, at time 1, the population = initial population * EXP (−1 * decline rate) = 1,000 * e ^ (−1 * 0.003889) = 1,000 * 2.71828 ^ (−0.003889) = 1,000/(2.71828 ^ 0.003889) = 1,000/1.003896 = 996.119. This is why it is referred to as an exponential decline.

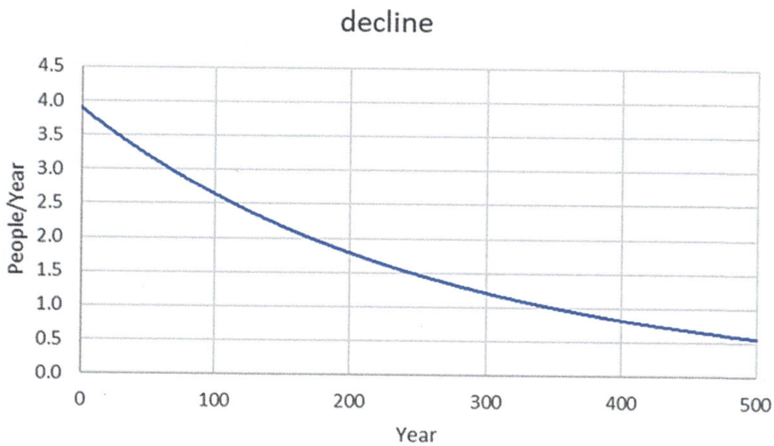

Fig. 3.18: The decline in the population model.

There is one more thing I would like to explain about exponential decline. This is counterintuitive. Let's conduct a thought experiment. Assuming the birth rate is zero, there will be no births. If we start with 1,000 people in the population at time zero and the life expectancy is 72 years, what do you expect the population to be in the year 72?

You might think that in year 72, the population would be zero. But if you were using system dynamics to calculate the population decline, you would be wrong. Let's look at the model. Figure 3.19 shows the Vensim model, and Fig. 3.20 shows the Excel model.

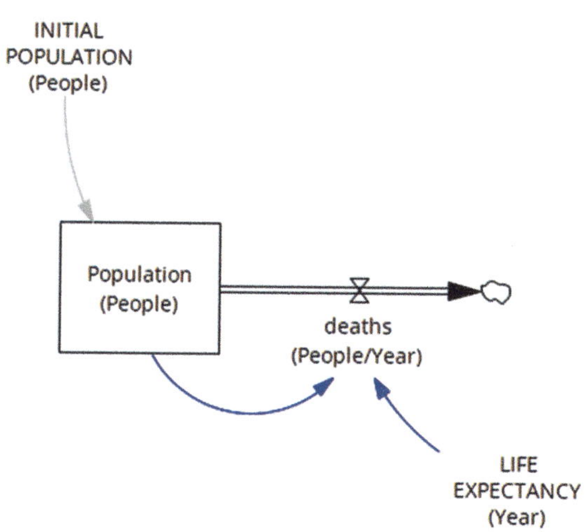

Fig. 3.19: Vensim population decline model with life expectancy.

SUM | fx =B2/E$5

	A	B	C	D	E	F	G
1	Time (Year)	Population Approx. (people)	decline (people/ Year)	PARAMETER	VALUES	UNITS	Population Exact (people)
2	0	1000.0000	=B2/E$5	INITIAL TIME	0	Year	1000.0000
3	1	986.1111	13.69599	TIME STEP	1	Year	986.2071
4	2	972.4151	13.50577	INITIAL VALUE	1000.0	People	972.6045
5	3	958.9094	13.31819	DECLINE RATE	72	Year	959.1895
6	4	945.5912	13.13321				945.9595
7	5	932.4580	12.95081				932.9120
8	6	919.5072	12.77093				920.0444
9	7	906.7362	12.59356				907.3543
10	8	894.1427	12.41865				894.8393
11	9	881.7240	12.24617				882.4969
12	10	869.4779	12.07608				870.3247

Fig. 3.20: Excel population decline model with life expectancy.

If we scroll down column B to year 72, we see that the population estimated by the system dynamics model is 365.3098 (see Fig. 3.21). How did the model come up with such a strange result?

	A	B	C	D	E	F	G
1	Time (Year)	Population Approx. (people)	decline (people/ Year)	PARAMETER	VALUES	UNITS	Population Exact (people)
65	63	414.3131	5.75435				416.86202
66	64	408.5588	5.67443				411.11229
67	65	402.8844	5.59562				405.44187
68	66	397.2887	5.51790				399.84965
69	67	391.7708	5.44126				394.33457
70	68	386.3296	5.36569				388.89556
71	69	380.9639	5.29117				383.53157
72	70	375.6727	5.21768				378.24157
73	71	370.4550	5.14521				373.02452
74	72	365.3098	5.07375				367.87944

Fig. 3.21: Excel population decline model results at year 72.

This is because of the exponential formula in the population decline model. The exact value for the population in year 72 is population = initial population * EXP (−time/life expectancy) = 1,000 * e ^ (−72/72) = 1,000 * 2.71828 ^ (−1) = 1,000/2.71828 = 367.879 people.

This example illustrates a key insight about exponential decline: the population does not decrease linearly but instead decreases gradually. Even after 72 years, when one might expect the population to be zero given no births and a life expectancy of 72 years, the exponential decline model shows that approximately 368 people remain. This result stems from the fact that the population declines proportionally over time. Understanding this principle is crucial in system dynamics modelling, as it highlights the fundamental behaviour of exponential processes in real-world systems.

3.7 Balancing Loops

Balancing loops are often considered goal-seeking. Exponential decline is a balancing loop. For example, if the birth rate is less than 1/life expectancy, then deaths will exceed births, resulting in a decline in the population. However, a decrease in the population leads to a reduction in both births and deaths. However, the number of births will still be less than the number of deaths, and the population will decline. So, even though the population will gradually decline, the rate of decline will decrease as it declines. The population will gradually go to zero but never actually reach zero. In this case, the goal is zero population.

This seems like a bad result, but balancing loops should be a large part of your system dynamics models to keep the reinforcing loops in check. In general, they are constraints on your model. Sometimes, a balancing loop can help you get back on track if you've gotten off track. At other times, we may find that we would like to implement positive changes through effective policies, but we cannot have a significant impact due to the balancing loops that resist change.

In a population model, we can consider a situation in which a carrying capacity limits the population. With a positive growth rate, the population will continue to grow; however, as it approaches its carrying capacity, growth will slow and eventually reach a steady state, where it will remain stable at approximately zero. Figure 3.22 shows the structure of this model in Vensim.

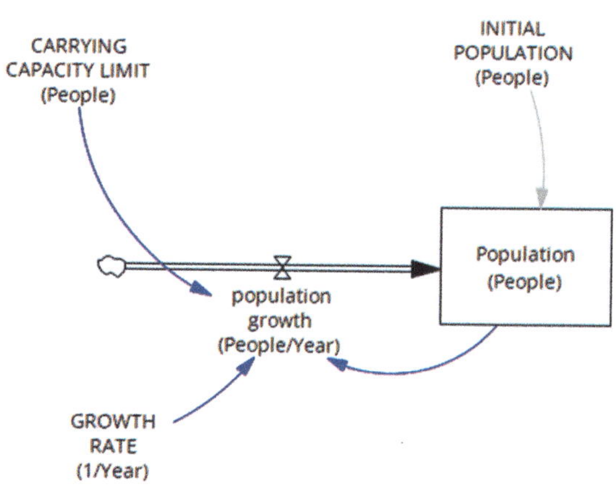

Fig. 3.22: Vensim version of the population growth model with a carrying capacity limit.

Figure 3.23 shows the Excel version of this model. We will set the initial population to 1,000 people, the growth rate to 0.02 people/people/year, and the carrying capacity to 10,000 people. We will revise the growth formula in the Excel model to growth = population * growth rate * (1–population/carrying capacity). At time 0, the growth is calculated as C2 * E$5 * (1–C2/E$6) (see Fig. 3.23). With this formula, if the population is small relative to the carrying capacity, growth will be dominated by the population * growth rate factor, resulting in nearly exponential growth. As the population approaches the carrying capacity limit, the factor (1–population/carrying capacity limit), which is expressed as people/people and commonly referred to as "dimensionless," approaches zero. When multiplying a dimensionless value by a value in units per year, the result remains in units per year. So, when this dimensionless value approaches zero, the growth rate approaches zero, corresponding to a rate of people/year.

SUM | =C2*E$5*(1-C2/E$6)

	A	B	C	D	E	F
1	Time (Year)	growth (people/ Year)	Population (people)	PARAMETERS	VALUES	UNITS
2	0	=C2*E$5*	1,000	START TIME	0	Year
3	1	18.28735	1,018	TIME STEP	1	Year
4	2	18.57796	1,036	INITIAL POPULATION	1,000	People
5	3	18.87182	1,055	GROWTH RATE	0.02	1/Year
6	4	19.16892	1,074	CARRYING CAPACITY LIMIT	10,000	People
7	5	19.46923	1,093			
8	6	19.77275	1,112			
9	7	20.07944	1,132			
10	8	20.38929	1,152			
11	9	20.70228	1,173			
12	10	21.01836	1,193			

Fig. 3.23: An Excel version of the population growth model with a carrying capacity limit.

Figure 3.24 shows the results of this model. We can see that for the period 0–110, the behaviour appears to be exponential growth, also known as increasing returns, because the growth at each time step is larger than the previous one. Then, after year 110, we see diminishing returns because the increase is more minor at each time step than in the previous one. By the year 400, the population will have approximately reached the carrying capacity limit of 10,000 people. This model represents the classic limits to growth model.

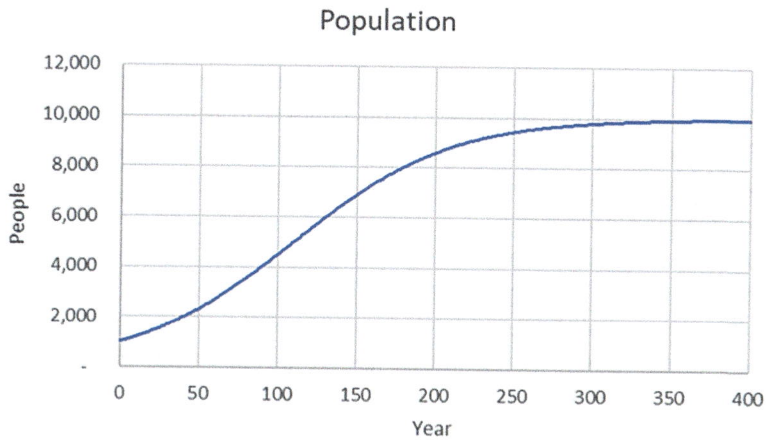

Fig. 3.24: The results of the population growth model with a carrying capacity limit.

In Fig. 3.25, we see the model's growth. We can see that the growth initially increases, peaks at 50 people/year at time 110, then declines and approaches zero at time 400.

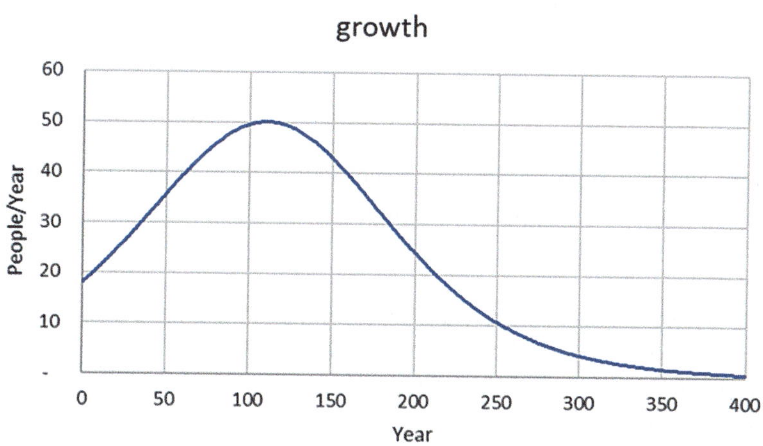

Fig. 3.25: The growth in the population model with a carrying capacity limit.

This is an example of a well-behaved model that transitions from a reinforcing loop with increasing returns to a balancing loop with diminishing returns, preventing the population from exploding.

3.8 Summary and Conclusion

In this chapter, we examined exponential growth and decline using the population model from Chapter 2. When births exceed deaths, the population grows; when deaths exceed births, it falls. We simplified the model using a growth-rate formula, used Excel's EXP function for an exact solution, and compared it with Euler integration to show how the time step affects accuracy.

We also introduced reinforcing feedback. The lily pond story and real-world examples, such as the growth of world population and compounding debt, illustrate how small changes can snowball into rapid growth – or collapse. To keep things in check, we discussed equilibrium – where inflows (births) match outflows (deaths) – and how adjusting birth rates and life expectancy can stabilize the system.

Exponential decline occurs when outflows exceed inflows. The population drops quickly at first, then more slowly, approaching – but never reaching – zero. Finally, we added a carrying capacity so growth starts fast, then slows as limits kick in, clarifying that "zero growth" means the population has levelled off, not that it is shrinking.

In the next chapter, we'll allow birth rates and life expectancy to change over time to reflect real trends in health and family size. We will build on the ideas of goal-seeking models and discuss a new model structure, the goal-gap model.

3.9 Discussion Questions

- In your context, where would misreading a reinforcing loop as positive create material risk? Cite an indicator that would validate its reinforcing.
- When would you accept Rule-of-72 approximations, and when must you show exact or simulated results?
- Show how a time-step choice can overstate or understate long-term performance claims. What's your time-step justification in an audit?
- Using the equilibrium condition, which lever (birth rate vs. life expectancy) is more feasible to shift in your domain, and why?
- Explain to a non-technical sponsor why declining to zero is asymptotic, not linear, and how that affects policy timelines.
- For a capacity-constrained system you know, specify the carrying-capacity driver and how it flips the loop from reinforcing to balancing.

3.10 Exercises

3.10.1 Growth rate reformulation, exact versus Euler

Task. Start with initial population = 1,000, birth rate = 0.022, life expectancy = 75. Compute the growth rate. In Excel, implement Euler with a time step of 1 and compute the

exact value using EXP (time * growth rate).
Deliverable: A 10-row table with population (Euler) and population (exact), plus the absolute error at time = 1.

3.10.2 Time step sensitivity
Task. Repeat exercise 1 with time step = 1/256 = 0.003906. Show that Euler and exact align to four decimal places by time = 1.
Deliverable. Brief note (<75 words) plus comparison at time = 1.

3.10.3 Lily pond doubling
Task. Build the lily pond model in Excel with initial lilies = 1, growth rate = 1/lillies/lillies/day, lily size = 0.01 m^2, pond size = 200 m^2. Add a column for fraction covered = (lilies * lily size)/pond size.
Deliverable. Show the day when coverage equals 0.5 and the day when coverage equals 1.0.

3.10.4 Doubling time: Rule of 72 versus model
Task. Using the rule of 72, estimate the doubling time and compare it to the modelled doubling interval.
Deliverable. Two numbers and one sentence explaining the variance.

3.10.5 Exponential decline paradox
Task. Set birth rate = 0.01, life expectancy = 75; calculate the decline rate and compute exact (time = 1) via EXP (–decline rate). Then, set the birth rate to 0, keep the life expectancy at 75, and report the population at time 75 using the exact formula.
Deliverable. A short table and two numeric answers (time = 1; time = 75) with a one-sentence interpretation.

3.10.6 Logistic (carrying-capacity) growth
Task. Implement growth = population * growth rate * (1–population/carrying capacity) with initial population = 500, growth rate = 0.05, and carrying capacity = 20,000. Plot population and growth over time.
Deliverable. Two Excel charts and a two-sentence takeaway on increasing and diminishing returns.

Chapter 4
Time-Varying Rates Using a Goal-Gap Model

4.1 Learning Objectives

- Explain why simple linear trend fits can look adequate in-sample yet fail for long-horizon forecasts, and identify warning signs of unsafe extrapolation.
- Describe the goal-gap (goal-seeking) feedback structure and why it behaves as a balancing loop that drives a variable towards a target.
- Formulate a generic goal-gap increase equation for any target (e.g. *change = (target level − current level) / time to change*) and implement it in Excel with Euler time stepping.
- Formulate a goal-gap decrease equation for metrics that should decline towards a floor (e.g. *change = (current level − target level) / time to change*) and implement it in Excel.
- Compare linear trend versus goal-gap projections; explain how goal-gap structures avoid impossible values (e.g. negatives, >100%) and enforce realistic asymptotic behaviour.
- Detect and prevent impossible states implied by naïve extrapolation by applying structural constraints and parameter bounds.
- Define and execute lightweight calibration procedures using historical data or reference modes, and articulate how calibration enhances credibility and traceability.
- Decide when to use trend fits versus feedback models for policy and planning, based on the decision horizon, stakes, and the availability of structural knowledge.

4.2 Introduction

Birth rates and life expectancies have been treated as constants, assuming they remain fixed over time. While this simplification can be helpful for short-term analysis, it fails to capture the long-term dynamics of population change. Historical data indicate that birth rate and life expectancy have evolved significantly with economic development, improvements in healthcare, social changes, and policy interventions. Modelling these variables as time-varying allows us to represent real-world trends and make more realistic projections.

This chapter explores approaches for modelling birth rates and life expectancies as dynamic variables that change over time. We first examine simple linear models that capture historical trends but can lead to unrealistic long-term projections. To address this issue, we introduce the goal-seeking balancing loop, known as the goal-gap model, which accounts for natural limits and gradual changes, thereby ensuring more

https://doi.org/10.1515/9783111541389-005

reasonable future projections. By comparing these modelling approaches, we highlight the importance of incorporating dynamic feedback mechanisms when analysing demographic transitions.

4.3 Life Expectancy Linear Model

It is well-known that life expectancy has increased in the last 70 years. Figure 4.1 shows data from the United Nations Population Prospects 2024 [38]. We can see a steady increase in life expectancy, from 46 years in 1950 to 73 years in 2023. The dip in 1960 was created by the Great Leap Forward in China, which resulted in millions of deaths from starvation and disease as the Chinese government abruptly transitioned from an agricultural economy to an industrial economy. COVID-19 created the dip in 2021. Otherwise, the growth in life expectancy is relatively steady.

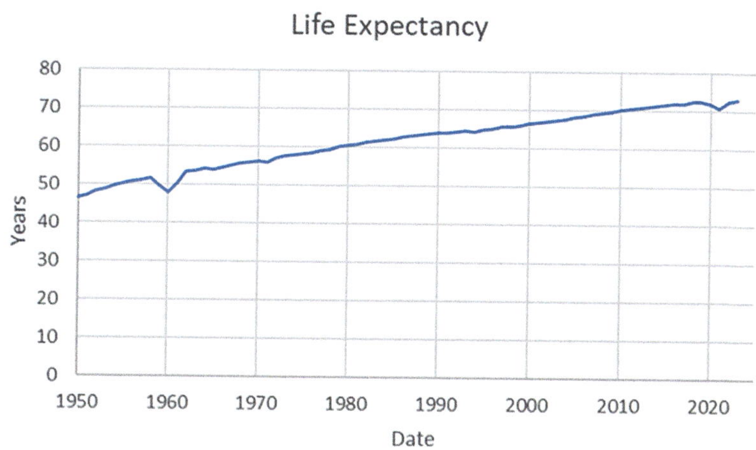

Fig. 4.1: Increase in life expectancy from 1950 to 2023.

We might be tempted to model this increasing trend using a statistical method such as linear regression. Figure 4.2 shows the Vensim version of the model, and Fig. 4.3 shows the Excel version. Notice that the increase in life expectancy inflow in Figs. 4.2 and 4.3 does not depend on the life expectancy stock; the rise in life expectancy is a constant.

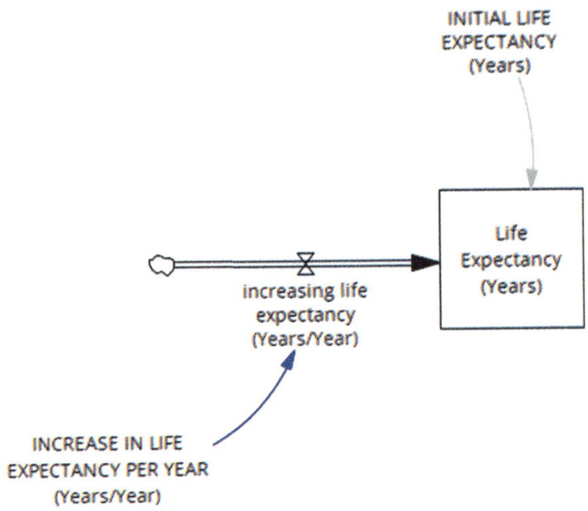

Fig. 4.2: Linear Vensim model of the increase in life expectancy.

	A	B	C	D	E	F
1	Date (Year)	increasing life expectancy (Years/Year)	Model Life Expectancy (Years)	PARAMETERS	VALUE	UNITS
2	1950	0.3558	48.6615	START TIME	1950	YEAR
3	1951	0.3558	49.0173	TIME STEP	1	YEAR
4	1952	0.3558	49.3731	INITIAL VALUE	48.6615	YEARS
5	1953	0.3558	49.7289	INCREASE PER YEAR	0.3558	YEARS/YEAR
6	1954	0.3558	50.0847			
7	1955	0.3558	50.4405			
8	1956	0.3558	50.7963			
9	1957	0.3558	51.1521			
10	1958	0.3558	51.5079			
11	1959	0.3558	51.8637			
12	1960	0.3558	52.2196			

Fig. 4.3: Linear Excel model of the increase in life expectancy.

Figure 4.4 illustrates that the results of the linear model align well with the historical data.

The problem arises when we attempt to extrapolate this model into the long term (see Fig. 4.5), which suggests that life expectancy in 2200 would be approximately 140 years. A significant technological breakthrough may make this possible.

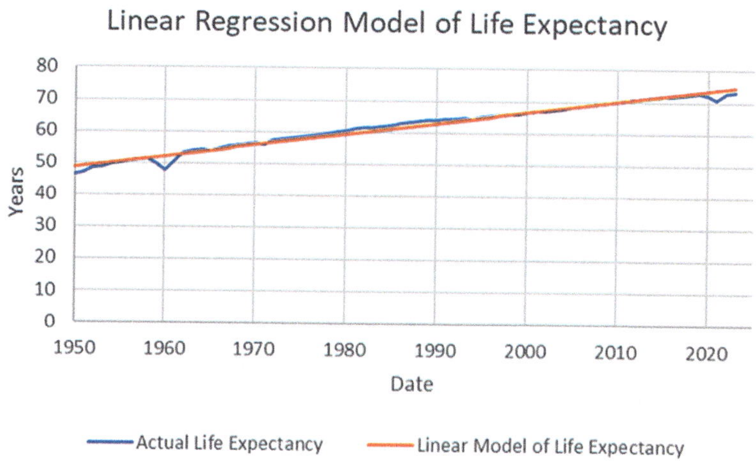

Fig. 4.4: Linear model results from 1950 to 2023.

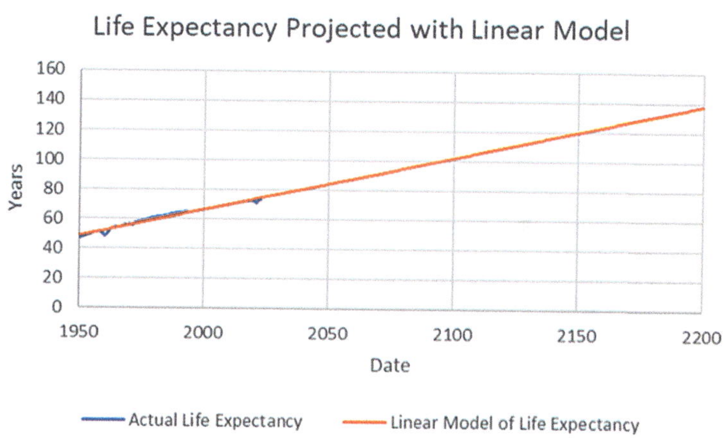

Fig. 4.5: Linear model projection of life expectancy from 1950 to 2200.

However, you can't predict technological breakthroughs. So, we will develop an alternative model that may not require a significant technological breakthrough.

4.4 Life Expectancy Goal-Gap Model

An alternative model of life expectancy is a non-linear growth model. In this case, we specify a long-term life expectancy. Life expectancy will approach the long-term value, but as it gets close, the increase will decline.

The goal-gap model is a goal-seeking system dynamics model that represents a system adjusting over time to move towards a predefined target or equilibrium state.

This behaviour is characteristic of a balancing loop, where the difference between the current and desired states drives corrective action. In the case of life expectancy, the model ensures that the variable approaches its long-term limits gradually and is controlled. The rate of change is proportional to the gap between the current value and the long-term goal, decreasing as the gap narrows. This feedback mechanism prevents unrealistic growth, ensuring a more stable, long-term projection. By incorporating a balancing loop, the goal-gap model accurately reflects the self-regulating nature of demographic trends, which are influenced by factors such as healthcare, economic development, and social aspects.

Figure 4.6 shows the Vensim goal-gap model. Notice that the inflow, which increases life expectancy, depends on life expectancy. The formula for increasing life expectancy is (long-term life expectancy – life expectancy)/time to change life expectancy. Figure 4.7 shows the Vensim interface for the increasing life expectancy formula. So, as life expectancy approaches its long-term value, the rate of increase in life expectancy approaches zero.

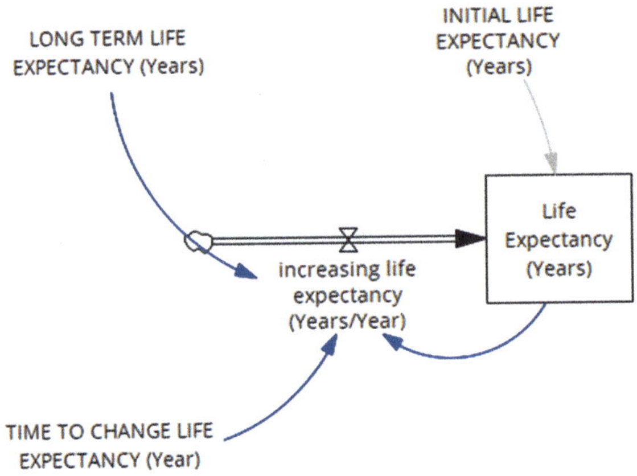

Fig. 4.6: Vensim goal-gap model of life expectancy.

Figure 4.8 shows the Excel version. In this case, the formula for increasing life expectancy at time zero is (E$5–C2)/E$6.

Figure 4.9 compares the goal-gap model results with the actual life expectancy values.

The value of the goal-gap model lies in its ability to project long-term life expectancy. Figure 4.10 shows the projection results for this goal-gap model. The projection that we can reach a world life expectancy of 80 years by 2050 may not be too far off the mark.

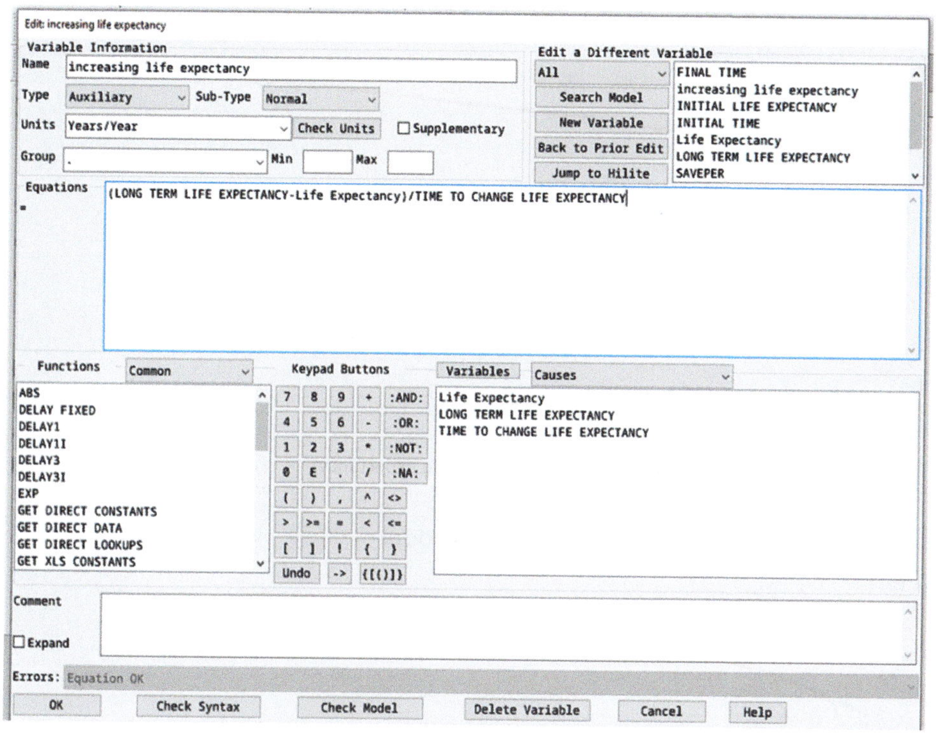

Fig. 4.7: Vensim interface for increasing life expectancy formula.

SUM | =(E$5-C2)/E$6

	A	B	C	D	E	F
1	Date (Year)	increasing life expectancy (Years/Year)	Model Life Expectancy (Years)	PARAMETERS	VALUE	UNITS
2	1950	=(E$5-C2)/E$6	46.3940	START TIME	1950	YEAR
3	1951	0.5011	46.8998	TIME STEP	1	YEAR
4	1952	0.4963	47.4009	INITIAL VALUE	46.394	YEARS
5	1953	0.4916	47.8972	LONG TERM VALUE	100	YEARS
6	1954	0.4870	48.3889	TIME TO CHANGE	105.9764	YEAR
7	1955	0.4824	48.8759			
8	1956	0.4779	49.3583			
9	1957	0.4733	49.8361			
10	1958	0.4689	50.3095			
11	1959	0.4645	50.7784			
12	1960	0.4601	51.2428			

Fig. 4.8: Excel goal-gap model of life expectancy.

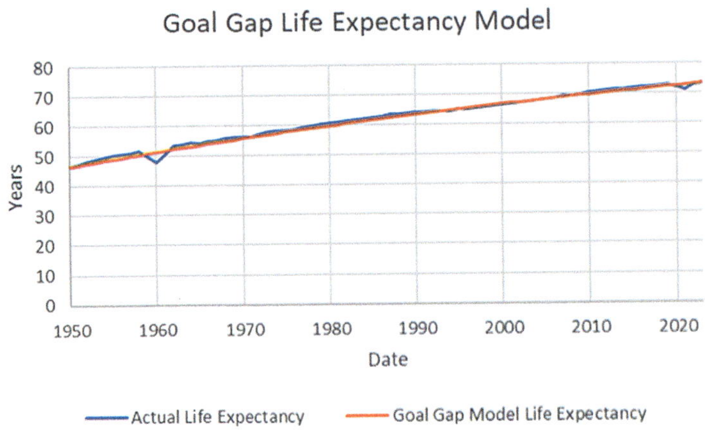

Fig. 4.9: Comparison of the goal-gap model with actual life expectancy.

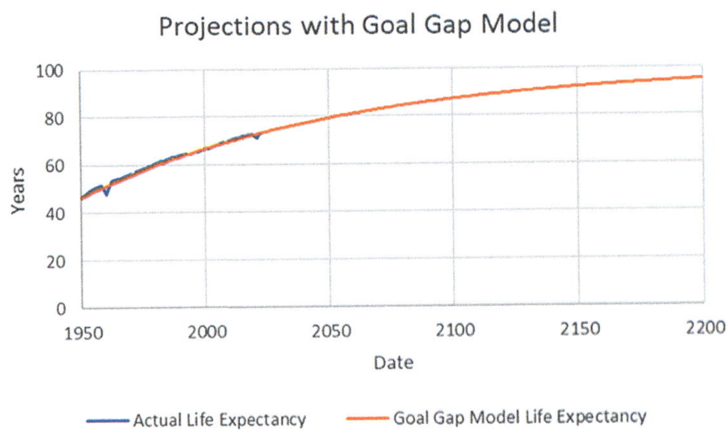

Fig. 4.10: Projection of life expectancy from the goal-gap model.

4.5 Linear Birth Rate Model

Figure 4.11 shows the historical world birth rate from 1950 to 2023. It shows that it has been steadily declining since the early 1960s.

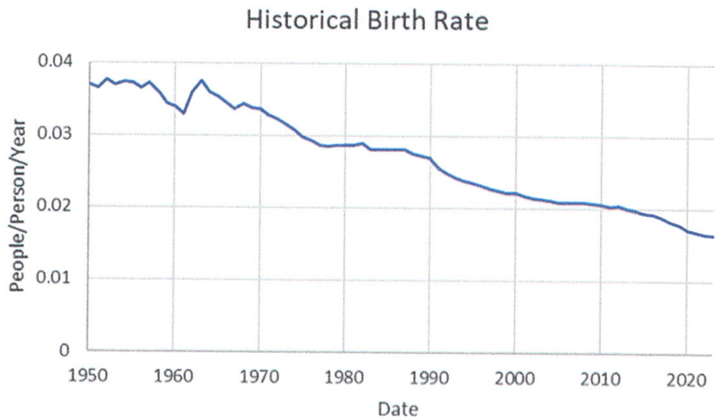

Fig. 4.11: Historical world birth rate.

Again, we might be tempted to model this with a linear regression. Figure 4.12 illustrates that the linear model provides a good fit for the data.

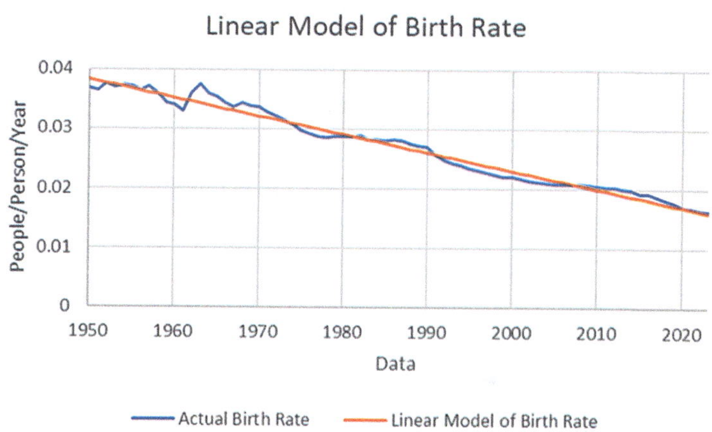

Fig. 4.12: Linear model of the historical world birth rate.

Again, the problem with the linear model comes when we project into the long term. The problem is even more serious than the linear life expectancy model. In Fig. 4.13, we observe that projecting the linear model into the future predicts a negative birth rate after 2075, which is physically impossible.

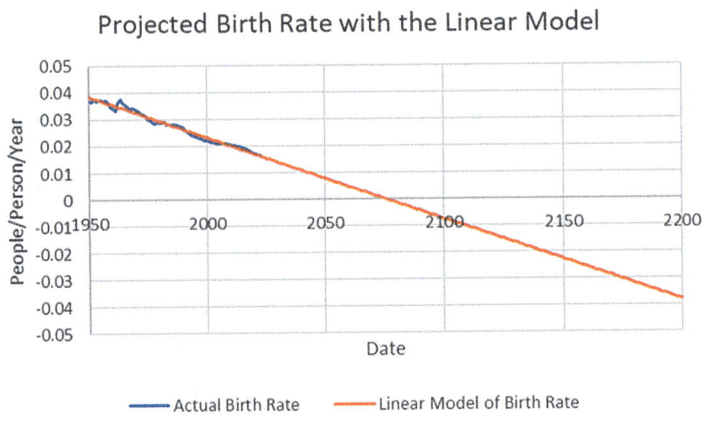

Fig. 4.13: Projected world birth rate with the linear model.

4.6 Goal-Gap Birth Rate Model

We will build a similar dynamic model for the time-varying birth rate. Figure 4.14 shows the Vensim model, and Fig. 4.15 shows the Excel version. The formula for the decreasing birth rate is (birth rate − long-term birth rate)/time to change birth rate. In Excel, the formula for time 0 is (B2 − E$5)/E$6. Figure 4.16 illustrates that the goal-gap model aligns well with the historical data.

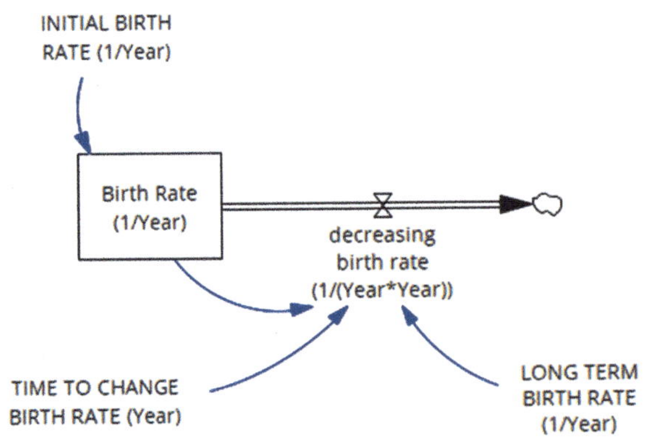

Fig. 4.14: Vensim goal-gap model for birth rate.

SUM | fx =(B2-E$5)/E$6

	A	B	C	D	E	F
1	Time (Year)	Goal- Gap Model of Birth Rate (1/Year)	decreasing birth rate (1/(Year*Year)	PARAMETERS	VALUES	UNITS
2	1950	0.04	=(B2-E$5)/E$6	START YEAR	1950	YEAR
3	1951	0.04	0.00054	TIME STEP	1	YEAR
4	1952	0.04	0.00053	INITIAL BIRTH RATE	0.042	1/YEAR
5	1953	0.04	0.00053	LONG-TERM BIRTH RATE	0.004	1/YEAR
6	1954	0.04	0.00052	TIME TO CHANGE BIRTH RATE	70	YEAR
7	1955	0.04	0.00051			
8	1956	0.04	0.00050			
9	1957	0.04	0.00050			
10	1958	0.04	0.00049			
11	1959	0.04	0.00048			
12	1960	0.04	0.00048			

Fig. 4.15: Excel goal-gap model for birth rate.

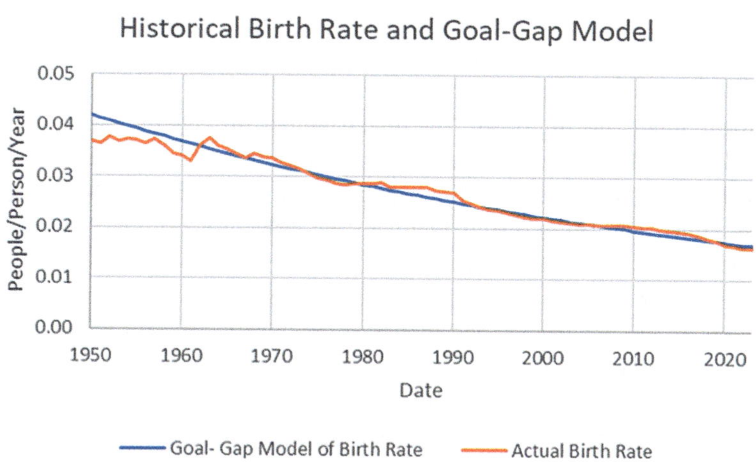

Fig. 4.16: Goal-gap model of historical world birth rate.

The value of the goal-gap model becomes apparent when we examine the projections (see Fig. 4.17). The birth rate is projected to continue declining over the next century, but it is not expected to become negative. Considering the recent declining trends, a projection of a birth rate of 0.008 people/people/ year in 2100 seems reasonable.

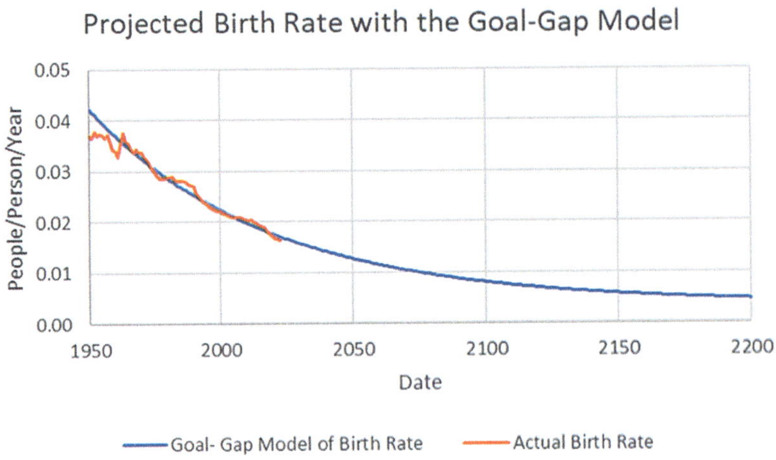

Fig. 4.17: Projected birth rate with the goal-gap model.

4.7 Conclusion

This chapter has explored the limitations of linear modelling for projecting demographic variables such as life expectancy and birth rates, and demonstrated the advantages of a goal-gap modelling approach. The linear models provided a reasonable fit to the historical data. They proved unreliable for long-term future projections, leading to implausible outcomes, such as a life expectancy of 140 years by 2200 and a negative birth rate after 2075. These results highlight the risks of assuming that past trends will continue indefinitely without constraints.

The goal-gap models, in contrast, offer a more realistic approach by incorporating natural limits (long-term life expectancy and long-term birth rate) towards which the variables asymptotically move. These models better reflect the biological, social, and economic factors that shape demographic transitions over time. The life expectancy model projects a more reasonable trajectory, reaching approximately 80 years by 2050, while the birth rate model ensures a continued decline to 0.008 by 2100 and never reaches negative values.

In the next chapter, we will extend this approach by applying the goal-gap model to real-world cases, analysing projections for the World, the USA, and Nigeria. These examples demonstrate how the model can be effectively utilized to comprehend demographic transitions across various regions.

In this chapter, we also introduced the concept of matching models to historical data to ensure their validity and reliability in projecting future trends. The goal-gap model successfully aligned with observed trends in life expectancy and birth rates, demonstrating its ability to replicate real-world dynamics. Adjusting model parameters to fit historical data is known as calibrating a system dynamics model, a crucial step in building credible simulations. We increase confidence in its future projections by ensuring the model behaves consistently with past data. We will explore the calibration process in more detail in Chapter 6.

4.8 Discussion Questions

- What governance check would you impose to prevent the publishing of linear long-run life expectancy projections like 140 years in 2200? Be specific.
- In your domain, how would you defend the long-term target and time to change parameters selected for a goal-gap model? Cite sources or precedents.
- Show how the life expectancy goal-gap inflow goes to ~ 0 as life expectancy approaches the long-term target. Why does that matter for communications?
- The linear birth rate fit projects negative values after 2075. What stakeholder harm would that cause if left unchallenged?
- Under what conditions would you still use a linear trend (for short-term operations or monitoring), and when must you escalate to goal-gap model?
- How would you quickly calibrate the goal-gap model using historical data before presenting forecasts to leadership? Deliver a three-step outline.

4.9 Exercises

4.9.1 Life expectancy: linear versus long-run realism
Task. Build the life expectancy linear model in Excel (constant increase per year). Extend to 2200.
Deliverable. One chart and a one-sentence risk statement.

4.9.2 Life expectancy: goal-gap build (Excel)
Task. Implement increase = (E$5−C2)/E$6 at time = 0, with E$5 = long-term life expectancy and E$6 = time to change life expectancy; simulate.
Deliverable. First 15 rows and a one-sentence justification.

4.9.3 Life expectancy: projection sanity check
Task. Using your goal-gap sheet, select reasonable parameters and project them to 2050; then report the resulting life expectancy.
Deliverable. Number and one-line justification.

4.9.4 Birth rate: linear versus goal-gap
Task. Fit a simple linear birth rate trend and extend to 2125; then build the goal-gap version (Decrease = (B2−E$5)/E$6 at time = 0) on a second sheet.
Deliverable. Two charts and a 2-sentence comparison.

4.9.5 Parameter sensitivity (time to change)
Task. In both life expectancy and birth rate goal-gap sheets, aim to halve and double the time to change.
Deliverable. A four-cell table listing time to reach 90% of the long-term target and a one-line takeaway.

4.9.6 Fit before forecast
Task. Using two historical anchor points for life expectancy and birth rate (start year and 2023 values), adjust long term and time to change to align the model curve with those points.
Deliverable. Screenshot of parameters and a one-paragraph calibration note.

Chapter 5
Making Projections with a System Dynamics Model

5.1 Learning Objectives

- Endogenize key rate parameters using goal-gap structures and integrate them into stock-flow models.
- Build an Excel stock-flow model with a parameters block, anchored references, and Euler time stepping.
- Calibrate with Solver to meet target conditions under bounded parameters, informed by external benchmarks.
- Diagnose inflow-outflow crossover and link it to peaks, plateaus, or declines in the focal stock.
- Communicate structure, assumptions, bounds, and calibration results in a stakeholder-ready artefact that aligns with standards.

5.2 Introduction

This chapter will explore how to make projections using a system dynamics model. We will apply the techniques discussed in the previous chapter to model the population dynamics of the world, as well as those of a developed nation (the United States) and a developing country (Nigeria). Building on the foundational principles of system dynamics, we will extend the population model from Chapter 2. This approach will also account for additional complexities, such as regional variations in birth and mortality rates, as well as migration patterns.

The United Nations Population Prospects [38] is a comprehensive and widely recognized database that provides demographic data for countries worldwide. It includes detailed information on population size, birth and death rates, life expectancy, and migration patterns, covering historical data from 1950 and making projections to 2100. This resource is essential for understanding global and regional demographic dynamics, as it reflects the latest estimates about demographic behaviours.

This book emphasizes the best practices in system dynamics modelling. Homer [39] suggests that collecting and immersing oneself in time-series data is a critical first step. We can ensure the model is grounded in empirical evidence by analysing historical patterns, referred to as Reference Modes. Fortunately, the UN Population Prospects provides a wealth of time-series data on global and national demographics, making it an invaluable resource for understanding population dynamics and validating models [38].

https://doi.org/10.1515/9783111541389-006

5.3 World Population Model

The United Nations projects the global population to reach approximately 9.7 billion by 2050 and peak at around 10.4 billion by 2100, after which it may decline. Figure 5.1 illustrates that the world population has increased significantly, from approximately 2.5 billion in 1950 to 8.1 billion in 2023, representing substantial growth over the past 73 years.

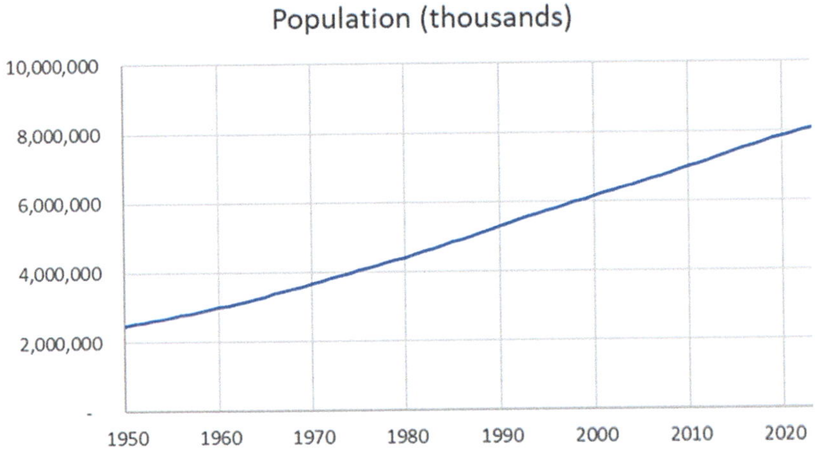

Fig. 5.1: Historical growth in world population from 1950 to 2023, in thousands.

Figure 5.2 illustrates that the number of births increased from approximately 91.4 million in 1950 to 131.6 million in 2023, while the number of deaths rose from 48.1 million to

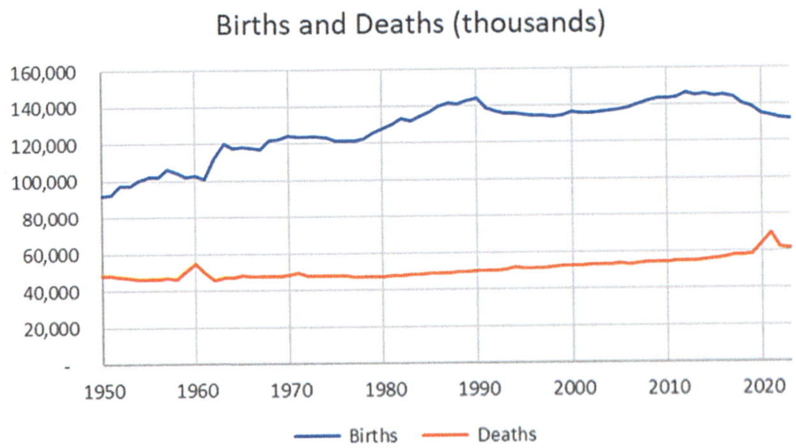

Fig. 5.2: Historical births and deaths from 1950 to 2023, in thousands.

61.3 million over the same period. Since the number of births each year consistently exceeds the number of deaths, the world population has continued to grow annually.

Figure 5.3 shows that the death rate has declined from 0.019 in 1950 to 0.008 in 2023. This trend reflects the steady increase in life expectancy and the growing number of children and young people in developing countries. However, the curve appears to be flattening, suggesting that the death rate may be approaching a lower limit and could soon start to increase due to ageing populations in many countries. Figure 5.3 also shows that the birth rate has significantly declined from 0.037 in 1950 to 0.016 in 2023. This substantial decrease indicates a convergence towards the death rate, suggesting that the gap between births and deaths is narrowing. If the trend continues, it could signal a demographic transition from population growth to decline. The birth rate may continue to decrease as developing countries develop. No country in the developed world has found a policy that can successfully encourage citizens to have more children.

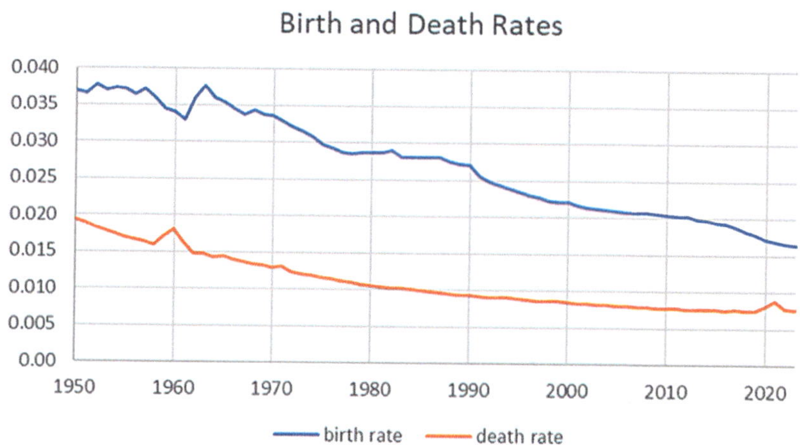

Fig. 5.3: Decreases in birth and death rates from 1950 to 2023.

We will build upon the population model introduced in the previous chapters. With a critical modification, we will incorporate dynamic birth and death rates that change over time rather than constant rates. The model will use time-varying stocks for birth and death rates, allowing them to evolve. These rates will be designed to gradually shift and eventually approach equilibrium values, reflecting the long-term trends of declining birth rates and stabilizing death rates observed in many populations. This approach will enable the model to capture population growth dynamics more accurately and to anticipate the conditions under which the population may peak and eventually decline.

Recall the population model developed in Chapter 2 (see Fig. 5.4) with a constant birth rate and life expectancy.

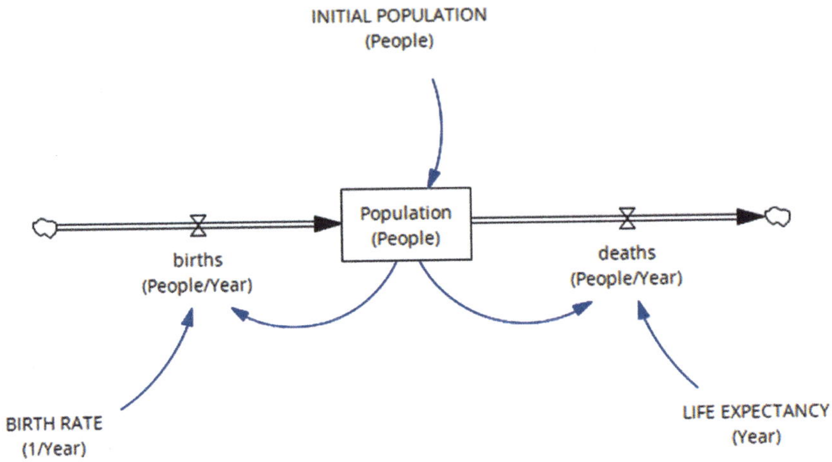

Fig. 5.4: The simple model of the population developed in Chapter 2.

The first step is to remove the constant values for birth rate and life expectancy (see Fig. 5.5). These constants represented fixed rates, which simplified the model but did not account for the dynamic nature of the demographic transition.

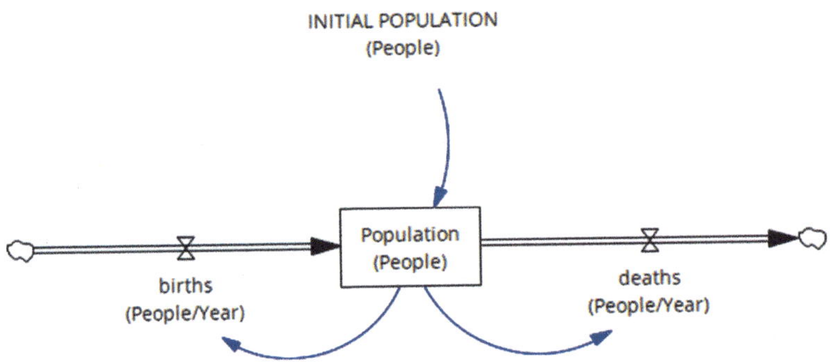

Fig. 5.5: Revising the population model.

We introduced in Chapter 4 a dynamic goal-gap model for the birth rate (see Fig. 5.6)

The formula for the decreasing birth rate is (long-term birth rate − current birth rate)/time to change. This is shown in the Vensim interface below (see Fig. 5.7). The crude birth rate, as provided by the UN Population Prospects, is expressed in units of births per 1,000 people [38]. The birth rate in our system dynamics model is written as ((people/people)/year) or 1/year. We are calculating the change in this value every year, so the units for the change in birth rate are (((people/people)/year)/year) or 1/(year * year).

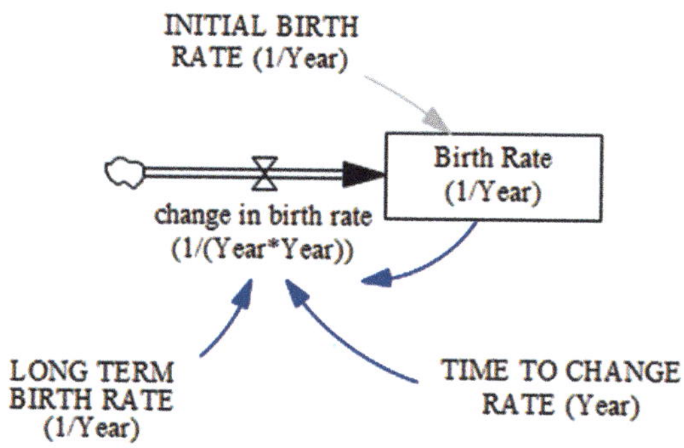

Fig. 5.6: A goal-gap model for the birth rate in our population model.

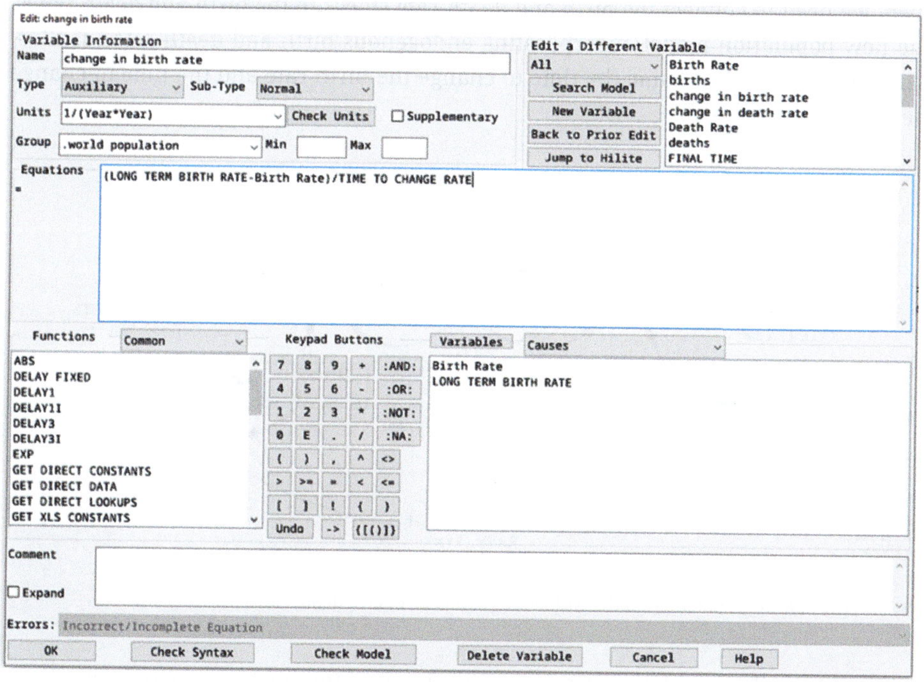

Fig. 5.7: Vensim interface for the change in birth rate flow.

We introduce a similar structure for the death rate represented as a stock, with the change in the death rate as the flow that adjusts the stock over time. We include three new constants: the initial death rate, the long-term death rate, and the time-to-change rate (see Fig. 5.8).

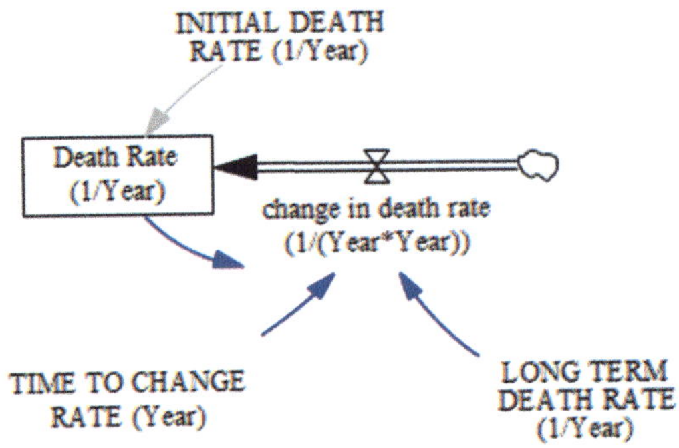

Fig. 5.8: A goal-gap model for the death rate in our population model.

Then, we need to connect the birth and death rate stocks to the birth and death flows. The new population model, incorporating endogenous birth and death rates, is illustrated in Fig. 5.9. We assume the time to change the birth rate and the time to change the death rate are equal.

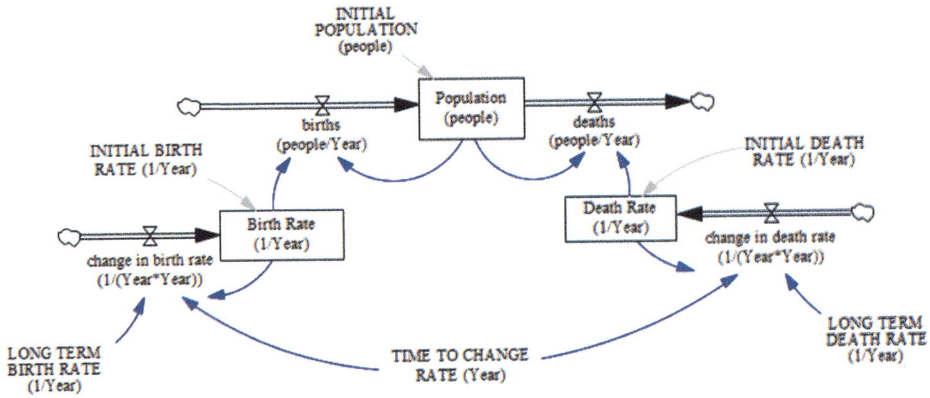

Fig. 5.9: The revised population model with endogenous birth and death rates.

In this model, the population reaches its peak when the birth rate equals the death rate, meaning the number of births equals the number of deaths. So, we will find the values of the long-term birth and death rates, so that the birth and death rates are equal in 2100. To achieve this, we must revise our Excel spreadsheet model by adding four new columns for the four additional endogenous variables and three new rows for the three additional exogenous variables. Then, we will use the Excel Solver add-in to find the appropriate exogenous values.

You will find the Solver under the Data tab, on the far right-hand side of the menu ribbon, under Analyze (see Fig. 5.10).

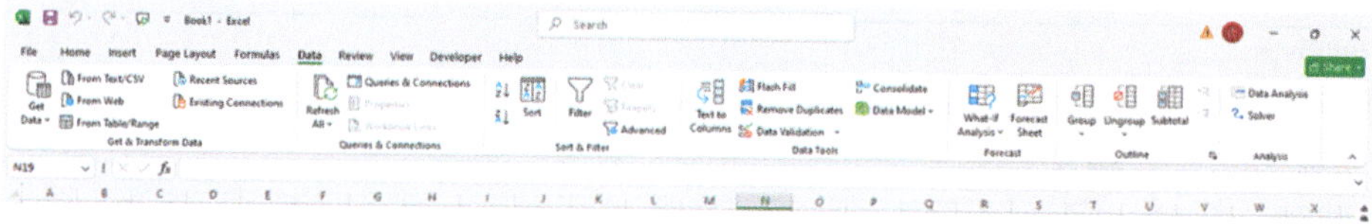

Fig. 5.10: Solver in the Data Analyze group.

If your version of Excel still needs to install the Solver add-in, you can install the Solver add-in manually. Open Excel and click on the File tab, then select Options at the bottom of the left-hand menu. In the Excel Options window, choose add-ins from the sidebar (see Fig. 5.11).

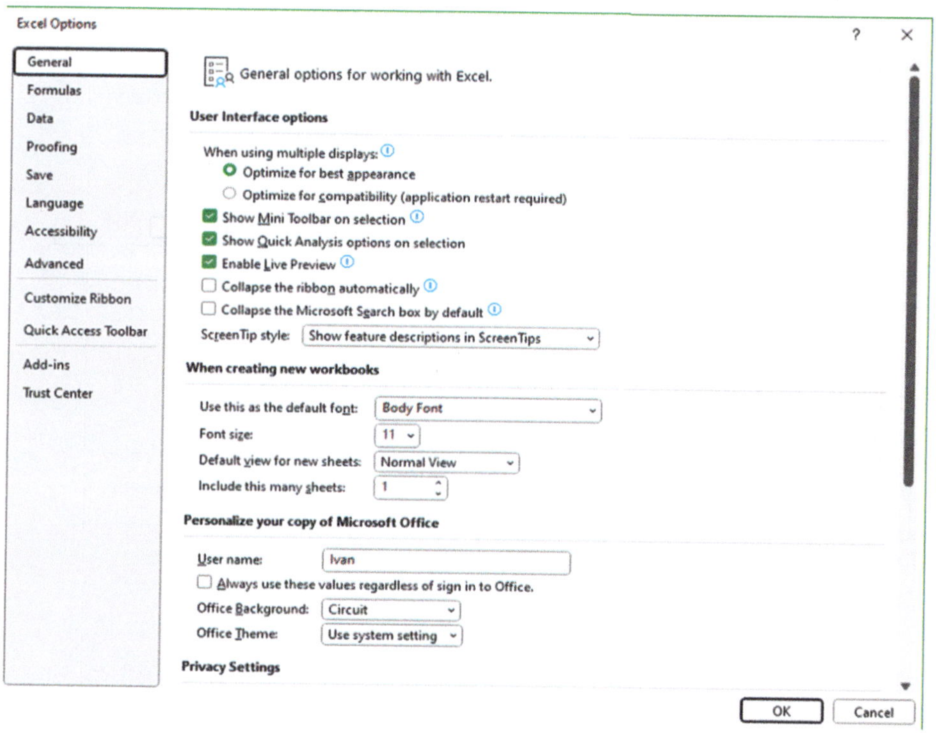

Fig. 5.11: File options.

At the bottom of the add-ins section, you'll see a drop-down menu labelled Manage; select Excel add-ins from this menu and click Go (see Fig. 5.12).

In the add-ins window that appears, check the box next to Solver add-in and click OK (see Fig. 5.13). Excel may take a moment to install the add-in, after which the Solver tool will be available under the Data tab in the Analyze group (see Fig. 5.10). If you still don't see Solver in the Data tab, restart Excel to finalize the installation.

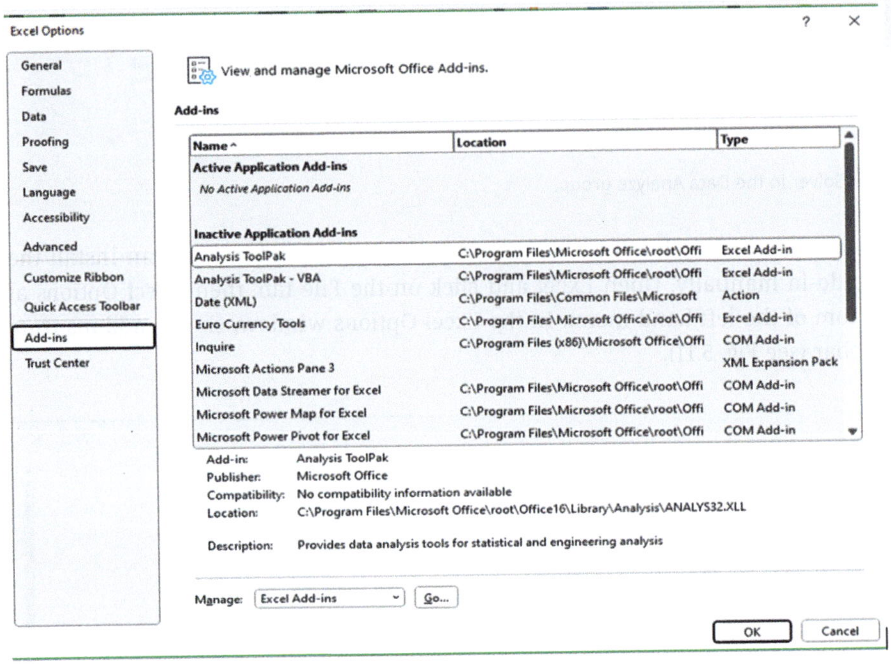

Fig. 5.12: Add-ins.

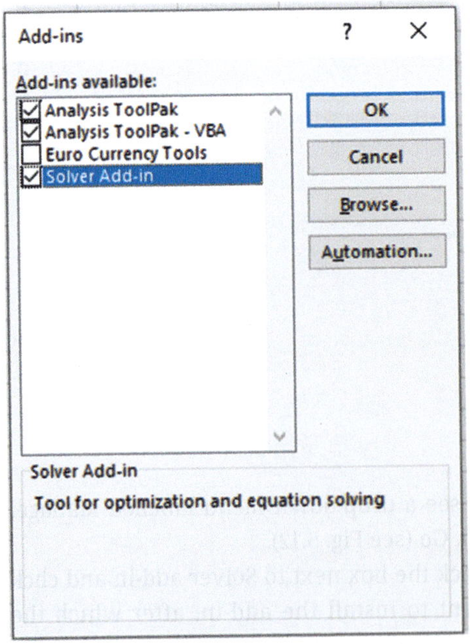

Fig. 5.13: Select Solver add-in.

Setting up a new population model in Excel with variable birth and death rates involves creating a spreadsheet with new columns for the updated rates. Figure 5.14 shows the setup.

	A	B	C	D	E	F	G	H
1	Time (Year)	change birth rate (1/(Year*Year)	Birth Rate (1/Year)	births (people/Year)	Population (people)	deaths (people/year)	Death Rate (1/Year)	change death rate (1/(Year*Year))
2								

Fig. 5.14: Set up of the new population model.

We will set the initial time to 2023 and the time step to 1 year. We will set the initial population to 8,056,506, the estimated world population in 2023, in thousands. We will put the initial birth rate to 0.01633, which corresponds to the crude birth rate in 2023. We will set the initial death rate to 0.00762, the crude death rate in 2023, and the time-to-change rates to 50 years, which is an arbitrary choice. For convenience, we set the long-term birth rate equal to the initial birth rate and the long-term death rate equal to the initial death rate (see Fig. 5.15). Later, we will calculate more realistic long-term birth and death rates.

I	J	K
PARAMETER	VALUES	UNITS
INITIAL TIME	2023	YEAR
TIME STEP	1	YEAR
INITIAL POPULATION	8,056,506	PEOPLE
INITIAL BIRTH RATE	0.01633	1/YEAR
INITIAL DEATH RATE	0.00762	1/YEAR
LONG TERM BIRTH RATE	0.01633	1/YEAR
LONG TERM DEATH RATE	0.00762	1/YEAR
TIME TO CHANGE RATES	50.0	YEAR

Fig. 5.15: The exogenous variables in the new population model.

We will set the initial year in the year column in cell A2 using the formula = J2, the initial population in the population column in cell E2 using the formula = J4, the initial birth rate in the birth rate column in cell C2, using the formula = J5, and the initial death rate in the death rate column in cell G2, using the formula = J6. Next, we will calculate the births for 2023 in cell D2 using the formula = C2 * E2, and the deaths in 2020 in cell F2 using the formula = E2 * G2 (see Fig. 5.16).

	A	B	C	D	E	F	G	H
1	Time (Year)	change birth rate (1/(Year*Year)	Birth Rate (1/Year)	births (people/Year)	Population (people)	deaths (people/year)	Death Rate (1/Year)	change death rate (1/(Year*Year))
2	2023		0.016	131,539	8,056,506	61,383	0.008	
3								

Fig. 5.16: The setup is similar to the original population model.

Now, we enter the formula for the change in the birth rate in cell B2 as = (J$7–C2)/J$9. This is the formula for the goal-gap model, where the goal is in cell J$7, and the gap is calculated as = (J$7–C2). This gap closes over time, and the rate at which it closes is determined by the value in cell J$9. However, we must assign a temporary value to the long-term birth rate and an arbitrary value to the time required to change the rate. Notice that we have anchored the cells J$7 and J$9 to retain their original values when we copy and paste them later (see Fig. 5.17).

B2 fx =(J$7-C2)/J$9

	A	B	C	D	E	F	G	H	I	J	K
1	Time (Year)	change birth rate (1/(Year*Year)	Birth Rate (1/Year)	births (people/Year)	Population (people)	deaths (people/year)	Death Rate (1/Year)	change death rate (1/(Year*Year))	PARAMETER	VALUES	UNITS
2	2023	=(J$7-C2)/J$9	0.016	131,539	8,056,506	61,383	0.008		INITIAL TIME	2023	YEAR
3									TIME STEP	1	YEAR
4									INITIAL POPULATION	8,056,506	PEOPLE
5									INITIAL BIRTH RATE	0.01633	1/YEAR
6									INITIAL DEATH RATE	0.00762	1/YEAR
7									LONG TERM BIRTH RATE	0.01633	1/YEAR
8									LONG TERM DEATH RATE	0.00762	1/YEAR
9									TIME TO CHANGE RATES	50.0	YEAR

Fig. 5.17: Calculation of the change in birth rate.

We enter a similar formula for the change in death rate in cell H2. Namely, = (J$8–G2)/J$9.

Then, we will update the year and the three stocks (population, birth rate, and death rate) for the next time step (2024, in this case) based on the 2023 values. We update the year to 2024 by adding J$3 (the time step) to the value in cell A2. That is, A3 contains the formula = A2 + J$3.

The population in 2024 is calculated as the population in 2023 plus the births in 2023 minus the deaths in 2023, multiplied by the time step. The formula in cell E3 would be = E2 +(D2-F2) * J$3 (see Fig. 5.18). The birth rate in 2024 is the birth rate in 2023 plus the change in the birth rate in 2023 multiplied by the time step. In cell C3, the formula is = C2 + B2 * J$3. Similarly, the death rate in 2024 is the death rate in 2023 plus the change in the death rate in 2023, multiplied by the time step. That is, the formula in cell G3 is = G2 + H2 * J$3.

E3 =E2+(D2-F2)*J$3

	A	B	C	D	E	F	G	H	I	J	K
1	Time (Year)	change birth rate (1/(Year*Year)	Birth Rate (1/Year)	births (people/Year)	Population (people)	deaths (people/year)	Death Rate (1/Year)	change death rate (1/(Year*Year))	PARAMETER	VALUES	UNITS
2	2023	0.00000	0.016	131,539	8,056,506	61,383	0.008		INITIAL TIME	2023	YEAR
3					=E2+(D2-F2)*J$3				TIME STEP	1	YEAR
4									INITIAL POPULATION	8,056,506	PEOPLE
5									INITIAL BIRTH RATE	0.01633	1/YEAR
6									INITIAL DEATH RATE	0.00762	1/YEAR
7									LONG TERM BIRTH RATE	0.01633	1/YEAR
8									LONG TERM DEATH RATE	0.00762	1/YEAR
9									TIME TO CHANGE RATES	50.0	YEAR

Fig. 5.18: Updating the stock variables.

Then, we update the flow variables for 2024 by copying and pasting the contents of cells B2, D2, F2, and H2 into the appropriate cells in row 3 (see Fig. 5.19).

	A	B	C	D	E	F	G	H
1	Time (Year)	change birth rate (1/(Year*Year)	Birth Rate (1/Year)	births (people/Year)	Population (people)	deaths (people/year)	Death Rate (1/Year)	change death rate (1/(Year*Year))
2	2023	0.00000	0.016	131,539	8,056,506	61,383	0.008	0.00000
3	2024	0.00000	0.016	132,684	8,126,662	61,917	0.008	0.00000
4								

Fig. 5.19: Copying and pasting the contents of the flows.

Now, we can copy the contents of cells A3 to H3, down the rows until the year is 2200. Notice that in the current simulation, the birth rate is 0.016, and the death rate is 0.008 (see Fig. 5.20). The values do not change because the long-term rates are equal to the initial rates.

Assuming the UN is correct, the world population is expected to peak in 2100. We aim to have the number of births equal the number of deaths in 2100. We can achieve that by adjusting the long-term birth and death rates. We can use Solver in Excel to set this condition and find the appropriate values.

	A	B	C	D	E	F	G	H
1	Time (Year)	change birth rate (1/(Year*Year)	Birth Rate (1/Year)	births (people/Year)	Population (people)	deaths (people/year)	Death Rate (1/Year)	change death rate (1/(Year*Year))
2	2023	0.00000	0.016	131,539	8,056,506	61,383	0.008	0.00000
3	2024	0.00000	0.016	132,684	8,126,662	61,917	0.008	0.00000
4	2025	0.00000	0.016	133,839	8,197,429	62,456	0.008	0.00000
5	2026	0.00000	0.016	135,005	8,268,812	63,000	0.008	0.00000
6	2027	0.00000	0.016	136,181	8,340,817	63,549	0.008	0.00000
7	2028	0.00000	0.016	137,366	8,413,448	64,102	0.008	0.00000
8	2029	0.00000	0.016	138,563	8,486,713	64,660	0.008	0.00000
9	2030	0.00000	0.016	139,769	8,560,615	65,223	0.008	0.00000
10	2031	0.00000	0.016	140,986	8,635,161	65,791	0.008	0.00000
11	2032	0.00000	0.016	142,214	8,710,356	66,364	0.008	0.00000
12	2033	0.00000	0.016	143,452	8,786,206	66,942	0.008	0.00000

Fig. 5.20: Copying and pasting row 3 down to row 179, where the year equals 2200.

We begin by calculating the difference between births and deaths in 2100. We will create a cell to calculate this difference. In cell L2, we put the formula = D82–F82 (see Fig. 5.21).

I	J	K	L
PARAMETER	VALUES	UNITS	DIFFERENCE (people/Year)
INITIAL TIME	2023	YEAR	136,775
TIME STEP	1	YEAR	
INITIAL POPULATION	8,056,506	PEOPLE	
INITIAL BIRTH RATE	0.01633	1/YEAR	
INITIAL DEATH RATE	0.00762	1/YEAR	
LONG TERM BIRTH RATE	0.01633	1/YEAR	
LONG TERM DEATH RATE	0.00762	1/YEAR	
TIME TO CHANGE RATES	50.0	YEAR	

Fig. 5.21: The difference between births and deaths in 2100.

Now, open Solver by going to the Data tab and selecting Solver. In the Solver parameters window, set the objective cell to the cell where the difference between births and deaths (L2) is calculated. Set the objective to a value of 0, as you want the difference to approach zero (see Fig. 5.22).

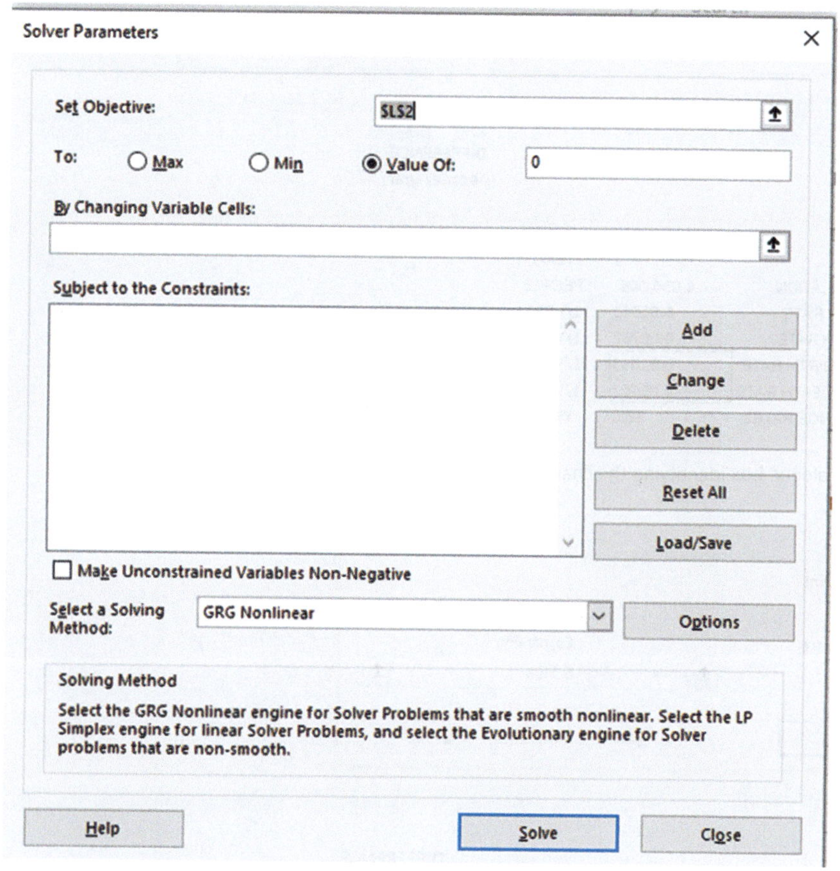

Fig. 5.22: Solver objective function set up.

In the "By Changing Variable Cells" box, select the cell containing the long-term birth rate in cell J7 and the long-term death rate in cell J8 (see Fig. 5.23). These are the values Solver will adjust to find when births minus deaths equals zero in 2100. That is, L2 equals zero.

Now, we will set the constraints. On the right-hand side of the Solver page, click Add. Then, in the Add Constraint dialogue box, we highlight the cells we want to constrain in the Cell Reference window and the cells we want to use as constraints under the Constraint window. We can set the constraint to be less than or equal to, or greater than or equal to, in the drop-down menu (see Fig. 5.24).

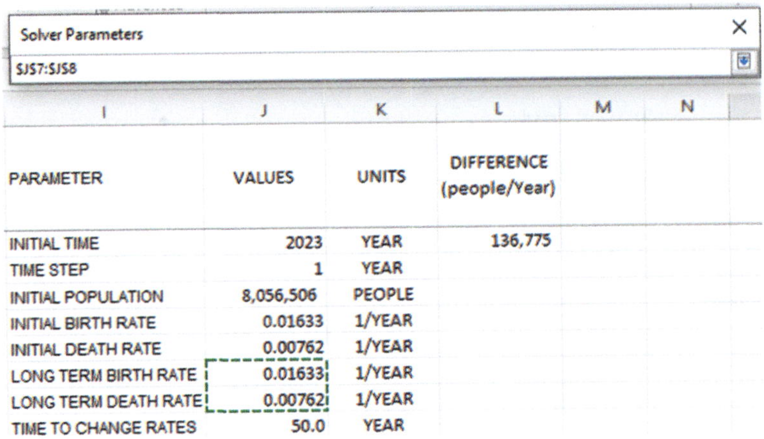

PARAMETER	VALUES	UNITS	DIFFERENCE (people/Year)
INITIAL TIME	2023	YEAR	136,775
TIME STEP	1	YEAR	
INITIAL POPULATION	8,056,506	PEOPLE	
INITIAL BIRTH RATE	0.01633	1/YEAR	
INITIAL DEATH RATE	0.00762	1/YEAR	
LONG TERM BIRTH RATE	0.01633	1/YEAR	
LONG TERM DEATH RATE	0.00762	1/YEAR	
TIME TO CHANGE RATES	50.0	YEAR	

Fig. 5.23: Dialogue box identifying the changing cells.

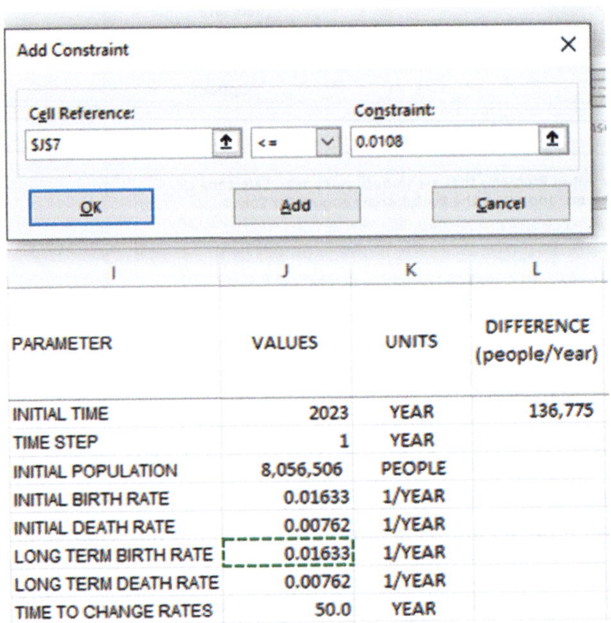

PARAMETER	VALUES	UNITS	DIFFERENCE (people/Year)
INITIAL TIME	2023	YEAR	136,775
TIME STEP	1	YEAR	
INITIAL POPULATION	8,056,506	PEOPLE	
INITIAL BIRTH RATE	0.01633	1/YEAR	
INITIAL DEATH RATE	0.00762	1/YEAR	
LONG TERM BIRTH RATE	0.01633	1/YEAR	
LONG TERM DEATH RATE	0.00762	1/YEAR	
TIME TO CHANGE RATES	50.0	YEAR	

Fig. 5.24: Dialogue box for one of the constraints.

We will put two constraints on the solution. The UN predicts that the birth rate in 2100 will be 0.0108, with a trend of decreasing birth rates. So, we set a constraint that the long-term birth rate would be less than 0.0108. Also, the UN believes the death rate in 2100 will be 0.0121 and will increase because of an ageing population. So, we set a constraint that the long-term death rate would be greater than 0.0121.

Note that the Solver automatically anchors the Objective Cell and the Changing Variable Cells, in this case, $L$2 and $J$7:$J$8. Figure 5.25 shows the completed Solver setup after adding the objective function, the changing variables, and the constraints.

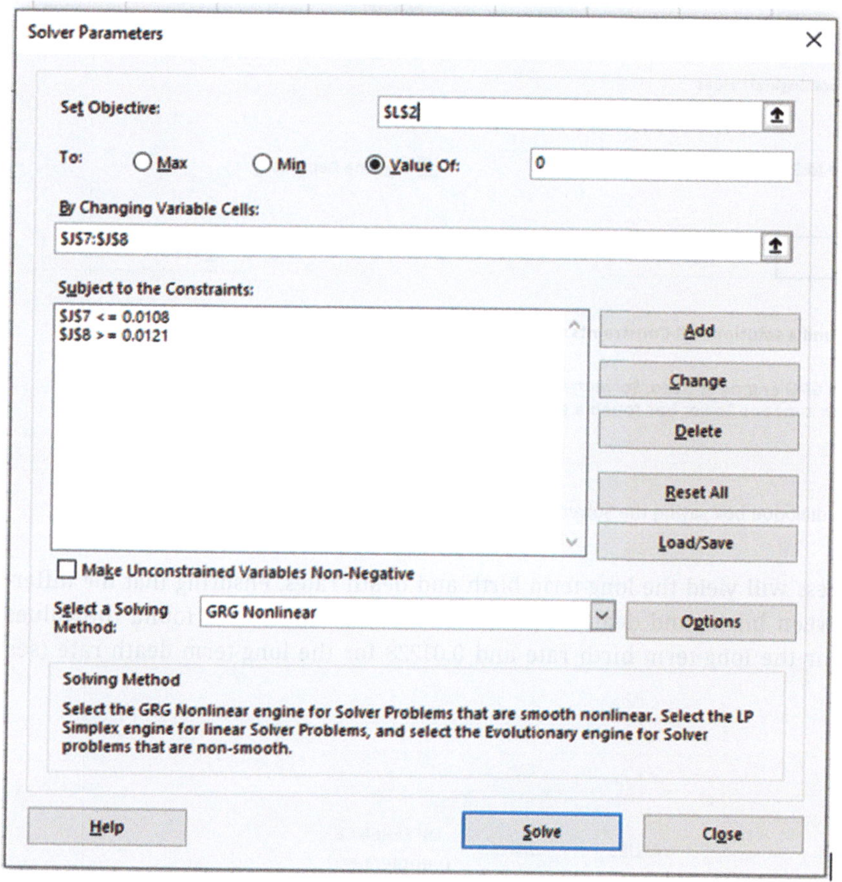

Fig. 5.25: Completed Solver setup.

Click Solve to allow Solver to find the values of long-term birth and death rates that make the difference between the births and deaths in 2100 equal to zero. Once Solver finds a solution, review the result and, if it meets your requirements, click OK to apply the solution (see Fig. 5.26).

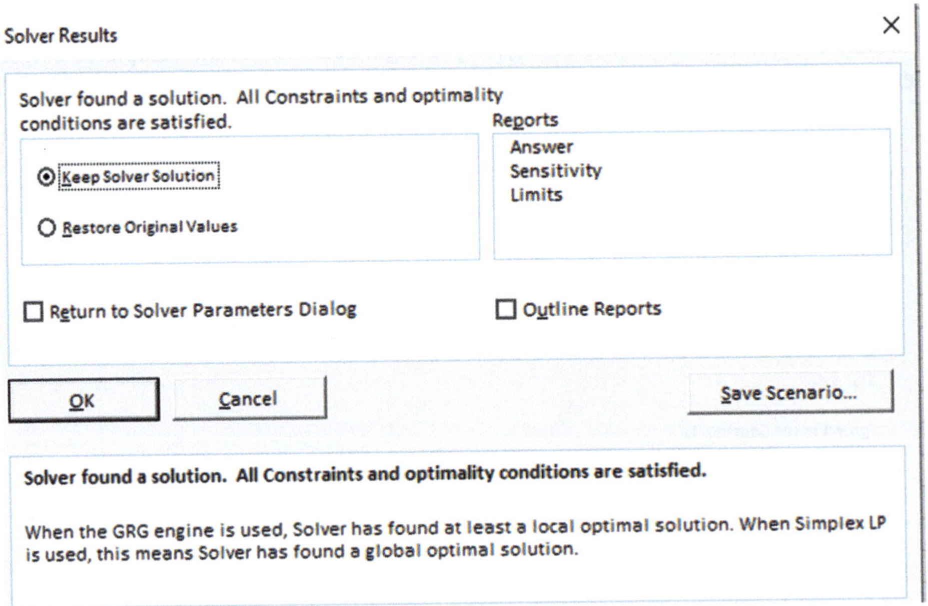

Fig. 5.26: A dialogue box saying the Solver found an optimal solution.

This process will yield the long-term birth and death rates, ensuring that the difference between births and deaths equals zero in 2100. The Solver found the values 0.00995 for the long-term birth rate and 0.01228 for the long-term death rate (see Fig. 5.27).

I	J	K	L
PARAMETER	VALUES	UNITS	DIFFERENCE (people/Year)
INITIAL TIME	2023	YEAR	(0)
TIME STEP	1	YEAR	
INITIAL POPULATION	8,056,506	PEOPLE	
INITIAL BIRTH RATE	0.01633	1/YEAR	
INITIAL DEATH RATE	0.00762	1/YEAR	
LONG TERM BIRTH RATE	0.00995	1/YEAR	
LONG TERM DEATH RATE	0.01228	1/YEAR	
TIME TO CHANGE RATES	50.0	YEAR	

Fig. 5.27: Results of the Solver.

Now, we can examine the peak population in 2100. The model projects that the world population will peak at 10.4 billion people, the same value estimated by the UN. Note that in 2100, the births equal 117,518 and the deaths equal 117,519. Additionally, we observe that the population is expected to continue growing until 2100, after which it is anticipated to decline (see Fig. 5.28).

74	2095	-0.00003	0.011	118,918	10,392,719	116,345	0.011	0.00002
75	2096	-0.00003	0.011	118,638	10,395,292	116,600	0.011	0.00002
76	2097	-0.00003	0.011	118,358	10,397,331	116,845	0.011	0.00002
77	2098	-0.00003	0.011	118,078	10,398,844	117,079	0.011	0.00002
78	2099	-0.00003	0.011	117,798	10,399,843	117,304	0.011	0.00002
79	2100	-0.00003	0.011	117,518	10,400,337	117,519	0.011	0.00002
80	2101	-0.00003	0.011	117,239	10,400,337	117,723	0.011	0.00002
81	2102	-0.00003	0.011	116,959	10,399,853	117,919	0.011	0.00002
82	2103	-0.00003	0.011	116,680	10,398,893	118,104	0.011	0.00002
83	2104	-0.00002	0.011	116,400	10,397,468	118,281	0.011	0.00002
84	2105	-0.00002	0.011	116,121	10,395,588	118,448	0.011	0.00002

Fig. 5.28: The peak values projected by the model for 2100.

Figure 5.29 illustrates the convergence of births and deaths in the model projections. The timeline spans from 1950 to 2200, integrating historical data and forecasts. Historical trends from 1950 to 2023 reveal significant increases in births and deaths. Beyond 2023, the model projects that future births will decline drastically. This seems implausible until we examine the trend in the birth rate. By 2100, the birth and death rates are expected to intersect, marking the peak of the population. After 2100, deaths surpass births, reflecting a shift towards population decline. Eventually, both the births and the deaths decline.

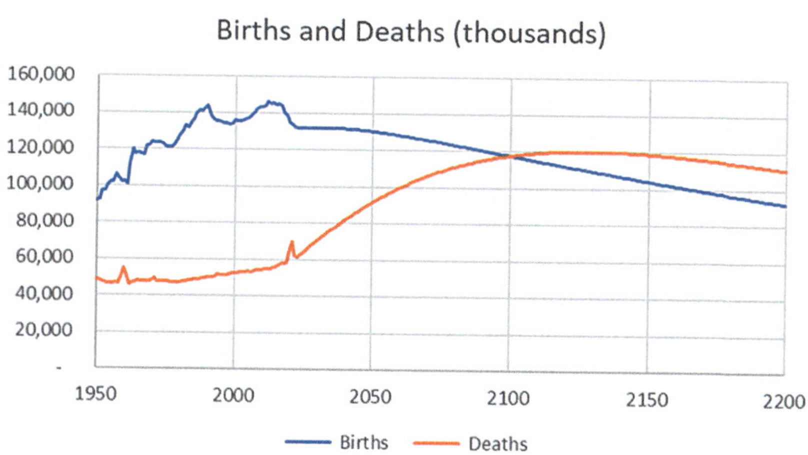

Fig. 5.29: Historical and projected births and deaths.

Figure 5.30 presents a timeline of historical and projected birth and death rates, highlighting past trends and future projections from 1950 to 2200. Historical data spanning 1950 to 2023 illustrate fluctuations in birth and death rates. From 2023 onwards, our model's projections are presented as smooth curves, consistent with a goal-gap approach, with birth and death rates gradually converging. By 2100, the birth and death rates are expected to intersect. Beyond 2100, the birth rate falls below the death rate, indicating a demographic transition. Both rates stabilize at 2200, suggesting they are approaching their long-term values. However, since the death rate exceeds the birth rate, the population is expected to decline steadily after 2100.

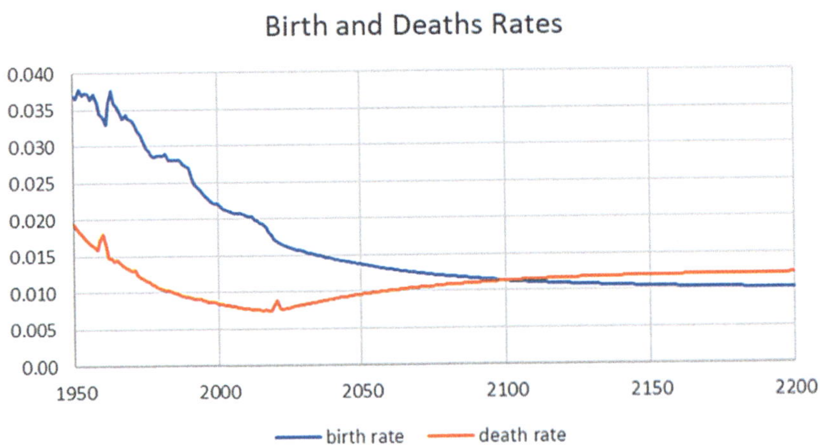

Fig. 5.30: Historical and projected birth and death rates.

Figure 5.31 illustrates the population trend, displaying historical and projected data from 1950 to 2200. The historical data from 1950 to 2023 capture the rapid population growth experienced during the latter half of the twentieth century and into the twenty-first century, driven by declining death rates and sustained high birth rates in many parts of the world. From 2023 onwards, the model's projections indicate a slowing growth rate, with the world population eventually peaking around 2100 at 10.4 billion, which aligns with the UN's forecasts. This peak marks the beginning of a gradual decline in population beyond 2100.

Remarkably, our simple model aligns precisely with the UN Population Prospects [38], despite there being no indication that our process of determining when births equal deaths would necessarily yield this result. This accuracy highlights the robustness of our approach, demonstrating how even a straightforward model can effectively capture complex global demographic trends.

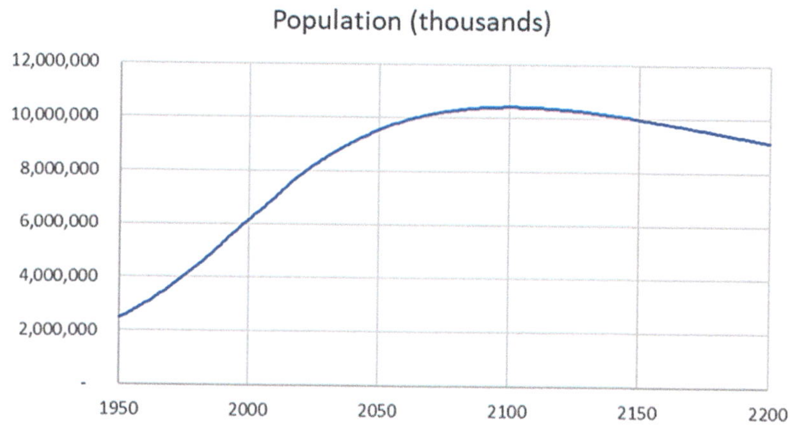

Fig. 5.31: Historical and projected population.

5.4 The US Population

To illustrate the US's population growth dynamics, we use a simple yet slightly different system dynamics model with a population stock and three flows – births, net migration, and deaths – as shown in Fig. 5.32.

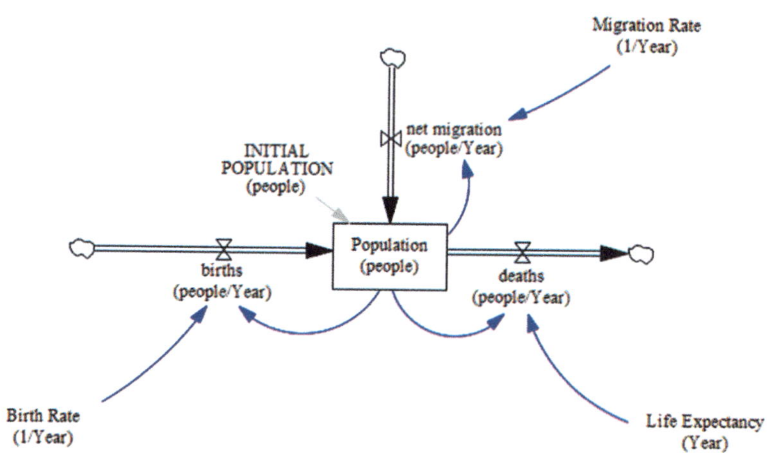

Fig. 5.32: A simple national population system dynamics model.

We found historical data on population, births, deaths, and net migration from 1950 to 2023 in the UN Population Prospects 2024 database [38]. Figure 5.33 shows the steady growth in the US's population, from 150 million in 1950 to 340 million in 2023.

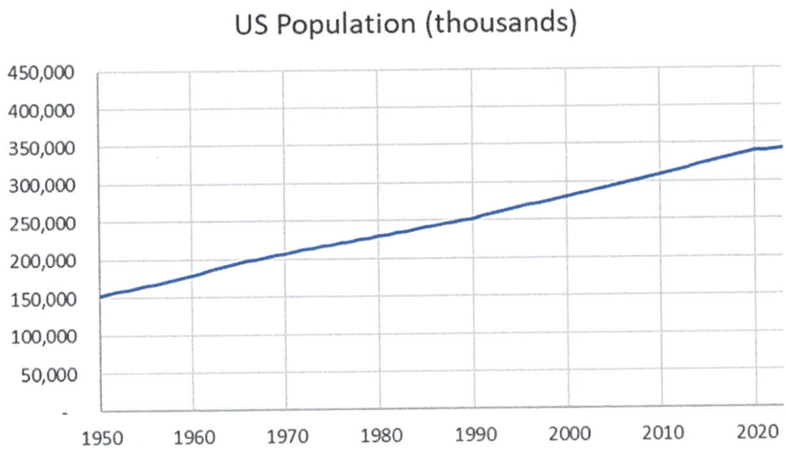

Fig. 5.33: Historical population in the US from 1950 to 2023.

While this trend appears linear, it will not continue indefinitely, as the US's population is expected to peak and then gradually decline.

The data shows that the US's life expectancy has steadily increased since 1950, except for the significant reduction in 2020 caused by COVID-19 (see Fig. 5.34).

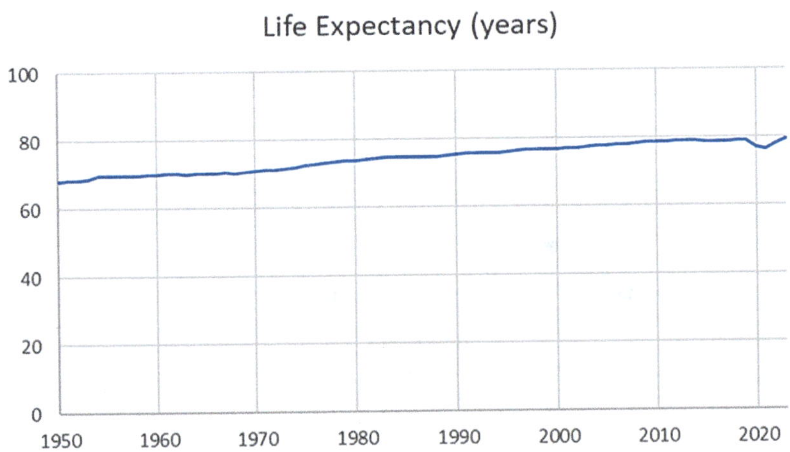

Fig. 5.34: Historical life expectancy in the US from 1950 to 2023.

Figure 5.35 shows the US's births, net migration, and deaths from 1950 to 2023. Births have fluctuated widely, but the trend has been relatively flat. Net migration has exhibited a relatively steady upward trend. The number of deaths in the US has seen a steadily increasing trend because, although life expectancy has increased, so has the population.

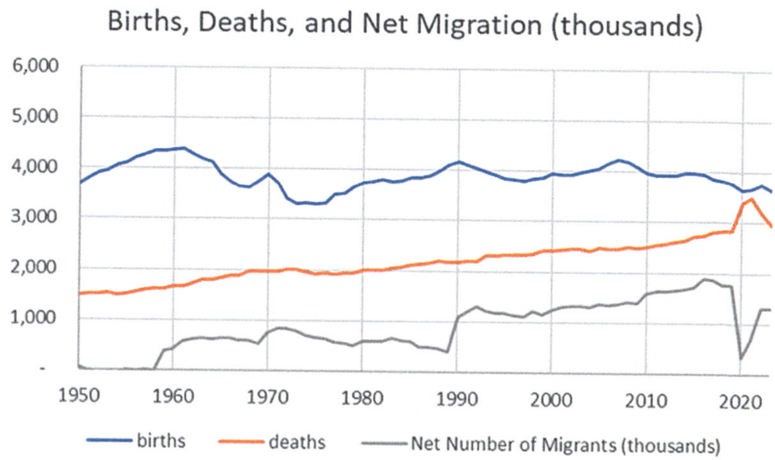

Fig. 5.35: Historical births, net migration, and deaths in the US from 1950 to 2023.

Figure 5.36 shows that the US has historically seen declining birth rates from 1950 to 2023. In the 1950s, the birth rate was relatively high, driven by the post-World War II baby boom. It saw a sharp decline in the 1960s, followed by a gradual decline in subsequent decades. Meanwhile, the death rate declined steadily but modestly over these 70 years, and the net migration rate has fluctuated but increased overall.

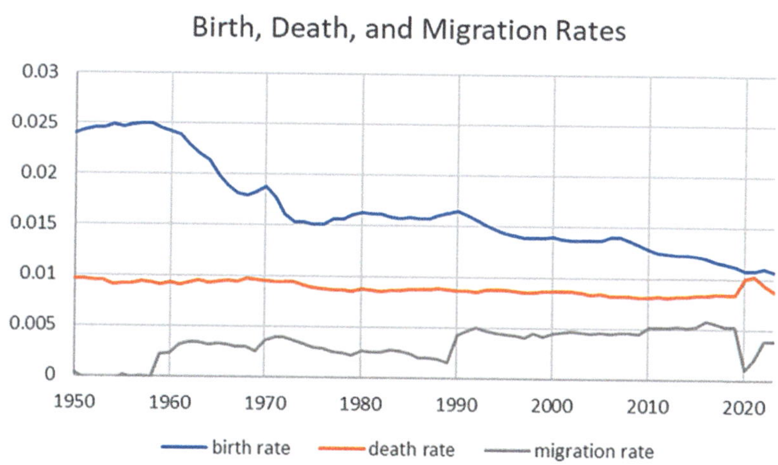

Fig. 5.36: Historical birth, net migration, and death rates in the US from 1950 to 2023.

Since net migration has been positive, we can add births and net migration to show growth patterns in the United States. Figure 5.37 illustrates the births plus net migration, and deaths in the US from 1950 to 2023. Births plus net migration, and deaths in

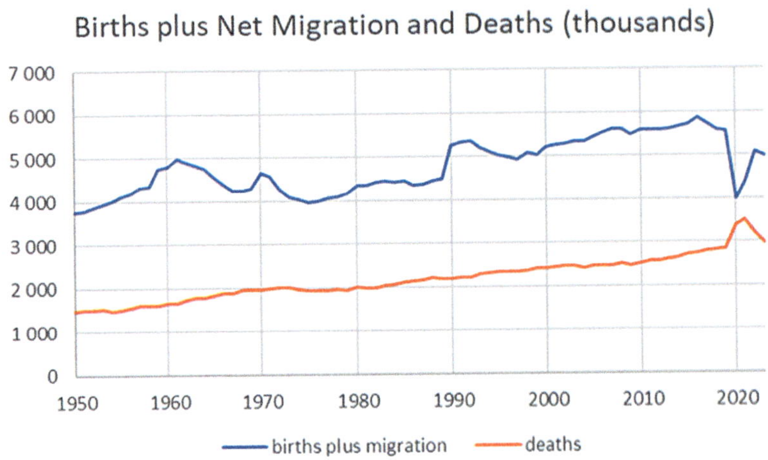

Fig. 5.37: Historical births plus net migration and deaths in the US from 1950 to 2023.

the United States have exhibited a steadily increasing trend, except for 2020, when COVID-19 had a significant but temporary impact.

Figure 5.38 shows that, even with a relatively high migration rate, the birth plus net migration rate is approaching the death rate, indicating that the population will eventually reach a peak.

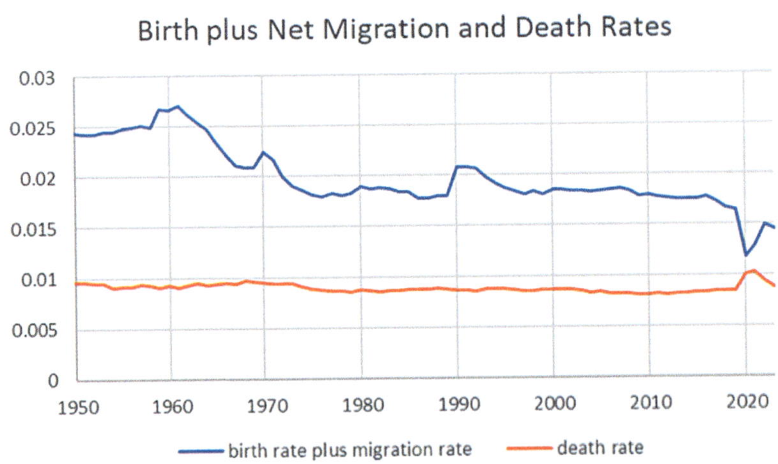

Fig. 5.38: Historical birth plus net migration and death rates in the United States from 1950 to 2023.

In our model of the US population, we extended the structure to include a time-varying net migration rate alongside time-varying birth and death rates. This approach enables dynamic adjustments in migration patterns that reflect historical trends and potential future shifts. We applied the same goal-gap model to the migration rate, taking into account both birth and death rates. This model incorporates a long-term target, or "goal," migration rate and gradually closes the gap between the current migration rate and this target. Using the goal-gap model (see Fig. 5.39) across all three rates (birth, death, and migration), we capture the unique population dynamics in the United States.

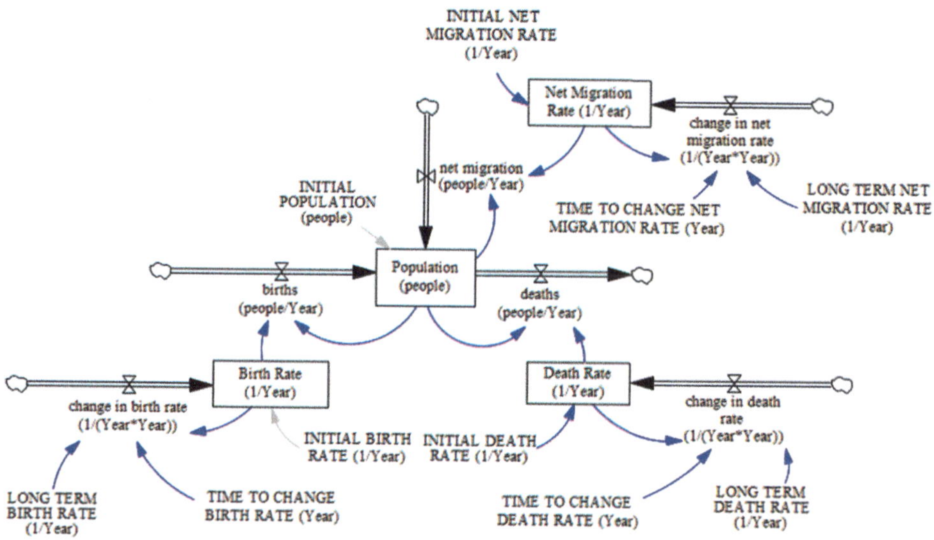

Fig. 5.39: The goal-gap structures used in the US population model.

We employ a different approach here than the previous world population model, as the UN Population Prospects suggests that the US population will still grow in 2100 [38]. So, the exact timing of the US population peak is uncertain. We aim to determine the long-term birth rate, long-term death rate, and long-term migration rate that align the model's population with the UN's 2100 projection of 421 million.

Figure 5.40 illustrates the parameters used to configure the US population model. We had to add two new exogenous variables for the initial net migration rate and the long-term net migration rate. We set the initial and long-term values to the 2023 values from the UN Population Prospects 2024 [38].

We added three columns to the spreadsheet: one for the net migration flow, one for the migration rate stock, and another for the change in migration rate flow. The flow uses a goal-gap formula to adjust the migration rate towards the long-term migration rate over time (Fig. 5.41).

L	M	N
PARAMETERS	VALUE	UNITS
INITIAL YEAR	2023	YEAR
TIME STEP	1	YEAR
INITIAL POPULATION	342,475	PEOPLE
INITIAL BIRTH RATE	0.01065	1/YEAR
INITIAL DEATH RATE	0.00866	1/YEAR
INITIAL MIGRATION RATE	0.00385	1/YEAR
LONG TERM BIRTH RATE	0.01065	1/YEAR
LONG TERM DEATH RATE	0.00866	1/YEAR
LONG TERM MIGRATION RATE	0.00385	1/YEAR
TIME TO CHANGE RATES	50	YEAR

Fig. 5.40: The setup of the US population model.

SUM =(M$10-J2)/M$11

	A	B	C	D	E	F	G	H	I	J	K	L	M	N
1	Year	change in birth rate	Birth Rate	births	Population	deaths	Death Rate	change in death rate	net migration	Net Migration Rate	change in migration rate	PARAMETERS	VALUE	UNITS
2	2023	0	0.01065	3,647	342,475	2,967	0.00866	0	1,319	0.00385	=(M$10-J2)	INITIAL YEAR	2023	YEAR
3												TIME STEP	1	YEAR
4												INITIAL POPULATION	342,475	PEOPLE
5												INITIAL BIRTH RATE	0.01065	1/YEAR
6												INITIAL DEATH RATE	0.00866	1/YEAR
7												INITIAL MIGRATION RATE	0.00385	1/YEAR
8												LONG TERM BIRTH RATE	0.01065	1/YEAR
9												LONG TERM DEATH RATE	0.00866	1/YEAR
10												LONG TERM MIGRATION RATE	0.00385	1/YEAR
11												TIME TO CHANGE RATES	50	YEAR

Fig. 5.41: The new columns for the net migration flow, net migration rate stock, and change in migration rate flow.

Figure 5.42 is the setup of the UN Estimate of the US population in 2100, the model estimate of the US population in 2100 under these initial conditions, and the difference between the UN estimate and the model estimate, which we will use as the objective and find the long-term parameter values to ensure the difference is zero.

O	P	Q
UN ESTIMATE	MODEL ESTIMATE	DIFFERENCE
421,007	536,070	-115,063

Fig. 5.42: The setup of the difference between the UN and model population estimates in 2100.

In the Excel Solver setup (see Fig. 5.43), we constrained the long-term birth rate to be less than the UN's projected birth rate for the US in 2100, 0.009291; the long-term death rate to be higher than the UN's projected death rate for the US in 2100, 0.010913; and the long-term migration rate to be lower than the UN's projected migration rate for the United States in 2100, 0.002911. Additionally, we set the time to change the rates to 50 years, ensuring a gradual transition consistent with long-term demographic trends.

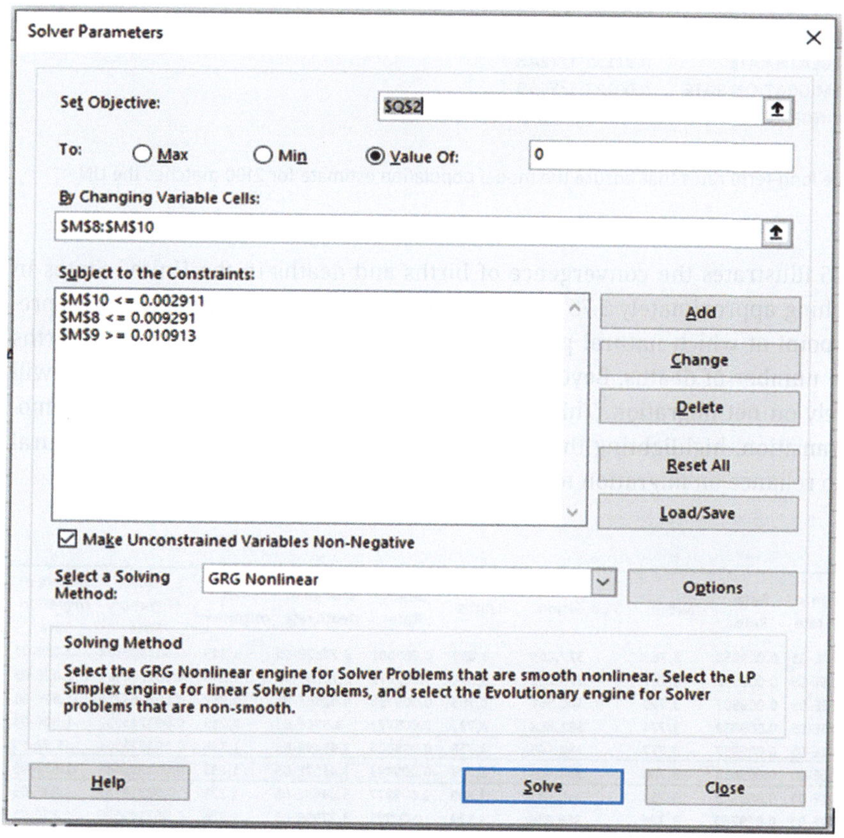

Fig. 5.43: The setup of the Excel Solver.

Figure 5.44 illustrates the long-term birth rate, long-term death rate, and long-term migration rate required for the model to align with the UN's 2100 US population projection of 421 million [38].

L	M	N	O	P	Q
PARAMETERS	VALUE	UNITS	UN ESTIMATE	MODEL ESTIMATE	DIFFERENCE
INITIAL YEAR	2023	YEAR	421,007	421,007	0
TIME STEP	1	YEAR			
INITIAL POPULATION	342,475	PEOPLE			
INITIAL BIRTH RATE	0.01065	1/YEAR			
INITIAL DEATH RATE	0.00866	1/YEAR			
INITIAL MIGRATION RATE	0.00385	1/YEAR			
LONG TERM BIRTH RATE	0.00865	1/YEAR			
LONG TERM DEATH RATE	0.01155	1/YEAR			
LONG TERM MIGRATION RATE	0.00227	1/YEAR			
TIME TO CHANGE RATES	50	YEAR			

Fig. 5.44: The long-term rates that ensure the model population estimate for 2100 matches the UN estimate.

Figure 5.45 illustrates the convergence of births and deaths in the United States in 2049, reaching approximately 3.78 million births and deaths. This intersection represents the point at which natural population growth ceases, as the number of births equals the number of deaths. Beyond this point, any increase in population size will rely entirely on net migration. This moment marks a key milestone in the US demographic transition, highlighting the shift from population growth driven by natural increase to reliance on migration to sustain growth.

	A	B	C	D	E	F	G	H	I	J	K
1	Year	change in birth rate	Birth Rate	births	Population	deaths	Death Rate	change in death rate	net migration	Net Migration Rate	change in migration rate
23	2044	-2.61E-05	0.009958	3,763	377,865	3,651	0.009661	3.7782E-05	1,249	0.003305624	-2.06E-05
24	2045	-2.56E-05	0.009932	3,767	379,227	3,678	0.009699	3.7026E-05	1,246	0.003284983	-2.02E-05
25	2046	-2.51E-05	0.009907	3,770	380,561	3,705	0.009736	3.6286E-05	1,242	0.003264756	-1.98E-05
26	2047	-2.46E-05	0.009882	3,774	381,868	3,732	0.009772	3.556E-05	1,239	0.003244932	-1.94E-05
27	2048	-2.41E-05	0.009857	3,777	383,149	3,758	0.009808	3.4849E-05	1,236	0.003225506	-1.9E-05
28	2049	-2.36E-05	0.009833	3,780	384,404	3,784	0.009843	3.4152E-05	1,233	0.003206468	-1.87E-05
29	2050	-2.31E-05	0.009809	3,783	385,633	3,809	0.009877	3.3469E-05	1,229	0.00318781	-1.83E-05
30	2051	-2.27E-05	0.009786	3,786	386,836	3,834	0.00991	3.2799E-05	1,226	0.003169526	-1.79E-05
31	2052	-2.22E-05	0.009764	3,788	388,014	3,858	0.009943	3.2143E-05	1,223	0.003151608	-1.76E-05
32	2053	-2.18E-05	0.009742	3,791	389,168	3,882	0.009975	3.1501E-05	1,220	0.003134048	-1.72E-05
33	2054	-2.13E-05	0.00972	3,794	390,296	3,906	0.010007	3.0871E-05	1,216	0.003116839	-1.69E-05

Fig. 5.45: The births equal the deaths in 2049.

Figure 5.46 illustrates graphically the convergence of births and deaths in the United States by approximately 2050.

Figure 5.47 illustrates the intersection of birth and death rates in the United States around 2050, highlighting a critical moment in the country's demographic evolution. The birth rate steadily declines due to falling fertility rates and changing societal

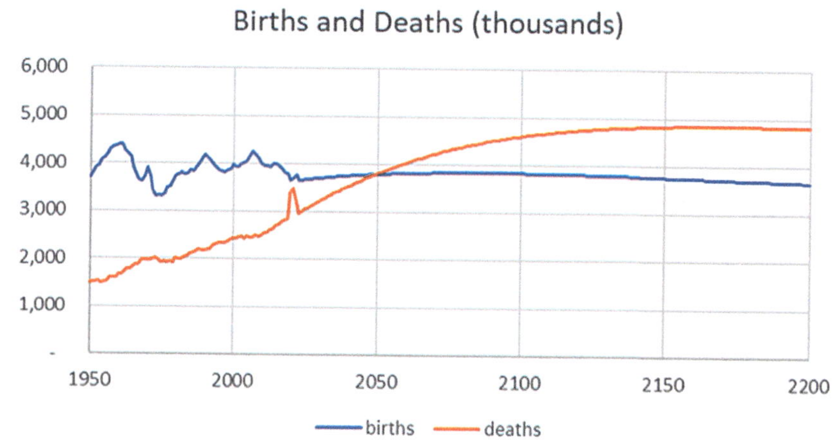

Fig. 5.46: The historical and projected births and deaths in the United States.

norms, while the death rate rises as the population ages. This intersection marks the point at which natural population growth ceases, as births no longer exceed deaths. Beyond 2050, the death rate is expected to exceed the birth rate, potentially signalling a shift towards population decline unless offset by migration. This trend aligns with historical data and long-term projections.

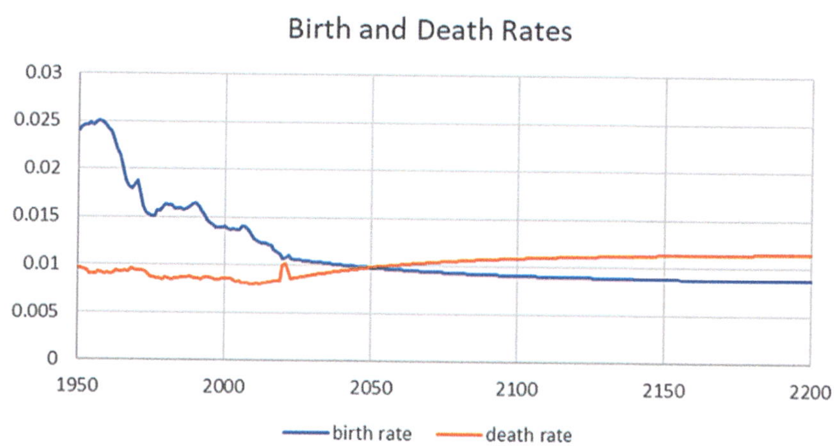

Fig. 5.47: The historical and projected birth and death rates in the United States.

In 2139, Fig. 5.48 shows that the projected births plus net migration in the United States amount to 4.806 million (comprising 3.772 million births and 1.034 million net migration), which is approximately equal to the projected number of deaths, 4.808 million. This near-equivalence signifies a critical demographic equilibrium, in which the combined impact of births and migration offsets the effects of deaths. This balance underscores the continuing importance of migration in sustaining the US population, even as births remain below deaths. It also reflects the long-term, with the population peaking at 426 million and then declining.

	A	B	C	D	E	F	G	H	I	J	K
1	Year	change in birth rate	Birth Rate	births	Population	deaths	Death Rate	change in death rate	net migration	Net Migration Rate	change in migration rate
113	2134	-4.24E-06	0.008865	3,780	426,378	4,794	0.011244	6.1324E-06	1,041	0.00244111	-3.35E-06
114	2135	-4.15E-06	0.008861	3,778	426,405	4,797	0.01125	6.0098E-06	1,039	0.002437759	-3.28E-06
115	2136	-4.07E-06	0.008857	3,777	426,426	4,800	0.011256	5.8896E-06	1,038	0.002434476	-3.22E-06
116	2137	-3.99E-06	0.008853	3,775	426,441	4,802	0.011262	5.7718E-06	1,037	0.002431259	-3.15E-06
117	2138	-3.91E-06	0.008849	3,774	426,450	4,805	0.011268	5.6563E-06	1,035	0.002428106	-3.09E-06
118	2139	-3.83E-06	0.008845	3,772	426,455	4,808	0.011273	5.5432E-06	1,034	0.002425016	-3.03E-06
119	2140	-3.75E-06	0.008841	3,770	426,453	4,810	0.011279	5.4323E-06	1,033	0.002421987	-2.97E-06
120	2141	-3.68E-06	0.008837	3,769	426,447	4,812	0.011284	5.3237E-06	1,032	0.00241902	-2.91E-06
121	2142	-3.6E-06	0.008834	3,767	426,435	4,814	0.01129	5.2172E-06	1,030	0.002416111	-2.85E-06
122	2143	-3.53E-06	0.00883	3,765	426,418	4,816	0.011295	5.1129E-06	1,029	0.002413261	-2.79E-06
123	2144	-3.46E-06	0.008827	3,764	426,396	4,818	0.0113	5.0106E-06	1,028	0.002410468	-2.74E-06

Fig. 5.48: The births plus net migration equals the deaths in 2139.

Figure 5.49 graphically highlights the intersection of births plus net migration with deaths in 2140. Births plus migration remain relatively steady, at approximately 5 million people per year, while deaths show an upward trend, gradually peaking before declining.

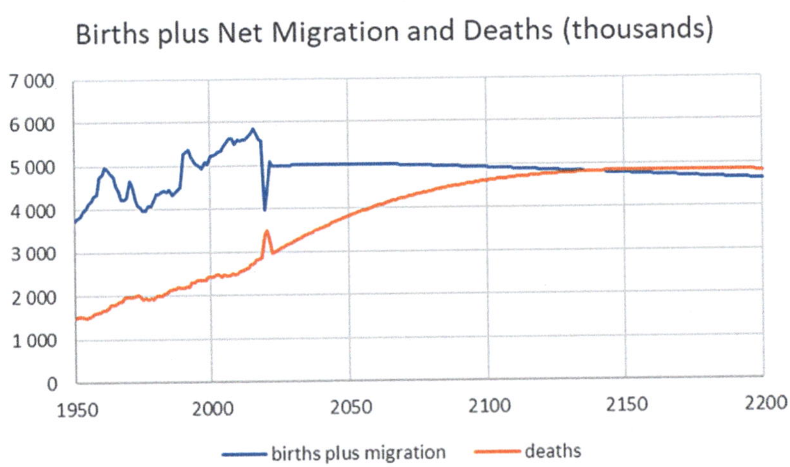

Fig. 5.49: The historical and projected births plus migration, and deaths in the United States.

Figure 5.50 illustrates the intersection of the birth plus migration and death rates in 2140. The birth plus migration rates approach equilibrium, while the death rate increases towards its equilibrium value. They intersect in 2140, and as we saw in the previous figure, in that year, the sum of births and migration equals the deaths.

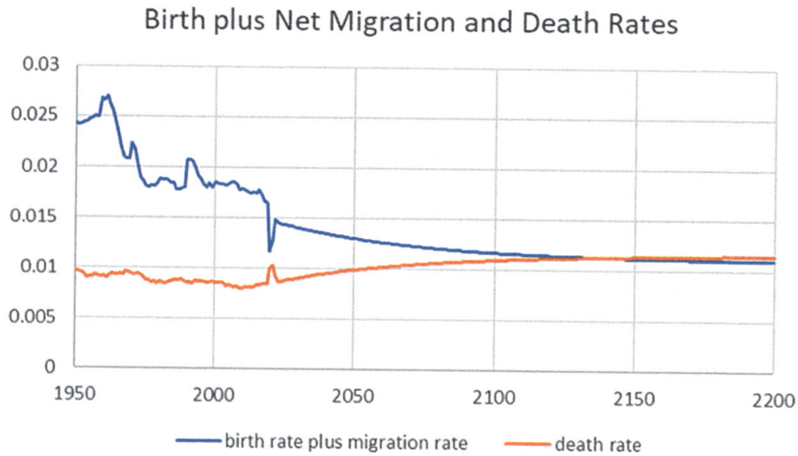

Fig. 5.50: The historical and projected birth plus net migration, and death rates.

Figure 5.51 shows the US population peaking at just over 426 million in 2140, driven by growth from births and net migration, which outpaced deaths. After 2140, the population declines slightly as deaths exceed the combined impact of births and migration, reflecting long-term demographic shifts.

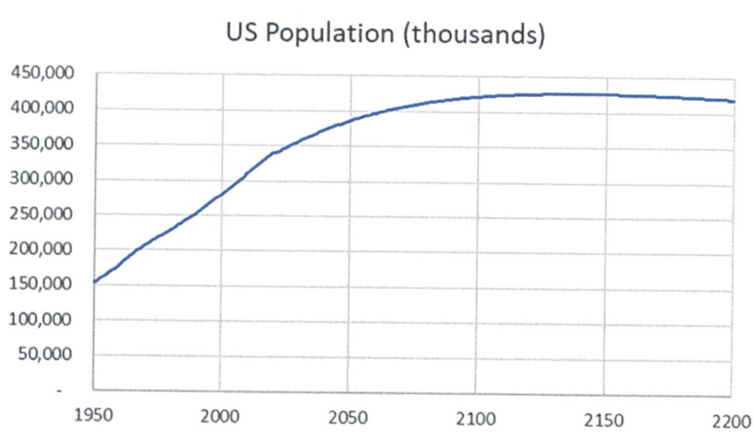

Fig. 5.51: The historical and projected US population.

Notice in Fig. 5.51 that the decline in the US population after 2140 is very gradual. This is because the difference between long-term births plus migration and the deaths is relatively small, as shown in Fig. 5.49.

5.5 Population of Nigeria

We will now convert this US population model to another country, Nigeria.

Sub-Saharan Africa continues to experience significant population growth, with Nigeria at the forefront as the continent's most populous country. As of 2024, Nigeria's population is estimated at around 225 million, driven by one of the world's highest birth rates. High fertility rates have fuelled the country's population growth. However, like many regions experiencing rapid demographic expansion, Nigeria's growth is expected to slow over the coming decades as fertility rates decline.

To illustrate Nigeria's population growth dynamics, we begin with the same simple system dynamics model used for the US, featuring a population stock and three flows: births, net migration, and deaths (see Fig. 5.52).

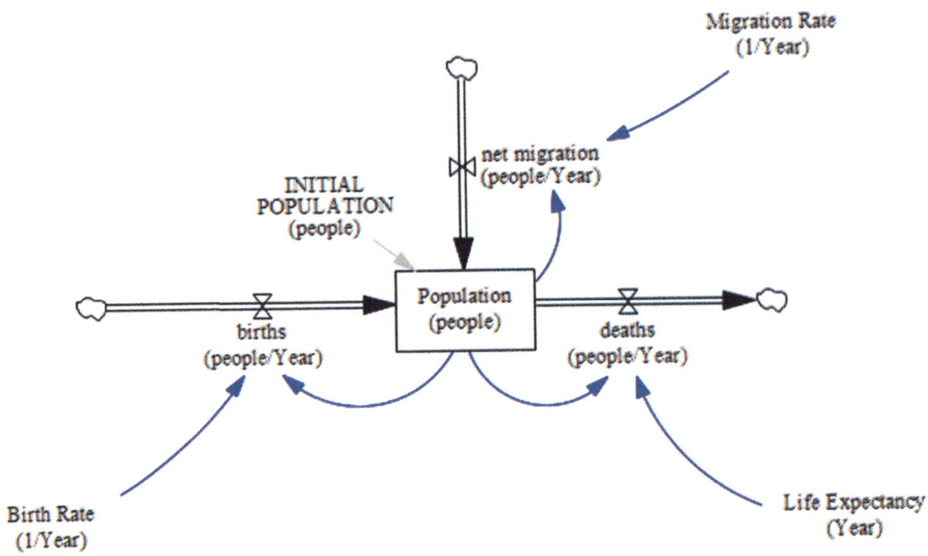

Fig. 5.52: A simple national population system dynamics model.

We obtained historical data on population, births, deaths, and net migration from 1950 to 2023, as well as projected values until 2100, from the United Nations Population Prospects 2024 database [38]. Figure 5.53 depicts Nigeria's population growth from 37 million in 1950 to 225 million in 2023, following an almost exponential trajectory. This rapid increase reflects high fertility rates, sustained over decades, and relatively low death rates due to improvements in healthcare and living conditions. The steep curve highlights Nigeria's position in the earlier stages of the demographic transition, where births significantly outpace deaths. This trend underscores the immense demographic momentum driving Nigeria's population growth.

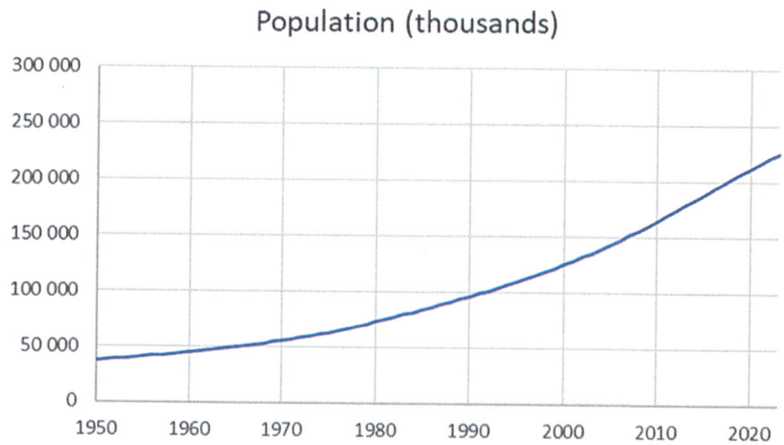

Fig. 5.53: Historical population estimates in Nigeria, from 1950 to 2023.

The data indicate that Nigeria's life expectancy has increased steadily since 1950, although it remains below the global average (see Fig. 5.54).

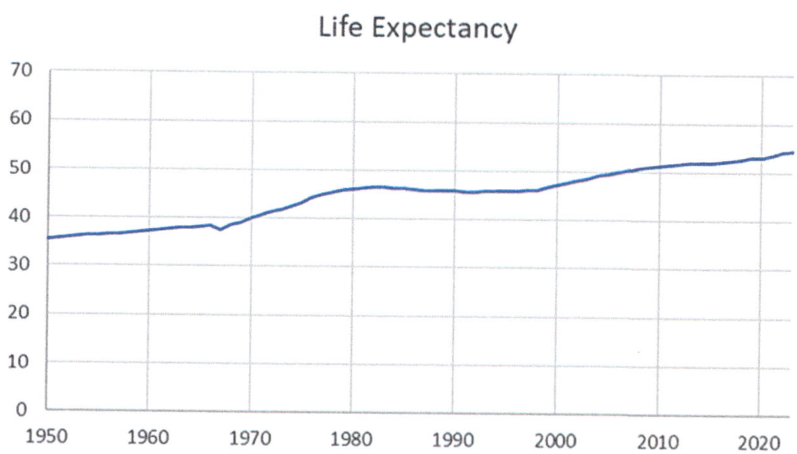

Fig. 5.54: Historical life expectancy in Nigeria from 1950 to 2023.

Figure 5.55 illustrates the widening gap between births and deaths in Nigeria from 1950 to 2023, driving the exponential population growth observed during this period. The high number of births in recent years suggests that millions of children are born in Nigeria, making the demographics unique.

Figure 5.56 illustrates that the birth rate peaked in the 1970s, declined gradually until 2010, and then dropped sharply until 2023. The death rate in Nigeria has steadily declined from 1950 to 2023. According to the UN Population Prospects, this downward

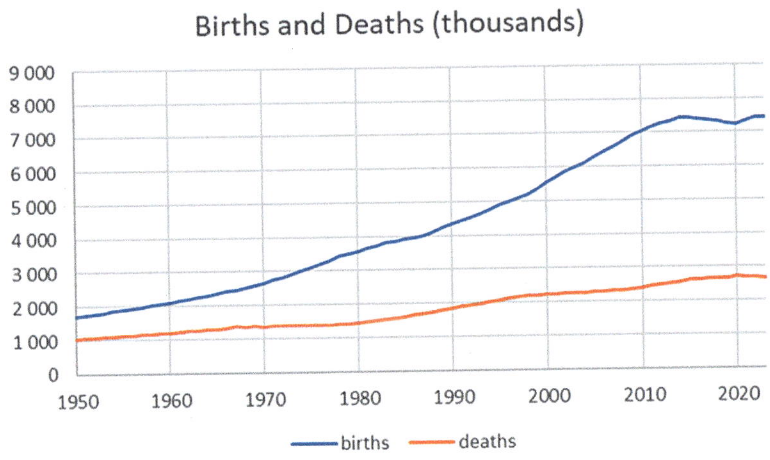

Fig. 5.55: Historical births and deaths in Nigeria from 1950 to 2023.

trend is expected to continue, with the death rate reaching a minimum in 2050 [38]. This extended decline highlights Nigeria's youthful population, but necessitates revising the death rate model in the Nigerian population simulation. The model must account for this continued reduction and incorporate a dynamic structure to reflect projected long-term mortality trends accurately.

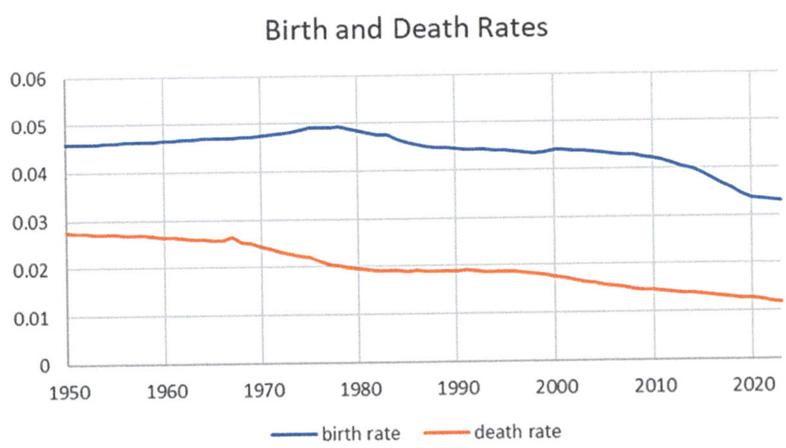

Fig. 5.56: Historical birth and death rates from 1950 to 2023.

Net migration has had a minimal impact on the population, as emigration and immigration have mainly offset each other. Figure 5.57 shows the historical net migration rate. A sharp outflow of Nigerians in 1983 might have been associated with the coup d'état that happened that year. There appears to be a slight decline in net migration after 1990. However, as we mentioned, the values are small.

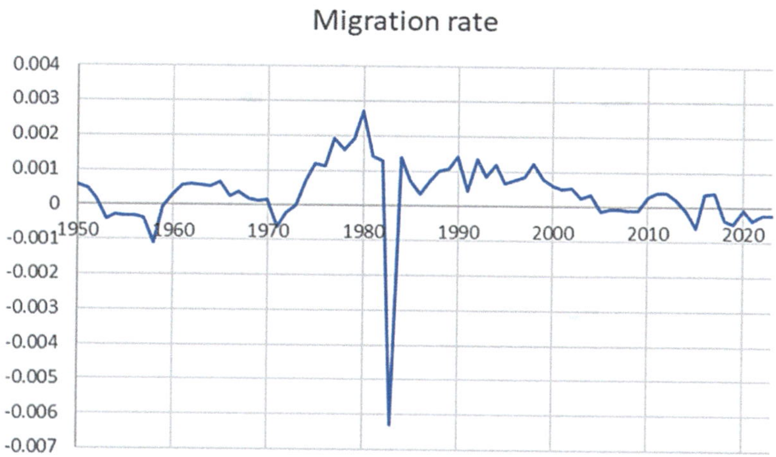

Fig. 5.57: Historical migration rate from 1950 to 2023.

The birth and net migration rates will be modelled for the Nigerian population model using the same goal-gap approach as the US model.

Our revised death rate model (Fig. 5.58) introduces a more dynamic structure with inflows and outflows to reflect Nigeria's unique demographic trends. The inflow, which represents an increase in the death rate, follows a goal-gap approach in which the death rate adjusts to a long-term target over a specified time period. Simultaneously, the model includes an outflow, referred to as a decrease in the death rate, which employs a goal-gap approach to represent the decline in the death rate over time towards a minimum death rate.

We introduce a transition factor, modelled as an additional goal-gap structure to manage the transition between these two goals. The transition factor begins at zero, meaning the death rate initially aligns with its minimum value. Over time, the transition factor gradually approaches its long-term value of one using another goal-gap model, shifting the orientation of the death rate model from the minimum death rate goal to the long-term death rate goal. This layered approach ensures that the model accurately captures the expected decline in the death rate to a minimum value, followed by an increase to a long-term equilibrium value. Since this is simply a combination of three goal-gap models, implementation is straightforward.

For the Nigerian model, we will utilize Excel Solver in a slightly different manner. We minimize the error between the model's projections and the UN Population Prospects for Nigeria [38], rather than aiming for an exact match. Specifically, we strive to minimize the squared error between the model's estimate of the death rate in 2050

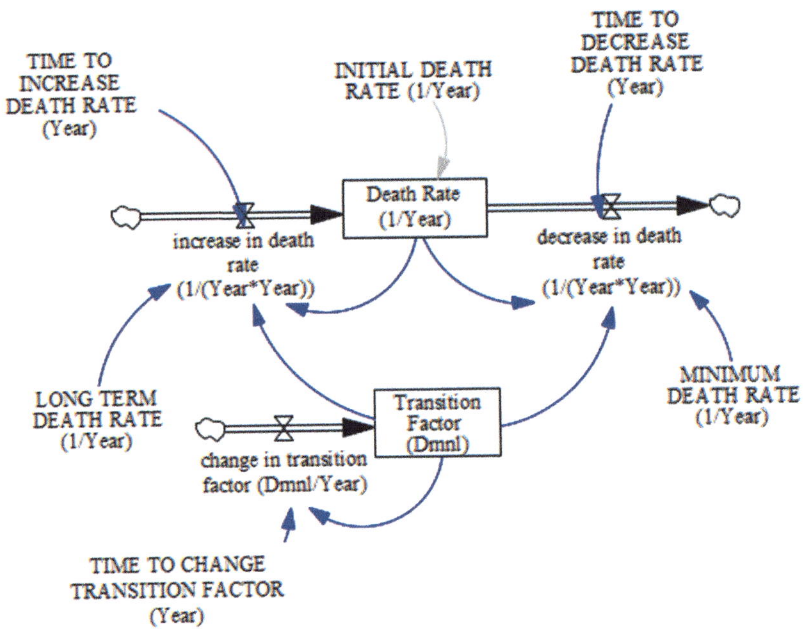

Fig. 5.58: Revised death rate model for Nigeria.

and the UN's projected value for that year, as well as the squared error between the model's estimate of the population in 2100 and the UN's projected value for that year.

Figure 5.59 illustrates the UN's projected death rate for 2050, the model's estimate, and the UN's projected population for 2100, in billions [38]. We present the population in billions to ensure the squared errors are comparable. The squared error is calculated as (UN projected value − model estimate) ^ 2, and we compute it for both the 2050 death rate and the 2100 population. This squaring ensures all errors are positive and amplifies more significant discrepancies, making them more influential in optimization. To minimize this error, the Solver adjusts the model parameters, such as birth, death, and migration rates. This ensures the model aligns closely with both the 2050 death rate and 2100 population projections.

R	S	T	U	V	W
YEAR	PARAMETER	UN ESTIMATE	MODEL ESTIMATE	SQUARED ERROR	SUM OF SQUARED ERROR
2050	Death Rate	0.01049	0.01134	0.00000	0.44974
2100	Population	0.47669	1.14732	0.44974	

Fig. 5.59: Setting up the objective function to minimize in Nigeria's population projection model.

Note that the model estimates are based on the Solver's starting conditions when the long-term values are set to 2023 values (see Fig. 5.60). We need to add an exogenous variable to the model. We add a minimum death rate. We set the long-term values to the initial values and the minimum death rate to the UN Prospects value for 2050 [38].

O	P	Q
PARAMETERS	VALUE	UNITS
INITIAL TIME	2023	YEAR
TIME STEP	1	YEAR
INITIAL POPULATION	225,495	PEOPLE
INITIAL BIRTH RATE	0.03295	1/YEAR
INITIAL MIGRATION RATE	-0.00023	1/YEAR
INITIAL DEATH RATE	0.01174	1/YEAR
LONG TERM BIRTH RATE	0.03295	1/YEAR
LONG TERM MIGRATION RATE	-0.00023	1/YEAR
MINIMUM DEATH RATE	0.01049	1/YEAR
LONG TERM DEATH RATE	0.01174	YEAR
TIME TO CHANGE RATES	50	YEAR

Fig. 5.60: Setting up the parameters in Nigeria's population model.

To incorporate the revised death rate model, we add four new columns to the worksheet: increase in death rate, decrease in death rate (flows), transition factor (stock), and change in transition factor (flow). The transition factor is initialized to zero, representing the initial alignment of the death rate model to minimize the death rate. The change in transition factor is calculated using the formula: (1–transition factor)/time to change rates (see Fig. 5.61). This ensures the transition factor gradually moves from 0 to 1 over the specified time, reflecting the shift from the minimum to the long-term death rate goal. The transition factor effectively serves as a weight in the death rate goal-gap models, with a value of 1 fully aligning the death rate with its long-term target.

SUM fx =(1-J2)/P$12

	A	B	C	D	E	F	G	H	I	J	K	L	M	N	O	P	Q
1	Year	change in birth rate	Birth Rate	births	Population	deaths	Death Rate	increase in death rate	decrease in death rate	Transition Factor	change in transition factor	migration	Migration Rate	change in migration rate	PARAMETERS	VALUE	UNITS
2	2023	0	0.032954	7,431	225,495	2,647	0.0117			0	P$12	-52	-0.0002	0.0000	INITIAL TIME	2023	YEAR
3															TIME STEP	1	YEAR
4															INITIAL POPULATION	225,495	PEOPLE
5															INITIAL BIRTH RATE	0.03295	1/YEAR
6															INITIAL MIGRATION RATE	-0.00023	1/YEAR
7															INITIAL DEATH RATE	0.01174	1/YEAR
8															LONG TERM BIRTH RATE	0.03295	1/YEAR
9															LONG TERM MIGRATION RATE	-0.00023	1/YEAR
10															MINIMUM DEATH RATE	0.01049	1/YEAR
11															LONG TERM DEATH RATE	0.01174	YEAR
12															TIME TO CHANGE RATES	50	YEAR

Fig. 5.61: Set up of new columns for the transition factor and the change in the transition factor.

The formula for the decrease in the death rate in Fig. 5.62 is based on a goal-gap model with a few small but significant changes: (death rate − minimum death rate)/ time to change rates * (1 − transition factor). The goal-gap portion of the formula suggests that the decrease in death rate is a positive outflow. Since the transition factor is initialized to zero, the (1 − transition factor) = 1 at time 0, but since the transition factor will gradually approach 1, this term will become smaller, and the emphasis on the decrease in the death rate will decline.

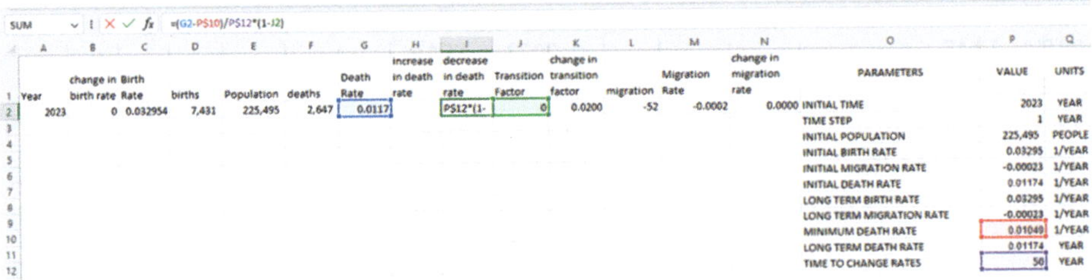

Fig. 5.62: Set up a new column for the decrease in the death rate flow.

The formula for the increase in the death rate in Fig. 5.63 is based on a goal-gap model with a small but significant addition: (long-term death rate − death rate)/time to change rates * transition factor. The goal-gap portion of the formula suggests that the increase in death rate is a positive inflow. Since the transition factor is initialized to zero but gradually approaches one, this term will become increasingly significant, making the emphasis on the rise in the death rate more pronounced.

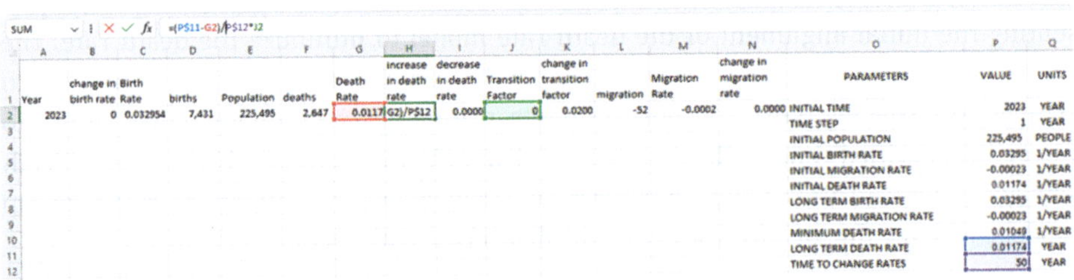

Fig. 5.63: Set up a new column for the increase in death rate flow.

Then, the death rate stock is updated for 2024 as the 2023 death rate plus the increase in the death rate minus the decrease in the death rate, multiplied by the time step (see Fig. 5.64).

To calibrate the model for Nigeria, we will use the Solver to minimize the sum of squared errors (SSEs) between the model's projections and the UN Population Prospects [38]. Note that in Fig. 5.65, the "Min" button is checked. We will adjust four parameters: the long-term birth rate, long-term migration rate, long-term death rate,

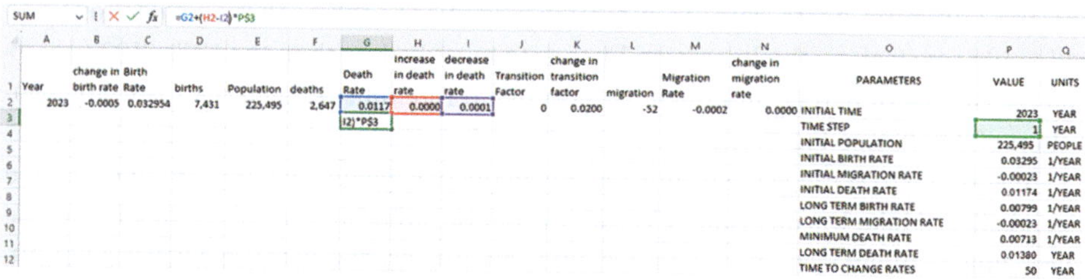

Fig. 5.64: Update of the death rate stock.

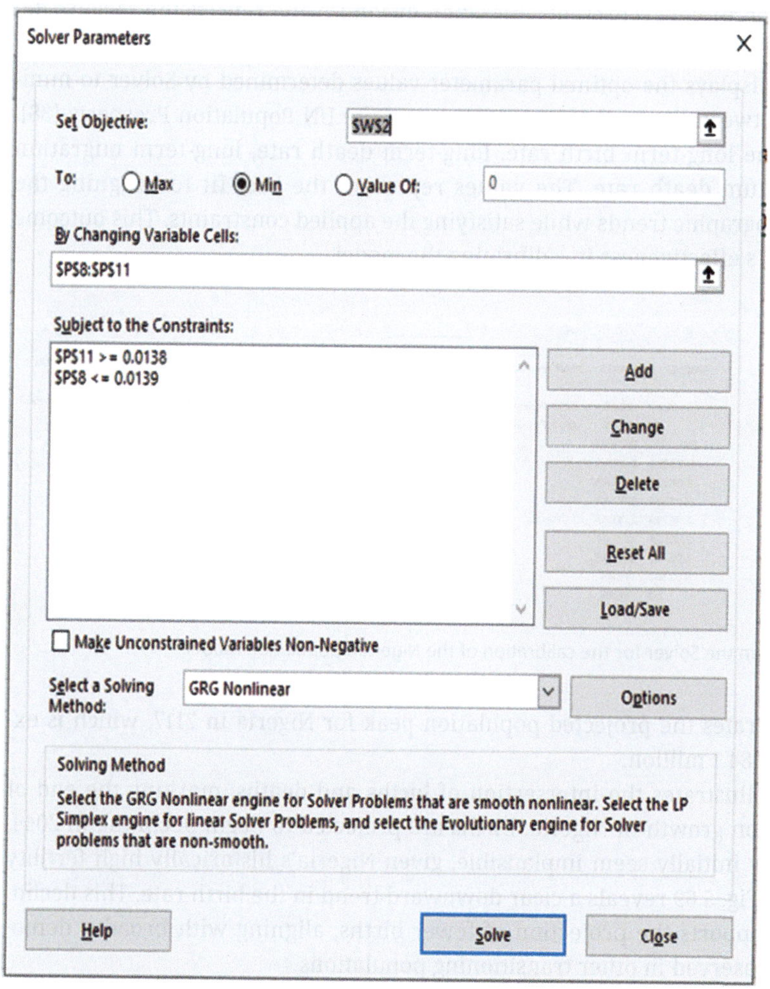

Fig. 5.65: Set up the Solver for calibrating the Nigerian population model.

and the minimum death rate. To maintain alignment with realistic projections, we will apply constraints: the long-term birth rate must be less than the UN's 2100 projection for Nigeria of 0.0139, and the long-term death rate must exceed the UN's 2100 projection of 0.0138 (see Fig. 5.65).

In addition to setting constraints for the model parameters, we need to uncheck the box labelled "Make Unconstrained Variables Non-Negative" in the Solver, just below the constraints window (see Fig. 5.65). This adjustment is crucial because Nigeria's net migration rate is negative, indicating a long-term outflow of migrants. By unchecking this box, we allow Solver to explore negative net migration values, which aligns with our long-term belief that Nigeria will continue to experience net emigration. This step ensures the model accurately represents migration dynamics and reflects the region's demographic realities.

Figure 5.66 displays the optimal parameter values determined by Solver to minimize the SSEs between the model's projections and the UN Population Prospects [38]. These include the long-term birth rate, long-term death rate, long-term migration rate, and minimum death rate. The values represent the best fit for aligning the model with demographic trends while satisfying the applied constraints. This outcome highlights Solver's effectiveness in calibrating the model.

O	P	Q	R	S	T	U	V	W
PARAMETERS	VALUE	UNITS	YEAR	PARAMETER	UN ESTIMATE	MODEL ESTIMATE	SQUARED ERROR	SUM OF SQUARED ERROR
INITIAL TIME	2023	YEAR	2050	Death Rate	0.01049	0.01047	0.00000	0.00000
TIME STEP	1	YEAR	2100	Population	0.47669	0.47669	0.00000	
INITIAL POPULATION	225,495	PEOPLE						
INITIAL BIRTH RATE	0.03295	1/YEAR						
INITIAL MIGRATION RATE	-0.00023	1/YEAR						
INITIAL DEATH RATE	0.01174	1/YEAR						
LONG TERM BIRTH RATE	0.00799	1/YEAR						
LONG TERM MIGRATION RATE	-0.00023	1/YEAR						
MINIMUM DEATH RATE	0.00713	1/YEAR						
LONG TERM DEATH RATE	0.01380	YEAR						
TIME TO CHANGE RATES	50	YEAR						

Fig. 5.66: Results from the Solver for the calibration of the Nigerian population model.

Figure 5.67 illustrates the projected population peak for Nigeria in 2117, which is expected to reach 484.1 million.

Figure 5.68 illustrates the intersection of births and deaths, marking the end of natural population growth in Nigeria. Births are projected to begin declining in 2044, a trend that may initially seem implausible, given Nigeria's historically high fertility rates. However, Fig. 5.69 reveals a clear downward trend in the birth rate. This declining birth rate supports the projection of fewer births, aligning with broader demographic trends observed in other transitioning populations.

	A	B	C	D	E	F	G	H	I	J	K	L	M	N
1	Year	change in birth rate	Birth Rate	births	Population	deaths	Death Rate	increase in death rate	decrease in death rate	Transition Factor	change in transition factor	migration	Migration Rate	change in migration rate
91	2112	-8.3E-05	0.012124	5,863	483,577	5,537	0.0115	0.0000	0.0000	0.8344	0.0033	-112	-0.0002	0.0000
92	2113	-8.1E-05	0.012041	5,825	483,790	5,552	0.0115	0.0000	0.0000	0.8377	0.0032	-112	-0.0002	0.0000
93	2114	-7.9E-05	0.01196	5,788	483,952	5,566	0.0115	0.0000	0.0000	0.8409	0.0032	-112	-0.0002	0.0000
94	2115	-7.8E-05	0.01188	5,751	484,062	5,579	0.0115	0.0000	0.0000	0.8441	0.0031	-112	-0.0002	0.0000
95	2116	-7.6E-05	0.011803	5,714	484,122	5,592	0.0115	0.0000	0.0000	0.8472	0.0031	-112	-0.0002	0.0000
96	2117	-7.5E-05	0.011726	5,677	484,133	5,604	0.0116	0.0000	0.0000	0.8503	0.0030	-112	-0.0002	0.0000
97	2118	-7.3E-05	0.011652	5,640	484,094	5,615	0.0116	0.0000	0.0000	0.8533	0.0029	-112	-0.0002	0.0000
98	2119	-7.2E-05	0.011578	5,604	484,008	5,626	0.0116	0.0000	0.0000	0.8562	0.0029	-112	-0.0002	0.0000
99	2120	-7E-05	0.011507	5,568	483,874	5,636	0.0116	0.0000	0.0000	0.8591	0.0028	-112	-0.0002	0.0000
100	2121	-6.9E-05	0.011436	5,532	483,694	5,646	0.0117	0.0000	0.0000	0.8619	0.0028	-112	-0.0002	0.0000
101	2122	-6.8E-05	0.011367	5,496	483,468	5,655	0.0117	0.0000	0.0000	0.8647	0.0027	-112	-0.0002	0.0000

Fig. 5.67: Results from the Nigerian population model projections.

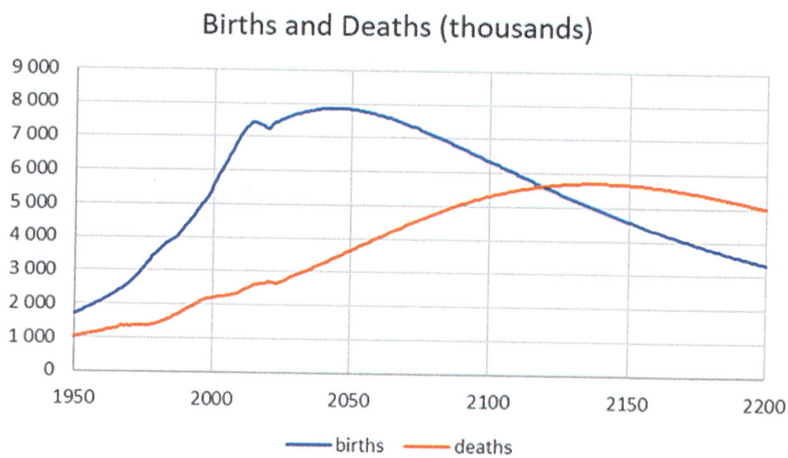

Fig. 5.68: Historical and projected births and deaths in Nigeria.

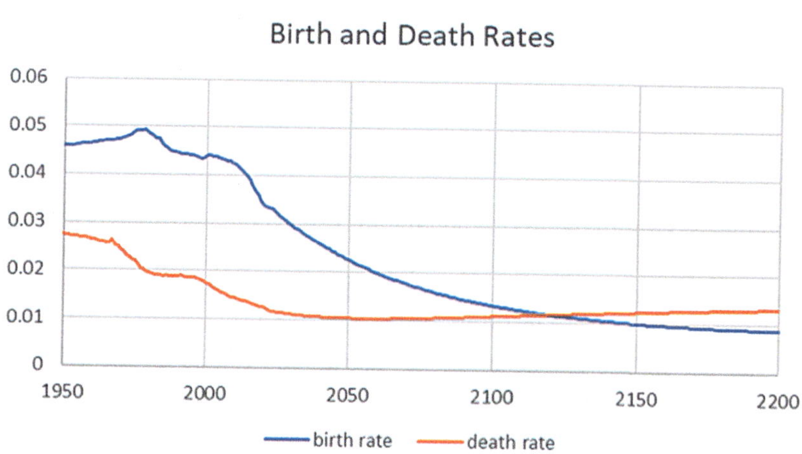

Fig. 5.69: Historical and projected birth and death rates in Nigeria.

Figure 5.69 clearly illustrates that the death rate is projected to continue declining after 2023, primarily due to Nigeria's youthful population. This trend is expected to reach a minimum of 0.01049 in 2050, marking the lowest mortality during this period. Following this minimum, the death rate is expected to gradually increase as demographic factors, such as an ageing population, become more prominent. This upward trajectory leads the death rate towards a long-term equilibrium value, aligning with broader demographic trends. This dynamic behaviour emphasizes the capture of short-term improvements and long-term stabilization in population projections.

Figure 5.70 illustrates Nigeria's population growth over time, highlighting a peak in 2117, at approximately 484 million. This marks the point at which natural population growth, driven by high fertility and declining mortality, begins to slow as the number of births and deaths converges. Following this peak, the population gradually declines. This reflects Nigeria's projected demographic transition.

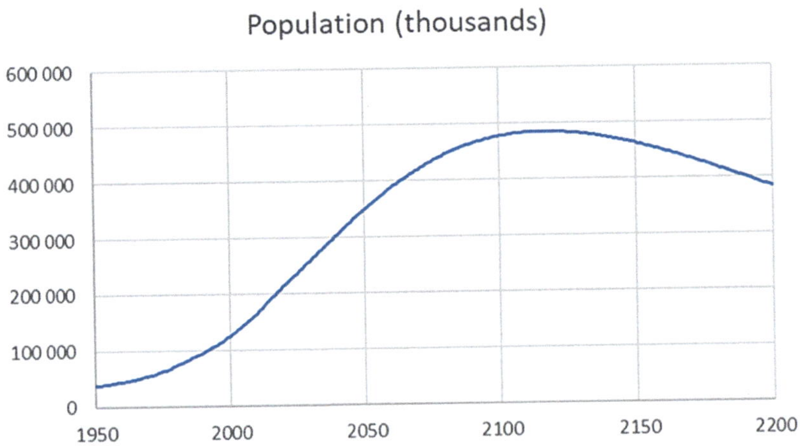

Fig. 5.70: Historical and projected population in Nigeria.

5.6 Summary

This chapter applies system dynamics to population projections for the world, the United States, and Nigeria, extending the Chapter 2 stock-and-flow model (births, deaths, and migration) with a goal-gap structure. The World model replicates UN trends and projects a 2100 peak of 10.4 billion. The US model incorporates dynamic net migration, illustrating growth sustained by migration, even as the natural increase halts, with a peak of ~ 426 million in 2140. The Nigerian model revises the death rate structure with a transition factor to capture short-term improvements and long-run stabilization, projecting a 2117 peak of ~ 484 million. Excel Solver calibration aligns the models with the UN estimates while preserving causal fidelity, thereby demonstrating accessible and defensible forecasting.

5.7 Discussion Questions

- For the world model, why is "births = deaths in 2100" an acceptable calibration target, and what risk does it avoid relative to free-fitting?
- In the US case, what governance guardrails justify the Solver bounds on long-term birth, death, and migration rates? Cite the specific bound logic.
- How would you brief executives on the expected decline in natural increase in the US by 2050 and the resulting reliance on migration?
- Defend the transition-factor construct in Nigeria's death-rate model versus a single goal-gap; where does the single-goal formulation mislead?
- Why is an SSE objective across two targets (2050 death rate; 2100 population) more robust than a single target for Nigeria?
- When (and how) do you justify allowing negative decision variables (e.g. migration rate) in Solver?
- The world model reproduces ~ 10.4 billion in 2100. What makes this convergence persuasive, and what doesn't?

5.8 Exercises

5.8.1 World model : endogenous rates and Solver.
Task. In Excel, implement goal-gap stocks for birth rate and death rate and connect them to births/deaths. Initialize 2023 values and update stocks using Euler and anchored references. Configure the Solver to set births minus deaths (2100) to 0 by varying long-term rates (keep the time to change fixed).
Deliverable. Spreadsheet (first 15 rows and a Solver dialogue screenshot) and the 2100 check (births ≈ deaths).

5.8.2 Stress test: parameter bounds
Task. Add Solver constraints for long-term birth rate ≤ UN 2100 birth rate and long-term death rate ≥ UN 2100 death rate; re-solve.
Deliverable. Table of bounds versus solution; Two-sentence justification of constraint directionality.

5.8.3 United States: introduce migration
Task. Add migration rate stock and net migration flow using a goal-gap formulation, setting a target of 421 million (2010) and utilizing Solver to achieve it within UN-aligned rate bounds.

Deliverable. Parameters block, Solver setup, and a short note on births ≈ deaths ~ 2050 and migration's role.

5.8.4 Nigeria: two-goal death rate with transition factor.
Task. Add columns for increase in death rate, decrease in death rate, transition factor, and change in transition factor. Use change in transition factor = (1 − transition factor)/time to change, decrease = (death rate − minimum death rate)/time to change * (1 − transition factor), increase = (long-term death rate − death rate)/time to change * transition factor. Update death rate (t + dt) = death rate + (increase − decrease) * dt. Configure SSE objective: (death rate 2050 − UN death rate 2050) ^ 2 + (population 2100 − UN population 2100) ^ 2. Uncheck "Make unconstrained variables non-negative" to permit negative migration.
Deliverable. Screenshot of formulas, SSE cell, constraints, and Solver dialogue.

5.8.5 Result interpretation: Nigeria.
Task. Report peak year and peak population, and identify the year of the births-deaths crossover. Provide a three-sentence management takeaway.

5.8.6 Communication artefact: world chart pack.
Task. Create a one-page chart pack: (A) births versus deaths (1950–2200), (B) birth and death rates (1950–2200), and (C) population trajectory with 2100 peak called out. Add one tight caption per chart.
Deliverable. PDF or slide deck with three charts and captions.

Chapter 6
Fitting Model Results to Time-Series Data

6.1 Learning Objectives

- Explain why reference modes (historical time series) are required before presenting forward scenarios, and justify the selection of an authoritative data source.
- Build an Excel calibration scaffold: align time bases, normalize units/scales, and create actual, model, and error columns.
- Configure Excel Solver to minimize the error metric within parameter bounds and structural constraints, documenting the setup for audit purposes.
- Implement goal-gap adjustments for key rates and, where warranted, use separate adjustment times (e.g. for distinct inflow vs. outflow processes); explain the rationale.
- Calibrate multiple outputs (e.g. a level and one or more rates) using weights/normalization, so no single series dominates the fit; interpret the resulting plots.
- Produce a stakeholder-ready summary (assumptions, parameter values, fit quality, limitations, and next-step improvements) suitable for inclusion in a management pack.

6.2 Introduction

In Chapter 5, we examined how system dynamics models can project future scenarios, offering powerful tools for planning and decision-making. These forward-looking insights are often the most exciting deliverables for clients. However, before clients can trust projections about the future, they usually need assurance that the model can accurately replicate the past. Establishing this credibility involves demonstrating that the model reflects historical data, showing that its structure and assumptions align with real-world dynamics. Achieving this alignment builds confidence in the model's validity and utility for future projections.

This chapter delves into the foundational practices of system dynamics modelling, emphasizing the critical importance of grounding models in empirical evidence. As Homer [39] highlights, the first step in building a credible model is to collect and thoroughly examine time-series data. These historical trends, known as reference modes, provide a blueprint for understanding the system's behaviour over time. By carefully analysing these patterns, modellers can create simulations that accurately reflect real-world dynamics, thereby reinforcing the model's reliability.

To achieve this, we will utilize Excel's Solver tool to calibrate a model against historical data. Calibration involves adjusting the model's parameters to align its outputs closely with observed data. We will revisit our population models for the world, the

https://doi.org/10.1515/9783111541389-007

United States, and Nigeria, but with a backward-looking approach. The UN Population Prospects provides a wealth of demographic data, serving as a robust foundation for this process [38]. By leveraging this data and applying the Solver, we will demonstrate how to refine the model, align it with historical trends, and build a compelling case for validity. Through this process, we will showcase technical techniques and highlight how thoughtful model calibration can strengthen stakeholder confidence and enhance the overall impact of system dynamics models.

6.3 The World Model

Let's revisit the world model we developed in Chapter 5, which utilized the goal-gap approach to estimate birth and death rates over time. In this chapter, we will introduce a pivotal modification to the model. Instead of using a single parameter to represent the adjustment time for birth and death rates, we will assign separate values for the time to change birth rate and time to change death rate (see Fig. 6.1). This adjustment enables us to capture more nuanced dynamics in population changes, reflecting the varying speeds at which birth and death rates respond to underlying factors.

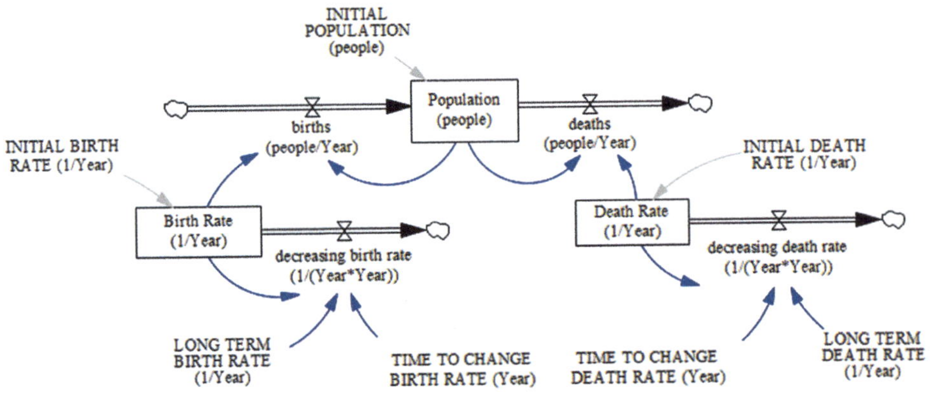

Fig. 6.1: The revised population model with separate times to change birth and death rates.

The UN Population Prospects provides detailed estimates of the world population, as well as birth and death rates, covering the period from 1950 to 2023 [38]. To build on this, let's revisit the graphical representation of the world population from Chapter 5 (see Fig. 6.2). We will also reference the graphical displays of global birth and death rates introduced in that chapter (see Fig. 6.3).

In this chapter, we will use the same population Excel Worksheet model introduced in Chapter 5, with a few critical adjustments to focus on historical data. Specifically, the model will begin in 1950, using an initial population of approximately 2.5 billion people, a birth rate of 0.03683, and a death rate of 0.01955 for that year.

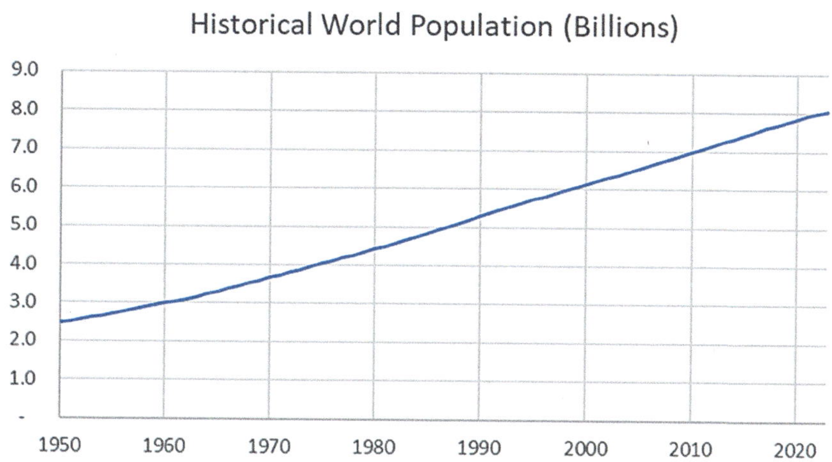

Fig. 6.2: Historical growth in world population from 1950 to 2023 in billions.

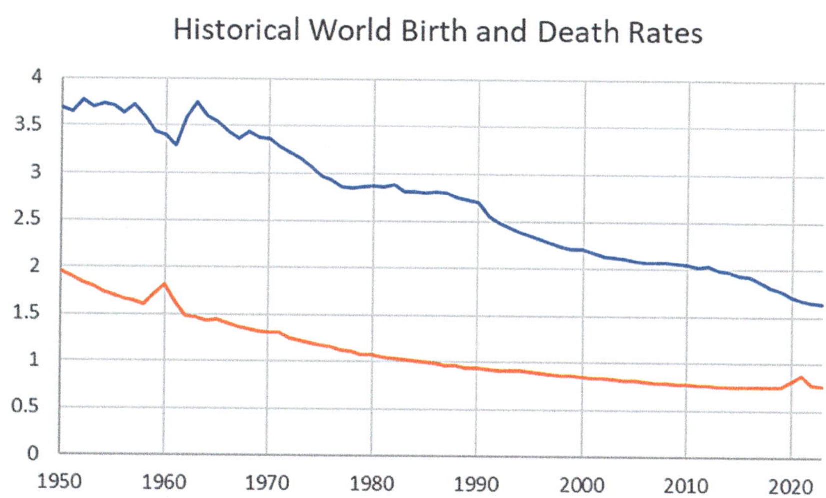

Fig. 6.3: Birth and death rates from 1950 to 2023.

These values, illustrated in Fig. 6.4, are the starting point for calibrating the model to align with historical trends.

To match the model to historical data, we will create two columns: one for the actual population values and another for the model's estimates. To simplify calculations, we will convert these population estimates into billions of people, a step we will explain in more detail shortly. Additionally, we will include a third column to calculate the squared error between the actual population and the model's estimate. The squared error is computed using the formula: (actual population – model estimate)^2. The setup, illustrated in Fig. 6.5, will help us evaluate how closely the model aligns with historical data.

	A	B	C	D	E	F	G	H	I	J
1	Year	change in birth rate	Birth Rate	births	Population	deaths	Death Rate	change in death rate	PARAMETER	VALUES
2	1950	0.00000	0.037	91,025	2,471,424	48,064	0.019	0.00000	INITIAL TIME	1950
3	1951	0.00000	0.037	92,607	2,514,385	48,900	0.019	0.00000	TIME STEP	1
4	1952	0.00000	0.037	94,217	2,558,092	49,750	0.019	0.00000	INITIAL POPULATION	2,471,424
5	1953	0.00000	0.037	95,855	2,602,560	50,615	0.019	0.00000	INITIAL BIRTH RATE	0.03683
6	1954	0.00000	0.037	97,521	2,647,800	51,494	0.019	0.00000	INITIAL DEATH RATE	0.01945
7	1955	0.00000	0.037	99,216	2,693,827	52,390	0.019	0.00000	LONG TERM BIRTH RATE	0.03683
8	1956	0.00000	0.037	100,941	2,740,653	53,300	0.019	0.00000	LONG TERM DEATH RATE	0.01945
9	1957	0.00000	0.037	102,696	2,788,294	54,227	0.019	0.00000	TIME TO CHANGE BIRTH RATES	50
10	1958	0.00000	0.037	104,481	2,836,763	55,169	0.019	0.00000	TIME TO CHANGE DEATH RATE	50

Fig. 6.4: The revised Excel population model, with separate times to change birth and death rates.

K	L	M	N
Year	Actual Population	Model Population	SE
1950	2.471424	2.47142	=(L2-M2)^2

Fig. 6.5: The calculation of the squared error between the actual population and the model estimate.

We will extend these columns by copying and pasting them down the worksheet to row 75, covering the years up to 2023 (see Fig. 6.6).

K	L	M	N
Year	Actual Population	Model Population	SE
2013	7.2468325	7.31930	0.00525
2014	7.33675467	7.44653	0.01205
2015	7.42647782	7.57597	0.02235
2016	7.51450593	7.70766	0.03731
2017	7.60260312	7.84165	0.05714
2018	7.68863279	7.97796	0.08371
2019	7.77117278	8.11664	0.11935
2020	7.85141462	8.25773	0.16509
2021	7.92258796	8.40127	0.22914
2022	7.98630882	8.54731	0.31472
2023	8.05650556	8.69589	0.40881

Fig. 6.6: The squared error for each year up to 2023.

Next, we will compute the total squared error from 1950 to 2023 (see Fig. 6.7).

K	L	M	N	O	P
Year	Actual Population	Model Population	SE	SSE	
1950	2.471424	2.47142	0.00000	=SUM(N2:N75)	
1951	2.51476169	2.51438	0.00000		
1952	2.55909238	2.55809	0.00000		
1953	2.6090803	2.60256	0.00004		
1954	2.65913217	2.64780	0.00013		
1955	2.71265755	2.69383	0.00035		
1956	2.76777003	2.74065	0.00074		
1957	2.82304995	2.78829	0.00121		
1958	2.88218672	2.83676	0.00206		
1959	2.94031262	2.88607	0.00294		
1960	2.99158808	2.93624	0.00306		

Fig. 6.7: The sum of the squared errors from 1950 to 2023.

We will follow the same approach for the birth rate and death rate. In this case, the crude birth and death rates have been estimated in units of people per 100 per year, aligning them with the population scale in billions for consistency (see Fig. 6.8).

Q	R	S	T	U	V	W	X
Actual Birth Rate	Model Birth Rate	SE	SSE	Actual Death Rate	Model Death Rate	SE	SSE
3.6831	3.6831	0	101.276	1.9448	1.9448	0	60.775
3.6464	3.6831	0.001347		1.899	1.9448	0.002098	
3.7681	3.6831	0.007225		1.8337	1.9448	0.012343	
3.6935	3.6831	0.000108		1.7934	1.9448	0.022922	
3.7301	3.6831	0.002209		1.7373	1.9448	0.043056	
3.7131	3.6831	0.0009		1.7019	1.9448	0.059	
3.6402	3.6831	0.00184		1.6627	1.9448	0.07958	
3.7165	3.6831	0.001116		1.6434	1.9448	0.090842	
3.5945	3.6831	0.00785		1.5979	1.9448	0.12034	
3.439	3.6831	0.059585		1.7102	1.9448	0.055037	
3.3951	3.6831	0.082944		1.8111	1.9448	0.017876	

Fig. 6.8: The squared errors for birth rate and death rate from 1950 to 2023.

Finally, we will calculate the total sum of squared errors (SSEs) by combining the squared error sums for population, birth rate, and death rate. This process is illustrated in Fig. 6.9.

L	M	N	O	P	Q	R	S	T	U	V	W	X	Y
Year	Actual Populati on	Model Populati on	SE	SSE	Actual Birth Rate	Model Birth Rate	SE	SSE	Actual Death Rate	Model Death Rate	SE	SSE	TSSE
1950	2.471424	2.47142	0.00000	0.07979	3.6831	4.038937	0.12662	1.290963	1.9448	1.974714	0.000895	0.162931	=P2+T2+X2
1951	2.514762	2.52244	0.00006		3.6464	3.988658	0.117141		1.899	1.923125	0.000582		

Fig. 6.9: The total sum of squared errors.

Next, we will use Excel's Solver tool to minimize the total SSEs by adjusting the initial and long-term values of the birth and death rates, as well as the time parameters governing their changes. The detailed process is illustrated in Fig. 6.10.

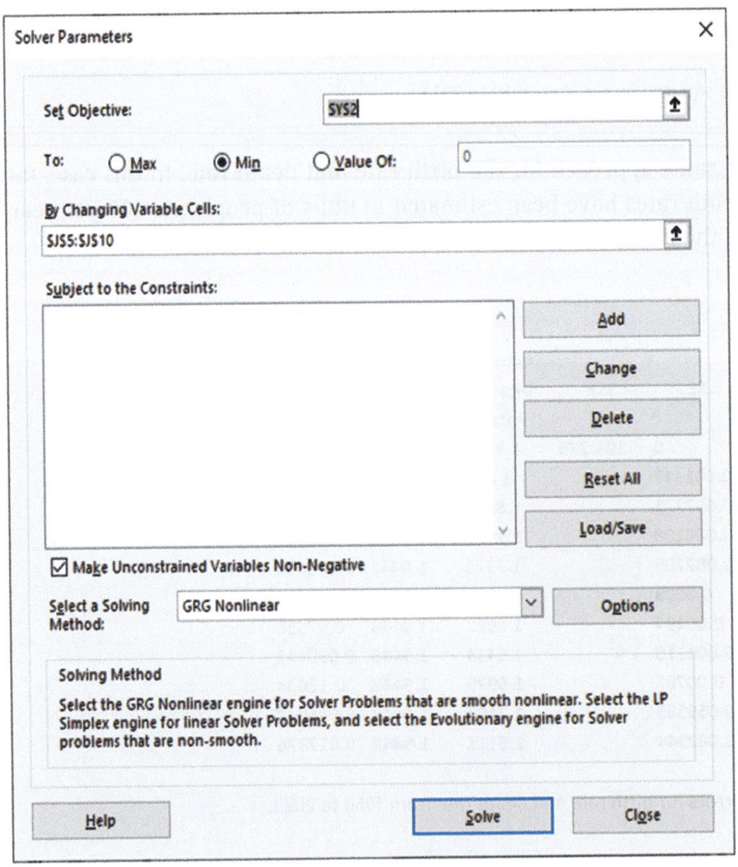

Fig. 6.10: The Solver setup for minimizing the total sum of squared error.

Figure 6.11 shows the results of the Solver minimization process.

I	J
PARAMETER	VALUES
INITIAL TIME	1950
TIME STEP	1
INITIAL POPULATION	2,471,424
INITIAL BIRTH RATE	0.03988
INITIAL DEATH RATE	0.01971
LONG TERM BIRTH RATE	0.00000
LONG TERM DEATH RATE	0.00662
TIME TO CHANGE BIRTH RATE	90
TIME TO CHANGE DEATH RATE	26

Fig. 6.11: The Solver results.

Figure 6.12 illustrates that the model aligns perfectly with the historical time series of the world population.

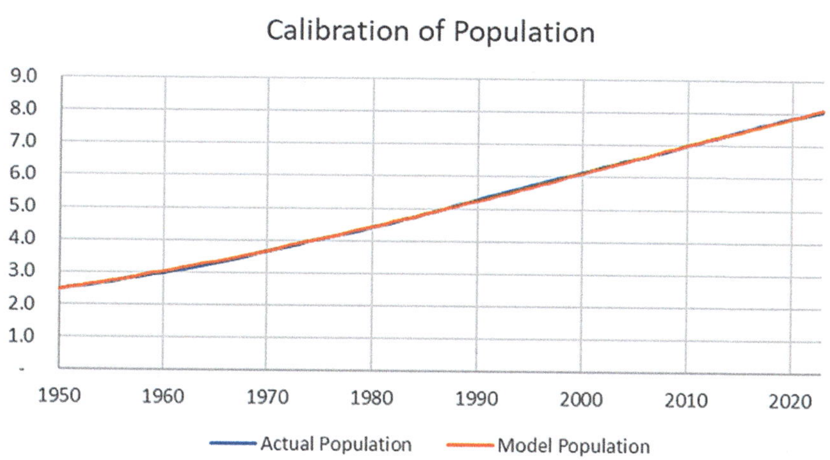

Fig. 6.12: A graphical comparison of the actual population and the model estimates.

Figure 6.13 compares the actual birth rate and the model's birth rate. While the model captures the overall trend, it struggles to accurately match the time-series data.

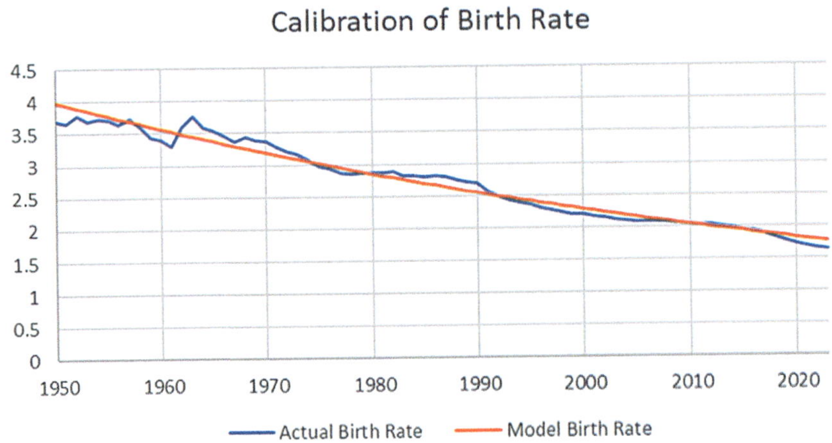

Fig. 6.13: A graphical comparison of the actual birth rate and the model estimates.

Figure 6.14 compares the actual death rate and the model's death rate. In this case, the model strongly aligns with the historical death rate time series.

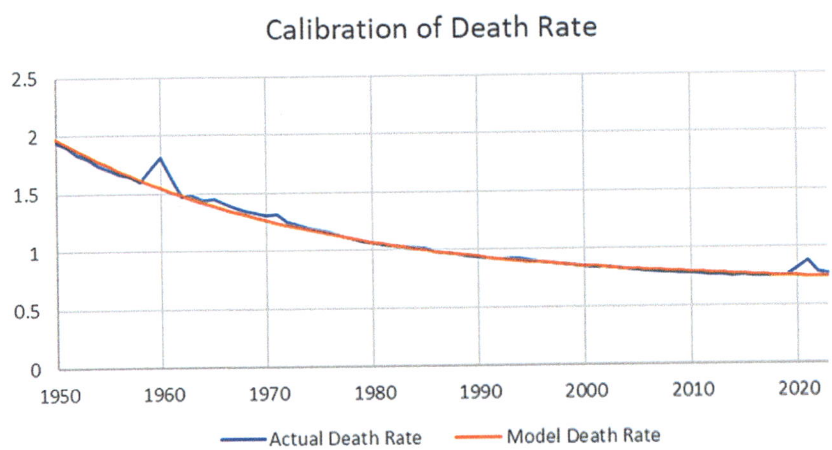

Fig. 6.14: A graphical comparison of the actual death rate and the model estimates.

System dynamics maps feedback, stocks, and delays to illustrate how today's conditions evolved and where current trends are likely to lead. The result is evidence-based foresight, enabling leaders to anticipate risks and target interventions.

6.4 US Population Model

Using UN Population Prospects data for the United States [38], we replicated historical population trends. The simulation closely matched observations (Fig. 6.15), confirming model fidelity and its utility for scenario analysis of demographic transitions and policy.

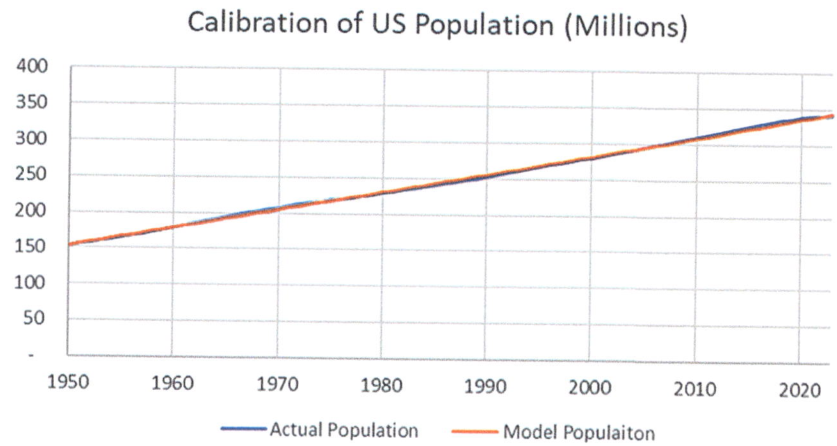

Fig. 6.15: A comparison of the US model's match with UN historical estimates of the population.

Beyond trends in total population, the model struggles to replicate certain demographic factors in population calculations accurately. Figure 6.16 illustrates the model

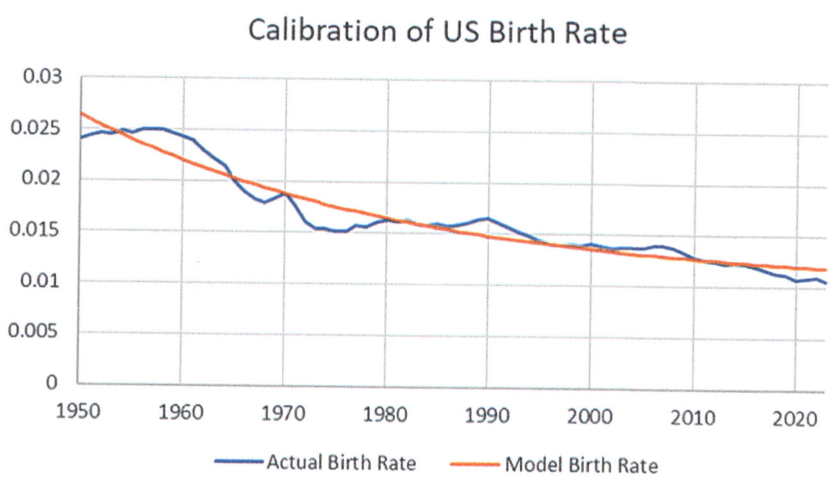

Fig. 6.16: A comparison of the US model's match of birth rates with UN historical estimates, with the goal-gap model.

of US birth rates over time, highlighting the challenge the goal-gap model faces in fully aligning with historical demographic data.

Figure 6.17 illustrates the model's reproduction of US death rates, which reasonably match historical trends, except for the impact of the COVID-19 pandemic in 2020 and 2021.

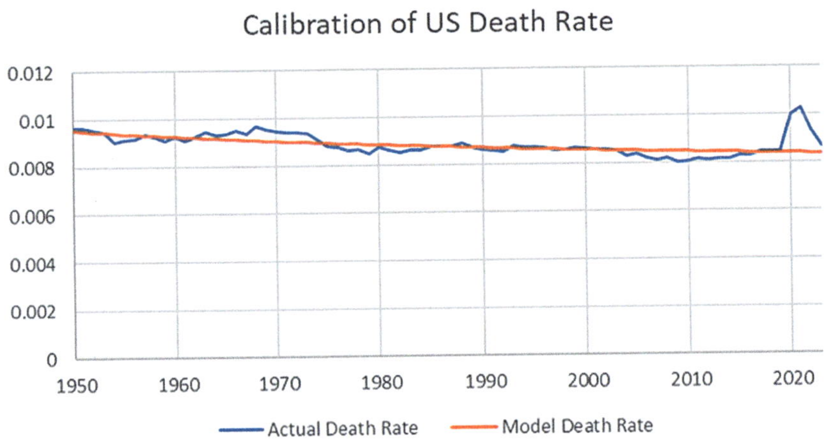

Fig. 6.17: A comparison of the USA model's match of death rates with UN historical estimates, with the goal-gap model.

Finally, Fig. 6.18 illustrates the challenges the goal-gap model faces in capturing the historical fluctuations in net migration.

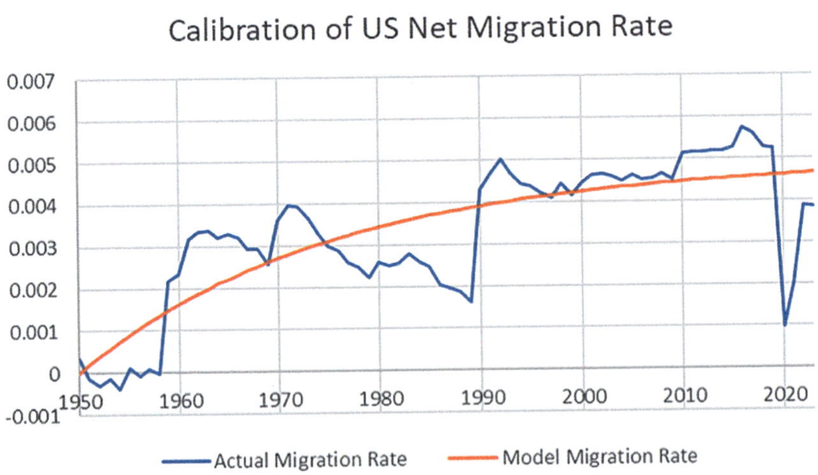

Fig. 6.18: A comparison of the USA model's match of net migration rates with UN historical estimates, with the goal-gap model.

Although the goal-gap model struggled to replicate certain demographic factors, such as birth rates and net migration patterns, it performed well overall in matching historical US population data. This overall match gives us confidence in the robustness and reliability of the goal-gap modelling approach for projecting population dynamics, even as it highlights areas for further refinement

6.5 The Nigerian Population Model

To finalize our evaluation of the goal-gap modelling approach, we will conduct one final calibration using historical demographic data for Nigeria, sourced from the UN Population Prospects [38]. With its dynamic and rapidly growing population, Nigeria offers a complex and unique context for testing the model's capabilities. This analysis will focus on how well the goal-gap model captures key demographic trends, including birth, death, and net migration patterns. By calibrating the model with Nigeria's data, we aim to assess its ability to accurately reflect the characteristics of a high-growth population and identify opportunities for further refinement.

Figure 6.19 illustrates the strong performance of the goal-gap model in replicating Nigeria's historical population data. The model matches observed trends exceptionally well, accurately capturing the country's demographic changes, rapid growth, and underlying dynamics. This alignment suggests that the model can reflect the complexities of a high-growth population. The close agreement between the simulated and historical data indicates that the goal-gap approach is a reliable tool for analysing and projecting population dynamics in Nigeria's unique and challenging demographic profile.

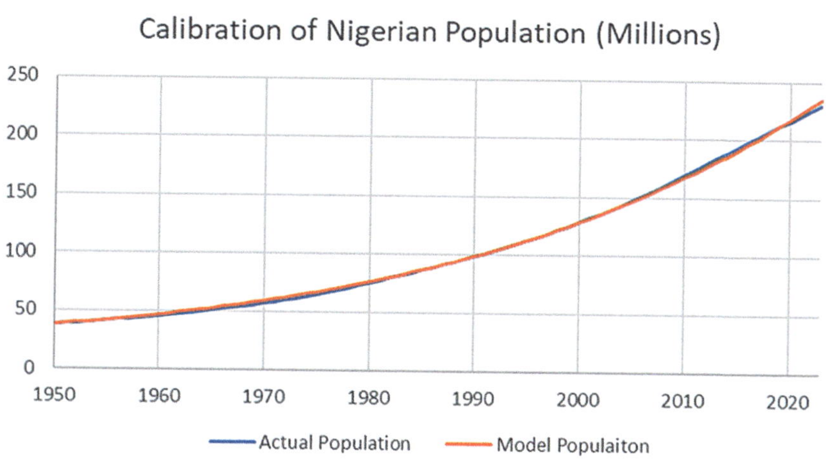

Fig. 6.19: A comparison of the Nigerian model's match with UN historical estimates of the population.

Beyond trends in total population, the model struggles to replicate certain demographic factors in population calculations accurately. Figure 6.20 highlights the model's reproduction of Nigerian birth rates over time, showcasing the difficulty the goal-gap model faces in fully aligning with historical demographic data.

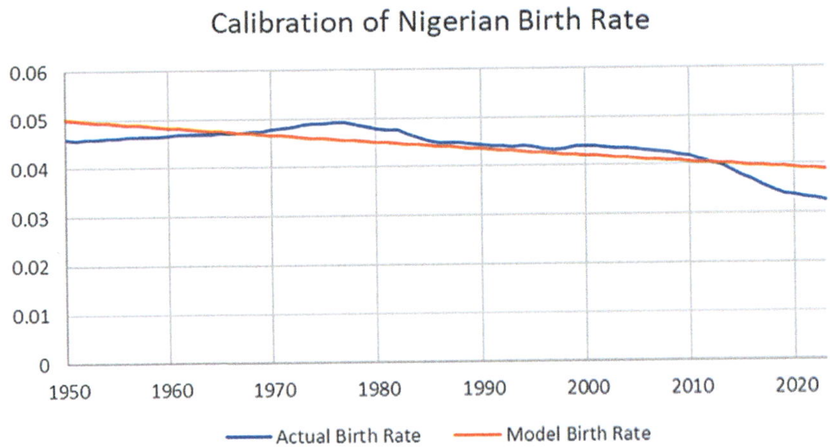

Fig. 6.20: A comparison of the Nigerian model's match of birth rates with UN historical estimates, with the goal-gap model.

Figure 6.21 illustrates the model's reproduction of Nigerian death rates, which reasonably matches historical trends.

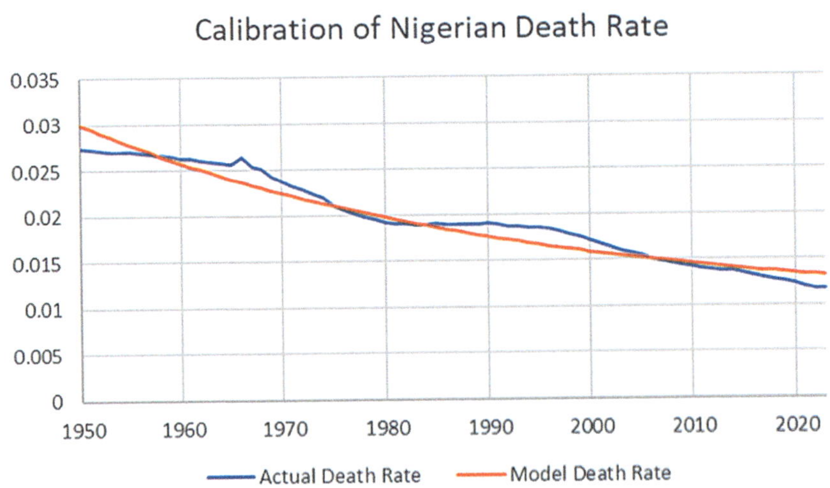

Fig. 6.21: A comparison of the Nigerian model's match of death rates with UN historical estimates, with the goal-gap model.

Finally, Fig. 6.22 illustrates the challenges the goal-gap model faces in capturing the historical fluctuations in net migration.

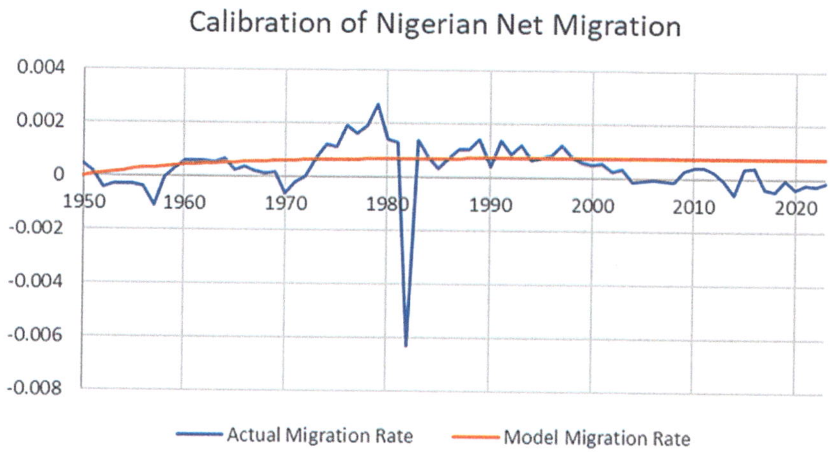

Fig. 6.22: A comparison of the Nigerian model's match of net migration rates with UN historical estimates, with the goal-gap model.

Calibrating the goal-gap model to Nigeria reveals strong replication of UN-reported population trends [38], particularly in terms of deaths and overall growth. However, it faces challenges due to historical variation in Nigerian birth rates and net migration, indicating a need for refinements. Despite this, the model remains a credible basis for projecting Nigeria's demographic change.

6.6 Summary

This chapter showed how to calibrate system dynamics models against historical time series to build credibility. Using UN data [38] and Excel Solver to minimize the SSE, we tuned the parameters of the world, the United States, and Nigeria models. The results demonstrated a strong fit for population and deaths, but a weaker fit for birth rate variation and net migration – especially in the case of Nigeria. This indicates scope for refinement. We conclude this discussion of population models by introducing, a new approach to modelling time-varying rates in the next chapter. This approach models birth, death, and migration using lookup functions to achieve a more accurate match to historical data.

6.7 Discussion Questions

- What minimum evidence of historical replication should be shown before presenting forward scenarios to stakeholders, and why?
- Why introduce separate times-to-change for birth versus death rates here, and what error modes does this mitigate?
- How do the unit choices (billions; births and deaths per 100 people per year) affect the comparability of squared errors across variables?
- Which parameters are appropriate decision variables in Solver for this chapter, and which must remain constrained for realism?
- World versus US versus Nigeria: where does the model align strongly, and where does it struggle? What does that imply structurally?
- Given the chapter's conclusion, what methodological pivot is proposed next to improve fit, and why?

6.8 Exercises

6.8.1 Build the calibration scaffold
Task. In Excel, add actual, model, and squared error columns, starting at 1950 with the provided 1950 values from this chapter. Convert the population to billions and the rates to per 100 per year.
Deliverable. Screenshot of the first 10 rows and the cell computing SSE (1950–2023).

6.8.2 Compute per-series SSE and total SSE
Task. Calculate separate SSEs for population, birth rate, and death rate and a total SSE cell.
Deliverable. Small summary table (four cells).

6.8.3 Solver minimization
Task. Use Solver to minimize total SSE, varying initial and long-term birth and death rates and time to change parameters. Save the Solver dialogue and results.
Deliverable. Solver setup screenshot and graphical comparisons before and after SSE minimization.

6.8.4 Separate adjustment times
Task. Replace a single adjustment time with two parameters: time to change birth rate and time to change death rate; re-solve.
Deliverable. Parameter block screenshot and note on SSE change.

6.8.5 World model read-out
Task. After calibration, export three charts: population, birth rate, and death rate (actual vs. model).
Deliverable. Charts and a three-sentence executive read-out describing fit quality (substantial population, death rate fit quality, and birth rate challenges).

6.8.6 US replication
Task. Apply the same format to the US series (1950–2023) and rerun Solver.
Deliverable. SSE table and one chart; one to two lines on fit quality.

6.8.7 Nigeria diagnostic
Task. Calibrate Nigeria and document which output(s) are hardest to match.
Deliverable. One-paragraph diagnostic plus a "next-step" suggestion.

6.8.8 One-page calibration memo
Task. Draft a 150- to 200-word memo summarizing data source, parameters varied, SSE, fit graphs, and concerns.
Deliverable. Text block suitable for a steering committee appendix.

Chapter 7
Lookup Tables

7.1 Learning Objectives

- Explain when lookup tables are preferable to single-parameter goal-gap dynamics to reproduce historical variability.
- Build a time-indexed lookup for one or more rates (e.g. every 10 years) and interpolate intermediate years.
- Implement robust linear interpolation in Excel using IF bounds and FORECAST/OFFSET/MATCH, with anchored ranges.
- Configure Solver to minimize total sum of squared error (SSE) by adjusting lookup values while enforcing structural and realism constraints.
- Update lookup ranges and formulas when extending the horizon (e.g. beyond 2030) and avoid unrealistic extrapolations (e.g. exponential growth from a birth rate exceeding a death rate).
- Calibrate multiple outputs (levels and rates) and reconcile trade-offs among fits (e.g. strong level fit vs. rate detail).
- Produce scenario extensions by applying controlled multipliers to post-horizon breakpoints (e.g. enforce a crossover year), and quantify impacts on peaks/declines.
- Document a stakeholder-ready summary: data source, lookup structure, interpolation method, Solver setup, fit quality, and scenario caveats.

7.2 Introduction

Chapter 6 explored the calibration of a simple goal-gap population system dynamics model using historical data. Calibration is a critical step in establishing a model's credibility, as it demonstrates that the model can accurately replicate past trends, building confidence in its validity and utility for future projections. This alignment is often a key requirement for clients and stakeholders before they can trust the model's insights and recommendations.

To achieve calibration, we utilized Excel's Solver tool to minimize the total SSEs between the model's estimates and historical data spanning the period from 1950 to 2023. This process involved adjusting the long-term values of birth, death, and net migration rates. While the goal-gap model effectively replicates overall population trends for the three cases studied (global, the United States, and Nigerian populations), it fell short of accurately capturing the finer details of demographic patterns, such as birth rate fluctuations, death rate, and net migration. These discrepancies

https://doi.org/10.1515/9783111541389-008

highlighted the need for a more refined approach to improve the model's performance in replicating complex demographic dynamics.

To address these limitations, we will now turn to an alternative approach that leverages an essential feature of system dynamics: lookup tables. Unlike the goal-gap model, which relies on adjusting a limited set of parameters, the use of lookup tables allows for the direct incorporation of observed historical trends into the model. This flexibility enables a more precise representation of the dynamic changes in demographic variables over time, offering a closer match to historical data.

However, implementing lookup tables in Excel presents a new layer of complexity. Developing these tables requires careful consideration of the equation's structure. Despite these challenges, lookup tables have the potential to significantly enhance the model's accuracy, especially in capturing the variability of demographic trends such as birth and death rates and migration patterns. This chapter will delve into the technical aspects of creating and calibrating a lookup table-based population model using Excel Solver. Through this process, we will demonstrate how this refined approach can provide more reliable and nuanced projections, strengthening the overall utility of system dynamics modelling for demographic analysis.

7.3 The World Model

The goal-gap model reasonably matched the historical time-series data. It had minor problems matching the birth rate data. We will describe how to modify the population model to incorporate lookup tables, thereby obtaining even more accurate estimates of birth and death rates. Figure 7.1 shows the world population model with lookup

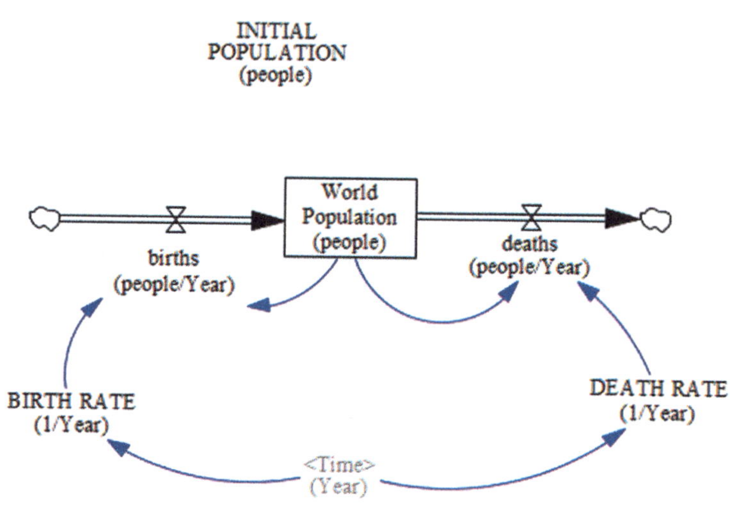

Fig. 7.1: World population model with lookup tables.

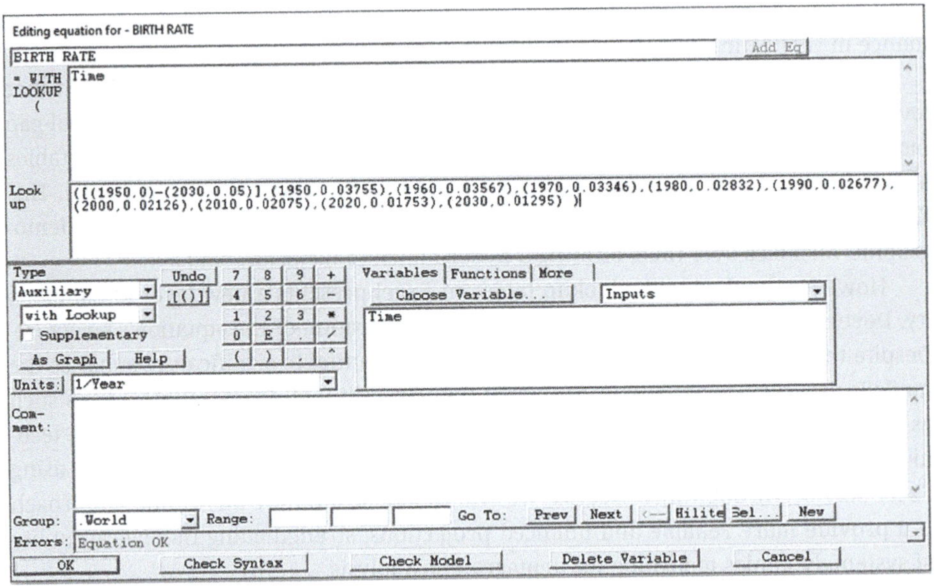

Fig. 7.2: Vensim implementation of the birth rate lookup table.

tables in Vensim. Notice that the birth and death rates are functions of time. Figures 7.2 and 7.3 show the Vensim implementation of lookup tables.

Figure 7.4 shows the improved alignment between the world historical birth rate and the lookup table estimates. Similarly, Fig. 7.5 depicts the match for world historical death rates.

Figure 7.6 displays the results of the Solver minimization of the SSEs for the optimal values of birth and death rates, calculated every 10 years. Figure 7.7 illustrates the Solver setup, where we minimize the total SSEs in cell $Y$2. However, this time, we changed the cells $J$2:$K$10.

The challenge of using lookup tables is the complexity of the Excel formula for linear interpolation. Figure 7.8 illustrates the formula in the function line, showing that it is located in cell B2 for the 1950 birth rate. The formula uses the year value in A2 and the columns of values in I2 to I10 and J2 to J10.

We have a data table, but we need to estimate values between two points within it. This is called interpolation. For example, we have birth rates from 1950 in 10-year intervals up to 2030. But what if we want to know the birth rate in 1965? We do that with linear interpolation.

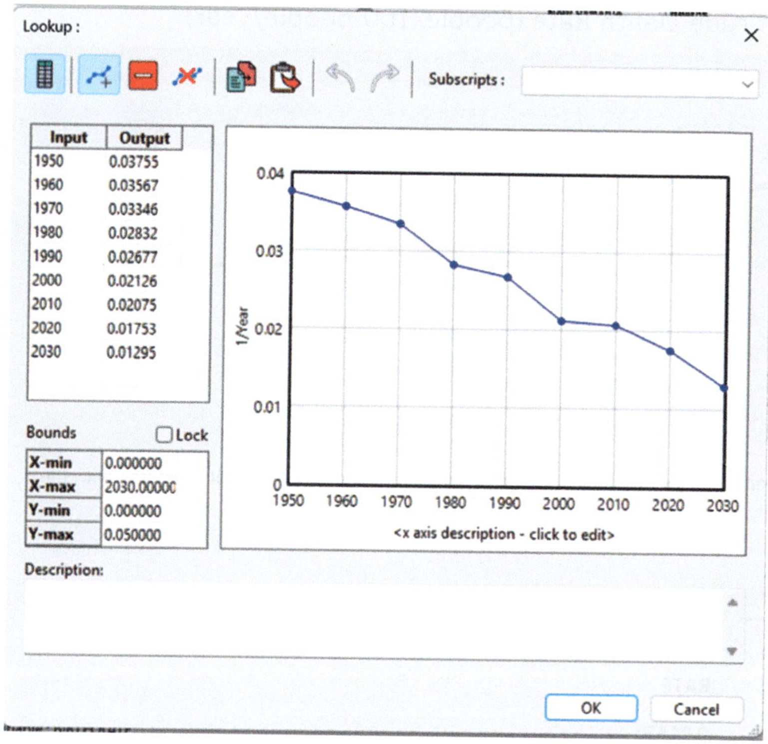

Fig. 7.3: The values for birth rate in the lookup table are displayed graphically.

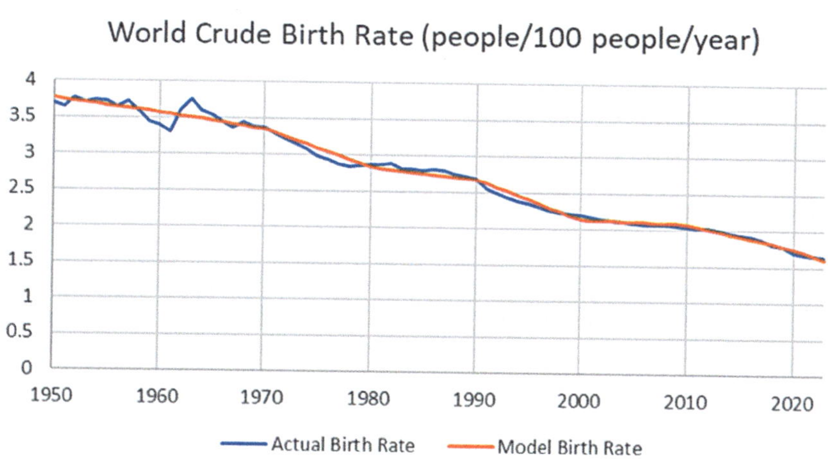

Fig. 7.4: A comparison of the world model's match of birth rates with UN historical estimates, with the lookup table model.

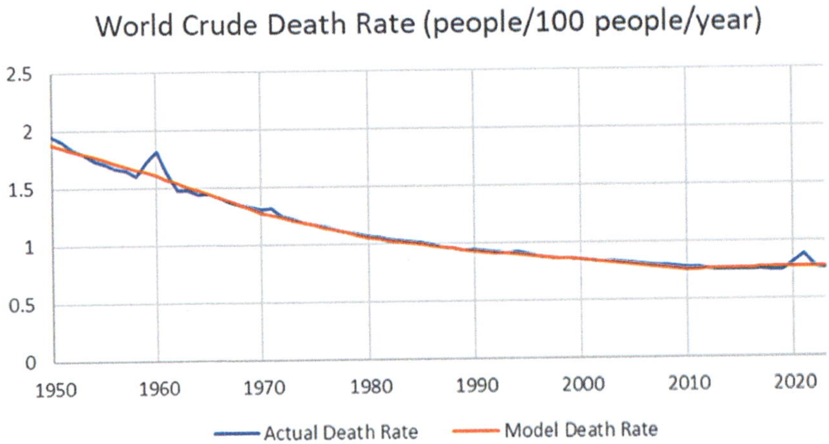

Fig. 7.5: A comparison of the world model's match of death rates with UN historical estimates, with the lookup table model.

I	J	K
YEAR	BIRTH RATE	DEATH RATE
1950	0.03755	0.01875
1960	0.03567	0.01606
1970	0.03346	0.01275
1980	0.02832	0.01051
1990	0.02677	0.00926
2000	0.02126	0.00846
2010	0.02075	0.00755
2020	0.01753	0.00775
2030	0.01295	0.00820

Fig. 7.6: The lookup table values that minimize the total sum of squared error.

Linear interpolation assumes the values between two points lie on a straight line. If you know two points, you can estimate a value for any point between them. Here's the basic idea:

1. Draw a straight line between your closest points (e.g. at 1960 and 1970).
2. Use math to find where the value for your desired point (e.g. 1965) falls on that line.

The formula with these points is: (1960, 0.03567) and (1970, 0.03346). Since 1965 is between 1960 and 1970, the interpolated value is 0.034565, calculated as follows: 0.03567 + (0.03346 – 0.03567) * (1970 – 1965)/(1970 – 1960).

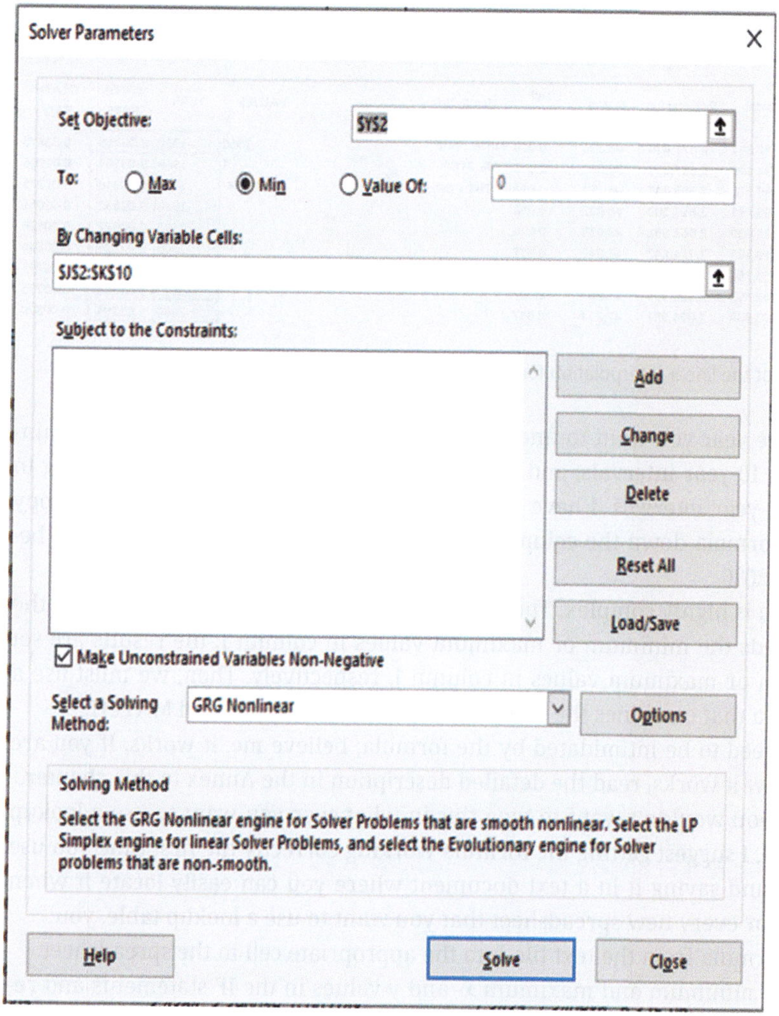

Fig. 7.7: The Solver is set up to find the values of the lookup table that minimize the total sum of squared error.

The linear interpolation equation above can be implemented directly in Microsoft Excel, provided the tabulated values are monotonic in x, the x-values are sorted, and no two x-values are equal. However, this approach is cumbersome if you have many y-values to calculate and a table of values for both x-values and y-values. So, you can use the following formula instead:

=IF($A2<=$I$2,$J$2,IF($A2>=$I$10,$J$10,FORECAST($A2,OFFSET($J$2:$J$10,MATCH($A2,$I$2:$I$10,1)–1,0,2),OFFSET($I$2:$I$10,MATCH($A2,$I$2:$I$10,1)–1,0,2))))

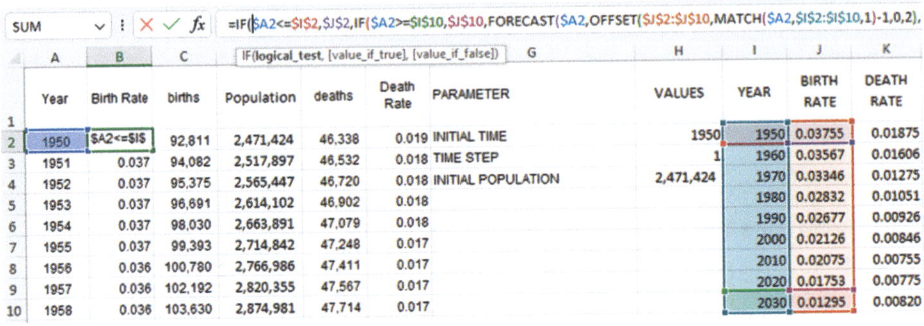

	A	B	C	D	E	F	G	H	I	J	K
1	Year	Birth Rate	births	Population	deaths	Death Rate	PARAMETER	VALUES	YEAR	BIRTH RATE	DEATH RATE
2	1950	$A2<=$I$	92,811	2,471,424	46,338	0.019	INITIAL TIME	1950	1950	0.03755	0.01875
3	1951	0.037	94,082	2,517,897	46,532	0.018	TIME STEP	1	1960	0.03567	0.01606
4	1952	0.037	95,375	2,565,447	46,720	0.018	INITIAL POPULATION	2,471,424	1970	0.03346	0.01275
5	1953	0.037	96,691	2,614,102	46,902	0.018			1980	0.02832	0.01051
6	1954	0.037	98,030	2,663,891	47,079	0.018			1990	0.02677	0.00926
7	1955	0.037	99,393	2,714,842	47,248	0.017			2000	0.02126	0.00846
8	1956	0.036	100,780	2,766,986	47,411	0.017			2010	0.02075	0.00755
9	1957	0.036	102,192	2,820,355	47,567	0.017			2020	0.01753	0.00775
10	1958	0.036	103,630	2,874,981	47,714	0.017			2030	0.01295	0.00820

Fig. 7.8: The setup of the linear interpolation formula in the Excel spreadsheet.

Where $A2 is the year you want to find the birth rate, $I$2:$I$10 are the cells containing the years in 10-year intervals, and $J$2:$J$10 are the birth rates corresponding to each of these 10-year intervals. I have anchored the table values so that you can copy and paste this formula down the column to calculate the birth rate for every year between 1950 and 2030.

The formula is highly complex. The two IF statements state that if the value in the A column exceeds the minimum or maximum values in column I, the results are set to the minimum or maximum values in column J, respectively. Then, we must use a complex formula that combines the functions FORECAST, OFFSET, and MATCH.

You don't need to be intimidated by the formula; believe me, it works. If you are interested in how it works, read the detailed description in the Annex to this chapter.

Of course, you wouldn't want to type this in whenever you want to use a lookup table. Therefore, I suggest getting the formula working correctly the first time you use a lookup table and saving it in a text document where you can easily locate it when needed. Then, for every new spreadsheet that you want to use a lookup table, you:

1. Copy the formula from the text file into the appropriate cell in the spreadsheet.
2. Replace the minimum and maximum *x*- and *y*-values in the IF statements and replace the *x*-column I2:I10 and *y*-column J2:J10 with the ranges of your table into the appropriate places in the FORECAST, OFFSET, and MATCH functions.
3. Replace A2 with the *x*-value for which you're trying to estimate the *y*-value.

Excel will calculate your interpolated value in any system dynamics model you build. And that's it, now you can implement lookup tables in Excel.

With the lookup tables, we achieve an excellent fit between the historical population and the model-estimated world population, as shown in Fig. 7.9.

If we do nothing more, the birth rate in 2030 (0.01295) will still exceed the death rate (0.00820). The lookup table formula will use these values for all the values beyond 2030, resulting in exponential growth. However, to develop more realistic scenarios, we can extend the lookup table beyond 2030 and select values for the birth rate and death rate that are more realistic.

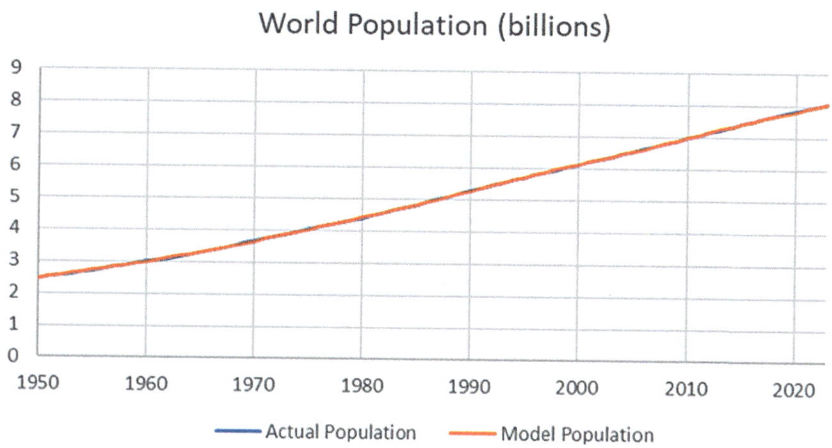

Fig. 7.9: A comparison of the world model's match of population with UN historical estimates with the lookup table model.

We extended the birth, death, and net migration rates in the lookup table for 2050, 2100, 2150, and 2200. To do this, we had to update the lookup table formula to include the cells I11:I15, J11:J15, and K11:K15. The new formula is:

=IF($A2<=$I$2,$J$2,IF($A2>=$I$15,$J$15,FORECAST($A2,OFFSET($J$2:$J$15,MATCH($A2,$I$2:$I$15,1)–1,0,2),OFFSET($I$2:$I$15,MATCH($A2,$I$2:$I$15,1)–1,0,2))))

We used the Solver to find a multiplier to obtain a birth rate that equalled the death rate in 2100. The value we found was 1.121. By dividing the birth rate in 2030 by 1.121 and multiplying the death rate in 2030 by 1.121, we obtain the values for 2050. So, the birth rate equals 0.01155, and the death rate is 0.00919. Then, we again divided the 2050 birth rate by 1.121 and obtained a 2100 birth rate of 0.01031. We then multiplied the 2050 death rate by 1.121 to get 0.01031. Then we continued by dividing the birth rate by 1.121 and multiplying the death rate by the same value for both 2150 and 2200. Figure 7.10 shows these values.

Figure 7.11 graphically illustrates the projected birth and death rates, showing that the birth rate equals the death rate in 2100, and subsequently, the death rate exceeds the birth rate. This appears to be a realistic extension of the birth and death rates, as evidenced by the values from 1950 to 2030 in the lookup table, which were calculated using a fit to historical data. This will lead to a worldwide demographic transition, as expected. It also means that the population will stop growing exponentially, eventually peak, and then decline. Figure 7.12 illustrates the projected world population for this scenario.

I	J	K
YEAR	BIRTH RATE	DEATH RATE
1950	0.03755	0.01875
1960	0.03567	0.01606
1970	0.03346	0.01275
1980	0.02832	0.01051
1990	0.02677	0.00926
2000	0.02126	0.00846
2010	0.02075	0.00755
2020	0.01753	0.00775
2030	0.01295	0.00820
2050	0.01155	0.00919
2100	0.01031	0.01031
2150	0.00919	0.01155
2200	0.00820	0.01295

Fig. 7.10: Extension of the lookup table model to 2200.

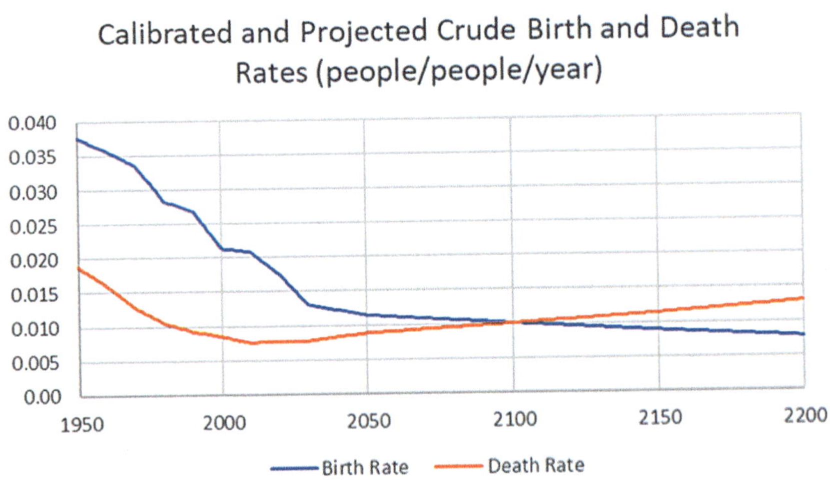

Fig. 7.11: Calibrated and projected birth and death rates for the world population model with the extended lookup table.

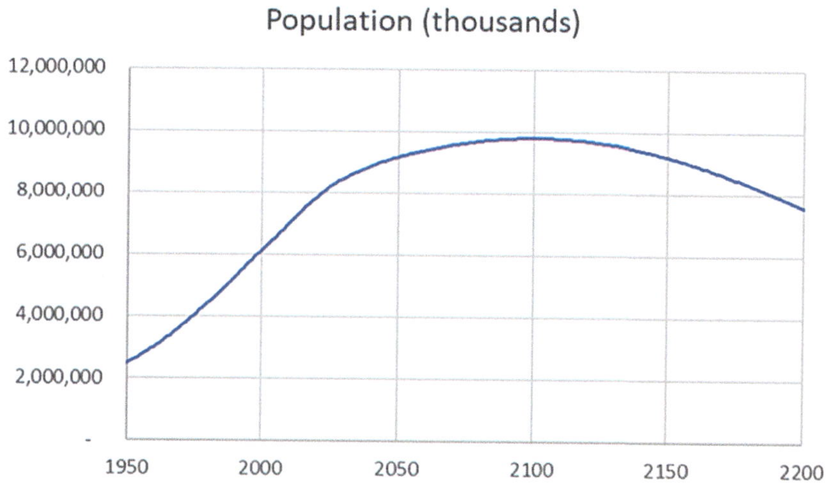

Fig. 7.12: Calibrated and projected population for the world with the extended lookup table.

7.4 The US Population Model

Building on the success of the world population model, this section applies a similar process to develop a refined demographic model for the United States using lookup tables. Like the world model, the initial goal-gap approach demonstrated reasonable alignment with total population trends when calibrated against historical data from the UN Population Prospects [38]. However, the goal-gap model struggled to accurately represent key demographic variables, such as birth, death, and net migration rates, leading to potential distortions in long-term projections.

Figure 7.13 shows the improved alignment between the historical birth rate and the lookup table estimates. Similarly, Fig. 7.14 depicts the match for historical death rates and the calibrated lookup table values. Figure 7.15 compares historical net migration rates and the calibrated values.

With the lookup tables, we obtain an excellent fit between the historical population and the model estimate for the US population, as shown in Fig. 7.16.

If we do nothing more, the birth rate in 2030 will still exceed the death rate. The lookup table formula will use these values for all the values beyond 2030, resulting in exponential growth.

However, as with the world model, we can build more realistic scenarios by extending the lookup table beyond 2030 and selecting values for the birth and death rates that are more realistic. Figure 7.17 graphically illustrates the birth and death rates, showing that the birth rate equals the death rate in 2050, after which the death rate exceeds the birth rate. This appears to be a realistic extension of the birth and death rates, as evidenced by the values from 1950 to 2030 in the lookup table, which

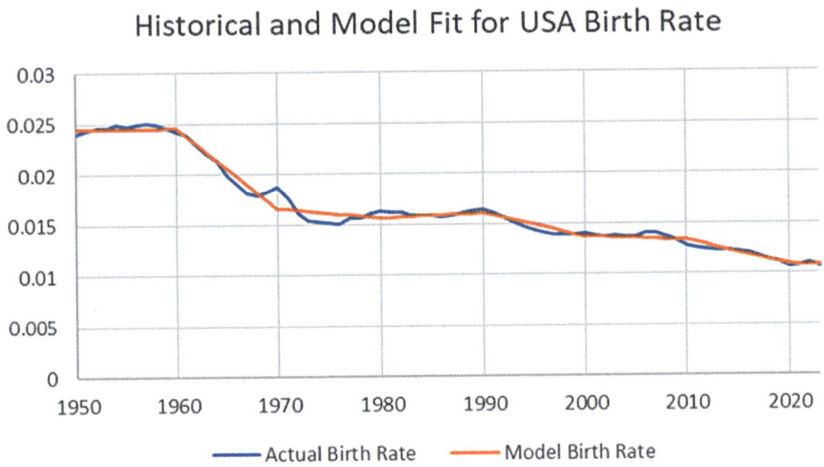

Fig. 7.13: A comparison of the US model's match of birth rates with UN historical estimates, with the lookup table model.

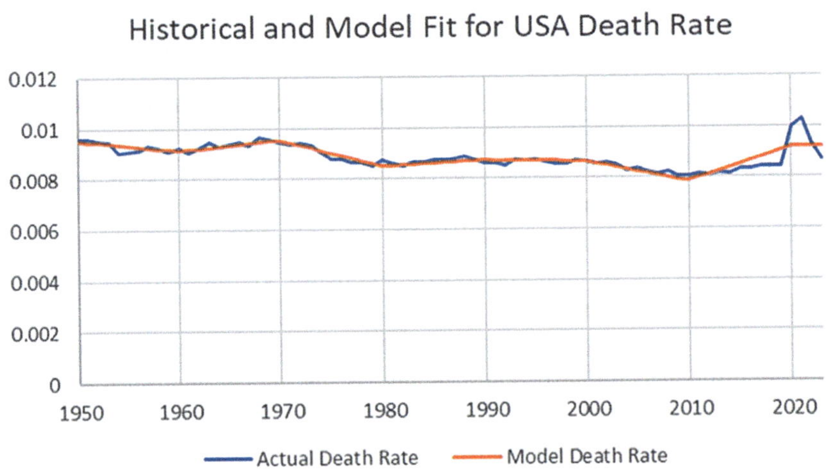

Fig. 7.14: A comparison of the US model's match of death rates with UN historical estimates, with the lookup table model.

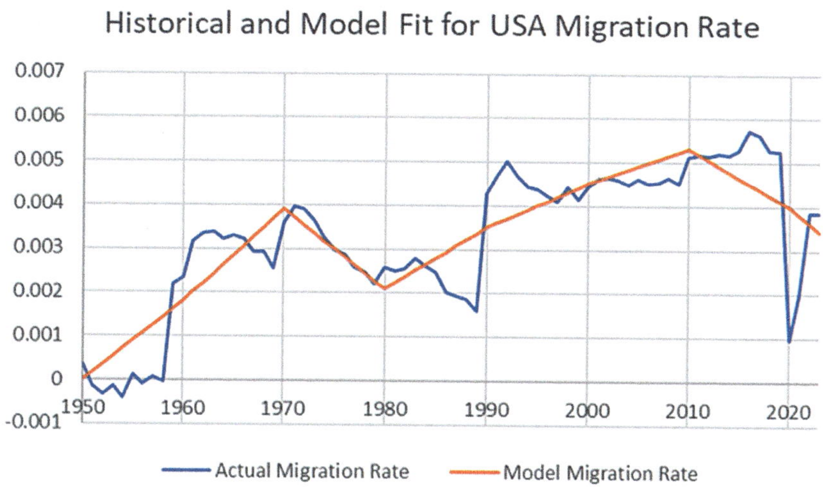

Fig. 7.15: A comparison of the US model's match of net migration rates with UN historical estimates, with the lookup table model.

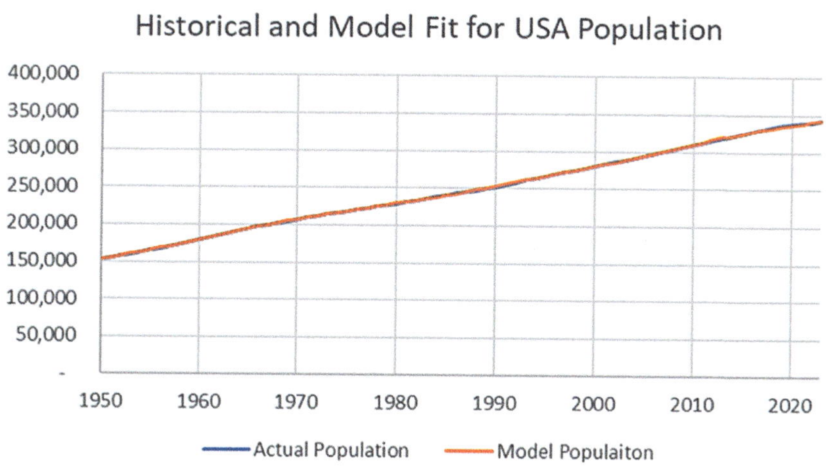

Fig. 7.16: A comparison of the US model's match of population with UN historical estimates, with the lookup table model.

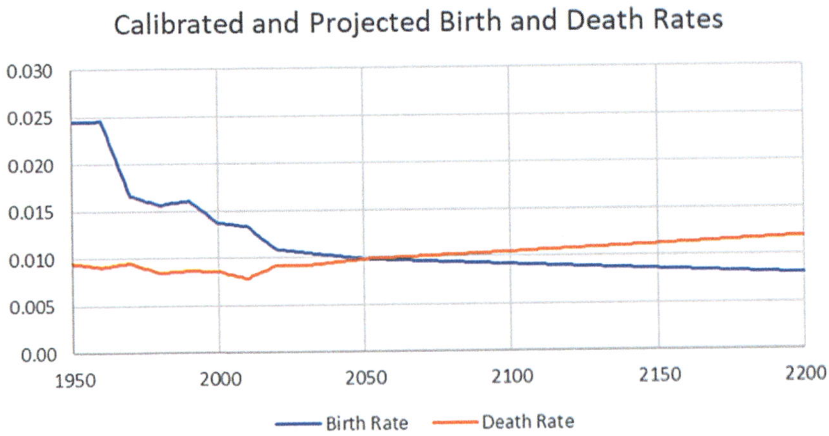

Fig. 7.17: Calibrated and projected birth and death rates in the United States with the extended lookup table.

were calculated using a fit to historical data. This will lead to a demographic transition in the United States, which we would expect. It also means that the population will eventually peak. Figure 7.18 shows the projected US population for this scenario.

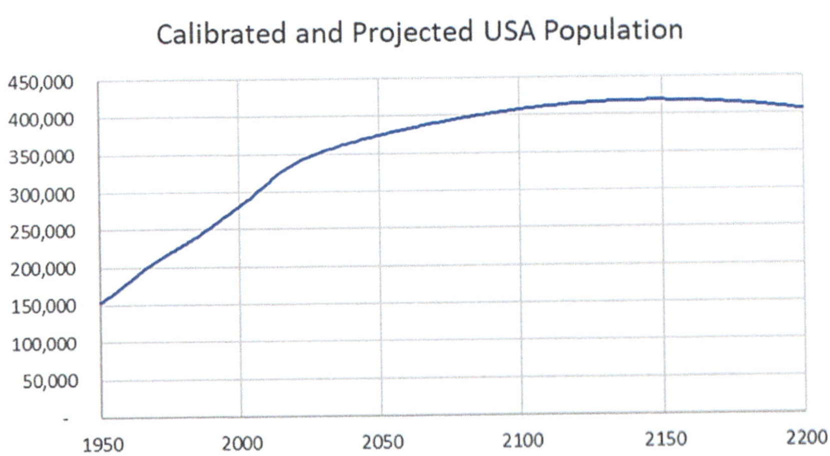

Fig. 7.18: Calibrated and projected population for the United States with the extended lookup table.

7.5 The Nigerian Model

The results from the US model highlight that the lookup table approach better aligns the model with historical data. We will repeat the calibration process with the Nigerian model. Figure 7.19 shows the improved alignment between the historical birth rate and the lookup table estimates. Similarly, Fig. 7.20 shows the match with historical death rates, and Fig. 7.21 shows the alignment with historical net migration rates.

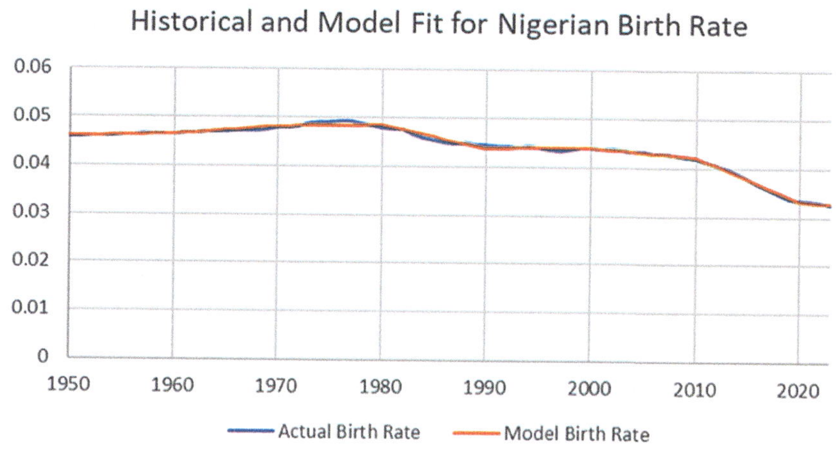

Fig. 7.19: A comparison of the Nigerian model's match of birth rates with UN historical estimates, with the lookup table model.

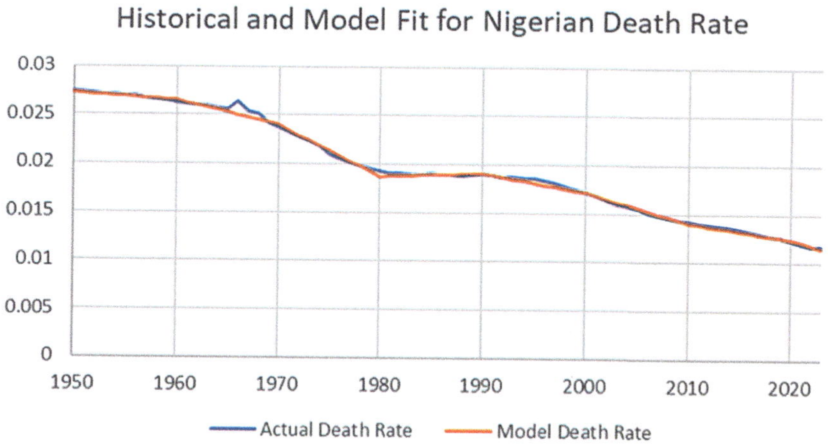

Fig. 7.20: A comparison of the Nigerian model's match of death rates with UN historical estimates, with the lookup table model.

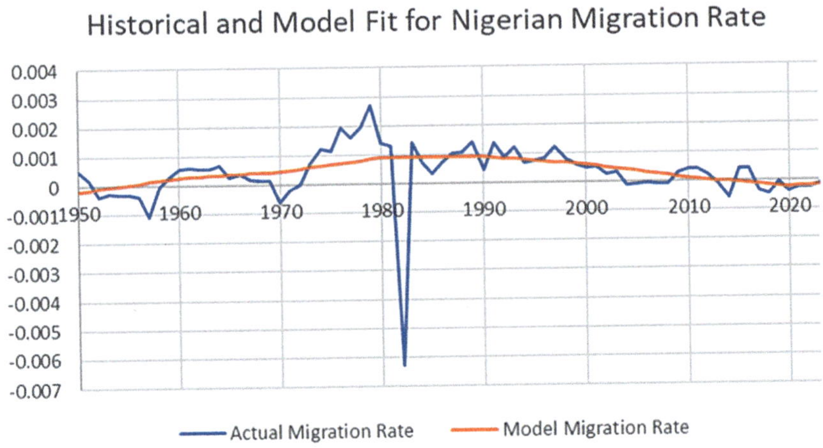

Fig. 7.21: A comparison of the Nigerian model's match of net migration rates with UN historical estimates, with the lookup table model.

With these lookup tables, we obtain an excellent fit between the historical population growth and the model-estimated Nigerian population, as shown in Fig. 7.22.

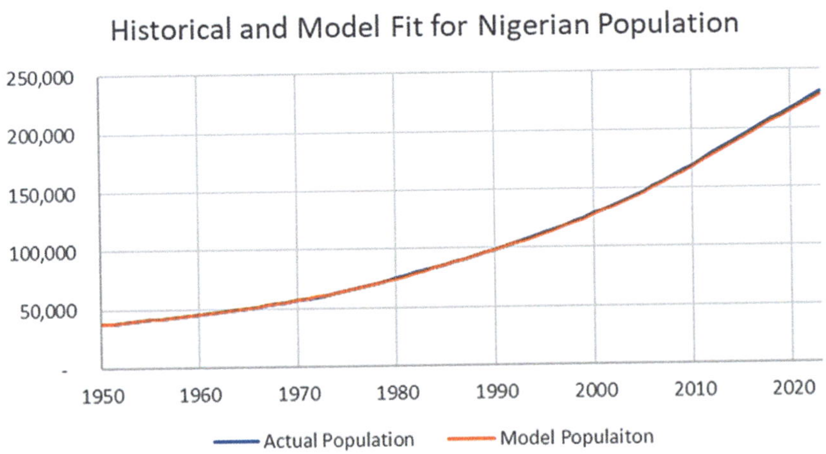

Fig. 7.22: A comparison of the Nigerian model's match of population with UN historical estimates with the lookup table model.

If we do nothing more, the birth rate in 2030 will still exceed the death rate. The lookup table formula will use these values for all the values beyond 2030, resulting in continued exponential growth. Again, we extended the birth, death, and net migration rates in the lookup table for 2050, 2100, 2150, and 2200.

Figure 7.23 graphically illustrates the projected birth and death rates, showing that the birth rate equals the death rate in 2150. Following this, the death rate exceeds the birth rate. This appears to be a realistic extension of the birth and death rates, as evidenced by the values from 1950 to 2030 in the lookup table, which were calculated using a fit to historical data. This will lead to a demographic transition in Nigeria, which we would expect. It also means that the population will eventually peak. Figure 7.24 illustrates the projected Nigerian population for this scenario.

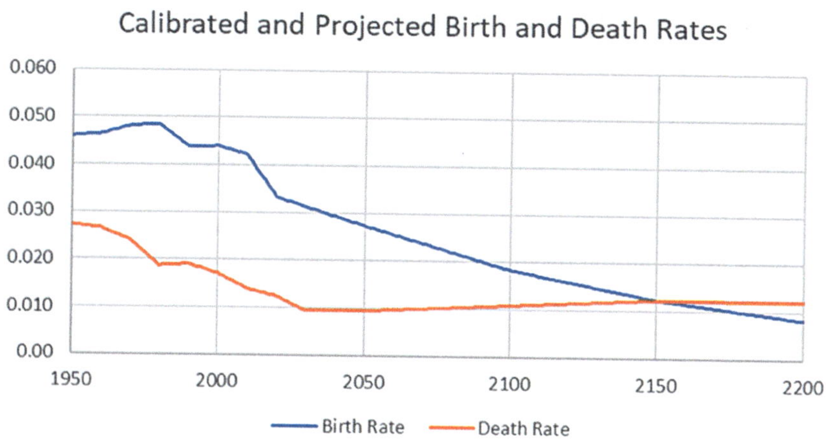

Fig. 7.23: Projected birth and death rates in Nigeria with the extended lookup table.

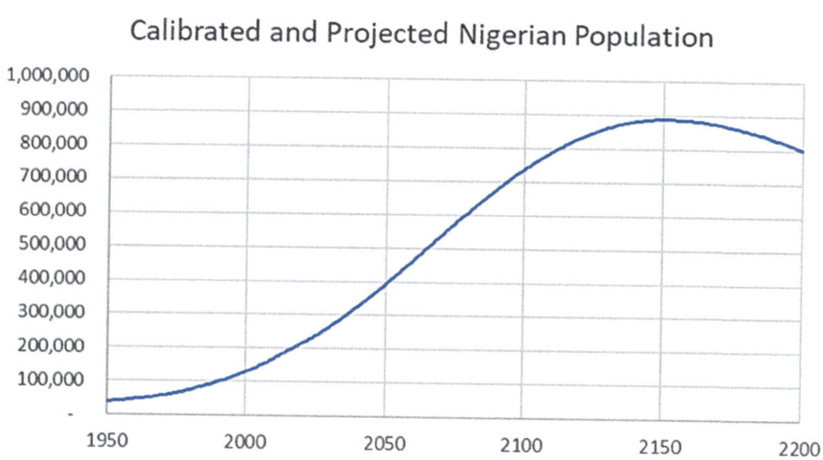

Fig. 7.24: Calibrated and projected population for Nigeria with the extended lookup table.

7.6 Conclusion

In this chapter, we explored the use of lookup tables to enhance the accuracy and robustness of demographic system dynamics models. The goal-gap approach discussed in the previous chapter had limitations in replicating detailed demographic patterns, such as birth, death, and net migration rates. By introducing lookup tables, we significantly improved the model's alignment with historical data and its ability to produce realistic projections.

The chapter also detailed the technical implementation of lookup tables in Excel, including the use of complex formulas for linear interpolation. We guided the adaptation of the formula for new models, emphasizing their utility in automating calculations and improving model precision.

Beyond calibration, we extended each model to project future demographic trends. By adjusting birth, death, and net migration rates beyond 2030, we demonstrated the potential to create realistic scenarios of demographic transitions, including a population peak and eventual decline. These scenarios highlight the flexibility of lookup tables in supporting scenario analysis and enabling stakeholders to explore alternative futures.

7.7 Discussion Questions

- What specific reference-mode features (trend shifts, inflections) argue for a lookup-table approach over a goal-gap approach?
- What are the failure modes of interpolation in spreadsheets (unsorted *x*, duplicates, drifting ranges, unanchored references), and how will you prevent them?
- If the model fits stocks well but not rates, is that a parameterization or a structure problem? What evidence would you bring to a review board?
- How should bounds be set on lookup values (e.g. non-negativity and ceiling/floor) so Solver can search productively without producing nonsense?
- When extending beyond the last historical point, what's the minimum governance you require to avoid baking in unrealistic growth/decline?
- What constitutes a persuasive scenario pack (e.g. crossover year, peak timing/magnitude, and sensitivity to multipliers), and what belongs in the executive readout?

7.8 Exercises

7.8.1 Lookup scaffold and interpolation
Task. Create a 10-year grid of breakpoints (e.g. 1950 . . . 2030) and implement a yearly interpolated series using the formula in this chapter.
Deliverable. First 15 rows and the exact formula used.

7.8.2 SSE minimization with lookup values
Task. Add actual versus model and squared error columns. Use Solver to minimize total SSE by changing the lookup *y*-values (breakpoints).
Deliverable. Solver dialogue screenshot and results graphs before and after SSE minimization.

7.8.3 Multi-output fit
Task. Calibrate two rate lookups (e.g. "birth" and "death") that drive a stock trajectory. Optimize a weighted SSE across (stock, rate1, rate2).
Deliverable. Weight table; SSE by series; total SSE.

7.8.4 Horizon extension
Task. Extend the lookup grid to 2050, 2100, 2150, and 2200. Update formulas and named ranges once (no hard-coded cell edits).
Deliverable. Screenshot of updated formula.

7.8.5 Enforce a crossover scenario
Task. Introduce a multiplier on post-2030 lookup breakpoints to force a specified crossover year (e.g. Rate A = Rate B in 2100). Solve for the multiplier.
Deliverable. Target year, solved multiplier, and a one-paragraph rationale.

7.8.6 Robustness and guardrails
Task. Deliberately break an assumption (unsort *x*; duplicate *x*; remove anchoring) and note the failure symptom. Fix it by adding a data validation or formula guard.
Deliverable. Before/after screenshots and brief root-cause notes.

7.8.7 Sensitivity to breakpoint density
Task. Compare coarse (20-year) versus fine (10-year) breakpoint grids. Refit both and summarize SSE, parameter count, and preferred design.
Deliverable. Three-row table (grid/parameters/SSE/preference and why).

7.8.8 Executive one-pager
Task. Write 150–200 words covering: data source, lookup structure, interpolation method, Solver setup, fit quality, post-2030 scenario logic, and key risks.
Deliverable. Text suitable for a steering committee appendix.

Annex

Understanding Interpolation in Excel

We have a table of data, but we need to estimate a value between two points in that table. This is called interpolation. For example, imagine we have the birth rates for 1950 in 10-year intervals until 2030. But what if we want to know the birth rate in 1965? We do that with linear interpolation. If you have two points, ($X1$, $Y1$) and ($X2$,

$Y2$) and a value X between $X1$ and $X2$, then the interpolated value corresponding to $X = Y1 + (Y2 - Y1) * (X - X1)/(X2 - X1)$.

The linear interpolation equation above can be implemented directly in Microsoft Excel, provided the tabulated values are monotonic in *x*; the *x*-values are sorted, and no two are equal. However, this approach is cumbersome if you have many *y*-values to calculate and a table of both *x*- and *y*-values. So, you can use the following formula instead:

=FORECAST (A2, OFFSET (M2:M10, MATCH (A2, L2:L10,1)−1,0,2), OFFSET (L2:L10, MATCH (A2, L2:L10,1)−1,0,2)))

This formula calculates the *y*-value corresponding to the *x*-value in cell A2 when we have a table of *x*-values (L2:L10) and *y*-values (M2:M10).

The formula can be understood if we break it into three main parts:

1. FORECAST function: Calculates the interpolated value using a straight-line formula.
2. MATCH function: Find the closest *x*-value in the table smaller than the value you want to estimate.
3. OFFSET function: Points to the *x*- and *y*-values just above and below your estimated value.

How Each Part Works:

1. FORECAST function: This does the actual interpolation. It needs three inputs:
   - "New *X*": The value you're estimating. (1965)
   - "Known *y* pair": The *y*-values just above and below your target value. (0.0266 and 0.0166)
   - "Known *x* pair": The *x*-values just above and below your target value. (1960 and 1970)
2. MATCH function: Finds the position of the largest *x*-value in the table still smaller than "New *X*" (1960)
3. OFFSET function: Takes the position from the MATCH function and creates a small range of two values (the *x*- and *y*-values just above and below your target). (1960 and 1970 for *x*) and (0.0266 and 0.0166 for *y*)

The formula combines these parts to calculate the interpolated value. It utilizes the FORECAST function to perform the calculations, while MATCH and OFFSET locate the exact table values required for the calculation. This method is efficient and produces accurate results.

We make a small change to ensure we don't exceed the *x*-range. We add two IF statements before the FORECAST to ensure that if the A value is less than the minimum value (L2), the output is the corresponding value M2. If the A value exceeds the largest value (L10), the output equals the corresponding value M10. In the equation below, I have also anchored the table cells so that we can copy and paste them down the columns.

=IF($A2<=$L$2,$M$2,IF($A2>=$L$10,$M$10,FORECAST($A2,OFFSET($M$2:$M$10, MATCH($A2,$L$2:$L$10,1)−1,0,2),OFFSET($L$2:$L$10,MATCH($A2,$L$2:$L $10,1)−1,0,2))))

Chapter 8
Modelling Delays

8.1 Learning Objectives

- Explain why delays (action → effect lags) shape stability, responsiveness, and stakeholder expectations; distinguish intended versus delayed unintended effects and perceptual delays.
- Implement a first-order delay as a balancing adjustment (goal-gap) in Vensim (DELAY1I) and replicate it in Excel using IF step input and Euler integration.
- Implement a third-order delay using Vensim (DELAY3) or an explicit three-stock chain, and translate the formulas into Excel.
- Select an appropriate time step (dt), justify powers-of-two (e.g. 0.25) for grid regularity and accuracy, and verify convergence.
- Build a client-facing spreadsheet Interface (Interface/Graphs/Model), link parameters, and hide internal mechanics without losing traceability.
- Model step changes in a target signal (policy implementation) and describe the resulting delayed response curve.
- Apply delay structures to an operational disruption (e.g. a supply chain) and encode the disruption window to assess its impacts on service levels.
- Produce a concise, stakeholder-ready narrative that sets realistic timing expectations for results in the event of a delay.

8.2 Introduction

In system dynamics, understanding the role of delays is essential for accurately capturing the behaviour of complex systems. Delays refer to the time lags between actions and their observable effects within a system. These temporal gaps can significantly influence how a system responds to changes, making it crucial to account for them in any dynamic model. Delays impact system behaviour in various ways, often determining the stability and responsiveness of the system.

Leaders often expect immediate results from their policies, but policies take time to produce system-wide changes. Emphasizing delays is crucial to setting realistic expectations and maintaining trust, as outcomes unfold gradually. Delays can arise from processes like legislation, stakeholder adaptation, and inherent system inertia. By emphasizing these time lags in our models, leaders can better anticipate the progression of their initiatives, make informed adjustments, and implement supportive measures. This understanding enables more strategic policymaking, ensuring that long-term goals are achieved sustainably.

https://doi.org/10.1515/9783111541389-009

Every action within a system generates both intended and unintended consequences. While leaders may implement policies expecting immediate positive outcomes, these actions can also lead to unforeseen adverse effects that emerge over time. For example, introducing a subsidy to boost a particular industry may initially increase production and employment, fulfilling the intended goals. However, delayed unintended consequences might include market distortions, resource depletion, or environmental impacts that were not anticipated at the outset. These adverse effects often become apparent only after the policy has been in place for months or years, underscoring the importance of modelling delays. By accounting for both the immediate benefits and the delayed drawbacks, system dynamics models can provide a more comprehensive understanding of a policy's full range of impacts, enabling leaders to make more informed and balanced decisions.

Delays in perceiving changes within a system can significantly influence its overall behaviour and outcomes. In Forrester's *Urban Dynamics* [2], for instance, the attractiveness of a city to migrants does not translate into immediate population growth. Instead, there is a lag between when a city's appeal increases and when migrants become aware of and decide to move there. This perceptual delay means that migration patterns do not instantly reflect the effects of improved amenities, job opportunities, or better living conditions. As a result, the city may experience gradual population changes rather than swift shifts, allowing time for other factors to interact and potentially create overshooting or undershooting effects in population growth. Understanding and modelling these perceptual delays is crucial for accurately predicting and managing the dynamic behaviour of systems, ensuring that policies and planning measures account for the time it takes for changes to be recognized and acted upon by individuals within the system.

This chapter will equip you with the tools to model delays effectively using Excel. You will learn how to identify different types of delays, implement them using Excel's features, and analyse their impact on your models. By integrating delay structures into your system models, you can achieve a more realistic and nuanced understanding of how real-world systems operate over time. Additionally, this chapter will demonstrate how modelling delays fit into the broader context of the book, enhancing your overall ability to build robust and insightful system dynamics models.

By the end of this chapter, you will have a solid foundation in delay modelling, enabling you to create more accurate and reliable simulations that reflect the temporal complexities of the systems you study.

8.3 First-Order Delays

In the previous chapters, we explored how first-order delays affect key parameters in our population model, precisely the time required to adjust birth and death rates. These first-order delays represent the simplest type of time lag, in which the response to a change occurs gradually rather than instantaneously. Understanding these delays is crucial, as they can significantly influence the dynamics and stability of the entire system. By starting with first-order delays and expanding into these practical techniques, you will gain a robust understanding of how to model delays in system dynamics using Excel. This foundation will prepare you to tackle more advanced delay structures and apply these principles to various real-world scenarios.

To illustrate the impact of a first-order delay in policy implementation, let us assume that a new policy was enacted in 2025. This policy is designed to improve a specific system variable – such as productivity, resource allocation, or public health outcomes – by 20% relative to its steady-state value. In our model, we will represent this policy change as a step function, meaning the improvement is introduced abruptly at the time of implementation. Using a step function, we create a clear and immediate shift in the variable's desired value, providing a baseline from which we can observe how delays influence the system's response over time.

Figure 8.1 shows a Vensim implementation for this model.

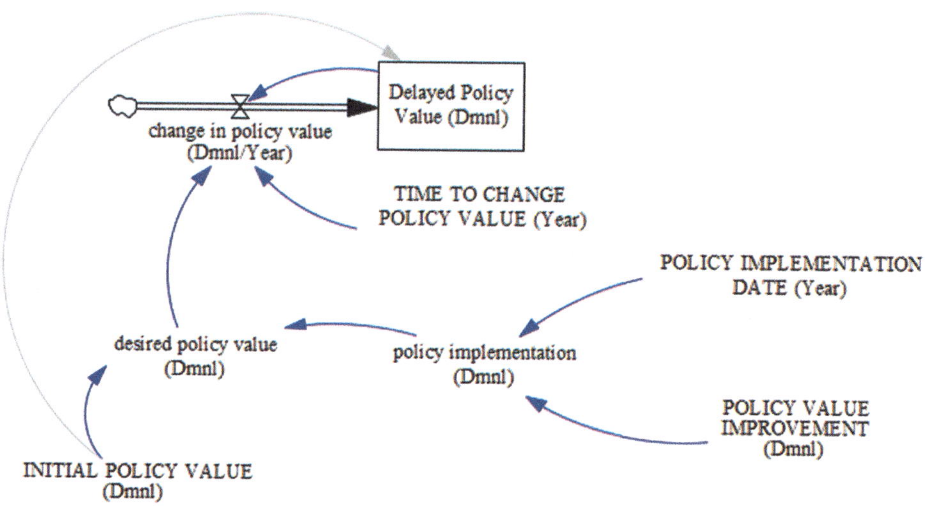

Fig. 8.1: A Vensim implementation of a first-order delay.

We have exogenous values for the initial policy value of 1, policy value improvement of 0.2, policy implementation date of 2025, and time to implement the policy of 10. The endogenous calculation for policy implementation is 1 + STEP (policy value improvement, policy implementation date).

The STEP function in Vensim returns zero before the policy implementation date and policy value improvement after it.

The endogenous calculation for the desired policy value = initial policy value * policy implementation. We have the endogenous calculation of the change in policy value: (desired policy value – delayed policy value)/time to change policy value. The delayed policy value is set to the initial policy value as of 2020, and then, for each step, it is updated using the Euler integration method.

In Vensim, there is a built-in function called DELAY1I. This model would be implemented with the equation DELAY1I (desired policy value, time to change policy value, initial policy value).

We will implement this in Excel. We will begin by setting up the columns for the endogenous values and the exogenous parameters (see Fig. 8.2).

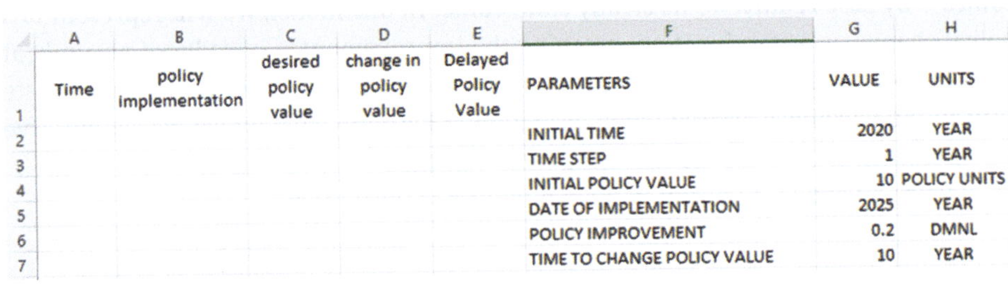

	A	B	C	D	E	F	G	H
1	Time	policy implementation	desired policy value	change in policy value	Delayed Policy Value	PARAMETERS	VALUE	UNITS
2						INITIAL TIME	2020	YEAR
3						TIME STEP	1	YEAR
4						INITIAL POLICY VALUE	10	POLICY UNITS
5						DATE OF IMPLEMENTATION	2025	YEAR
6						POLICY IMPROVEMENT	0.2	DMNL
7						TIME TO CHANGE POLICY VALUE	10	YEAR

Fig. 8.2: Set up the Excel spreadsheet for the first-order delay.

As in the previous chapters, we set the time in A2 to the initial time in G2 and the time in A3 = A2 + G$3. Then, we will specify the policy implementation function in cell B2 as follows: IF (A2 < E$5, 1, 1 + E$7). This is a simple if-then-else statement. If the year in cell A2 is less than the date of implementation, then the if statement returns the value one, and if A2 is greater than or equal to the date of implementation, the if statement will return the value one plus the policy improvement (see Fig. 8.3).

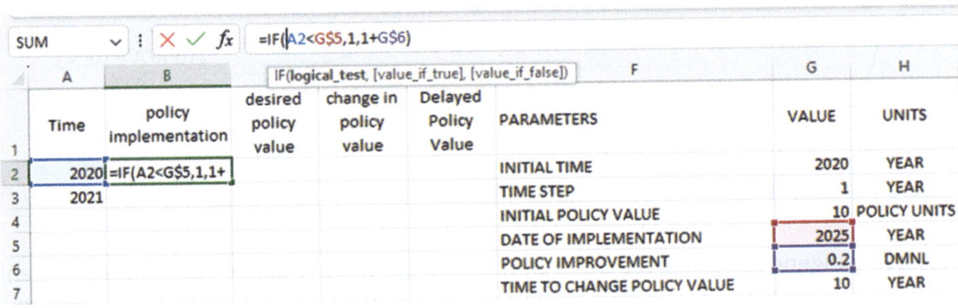

SUM | =IF(A2<G$5,1,1+G$6)

IF(logical_test, [value_if_true], [value_if_false])

	A	B	C	D	E	F	G	H
1	Time	policy implementation	desired policy value	change in policy value	Delayed Policy Value	PARAMETERS	VALUE	UNITS
2	2020	=IF(A2<G$5,1,1+				INITIAL TIME	2020	YEAR
3	2021					TIME STEP	1	YEAR
4						INITIAL POLICY VALUE	10	POLICY UNITS
5						DATE OF IMPLEMENTATION	2025	YEAR
6						POLICY IMPROVEMENT	0.2	DMNL
7						TIME TO CHANGE POLICY VALUE	10	YEAR

Fig. 8.3: The formula for policy implementation.

Then, we enter the formula C2 = G$4 * B2, multiplying the initial policy value by the policy implementation (see Fig. 8.4). The value in C2 will equal the initial policy value because the policy will not be implemented until 2025.

C2 | f_x =G$4*B2

	A	B	C	D	E	F	G	H
1	Time	policy implementation	desired policy value	change in policy value	Delayed Policy Value	PARAMETERS	VALUE	UNITS
2	2020	1	=G$4*B2			INITIAL TIME	2020	YEAR
3	2021					TIME STEP	1	YEAR
4						INITIAL POLICY VALUE	10	POLICY UNITS
5						DATE OF IMPLEMENTATION	2025	YEAR
6						POLICY IMPROVEMENT	0.2	DMNL
7						TIME TO CHANGE POLICY VALUE	10	YEAR

Fig. 8.4: The formula for the desired policy value.

Then, we enter the initial policy value in cell E2 = G4 and the formula for changing the policy value, D2 = (C2 – E2)/G$7 (see Fig. 8.5), which is identical to the formula we used in the previous chapters (desired policy value – delayed policy value)/time to change policy value.

SUM | f_x =(C2-E2)/G$7

	A	B	C	D	E	F	G	H
1	Time	policy implementation	desired policy value	change in policy value	Delayed Policy Value	PARAMETERS	VALUE	UNITS
2	2020	1	10	=(C2-E2)/	10	INITIAL TIME	2020	YEAR
3	2021					TIME STEP	1	YEAR
4						INITIAL POLICY VALUE	10	POLICY UNITS
5						DATE OF IMPLEMENTATION	2025	YEAR
6						POLICY IMPROVEMENT	0.2	DMNL
7						TIME TO CHANGE POLICY VALUE	10	YEAR

Fig. 8.5: The formula for the change in policy value.

Then, we update the value for the delayed policy value using the Euler integration formula E3 = E2 + G$3 * D2 (see Fig. 8.6). That is, the value for the delayed policy value in 2021 equals the delayed policy value in 2020 plus the time step times the change in policy value.

E3 | f_x =E2+G$3*D2

	A	B	C	D	E	F	G	H
1	Time	policy implementation	desired policy value	change in policy value	Delayed Policy Value	PARAMETERS	VALUE	UNITS
2	2020	1	10	0	10	INITIAL TIME	2020	YEAR
3	2021				=E2+G$3*D2		1	YEAR
4						INITIAL POLICY VALUE	10	POLICY UNITS
5						DATE OF IMPLEMENTATION	2025	YEAR
6						POLICY IMPROVEMENT	0.2	DMNL
7						TIME TO CHANGE POLICY VALUE	10	YEAR

Fig. 8.6: The formula for updating the delayed policy value.

Then, we copy the cells B2:D2 into the cells B3:D3, updating the other endogenous variables for 2021 (see Fig. 8.7).

	A	B	C	D	E	F	G	H
1	Time	policy implementation	desired policy value	change in policy value	Delayed Policy Value	PARAMETERS	VALUE	UNITS
2	2020	1	10	0	10	INITIAL TIME	2020	YEAR
3	2021	1	10	0	10	TIME STEP	1	YEAR
4						INITIAL POLICY VALUE	10	POLICY UNITS
5						DATE OF IMPLEMENTATION	2025	YEAR
6						POLICY IMPROVEMENT	0.2	DMNL
7						TIME TO CHANGE POLICY VALUE	10	YEAR

Fig. 8.7: Copying the endogenous formulae for 2020 into the cells for 2021.

Then, we copy the cells A3:E3, down the columns, to finish the system dynamics model (see Fig. 8.8).

	A	B	C	D	E
1	Time	policy implementation	desired policy value	change in policy value	Delayed Policy Value
2	2020	1	10	0	10
3	2021	1	10	0	10
4	2022	1	10	0	10
5	2023	1	10	0	10
6	2024	1	10	0	10
7	2025	1.2	12	0.2	10
8	2026	1.2	12	0.18	10.2
9	2027	1.2	12	0.162	10.38
10	2028	1.2	12	0.1458	10.542
11	2029	1.2	12	0.13122	10.6878
12	2030	1.2	12	0.118098	10.81902

Fig. 8.8: Copying the endogenous formulae for 2020 into the cells for 2021.

Figure 8.9 shows the results of the first-order delay model. The policy will be gradually implemented after 2025.

By mastering first-order delays through these practical techniques, you are equipped to model higher-order delay structures and apply these principles to various real-world scenarios, which we will discuss in the next section.

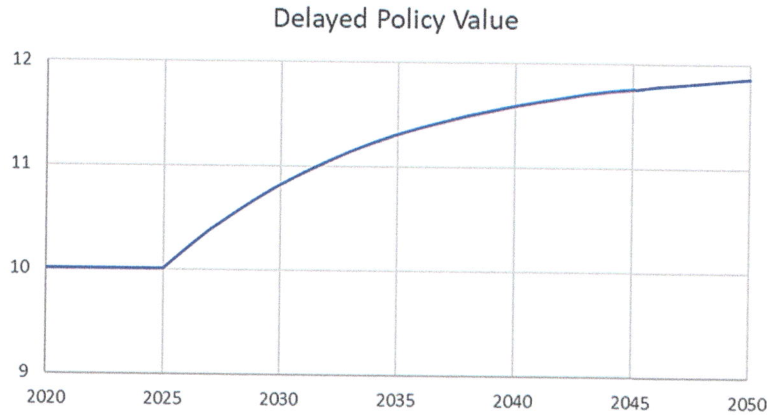

Fig. 8.9: The results of a first-order delay model.

8.4 Third-Order Delays

We can model any order delay, but we will discuss third-order delays here, as they are a standard Vensim function used in system dynamics. In Vensim, third-order delays can be implemented using the built-in function DELAY3. Figure 8.10 shows a more explicit implementation of third-order delays as a stock-and-flow diagram. We have four exogenous values: initial policy value = 1, policy improvement = 0.2, policy implementation date = 2025, and total delay = 12. The single order delay = 12/3 = 4 years, and the policy implementation = 1 + STEP (policy value, policy implementation date) and the desired policy value = initial policy value * policy implementation.

Now that we know how to model a first-order delay, implementing third-order delays in Excel is straightforward. We have four more endogenous variable columns for second-order change, second-order policy value, third-order change, and third-order policy value (see Fig. 8.11).

We set A2 = K2 and A3 = K2 + K$3. Next, we implement the policy using the IF statement: B2 = IF (A2 < K$7, 1, 1 + K$5). Then, we calculate the desired policy value, C2, as K$4 * B2. The first-order policy value for 2020 is in cell E2 = K4, the second-order policy value for 2020 is in cell G2 = K4, and the third-order policy value for 2020 is in cell I2 = K4 (see Fig. 8.12).

Then the first-order change is (desired policy value – first-order policy value)/(total delay time/3), that is, D2 = (C2 – E2)/(K$7/3). The second-order change is (first-order policy value – second-order policy value)/(total delay time/3), that is F2 = (E2 – G2)/(K$7/3) and the third-order change is (second-order policy value – third-order policy value)/(total delay time/3), that is H2 = (G2 – I2)/(K$7/3) (see Fig. 8.13).

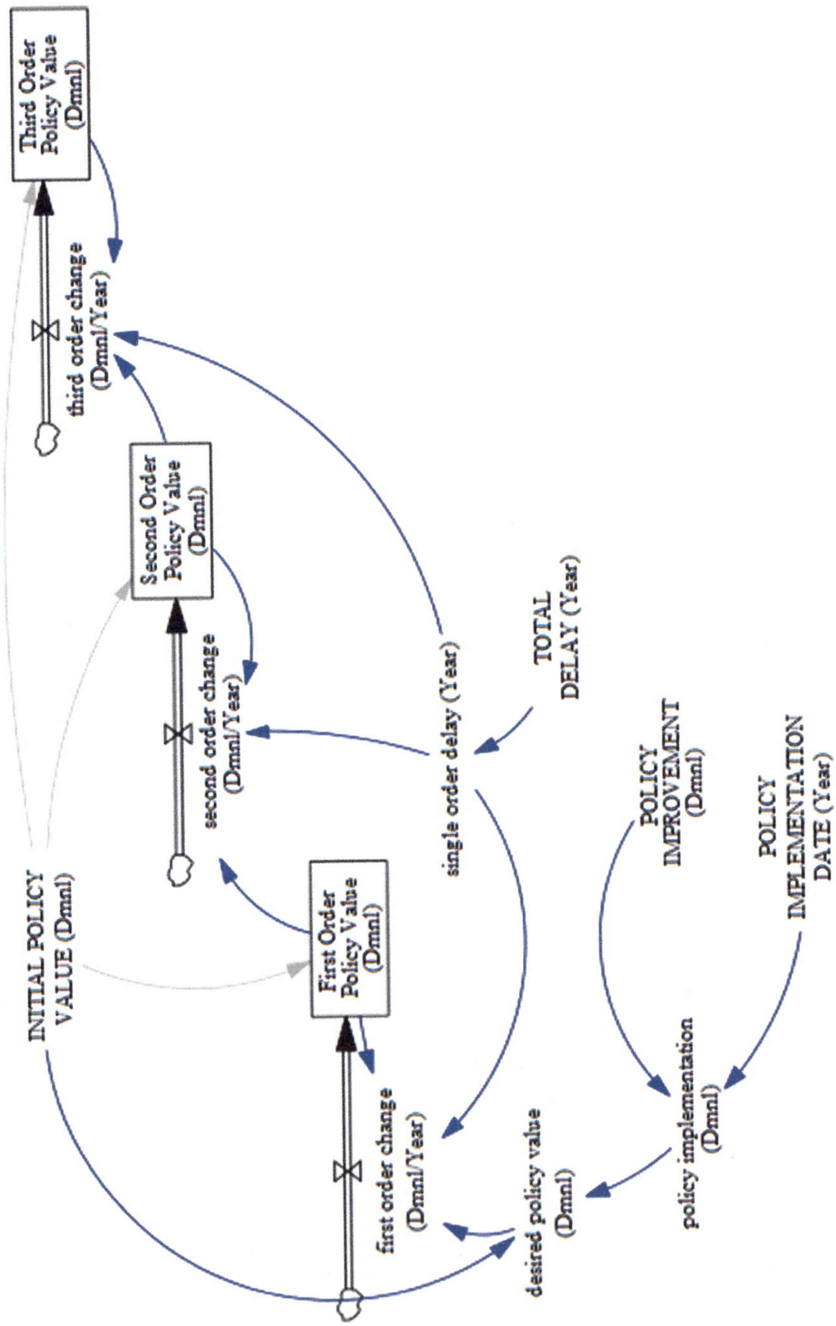

Fig. 8.10: The explicit model of a third-order delay in Vensim.

	A	B	C	D	E	F	G	H	I	J	K	L
1	Time	policy implementation	desired policy value	first order change	First Order Policy Value	second order change	Second Order Policy Value	third order change	Third Order Policy Value	PARAMETERS	VALUE	UNITS
2										INITIAL TIME	2020	YEAR
3										TIME STEP	1	YEAR
4										INITIAL POLICY VALUE	1	POLICY UNITS
5										POLICY IMPROVEMENT	0.2	POLICY UNITS
6										POLICY IMPLEMENTATION DATE	2025	YEAR
7										TOTAL DELAY TIME	12	YEAR

Fig. 8.11: The setup of the third-order delay model in Excel.

	A	B	C	D	E	F	G	H	I	J	K	L
1	Time	policy implementation	desired policy value	first order change	First Order Policy Value	second order change	Second Order Policy Value	third order change	Third Order Policy Value	PARAMETERS	VALUE	UNITS
2	2020	1	1		1		1		1	INITIAL TIME	2020	YEAR
3	2021									TIME STEP	1	YEAR
4										INITIAL POLICY VALUE	1	POLICY UNITS
5										POLICY IMPROVEMENT	0.2	POLICY UNITS
6										POLICY IMPLEMENTATION DATE	2025	YEAR
7										TOTAL DELAY TIME	12	YEAR

Fig. 8.12: The setup of the initial third-order delay model policy values.

SUM fx =(G2-I2)/(K$7/3)

	A	B	C	D	E	F	G	H	I	J	K	L
1	Time	policy implementation	desired policy value	first order change	First Order Policy Value	second order change	Second Order Policy Value	third order change	Third Order Policy Value	PARAMETERS	VALUE	UNITS
2	2020	1	1	0	1	0	1	=(G2-I2)/(	1	INITIAL TIME	2020	YEAR
3	2021									TIME STEP	1	YEAR
4										INITIAL POLICY VALUE	1	POLICY UNITS
5										POLICY IMPROVEMENT	0.2	POLICY UNITS
6										POLICY IMPLEMENTATION DATE	2025	YEAR
7										TOTAL DELAY TIME	12	YEAR

Fig. 8.13: The calculation of the third-order change.

Then, we update the three stocks (first-order policy value, second-order policy value, and third-order policy value) using the Euler integration formulae: E3 = E2 + $K$3 * D2, G3 = G2 + $K$3 * F2, and I3 = I2 + $K$3 * H2 (see Fig. 8.14).

SUM fx =I2+$K$3*H2

	A	B	C	D	E	F	G	H	I	J	K	L
1	Time	policy implementation	desired policy value	first order change	First Order Policy Value	second order change	Second Order Policy Value	third order change	Third Order Policy Value	PARAMETERS	VALUE	UNITS
2	2020	1	1	0	1	0	1	0	1	INITIAL TIME	2020	YEAR
3	2021				1		1		=I2+$K$3*	TIME STEP	1	YEAR
4										INITIAL POLICY VALUE	1	POLICY UNITS
5										POLICY IMPROVEMENT	0.2	POLICY UNITS
6										POLICY IMPLEMENTATION DATE	2025	YEAR
7										TOTAL DELAY TIME	12	YEAR

Fig. 8.14: The calculation of the third-order policy value in 2021 using Euler integration.

Then, we copy the endogenous variables for 2020 in cells B2:D2, F2, and H2 down to the 2021 rows B3:D3, F3, and H3 (see Fig. 8.15).

	A	B	C	D	E	F	G	H	I	J	K	L
1	Time	policy implementation	desired policy value	first order change	First Order Policy Value	second order change	Second Order Policy Value	third order change	Third Order Policy Value	PARAMETERS	VALUE	UNITS
2	2020	1	1	0	1	0	1	0	1	INITIAL TIME	2020	YEAR
3	2021	1	1	0	1	0	1	0	1	TIME STEP	1	YEAR
4										INITIAL POLICY VALUE	1	POLICY UNITS
5										POLICY IMPROVEMENT	0.2	POLICY UNITS
6										POLICY IMPLEMENTATION DATE	2025	YEAR
7										TOTAL DELAY TIME	12	YEAR

Fig. 8.15: The endogenous variables are updated for the next time step.

Then, we copy and paste the cells A3:I3 down the rows for as many years as we want to run the simulation (see Fig. 8.16).

	A	B	C	D	E	F	G	H	I	J	K	L
1	Time	policy implementation	desired policy value	first order change	First Order Policy Value	second order change	Second Order Policy Value	third order change	Third Order Policy Value	PARAMETERS	VALUE	UNITS
2	2020	1	1	0	1	0	1	0	1	INITIAL TIME	2020	YEAR
3	2021	1	1	0	1	0	1	0	1	TIME STEP	1	YEAR
4	2022	1	1	0	1	0	1	0	1	INITIAL POLICY VALUE	1	POLICY UNITS
5	2023	1	1	0	1	0	1	0	1	POLICY IMPROVEMENT	0.2	POLICY UNITS
6	2024	1	1	0	1	0	1	0	1	POLICY IMPLEMENTATION DATE	2025	YEAR
7	2025	1.2	1.2	0.05	1	0	1	0	1	TOTAL DELAY TIME	12	YEAR
8	2026	1.2	1.2	0.0375	1.05	0.0125	1	0	1			
9	2027	1.2	1.2	0.028125	1.0875	0.01875	1.0125	0.003125	1			
10	2028	1.2	1.2	0.021094	1.115625	0.021094	1.03125	0.007031	1.003125			
11	2029	1.2	1.2	0.01582	1.136719	0.021094	1.052344	0.010547	1.010156			
12	2030	1.2	1.2	0.011865	1.152539	0.019775	1.073438	0.013184	1.020703			

Fig. 8.16: The final third-order delay model.

Figure 8.17 shows the results of the third-order delay calculation.

Our clients probably do not need to see the details of the third-order delay calculations. In the example below, we will hide the model from the client in a separate spreadsheet. In general, our clients are not concerned with the specifics of our models. Once they have confidence in the model, they are primarily interested in results. However, we would like them to use the model themselves. In the next section, we will demonstrate how to create a clean interface for a model.

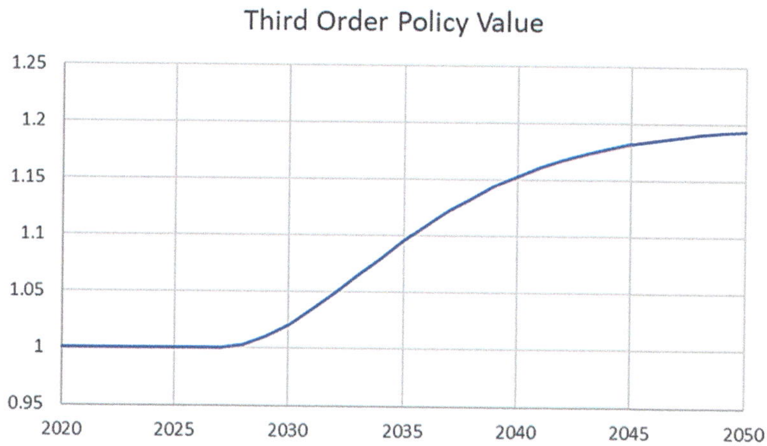

Fig. 8.17: Graphical display of the third-order delay model.

8.5 An Example Model of the Impact of Delays on a Small Business

In this example, we will consider a small sales and service business. They have two fleets of vehicles: seven cars for salespeople and 10 trucks for service people. They maintain these fleets themselves and have a small inventory of spare parts. If a car breaks down and they do not have the part in their inventory, they place an order with their supplier, which arrives in one day. Then they replace the part and return the vehicle to service.

They used an operations research optimization to determine the parts to hold in inventory. They found that with a 1-day delivery time, they can achieve 98% fleet availability for $15,000 in parts (see Fig. 8.18).

However, they experienced a four-month supply chain disruption in the first month, resulting in a 10-day delay in delivery. This significantly reduced fleet availability, from 98% to 48% (see Fig. 8.19), due to the $15,000 inventory.

This reduction in availability does not happen all at once. Instead, the availability decreases gradually as the vehicles break down over time, and there are no parts in inventory to fix them. We will assume this gradual decrease in fleet availability is a third-order delay with a delay time of three months. We will use the same third-order delay model as in Section 8.4 with one adjustment. We will use an embedded IF statement to implement the supply chain disruption. The formula for the availability impact = IF (Time < disruption start time, initial availability, IF (Time < disruption end time, availability reduction, initial availability)). So, in cell B2 = IF (A2 < J$7, J$4, IF (A2 < J$7, J$5, J$4)) as shown in Fig. 8.20.

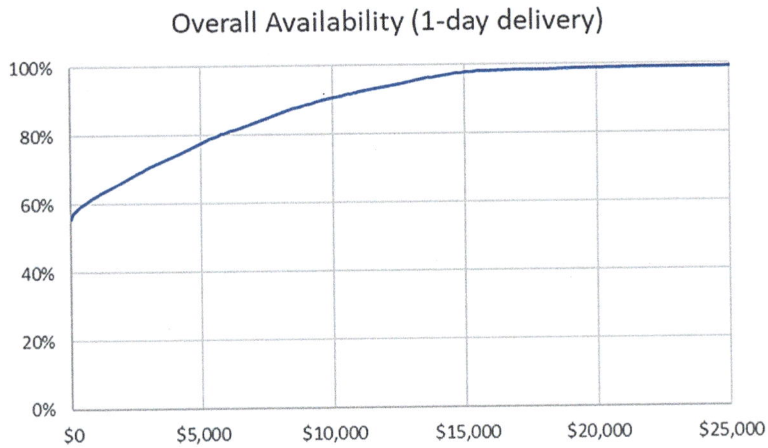

Fig. 8.18: Results of inventory optimization with 1-day delivery.

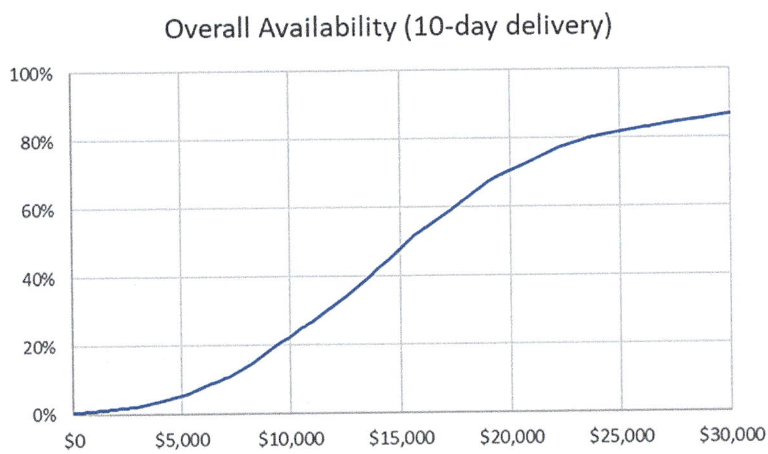

Fig. 8.19: Results of inventory optimization with 10-day delivery.

SUM | =IF(A2<J$6,J$4,IF(A2<J$7,J$5,J$4))

IF(logical_test, [value_if_true], [value_if_false])

	A	B	C	D	E	F	G	H	I	J	K
1	Month	Availability Impact	first order delay change	First Order Availability Impact	second order delay change	Second Order Availability Impact	third order delay change	Third Order Availability Impact	PARAMETERS	VALUE	UNITS
2	0	=IF(A2<J$6,	0%	98%	0%	98%	0%	98%	INITIAL TIME	0	MONTH
3	0.25	98%	0%	98%	0%	98%	0%	98%	TIME STEP	0.25	MONTH
4	0.5	98%	0%	98%	0%	98%	0%	98%	INITIAL AVAILABILITY	0.98	DMNL
5	0.75	98%	0%	98%	0%	98%	0%	98%	AVAILABILITY REDUCTION	0.48	DMNL
6	1	48%	-50%	98%	0%	98%	0%	98%	DISRUPTION START DATE	1	MONTH
7	1.25	48%	-38%	86%	-13%	98%	0%	98%	DISRUPTION END DATE	4	MONTH
8	1.5	48%	-28%	76%	-19%	95%	-3%	98%	TOTAL DELAY TIME	3	MONTH

Fig. 8.20: The third-order delay model for assessing the impact of supply chain disruptions on availability.

We now build an interface for the model. We start by naming three spreadsheets: Interface, Graphs, and Model (see Fig. 8.21).

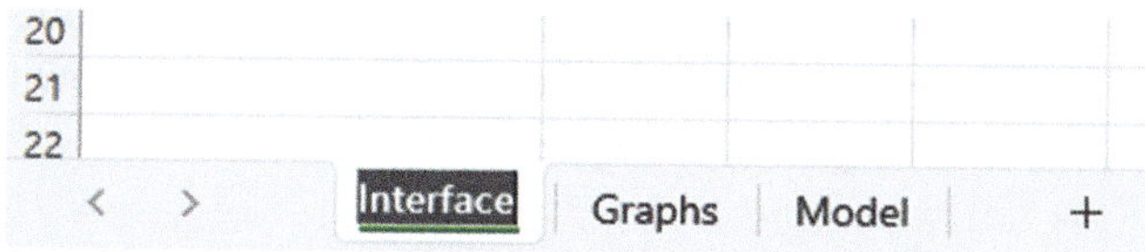

Fig. 8.21: Setting up the Interface and Graphs spreadsheets.

In the Interface spreadsheet, we put the model's parameters in columns A, B, and C (see Fig. 8.22). Next, we link the parameter cells in the Model spreadsheet to the corresponding cells in the Interface spreadsheet. To do this, type = in the appropriate cell in the Model spreadsheet, navigate to the relevant cell in the Interface spreadsheet, click on it, and press return (see Fig. 8.23).

	A	B	C
1	PARAMETERS	VALUE	UNITS
2	INITIAL TIME	0	MONTH
3	TIME STEP	0.25	MONTH
4	INITIAL AVAILABILITY	0.98	DMNL
5	AVAILABILITY IMPACT	0.48	DMNL
6	DISRUPTION START DATE	1	MONTH
7	DISRUPTION END DATE	4	MONTH
8	DELAY TIME	3	MONTH

Fig. 8.22: Setting up the parameter values in the Interface spreadsheet.

J2 =Interface!B2

	A	B	C	D	E	F	G	H	I	J	K
1	Month	Availability Impact	first order delay change	First Order Availability Impact	second order delay change	Second Order Availability Impact	third order delay change	Third Order Availability Impact	PARAMETERS	VALUE	UNITS
2	0	98%	0%	98%	0%	98%	0%	98%	INITIAL TIME	0	MONTH
3	0.25	98%	0%	98%	0%	98%	0%	98%	TIME STEP	0.25	MONTH
4	0.5	98%	0%	98%	0%	98%	0%	98%	INITIAL AVAILABILITY	0.98	DMNL
5	0.75	98%	0%	98%	0%	98%	0%	98%	AVAILABILITY REDUCTION	0.48	DMNL
6	1	48%	-50%	98%	0%	98%	0%	98%	DISRUPTION START DATE	1	MONTH
7	1.25	48%	-38%	86%	-13%	98%	0%	98%	DISRUPTION END DATE	4	MONTH
8	1.5	48%	-28%	76%	-19%	95%	-3%	98%	TOTAL DELAY TIME	3	MONTH

Fig. 8.23: Linking the parameters in the Model spreadsheet with the parameters in the Interface spreadsheet.

Now, we will clean up the Interface spreadsheet. We remove the spreadsheet frames, as shown in Fig. 8.24. To do this, click on an open cell, such as D1, and then press "CTRL-a" to highlight all cells in the spreadsheet. Next, click on the paint can and select the white square. Then, we highlight the parameter cells, click on the frame button, and click on "All Borders" to frame just the cells with the parameters, as shown in Fig. 8.25. Figure 8.26 shows the cleaned-up Interface spreadsheet.

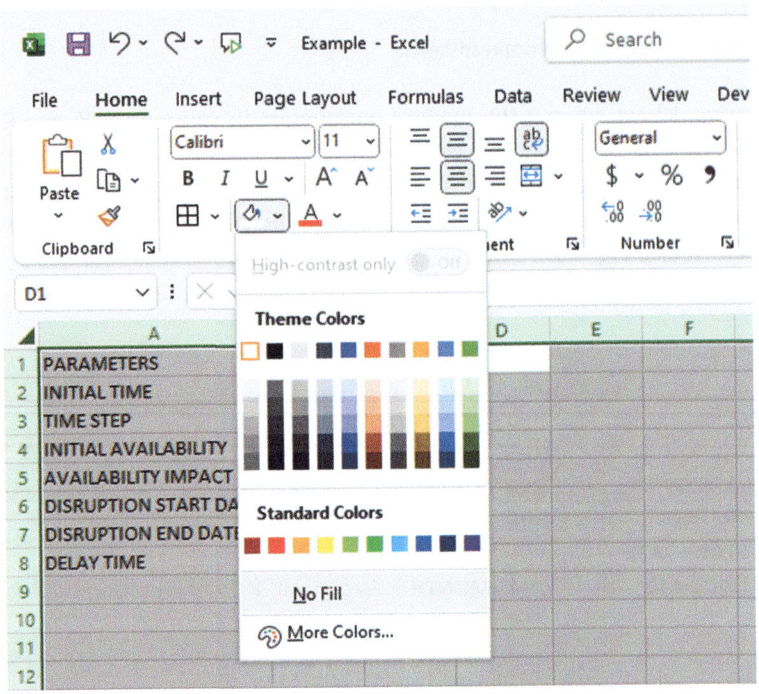

Fig. 8.24: Removing the cell borders on the Interface spreadsheet.

Now, we will set up the Graphs spreadsheet. We will reference the cells in column A of the Graphs spreadsheet with the corresponding cells in column A of the Model spreadsheet for the time values. Then, we will reference the cells in column B of the Graphs spreadsheet with those in column H in the Model spreadsheet (see Fig. 8.27). Then, we generate a results graph from columns A and B in the Graphs spreadsheet (see Fig. 8.28).

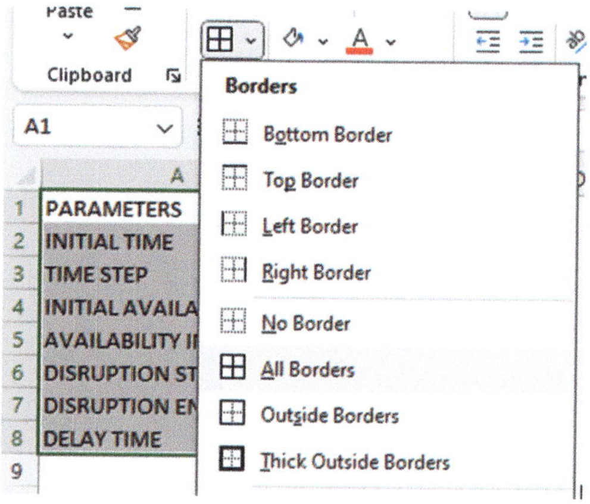

Fig. 8.25: Putting solid borders on the parameter cells in the Interface spreadsheet.

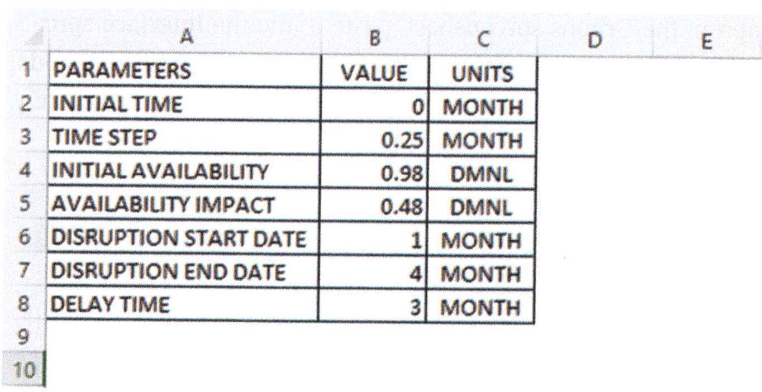

	A	B	C	D	E
1	PARAMETERS	VALUE	UNITS		
2	INITIAL TIME	0	MONTH		
3	TIME STEP	0.25	MONTH		
4	INITIAL AVAILABILITY	0.98	DMNL		
5	AVAILABILITY IMPACT	0.48	DMNL		
6	DISRUPTION START DATE	1	MONTH		
7	DISRUPTION END DATE	4	MONTH		
8	DELAY TIME	3	MONTH		
9					
10					

Fig. 8.26: Cleaned up list of parameters in the Interface worksheet.

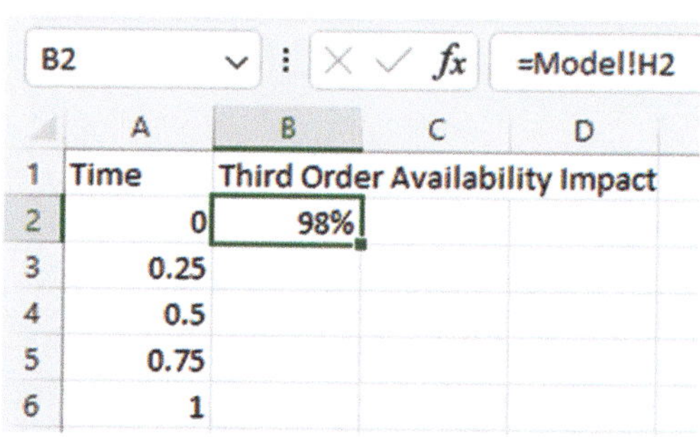

Fig. 8.27: Linking the Graphs spreadsheet to the Model spreadsheet.

Fig. 8.28: Graphic of the results in the Graphs spreadsheet.

Then we clean up the graph in the Graphs spreadsheet, paste it into the Interface spreadsheet, and enlarge it (see Fig. 8.29). This is a valuable tool for clients because all model parameters are visible, and when a parameter is changed, the graph updates immediately.

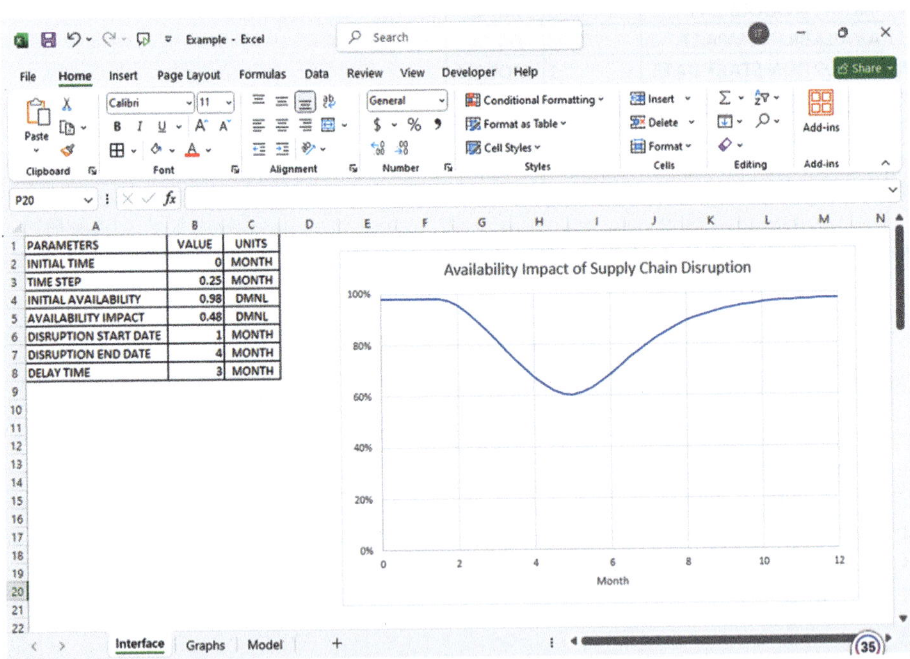

Fig. 8.29: The finished Interface spreadsheet.

8.6 Conclusions

In summary, this chapter equipped you with the skills to model delays of varying complexities using Excel. You learned how to implement first- and third-order delays and create interactive models tailored to client use. These techniques are fundamental for developing robust system dynamics models that accurately reflect the temporal intricacies of real-world systems. As you progress, these foundational skills will enable you to tackle more complex modelling challenges, apply advanced delay structures, and deliver insightful, actionable analyses to your clients.

In these first eight chapters, we have provided you with the fundamental principles of system dynamics modelling using Excel, utilizing simple examples with only a few stocks and flows. This solid foundation equips you to create models of any complexity you desire. In the upcoming chapters, we will build on these basics by presenting a series of case studies that demonstrate more intricate and comprehensive models, showcasing the full potential of system dynamics with Excel in real-world applications.

8.7 Discussion Questions

- When is a first-order delay sufficient, and when does a higher-order delay better capture observed smoothing/lag in your process? Cite your evidence.
- How would you justify the dt selection to an audit committee, and what's your convergence test?
- For a policy step input, what messaging prevents over-promising on near-term benefits given the modelled lag?
- In a client deliverable, what should be visible on the Interface worksheet versus what should be kept in the Model worksheet? How do you maintain trust without exposing every formula?
- In the supply-chain disruption example, which parameters most influence the timing of decline and recovery in service levels? How would you stress-test them?

8.8 Exercises

8.8.1 First-order delay: Excel build

Task. Implement a first-order delay with a policy step: policy implementation = IF (Time < start,1,1 + improvement), desired = initial * policy implementation, change = (desired−delayed)/delay time, Euler update for delayed.

Deliverable. First 12 rows, formulas, and a scatter chart of desired versus delayed.

8.8.2 Third-order delay: three-stock chain

Task. Create first/second/third-order stocks with per-stage change = (upstream−stock)/(total delay/3) and Euler updates for each stock.

Deliverable. Screenshot of formulas for one whole row and a chart of input versus third-order output.

8.8.3 Time-step sensitivity

Task. Re-run Exercise 8.8.2 with dt = 0.25 (or another 2^−*n*). Compare outputs at integer times; comment on accuracy versus run-time.

Deliverable. Two comparison rows and a two-sentence note.

8.8.4 Interface/Graphs/Model

Task. Split the workbook into Interface, Graphs, and Model. Link parameter cells from Interface to Model, link Graphs to Model results, and paste the chart into Interface.

Deliverable. Screenshots of named tabs and linked ranges.

8.8.5 Disruption window

Task. Add an embedded IF to apply an availability reduction only during a disruption window, then pipe that signal through your third-order delay chain.

Deliverable. Formula for the window, chart of availability over time, and two key numbers: minimum availability and the time required to recover to 90%.

8.8.6 Executive brief

Task. Write 120–150 words explaining why outcomes lag despite action, what delay order you used, what dt you chose, and the implications for timelines.

Deliverable. One paragraph suitable for leadership.

Introduction to Part 2: **Scaling Up System Dynamics Models in Excel**

Whenever I show people how to build system dynamics models in Excel using a simple population model, the first question I get is: "Can you use Excel for bigger, more complex models?" My answer is always yes, and I walk them through one of the case studies in this section to prove it.

Here, we apply what you learned in Part 1 to larger, real-world problems. Each chapter introduces a distinct problem and develops an Excel model to provide recommended solutions.

Each case study follows a structured format based on the System Dynamics Society's canonical style. The key sections in each case study include:

- Problem definition: Clearly stating the issue's importance and who is affected.
- Reference mode: Showing historical trends that describe how the system has behaved over time.
- Dynamic hypothesis: Using causal loop diagrams to explain the key feedback loops that drive system behaviour.
- Model formulation: Laying out the stock-and-flow structure, including equations.
- Calibration and validation: Checking that the model's results match real-world data.
- Base run analysis: Looking at what happens if there are no interventions in the system.
- Policy runs and sensitivity analysis: Testing different scenarios to see how changes affect outcomes.
- Conclusions: Summarize key findings and recommend possible actions.

Here's what you'll see in each case study:

- Chapter 9: ChatGPT Emissions: Development of policies to decouple AI expansion from CO_2 emissions [40].
- Chapter 10: Dairy Waste Treatment: Optimization of waste management, turning dairy farm waste into valuable resources like bio-fertilizer and biogas [41].
- Chapter 11: The Syrian Refugee Crisis: Examination of approaches to solve the refugee crisis created by the Syrian Civil War [42].
- Chapter 12: Diabetes Management in India: Examination of healthcare policies to control diabetes population growth in India [43].
- Chapter 13: Increasing Diversity in Organizations: Developing policies to increase the representation of minorities in the workforce and management in an organization [44].
- Chapter 14: Support to Women of Colour Entrepreneurs: Problem of high failure rate of women-of-colour-owned small businesses and policies to support women-of-colour entrepreneurs [45].

https://doi.org/10.1515/9783111541389-010

– Chapter 15: Canadian Oil Sands Industry Investment in ESG: The economic, social, and environmental impacts of the oil sands industry in Canada and investment strategies to reduce negative consequences [46].

By the end of this section, you'll have experience working with larger, more complex Excel models, see how system dynamics can handle real-world problems and gain the skills to adapt these methods to your challenges. The working models developed for this book are available at https://github.com/ivanwtaylor/Excel-Book.

Chapter 9
Reducing the Carbon Footprint of ChatGPT

9.1 Learning Objectives

- Frame the problem with a transparent reference mode and feedback hypothesis.
- Translate the stock-and-flow model to Excel, preserving units, structure, and causality.
- Parameterize inputs and re-link endogenous variables using robust cell references to ensure accuracy and consistency.
- Implement Euler integration for all stocks and validate first-step correctness and time-step adequacy.
- Establish clean workbook architecture (model, parameters, data, interface) with full traceability.
- Reproduce the reference mode in Excel, then calibrate via sum of squared error (SSE) minimization using Solver.
- Build a policy interface (e.g. efficiency, renewables), run scenarios, and compare them against the baseline.
- Quantify the impacts of interventions (e.g. target-year deltas and elasticities) and explain the structural drivers behind the outcomes.

9.2 Introduction

This case study [40] demonstrates how Excel can be used to implement a more complex system dynamics model without overwhelming the process. While system dynamics models can get pretty intricate, we've deliberately chosen a relatively straightforward case. That way, we can focus on the key ideas behind building and analysing dynamic systems in Excel without getting lost in unnecessary complexity.

One of the primary objectives is to demonstrate how a Vensim model can be systematically converted into an Excel model. Vensim is excellent for quickly creating and visualizing models using stock-and-flow diagrams. Still, Excel offers a more accessible platform, especially for sharing with people who may not be familiar with system dynamics. A transparent, structured process will show how the transition from Vensim to Excel can be applied to other models.

We also strongly emphasize the importance of proper model documentation. Throughout Part 2 of this book, we follow the standard approach recommended by the System Dynamics Society to ensure that models are structured, easy to follow, and adhere to best practices.

https://doi.org/10.1515/9783111541389-011

By the end of this case study, you'll see how Excel can handle more advanced models and walk away with a step-by-step understanding of converting a Vensim model into Excel while keeping everything well-documented and easy to interpret.

9.3 Problem Definition

The rapid growth of large language models (LLMs) such as ChatGPT is creating a significant environmental challenge [40]. Their widespread adoption has driven a steep rise in computational demand, resulting in rapidly increasing electricity consumption. Because much of this energy is still generated from fossil fuels, the associated carbon emissions are climbing at an unsustainable pace. If current trends continue unchecked, the scale of energy use and emissions from LLMs will pose a serious conflict between the benefits of artificial intelligence (AI) and the urgent global need to reduce greenhouse gases. This problem has far-reaching implications for climate policy, technology development, and industry practices, making it critical to understand the drivers of this growth and its long-term environmental consequences.

9.4 Reference Mode

Historical trends in the adoption and use of LLMs such as ChatGPT show a pattern of rapid, near-exponential growth in both user numbers and usage intensity over the past several years. Since its public launch, ChatGPT has experienced unprecedented adoption, reaching hundreds of millions of users in a short time. Monthly website visits and the number of queries per user have increased sharply as LLMs have become more integrated into personal, professional, and organizational workflows. This widespread uptake has been driven by the perceived utility of AI for tasks such as information retrieval, content generation, and customer interaction.

The reference mode of the number of visits per month, as shown in Fig. 9.1, highlights a critical dynamic. The reinforcing feedback of adoption growth and increased per-user engagement was offset by balancing effects from market saturation among early adopters. Eventually, the late adopters and the integration with the adopters' workflow kicked in, leading to exponential growth in monthly visits.

Our model will need to replicate this historical pattern before policymakers can have confidence in its use for decision-making.

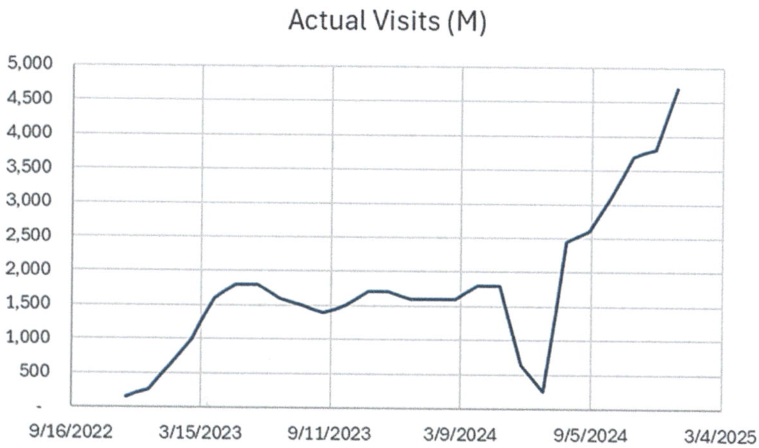

Fig. 9.1: Visits to ChatGPT from inception.

9.5 Dynamic Hypothesis

To understand how this reference mode may have been created, we utilize a causal loop diagram (Fig. 9.2). This diagram illustrates how various factors interact, forming feedback loops that either exacerbate problems or help bring them back under control. Some loops amplify adverse outcomes if left unchecked, while others help stabilize the system.

The causal loop diagram contains two main reinforcing feedback structures that drive growth in both adoption and usage of ChatGPT. The first, *AI Adoption Growth* (R1), begins with successful implementation experiences that increase the perceived value of the technology. This attracts more new users, increasing the number of active users and the total user base. As the user base grows, the likelihood of further successful implementations rises, creating a self-reinforcing cycle of adoption. The second, *Increased Usage Per User* (R2), is driven by integration into users' workflows. As users find more ways to incorporate the LLM into their daily tasks, the number of queries per user increases. Higher query volumes raise the perceived utility of the system, encouraging even deeper integration, which in turn further increases usage. Together, these loops result in exponential growth in computational demand, energy consumption, and emissions, unless counterbalancing forces are present.

The diagram also contains several balancing loops that limit this growth. *Market Saturation* (B1) constrains new user acquisition as the pool of potential adopters declines with the increasing total number of users. *Usage Limits* (B2) operate through cognitive capacity: as the number of queries per user increases, cognitive load rises, eventually reducing the user's ability or willingness to issue more queries. On the environmental side, *Energy Efficiency and Technological Advancements* (B3) act as a bal-

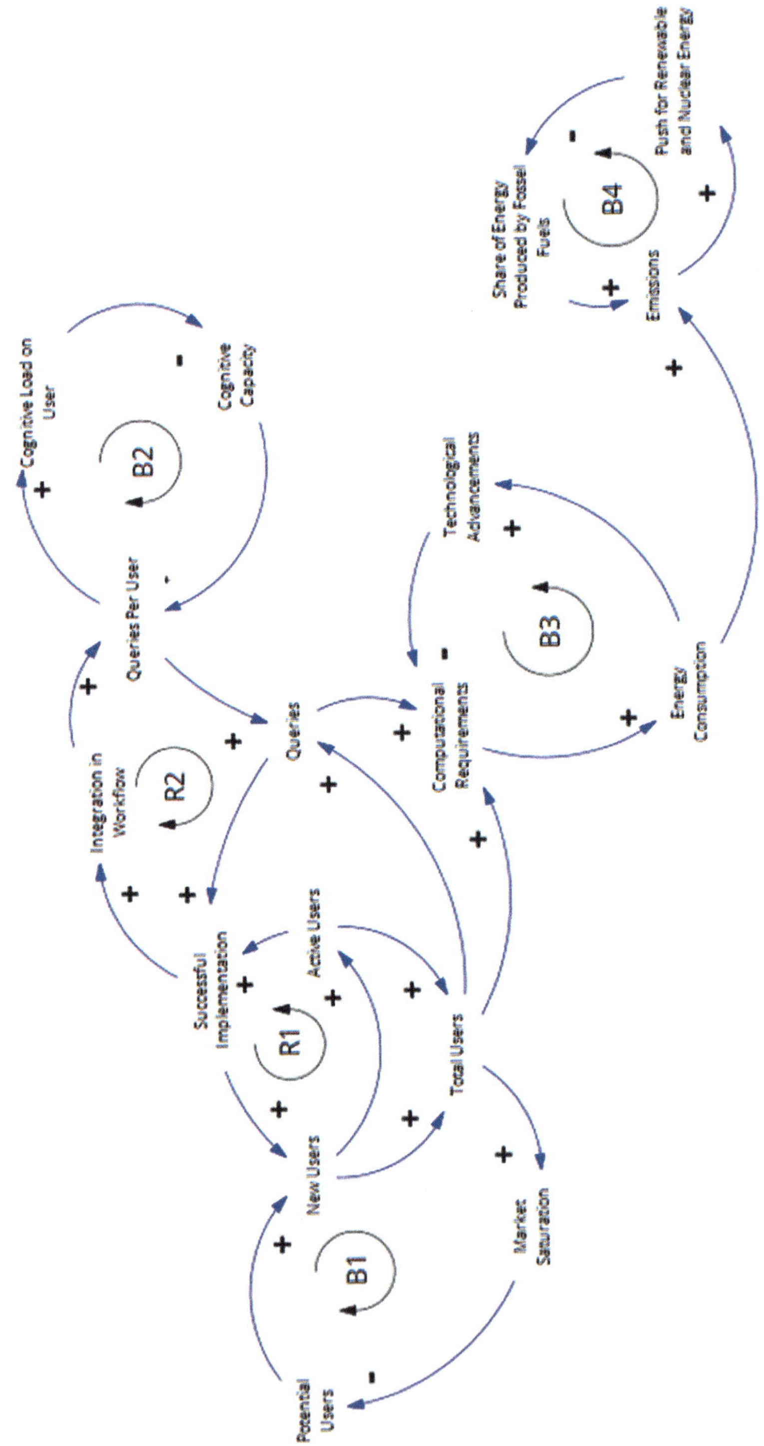

Fig. 9.2: Dynamic hypothesis for the ChatGPT emissions problem.

ancing loop: higher energy consumption creates pressure to improve the efficiency of hardware, algorithms, and infrastructure, thereby lowering energy use per query. Similarly, *Renewable Energy Adoption* (B4) functions as a balancing loop where higher emissions spur investment in renewable and nuclear energy, reducing the share of electricity from fossil fuels and lowering emissions over time. These balancing loops can slow or stabilize the system's environmental impact, but their effectiveness depends on their relative strength compared to the reinforcing loops driving adoption and usage growth.

9.6 Model Formulation

9.6.1 The System Dynamics Model in Vensim

The Vensim model simulates the growth of ChatGPT usage, as well as the resulting energy demand and carbon emissions. It links the number of users, visits per user, and queries per visit to total computational load, which determines energy consumption. That energy use, combined with the share of electricity from fossil fuels, drives CO_2 emissions. The model includes feedback loops where rising energy demand pressures improvements in energy efficiency, and higher emissions stimulate investment in renewable and nuclear energy production. Key parameters set limits on acceptable energy use and emissions, allowing the model to test how technological improvements and the adoption of clean energy can alter ChatGPT's long-term environmental impact.

At first glance, the Vensim model in Fig. 9.3 may look complex, but its structure is manageable. It contains seven stock variables: potential ChatGPT users, ChatGPT users, ChatGPT visits per user per month, queries per visit, energy per query, renewable and nuclear energy production, and carbon footprint. It contains six flows: new users, changes in visits per month per user, increases in queries per user, decreases in energy per query, increases in renewable and nuclear energy production, and CO_2 production. Our primary objective is to minimize CO_2 production. ChatGPT visits is our calibration variable. Renewable pressure and efficiency pressure are our policy levers, which can increase long-term renewable and nuclear energy production and decrease long-term energy per query, respectively.

We won't go deep into the details of the Vensim model here. This chapter focuses on how a more complex Vensim model can be translated into Excel, building on the simpler examples in Part 1. The step-by-step process outlined in the next section applies to any Vensim model, regardless of its complexity. If you want to gain some hands-on practice, try using these steps on one of the simpler models from earlier in the book.

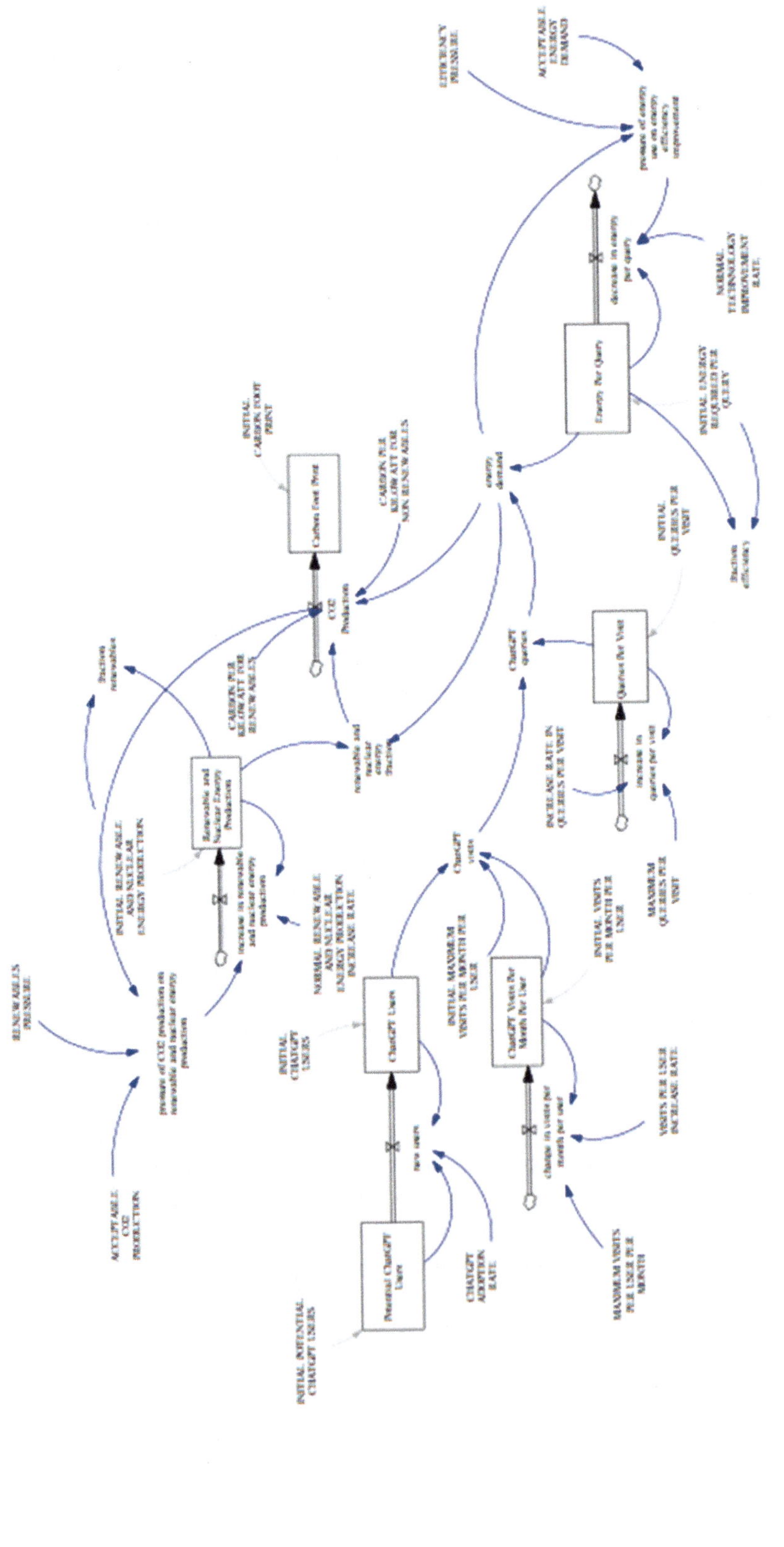

Fig. 9.3: Vensim model of ChatGPT emissions.

9.6.2 Translating the Vensim Model into an Excel Workbook

The following section describes the step-by-step process of converting a system dynamics model from Vensim to Excel. Although the model may appear complex initially, breaking it down into manageable steps makes the transition straightforward. This method ensures the original model's logic and structure are preserved, making it easier to customize, share, and analyze in Excel.

Step 1: Export Equations from Vensim

Open your Vensim model and locate the "Document All" button. Clicking it will generate a text window with all model equations listed in alphabetical order. Each variable is listed on three consecutive lines: its name, equation, and unit (see Fig. 9.4). This format facilitates easy transfer into Excel.

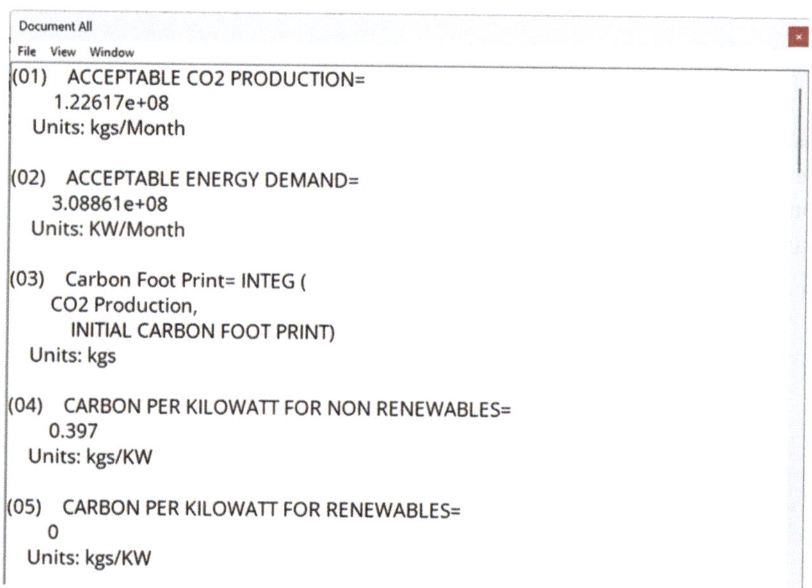

```
Document All
File View Window
(01) ACCEPTABLE CO2 PRODUCTION=
     1.22617e+08
  Units: kgs/Month

(02) ACCEPTABLE ENERGY DEMAND=
     3.08861e+08
  Units: KW/Month

(03) Carbon Foot Print= INTEG (
     CO2 Production,
       INITIAL CARBON FOOT PRINT)
  Units: kgs

(04) CARBON PER KILOWATT FOR NON RENEWABLES=
     0.397
  Units: kgs/KW

(05) CARBON PER KILOWATT FOR RENEWABLES=
     0
  Units: kgs/KW
```

Fig. 9.4: The Vensim equations for the ChatGPT model.

Step 2: Paste Equations into Excel

From the Vensim equations window, select Copy from the View menu. Create a new Vensim equations worksheet in Excel, click cell A1, and paste the copied equations into column A (see Fig. 9.5).

	A
1	(01) ACCEPTABLE CO2 PRODUCTION=
2	1.23E+08
3	Units: kgs/Month
4	
5	(02) ACCEPTABLE ENERGY DEMAND=
6	3.09E+08
7	Units: KW/Month
8	
9	(03) Carbon Foot Print= INTEG (
10	CO2 Production,
11	INITIAL CARBON FOOT PRINT)
12	Units: kgs
13	
14	(04) CARBON PER KILOWATT FOR NON RENEWABLES=
15	0.397
16	Units: kgs/KW

Fig. 9.5: The Vensim equations for the ChatGPT model in Excel.

Step 3: Transpose the Equations

Highlight the pasted content in column A (excluding the entire column – select the cells with content). In a new worksheet called *Model*, click cell A1 and choose Paste Special → Transpose. Then, select row 1, enable "Wrap Text," and centre the text vertically (see Fig. 9.6).

	A	B	C	D	E	F	G	H	I	J	K	L	M	N	O	P
1	(01) ACCEPTA BLE CO2 PRODUC TION=	1.23E+08	Units: kgs/Mont h		(02) ACCEPTA BLE ENERGY DEMAND =	3.09E+08	Units: KW/Mont h		(03) Carbon Foot Print= INTEG (	CO2 Productio n,	INITIAL CARBON FOOT PRINT)	Units: kgs		(04) CARBON PER KILOWAT T FOR NON RENEWA BLES=	0.397	Units: kgs/KW

Fig. 9.6: Transposed Vensim equations in Excel.

Step 4: Organize Parameters

Cut and paste all parameter cells (typically named in all caps) into separate columns for the parameter name, value, and unit to the right of the equations. Delete the original parameter columns. Place initial time and time step in rows 2 and 3 for convenience (see Fig. 9.7).

	X	Y	Z
1	PARAMETER	VALUE	UNITS
2	(30) INITIAL TIME = 0	0	Units: Month
3	(45) TIME STEP = 0.5	0.5	Units: Month [0,?]
4	(01) ACCEPTABLE CO2 PRODUCTION=	1.23E+08	Units: kgs/Month
5	(02) ACCEPTABLE ENERGY DEMAND=	3.09E+08	Units: KW/Month
6	(04) CARBON PER KILOWATT FOR NON RENEWABLES=	0.397	Units: kgs/KW
7	(05) CARBON PER KILOWATT FOR RENEWABLES=	0	Units: kgs/KW
8	(07) CHATGPT ADOPTION RATE=	4.36E-10	Units: 1/(Month*people)
9	(14) EFFICIENCY PRESSURE=	1	Units: Dmnl
10	(22) INCREASE RATE IN QUERIES PER VISIT=	0.0924485	Units: 1/Month
11	(23) INITIAL CARBON FOOT PRINT=	0.00E+00	Units: kgs
12	(24) INITIAL CHATGPT USERS=	1.00E+06	Units: people
13	(25) INITIAL ENERGY REQUIRED PER QUERY=	0.00396	Units: KW/queries
14	(26) INITIAL MAXIMUM VISITS PER MONTH PER USER=	5.35E+02	Units: visits/(Month*people)
15	(27) INITIAL POTENTIAL CHATGPT USERS=	6.14E+08	Units: people
16	(28) INITIAL QUERIES PER VISIT=	4.70178	Units: queries/visits
17	(29) INITIAL RENEWABLE AND NUCLEAR ENERGY PRODUCTION=	100000	Units: KW/Month
18	(31) INITIAL VISITS PER MONTH PER USER=	28.4277	Units: visits/(Month*people)

Fig. 9.7: Parameters of the ChatGPT model.

Step 5: Set Up the Structure

Insert columns A and B and enter the date and time headings. In each equation column, leave the variable name in row 1 cut and paste its units in row 2, and the formula (or initial value) in row 3. The flow variables go into row 4. Then delete the blank columns (see Fig. 9.8).

	A	B	C	D	E	F	G	H
1	Date	Time	(03) Carbon Foot Print= INTEG (	(06) change in visits per month per user=	(08) ChatGPT queries=	(09) ChatGPT Users= INTEG (	(10) ChatGPT visits=	(11) ChatGPT Visits Per Month Per User=
2			Units: kgs	Units: visits/(Mo nth*peopl e)/Month	Units: queries/M onth	Units: people	Units: visits/Mo nth	Units: visits/(Mo nth*peopl e)
3			INITIAL CARBON FOOT PRINT)	VISITS PER USER INCREAS E RATE*Ch	ChatGPT visits*Qu eries Per Visit	INITIAL CHATGPT USERS)	ChatGPT Users*(IN ITIAL MAXIMU	INITIAL VISITS PER MONTH
4			CO2 Productio n,			new users,		change in visits per month per user,

	I	J	K	L	M	N	O
1	(12) CO2 Productio n=	(13) decrease in energy per query=	(15) energy demand=	(16) Energy Per Query= INTEG (	(18) fraction efficiency =	(19) fraction renewabl es=	(20) increase in queries per visit=
2	Units: kgs/Mont h	Units: KW/(Mont h*queries)	Units: KW/Mont h	Units: KW/queri es	Units: fraction	Units: fraction	Units: queries/(Month*vi sits)
3	energy demand* (1- renewabl	NORMAL TECHNN OLOGY IMPROVE	ChatGPT queries*E nergy Per Query	INITIAL ENERGY REQUIRE D PER	Energy Per Query/INI TIAL	Renewabl e and Nuclear Energy	Queries Per Visit*INC REASE
4				- decrease in energy per query,			

Fig. 9.8: Excel row structure for variables.

Step 6: Convert the Parameters in the Model to Anchored Cell References

We will use a search-and-replace to convert the model's parameters to anchored cell references. First, we highlight row 3 where the equations are shown in text. In this case, the cells are A3 to W3 (see Fig. 9.9).

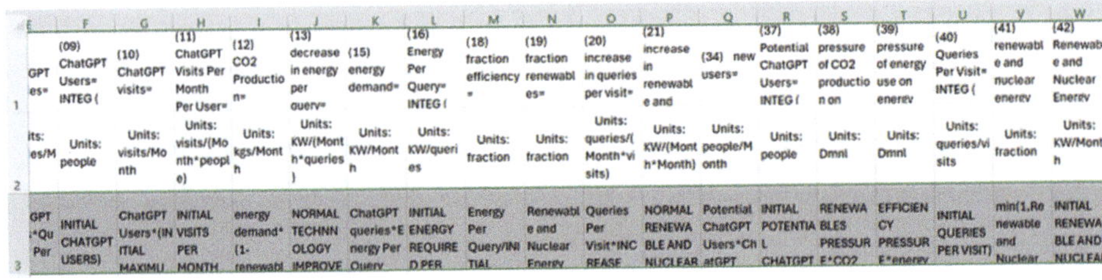

Fig. 9.9: Highlighted model equations in text in Excel.

Then we search and replace all the parameter names with anchored cell references as shown in Fig. 9.10.

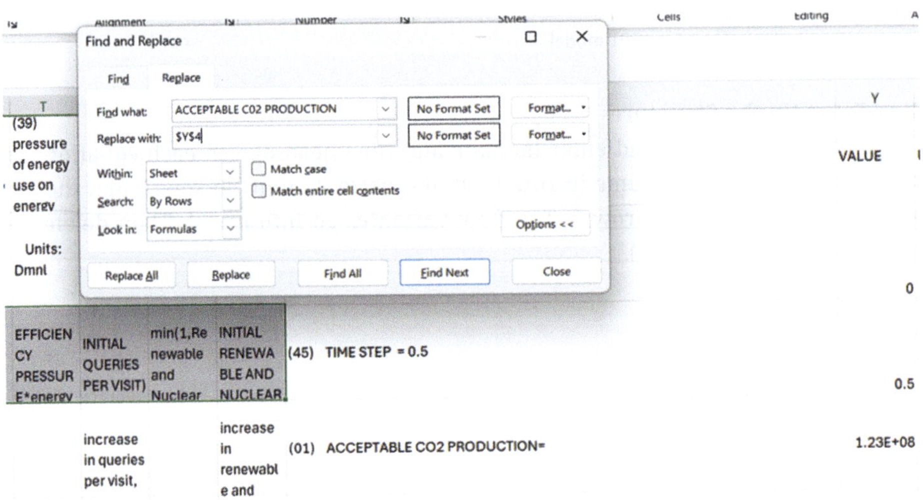

Fig. 9.10: Find and replace the parameter cell references in the model.

Step 8: Convert the Variable Names in Non-Anchored Cell References

In this case, we highlight cells A3 to W4 (see Fig. 9.11).

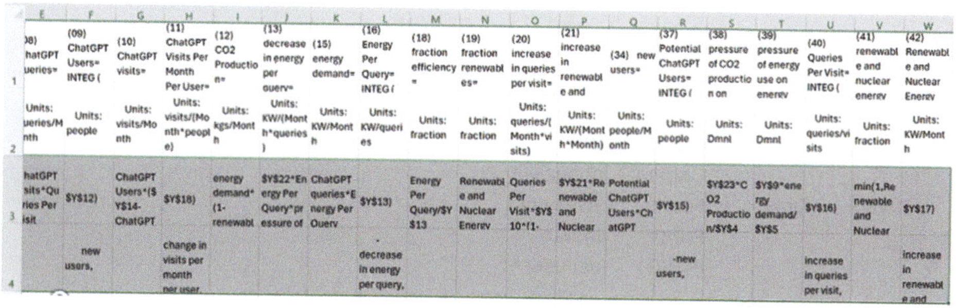

Fig. 9.11: Endogenous variables in Excel.

Then, we identify and replace the variable names with the appropriate non-anchored cell references in the model (see Fig. 9.12).

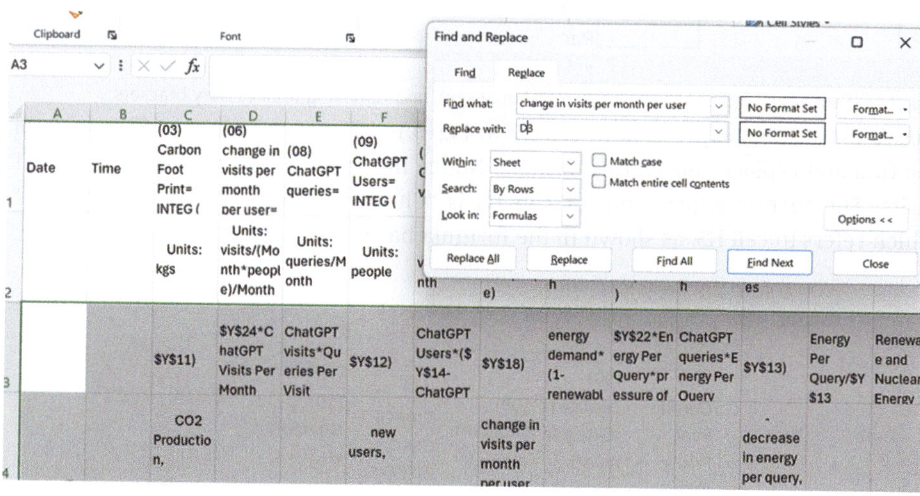

Fig. 9.12: Converting variable names into non-anchored cell references.

Step 9: Clean Up the Excel Formulas at Time 0

We need to clean up the Excel formulae. First, we need to add an equal sign (=) at the start in the formula bar and remove any extra spaces and brackets (see Fig. 9.13). Compare the value $Y$11) in cell C3 of Fig. 9.12 with the value = $Y$11 in the formula bar of Fig. 9.13.

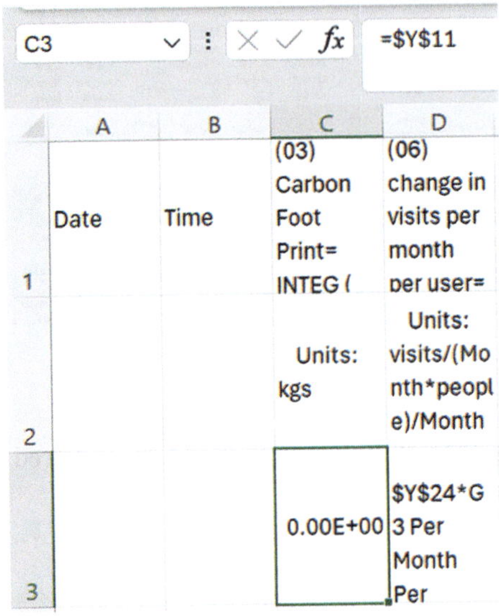

C3 | fx =$Y$11

	A	B	C	D
1	Date	Time	(03) Carbon Foot Print= INTEG (	(06) change in visits per month per user=
2			Units: kgs	Units: visits/(Month*people)/Month
3			0.00E+00	$Y$24*G3 Per Month Per

Fig. 9.13: Removing leading spaces, adding an equal sign, and removing unnecessary brackets.

Notice the strange expression in cell D3 in Fig. 9.14 "G3 per month per." The order of the find-and-replace caused this mistake. Notice in Fig. 9.14, column G is for ChatGPT visits. The correct expression for cell D3 is "ChatGPT Visits per month per user," which refers to cell H3, as shown in the formula bar in Fig. 9.15.

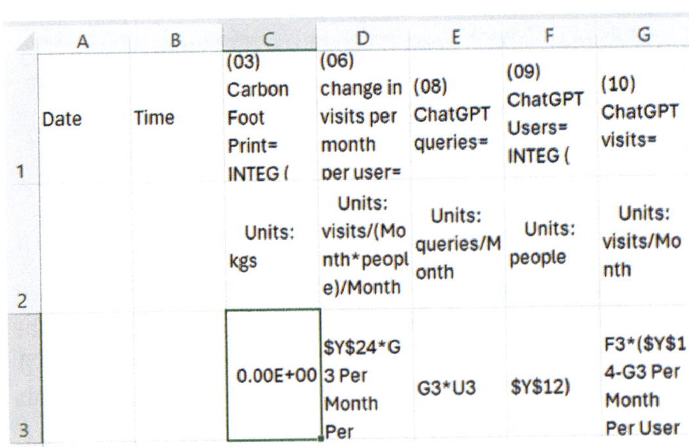

	A	B	C	D	E	F	G
1	Date	Time	(03) Carbon Foot Print= INTEG (	(06) change in visits per month per user=	(08) ChatGPT queries=	(09) ChatGPT Users= INTEG (	(10) ChatGPT visits=
2			Units: kgs	Units: visits/(Month*people)/Month	Units: queries/Month	Units: people	Units: visits/Month
3			0.00E+00	$Y$24*G3 Per Month Per	G3*U3	$Y$12)	F3*($Y$14-G3 Per Month Per User

Fig. 9.14: Cells for column G have the label "ChatGPT Visits."

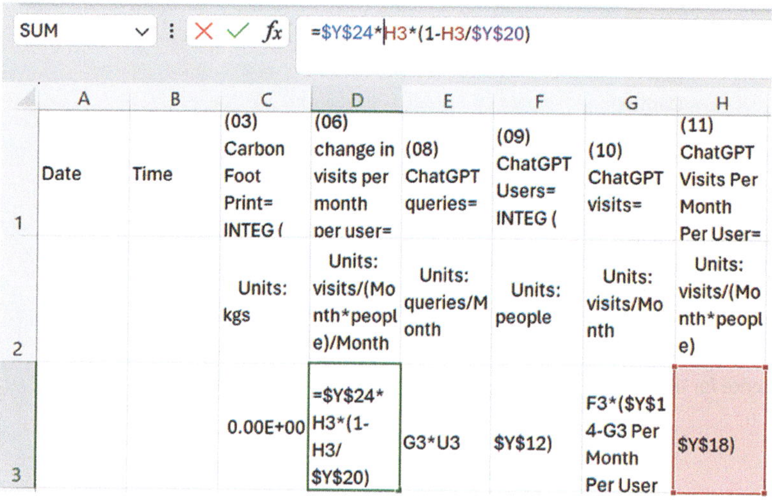
SUM | =$Y$24*H3*(1-H3/$Y$20)

	A	B	C	D	E	F	G	H
1	Date	Time	(03) Carbon Foot Print= INTEG (	(06) change in visits per month per user=	(08) ChatGPT queries=	(09) ChatGPT Users= INTEG (	(10) ChatGPT visits=	(11) ChatGPT Visits Per Month Per User=
2			Units: kgs	Units: visits/(Month*people)/Month	Units: queries/Month	Units: people	Units: visits/Month	Units: visits/(Month*people)
3			0.00E+00	=$Y$24*H3*(1-H3/$Y$20)	G3*U3	$Y$12)	F3*($Y$14-G3 Per Month Per User	$Y$18)

Fig. 9.15: Corrected formula for cell D3.

We continue cleaning up the formula until we have finished row 3 in the model. When we are finished, all the values in row 3 should be numeric (see Fig. 9.16). Notice we have added the initial time in cell B3 and the initial date in cell A3.

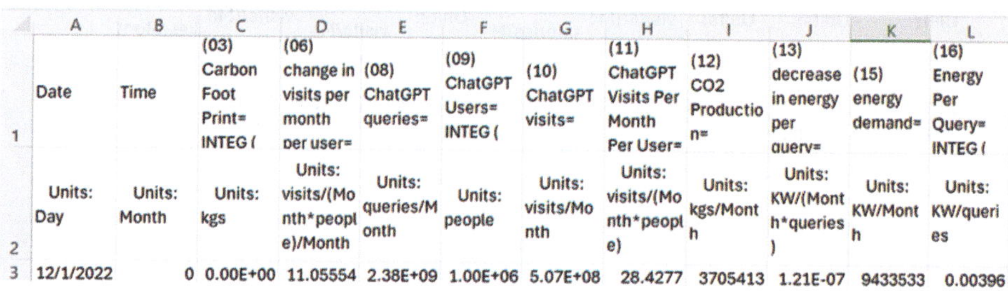

	A	B	C	D	E	F	G	H	I	J	K	L
1	Date	Time	(03) Carbon Foot Print= INTEG (	(06) change in visits per month per user=	(08) ChatGPT queries=	(09) ChatGPT Users= INTEG (	(10) ChatGPT visits=	(11) ChatGPT Visits Per Month Per User=	(12) CO2 Production=	(13) decrease in energy per query=	(15) energy demand=	(16) Energy Per Query= INTEG (
2	Units: Day	Units: Month	Units: kgs	Units: visits/(Month*people)/Month	Units: queries/Month	Units: people	Units: visits/Month	Units: visits/(Month*people)	Units: kgs/Month	Units: KW/(Month*queries)	Units: KW/Month	Units: KW/queries
3	12/1/2022	0	0.00E+00	11.05554	2.38E+09	1.00E+06	5.07E+08	28.4277	3705413	1.21E-07	9433533	0.00396

Fig. 9.16: Numeric values for time 0.

Step 10: Update the Stocks for the First-Time Step Using Euler Integration

Figure 9.17 shows the flow expressed as a cell reference. However, for Euler integration, we need to take the value from the previous time step and add the flow multiplied by the time step, as shown in Fig. 9.18. That is, = C3 + I3 * $Y$3.

	A	B	C
1	Date	Time	(03) Carbon Foot Print= INTEG (
2	Units: Day	Units: Month	Units: kgs
3	12/1/2022	0	0.00E+00
4	12/16/2022	0.5	I3,

Fig. 9.17: Cell reference for a flow.

SUM | fx =C3+I3*$Y$3

	A	B	C	D	E	F	G	H	I
1	Date	Time	(03) Carbon Foot Print= INTEG (	(06) change in visits per month per user=	(08) ChatGPT queries=	(09) ChatGPT Users= INTEG (	(10) ChatGPT visits=	(11) ChatGPT Visits Per Month Per User= INTEG (	(12) CO2 Production=
2	Units: Day	Units: Month	Units: kgs	Units: visits/(Month*people)/Month	Units: queries/Month	Units: people	Units: visits/Month	Units: visits/(Month*people)	Units: kgs/Month
3	12/1/2022	0	0.00E+00	11.05554	2.38E+09	1.00E+06	5.07E+08	28.4277	3705413
4	12/16/2022	0.5	=C3+I3*			Q3,		D3,	
5			$Y$3						

Fig. 9.18: Updating a stock for the first time step.

We repeat this for all of the stocks.

Step 11: Update All the Non-Stock Variables for the First-Time Step

We then update all the non-stock variables for the first-time step by copying and pasting the values in row 3 into row 4 (see Fig. 9.19).

	A	B	C	D	E	F
1	Date	Time	(03) Carbon Foot Print= INTEG (	(06) change in visits per month per user=	(08) ChatGPT queries=	(09) ChatGPT Users= INTEG (
2	Units: Day	Units: Month	Units: kgs	Units: visits/(Month*people)/Month	Units: queries/Month	Units: people
3	12/1/2022	0	0.00E+00	11.05554	2.38E+09	1.00E+06
4	12/16/2022	0.5	1.85E+06	13.05684	0	1.13E+06

Fig. 9.19: Update the non-stock variables for the first time step.

Step 12: Copy and Paste the Values in the First-Time Step (Row 4) Down the Columns

We can complete the model by copying the values in row 4 down the columns (see Figs. 9.20 and 9.21).

	A	B	C	D	E	F	G	H	I	J	K	L	M	N
1	Date	Time	(03) Carbon Foot Print= INTEG (	(06) change in visits per month per user=	(08) ChatGPT queries=	(09) ChatGPT Users= INTEG (	(10) ChatGPT visits=	(11) ChatGPT Visits Per Month Per User= INTEG (	(12) CO2 Production=	(13) decrease in energy per query=	(15) energy demand=	(16) Energy Per Query= INTEG (	(18) fraction efficiency =	(19) fraction renewables=
2	Units: Day	Units: Month	Units: kgs	Units: visits/(Month*people)/Month	Units: queries/Month	Units: people	Units: visits/Month	Units: visits/(Month*people)	Units: kgs/Month	Units: KW/(Month*queries)	Units: KW/Month	Units: KW/queries	Units: fraction	Units: fraction
3	12/1/2022	0	0.00E+00	11.05554	2.38E+09	1.00E+06	5.07E+08	28.4277	3705413	1.21E-07	9433533	0.00396	1	1
4	12/16/2022	0.5	1.85E+06	13.05684	2.71E+09	1.13E+06	5.68E+08	33.9554691	4216826	1.37E-07	10721728	0.0039599	0.999985	1.000015

Fig. 9.20: Copying the values in row 4.

	A	B	C	D	E	F	G	H	I	J	K	L	M	N
1	Date	Time	(03) Carbon Foot Print= INTEG (	(06) change in visits per month per user=	(08) ChatGPT queries=	(09) ChatGPT Users= INTEG (	(10) ChatGPT visits=	(11) ChatGPT Visits Per Month Per User= INTEG (	(12) CO2 Production=	(13) decrease in energy per query=	(15) energy demand=	(16) Energy Per Query= INTEG (	(18) fraction efficiency =	(19) fraction renewables=
2	Units: Day	Units: Month	Units: kgs	Units: visits/(Month*people)/Month	Units: queries/Month	Units: people	Units: visits/Month	Units: visits/(Month*people)	Units: kgs/Month	Units: KW/(Month*queries)	Units: KW/Month	Units: KW/queries	Units: fraction	Units: fraction
3	12/1/2022	0	0.00E+00	11.05554	2.38E+09	1.00E+06	5.07E+08	28.4277	3705413	1.21E-07	9433533	0.00396	1	1
4	12/16/2022	0.5	1.85E+06	13.05684	2.71E+09	1.13E+06	5.68E+08	33.9554691	4216826	1.37E-07	10721728	0.0039599	0.999985	1.000015
5	12/31/2022	1	3.96E+06	15.35816	3.07E+09	1.29E+06	6.36E+08	40.4838872	4785485	1.56E-07	12154121	0.0039599	0.999967	1.000032
6	1/15/2023	1.5	6.35E+06	17.97882	3.47E+09	1.46E+06	7.1E+08	48.1629686	5413770	1.76E-07	13736704	0.0039598	0.999948	1.000052
7	1/30/2023	2	9.06E+06	20.92814	3.91E+09	1.65E+06	7.9E+08	57.1523782	6102694	1.98E-07	15472033	0.0039597	0.999925	1.000074

Fig. 9.21: Pasting the values in row 4 down the columns.

You might wonder: why go through all this instead of just staying in Vensim? There are a few good reasons. In Excel, you can see all your parameters simultaneously, making it easier to manage scenarios without forgetting to reset values. It also aids in debugging, as logic errors are easier to catch when scanning formulas directly. While Excel has its quirks, working this way gives you complete transparency and control, especially when sharing models with others who may not use Vensim.

9.7 Model Calibration

As discussed in Part 1, calibration is a core part of system dynamics modelling. Using publicly available records, we collected time-series data on visits to ChatGPT from December 2022 to December 2024 (see Fig. 9.1) and compared it with the model's values.

To carry out the calibration, we created a worksheet called *DATA* with two primary columns: one for the actual ChatGPT visit values and one for the simulated values generated by the model (from column G in the *Model* worksheet, as shown in Fig. 9.21). We converted the actual and simulated values to millions of visits. For each value, we subtracted the model value from the actual value, squared the difference, and then summed these squared differences across the dataset. The result is a total squared error that reflects how closely the model matches real-world data (see Fig. 9.22).

	A	B	C	D	E
1	DATE	Actual Visits (M)	Model Visits (M)	SE	SSE
2	12/1/2022	153	523	1.37E+05	8.64E+06
3	12/16/2022	209	586	1.42E+05	
4	12/31/2022	266	655	1.52E+05	
5	1/15/2023	441	731	8.39E+04	
6	1/30/2023	616	812	3.84E+04	
7	2/15/2023	808	899	8.30E+03	
8	3/2/2023	1,000	991	7.72E+01	
9	3/17/2023	1,300	1,087	4.52E+04	
10	4/1/2023	1,600	1,186	1.71E+05	

Fig. 9.22: Calculating squared error.

Then we linked the SSEs to the model worksheet and used Solver to find the minimum value (see Fig. 9.23). Figure 9.24 shows the fit.

With the calibrated parameters, we can have confidence in using this model for policy analysis.

AB1 | f_x =Data!$E$2

	X	Y	Z	AA	AB
1	PARAMETER	VALUE	UNITS	SSE	8.64E+06
2	(30) INITIAL TIME = 0	0	Units: Month		
3	(45) TIME STEP = 0.5	0.5	Units: Month [0,?]		
4	(01) ACCEPTABLE CO2 PRODUCTION=	1.23E+08	Units: kgs/Month		
5	(02) ACCEPTABLE ENERGY DEMAND=	3.09E+08	Units: KW/Month		
6	(04) CARBON PER KILOWATT FOR NON RENEWABLES=	0.397	Units: kgs/KW		
7	(05) CARBON PER KILOWATT FOR RENEWABLES=	0	Units: kgs/KW		
8	(07) CHATGPT ADOPTION RATE=	4.36E-10	Units: 1/(Month*people)		
9	(14) EFFICIENCY PRESSURE=	1	Units: Dmnl		
10	(22) INCREASE RATE IN QUERIES PER VISIT=	0.0924485	Units: 1/Month		

Fig. 9.23: Linking the sum of squared error from the data worksheet.

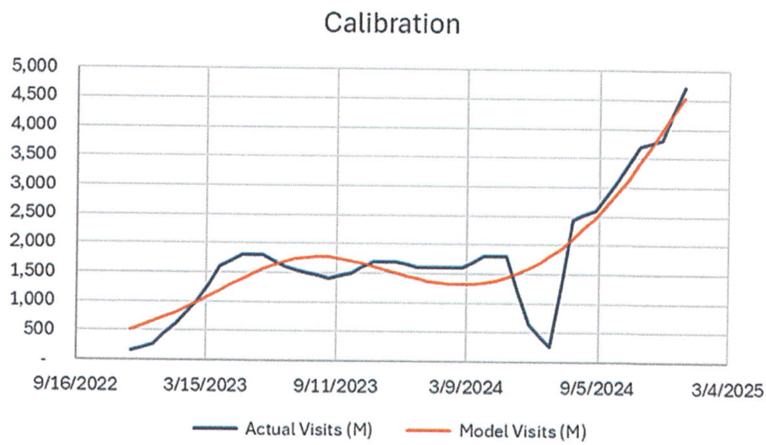

Fig. 9.24: The results of the calibration.

9.8 Policy Results

We developed an interface worksheet that incorporates policy levers, including efficiency pressure (a parameter designed to encourage ChatGPT developers to reduce the energy required per query) and renewables pressure (a parameter that promotes the use of renewable energy sources). Graphs illustrate the trend in CO_2 production in megatons/month, the relative increase in renewable energy production, and the corresponding reduction in energy requirements per query. There are also numerical values of the relative increase in renewable energy and the relative decrease in energy required per query in 2032. Policy analysts can experiment with the pressure to use renewables or reduce the energy needed per query to see how that affects long-term CO_2 emissions. They can also set goals for improvements in renewables and energy reduction, and use the Solver to determine the necessary pressure values to achieve those goals, and then see how that affects CO_2 production. Figure 9.25 shows the interface worksheet.

Fig. 9.25: The interface worksheet.

9.8.1 The Baseline Run

Figure 9.25 shows the baseline run with no pressure on either efficiency or renewables. CO_2 production appears to reach a steady state at 92 megatons/month.

9.8.2 Efficiency Pressure

Figure 9.26 shows the results for efficiency increase goals of 25%, 50%, and 75%; CO_2 production decreases by 26%, 52%, and 78% in 2032 compared to the baseline, respectively.

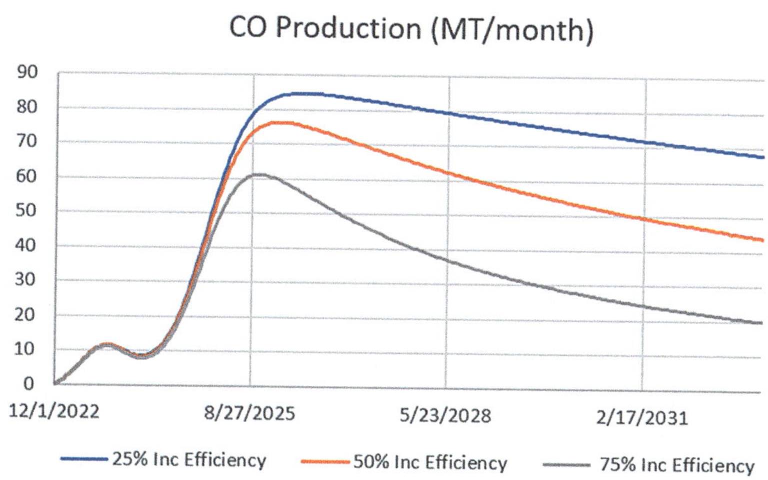

Fig. 9.26: Increasing energy efficiency.

9.8.3 Renewables Pressure

Fig. 9.27 illustrates the results obtained by increasing the use of renewables to 250%, 500%, and 750% of the baseline. CO_2 production decreased by 11%, 22%, and 32%, respectively, in 2032 compared to the baseline.

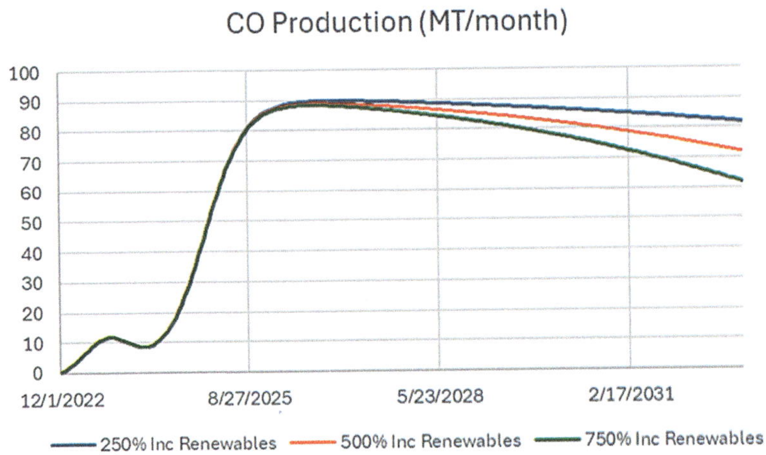

Fig. 9.27: Increasing the use of renewables.

9.9 Conclusion

This case study has demonstrated that Excel is a powerful and accessible platform for building, calibrating, and analysing system dynamics models. While specialized tools like Vensim excel at rapid model construction and visualization, Excel offers transparency, flexibility, and universality that is hard to match. By systematically converting a complex Vensim model into Excel, we have demonstrated that even models with multiple feedback loops and numerous stocks and flows can be effectively implemented in a spreadsheet without compromising structure or clarity.

Excel's strengths lie in its broad accessibility and ease of customization. It allows all model elements (parameters, equations, outputs, and calibration data) to be viewed, modified, and shared without requiring specialized software. This makes it an ideal medium for engaging stakeholders who may not have system dynamics expertise but are comfortable with spreadsheets. Excel also facilitates rigorous scenario testing and sensitivity analysis through built-in tools, such as Solver, while keeping the underlying logic completely transparent for validation and peer review.

Ultimately, the value of using Excel for system dynamics modelling is not in replacing dedicated modelling software, but in complementing it. Excel serves as a universal language for communicating model logic, testing policy scenarios, and involving decision-makers directly in the modelling process. By mastering the translation process from tools like Vensim to Excel, modellers can bridge the gap between technical analysis and practical application, ensuring that system dynamics insights are not only generated but also understood, trusted, and acted upon.

9.10 Discussion Questions

- Why must the model reproduce the ChatGPT visits reference mode before you brief policy options? What constitutes a "minimum viable" fit (e.g. SSE threshold + visual alignment) for decision rights?
- In early growth, do R1 (adoption growth) and R2 (usage per user) overwhelm B1/B2 (saturation/cognitive limits)? Post-inflection, when do B3/B4 (efficiency/clean energy) become material to outcomes? Implications for lever timing.
- What controls (anchored parameter cells, equation transparency, Solver traceability) make Excel a lower-friction delivery vehicle versus Vensim for stakeholder review and audit? Be specific about change control.
- The baseline stabilizes near ~92 megatons CO_2/month. What structural drivers set that plateau, and which real-world signals would trigger model recalibration (grid mix shifts, workload growth, rebound)?
- Compare marginal abatement from efficiency pressure vs. renewables pressure for 2032. Which lever has higher elasticity and why (hardware/algorithmic learning vs. grid decarbonization pace)? Cite chapter evidence.
- How would you detect and mitigate rebound (efficiency boosts → more queries) and market/operational constraints (renewables integration limits) in the workbook and in the narrative?

9.11 Exercises

9.11.1 Structure read-across: Vensim → Excel (ChatGPT model)
Task. Sketch the stock/flow for users, visits/user, queries/visit, energy/query, renewables, and CO_2; map to Excel sheets/ranges (model, parameters, data, and interface).
Deliverable. Screenshots of worksheets with named columns.

9.11.2 Equation ingestion and anchoring
Task. Export equations ("Document All"), paste → transpose, separate parameters (name/value/unit), and convert to anchored cell refs; convert endogenous variable references; clean row-3 time-zero formulas.
Deliverable. Before/after screenshots of the model sheet header rows.

9.11.3 Euler integration correctness
Task. Convert each stock to Euler form (previous + flow * time step) for the first simulated row, then fill down.
Deliverable. Example formulas for two stocks (users and carbon footprint) with comments.

9.11.4 Calibration worksheet (visits)
Task. Build DATA with actual visits vs. model visits (millions), compute pointwise squared errors and total SSE; chart actual vs. model; link SSE into model; set up Solver to minimize SSE over selected calibration parameters.
Deliverable. DATA screenshot (top 20 rows), SSE cell reference, chart image.

9.11.5 Policy interface and scenarios
Task. Create an INTERFACE with inputs for efficiency pressure and renewables pressure, and experiment with various pressure values. Plot CO_2 (megatons/month) versus baseline.
Deliverable. Interface screenshot and single multi-series chart.

9.11.6 One-factor sensitivity (2032 elasticity)
Task. Hold the model at baseline; vary efficiency pressure and renewables pressure independently by the same values. Compute the elasticities of 2032 CO_2.
Deliverable. Small 2×3 table (lever, pressures 0, 1) and a three-sentence interpretation.

9.11.7 Executive one-pager (board-pack ready)
Task. Draft 150–200 words: problem statement, method (Excel SD and SSE calibration), baseline (~92 megatons/month), levered outcomes (efficiency vs. renewables), and a governance recommendation (phased targets and recalibration cadence).
Deliverable. One-page executive brief.

Chapter 10
Eco-efficient Dairy Waste Treatment

10.1 Learning Objectives

- Articulate the business problem and sustainability opportunity in dairy waste, and why Excel is a pragmatic delivery vehicle for system dynamics models.
- Describe the feedback architecture that links herd dynamics, waste generation, treatment, and revenue.
- Explain the translation from Vensim structure to Excel implementation and the role of lookup tables for birthing/culling behaviour.
- Build and calibrate an Excel model using the sum of squared errors (SSEs) against time-series data for cows and calves, and interpret alignment graphs.
- Configure and run policy scenarios with phased parameter changes and read financial outcomes.
- Diagnose counterintuitive results as potential market saturation/diminishing returns and communicate guardrails.
- Summarize policy insights: Phased strategies outperform one-shot maximization, and matching capacity to market demand ensures stable economic outcomes.

10.2 Introduction

System dynamics is powerful. It helps us understand how complex systems behave over time – how changes ripple through feedback loops, trigger delays, and produce outcomes that often defy intuition. But power isn't the same as practicality. For many decision-makers, farm managers, and policy teams, advanced modelling software like Vensim can be a barrier: unfamiliar, expensive, or just not part of the everyday toolkit.

That's where Excel comes in.

Excel may not appear to be a simulation tool, but with a proper structure, it can be transformed into one. It offers a clear, customizable platform for building transparent, testable, and easy-to-adapt system dynamics models. More importantly, Excel is already widely used across agriculture, business, and government, eliminating the need for new software and a steep learning curve.

This chapter shows how Excel turns a system dynamics model from an academic exercise into a practical decision-support tool [41]. By translating a complex dairy waste management system into Excel, we make it accessible for anyone who needs to understand, test, and improve how waste is handled on the ground. Excel makes system dynamics real, whether you're optimizing policy, analysing trade-offs, or just trying to turn waste into value.

https://doi.org/10.1515/9783111541389-012

10.3 Problem Definition

Poor dairy waste management is a significant environmental issue, particularly in developing regions that lack adequate disposal systems. Standard methods, such as landfilling or open dumping, release harmful greenhouse gases and reduce the potential value of organic waste. The good news. With proper treatment, dairy waste can be converted into valuable products, such as biofertilizers and biogas. These reduce environmental damage and create new revenue streams.

This case study employs a system dynamics model to investigate various waste management options for a mid-sized dairy farm. It examines how improved waste collection, the choice between biofertilizer and biogas production, and targeted policy support can impact profits and emissions. The goal is to find the sweet spot, where sustainability and financial performance meet. The model is a practical tool for farm operators and policymakers seeking to adopt more sustainable agricultural practices.

10.4 Reference Mode

Two graphs illustrate changes in the farm's cow and calf numbers over 3 years. The first graph (Fig. 10.1) tracks the number of cows, starting at 465 in year 1 and increasing, albeit with numerous fluctuations, to 546 by year 3. The second graph (Fig. 10.2) shows the number of calves. It starts at 265, dips slightly in the first year (a classic "worse before better" pattern), then climbs sharply before peaking and dropping off a bit in year 3.

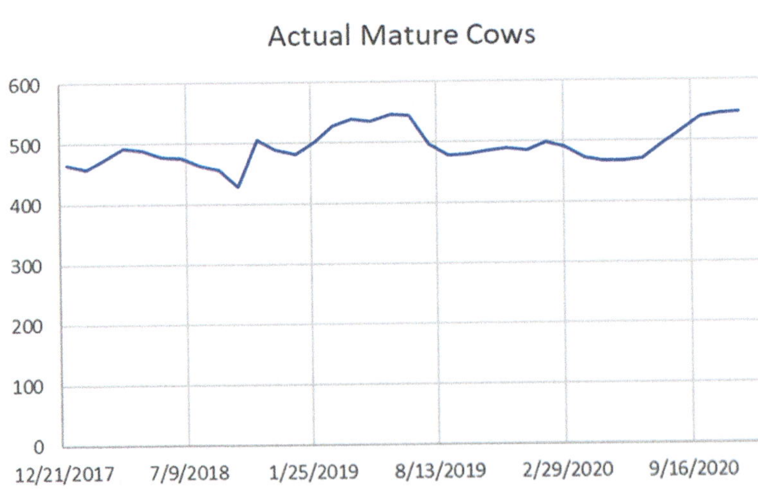

Fig. 10.1: Number of mature cows over time.

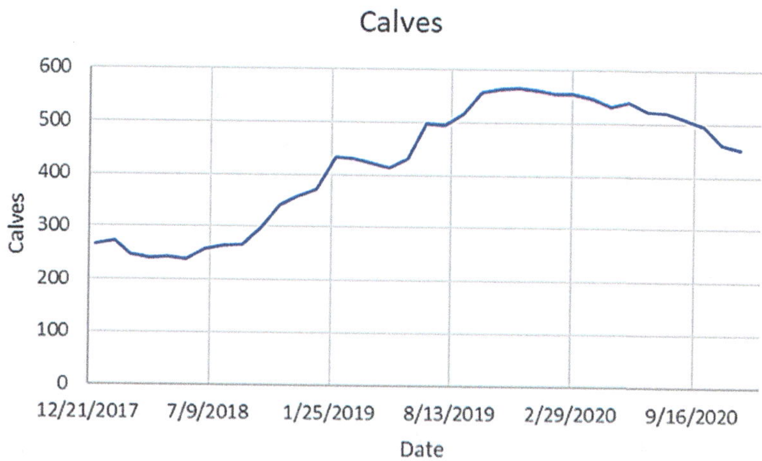

Fig. 10.2: Number of calves over time.

10.5 Dynamic Hypothesis

The system's behaviour is driven by a mix of closely connected feedback loops that reinforce and balance each other. These loops impact herd growth, the amount of waste produced, and the effectiveness with which that waste is converted into usable resources (see Fig. 10.3).

The core of the livestock system is a reinforcing loop (R1): more mature cows result in more calves, and over time, those calves mature into cows, further expanding the herd. This loop drives long-term growth.

But that growth doesn't go unchecked. A balancing loop (B1) kicks in as the herd expands; more mature cows also mean more culling, which brings the herd size back down. Together, these two loops (growth and control) create the fluctuating herd patterns we saw earlier in Figs. 10.1 and 10.2.

Herd size also directly affects the amount of dairy waste produced. More cows and calves mean more waste, which activates another set of balancing loops focussed on managing it.

Balancing loop B2 handles biofertilizer production. As waste accumulates, it is processed into biofertilizer, reducing untreated waste. B3 centres on raw dung waste, which is diverted into raw dung output, helping to reduce the backlog. B4 works the same way, but with biogas. More waste means more biogas production, thereby reducing the volume of leftover waste.

All three waste treatment paths (biofertilizer, biogas, and raw dung) feed into revenue generation. The more these outputs expand, the greater the income they generate. That financial return reinforces the value of treating waste properly and encourages further investment in treatment systems.

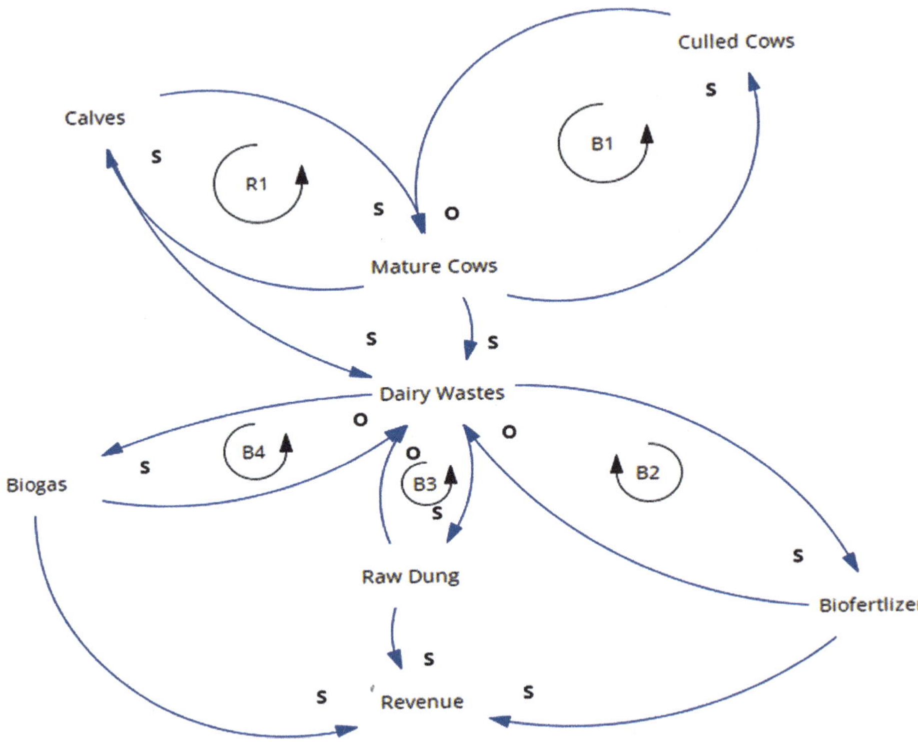

Fig. 10.3: Causal loop diagram of the dairy waste system.

This setup helps explain the system's behaviour over time: the early spike in calves, the eventual herd stabilization, and the rise in recovered resources. The takeaway is clear: to achieve both environmental and economic benefits, you must manage the herd sustainably and optimize waste treatment.

10.6 Model Formulation

10.6.1 The Vensim Model

Figure 10.4 shows the stock-and-flow structure of the system dynamics model built in Vensim. It maps out how the herd grows and shrinks over time, how dairy waste is produced, and how it is treated through biofertilizer, biogas, and raw dung. The model incorporates key feedback loops for reproduction, culling, waste processing, and revenue generation, enabling us to simulate the system's environmental and financial performance over time.

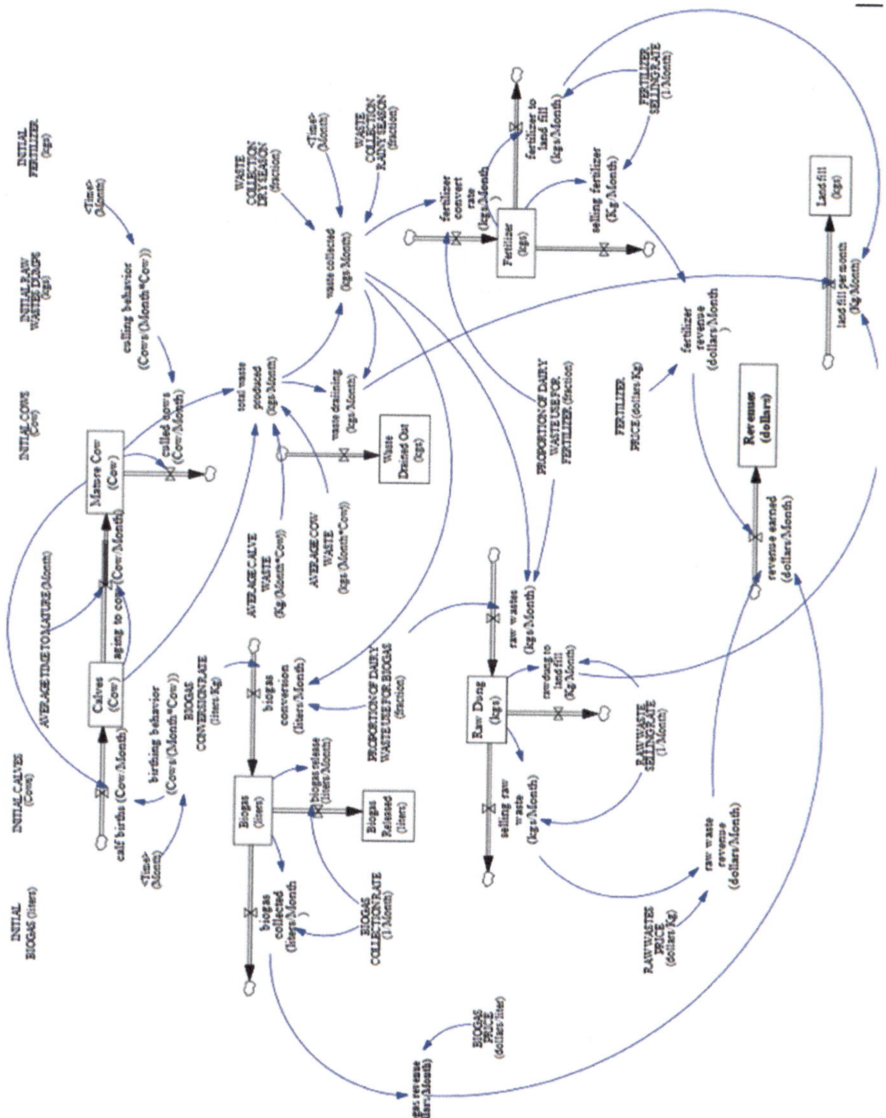

Fig. 10.4: Stock-and-flow diagram from the Vensim model.

10.6.2 The Excel Model

As in Chapter 9, we translated the Vensim model into Excel using the same step-by-step approach. While we don't walk through the conversion process here, the following few figures show the final result.

Figures 10.5–10.7 display the Excel version of the system dynamics model. It follows the same structure as the original Vensim model, capturing the key stock-and-flow relationships, herd growth, waste generation, and how that waste is converted into revenue-generating streams, such as biofertilizer, biogas, and raw dung.

	A	B	C	D	E	F	G	H	I	J	K	L
1	Time	(01) aging to cow=	(05) Biogas= INTEG (	(06) biogas collected =	(08) biogas conversion=	(11) biogas release=	(12) Biogas Released = INTEG (	(13) biogas revenue=	(14) birthing behavior = WITH LOOKUP (	(15) calf births=	(16) Calves= INTEG (	(17) culled cows=
2	Month	Cow/Month	liters	liters/Month	liters/Month	liters/Month	liters	dollars/ Month	Cows/Cow/Month	Cow/Month	Cow	Cow/Month
3	0	14.72222	0	0	115.479	0	0	0	0	0	265	2.79
4	0.25	14.51775	28.86975	20.20883	116.0164	8.660925	0	0.060626	0.002458	1.150458	261.3194	3.665867
5	0.5	14.33209	50.65642	35.45949	116.5054	15.19693	2.165231	0.106378	0.004917	2.314255	257.9776	4.550062
6	0.75	14.16518	67.11867	46.98307	116.9465	20.1356	5.964463	0.140949	0.007375	3.489419	254.9732	5.441128
7	1	14.0169	79.57562	55.70294	117.3403	23.87269	10.99836	0.167109	0.009833	4.674005	252.3042	6.337634

Fig. 10.5: Endogenous variables in the dairy waste model (set 1).

	A	M	N	O	P	Q	R	S	T	U	V	W
1	Time	(18) culling behavior = WITH LOOKUP (	(19) Fertilizer = INTEG (	(20) fertilizer convert rate=	(22) fertilizer revenue=	(24) fertilizer to land fill=	(32) Land fill= INTEG (	(33) land fill per month=	(34) Mature Cow= INTEG (	(37) Raw Dung= INTEG (	(38) raw dung to land fill=	(39) raw waste revenue=
2	Month	Cows/Cow/Month	kgs	kgs/Month	dollars/ Month	kgs/Month	kgs	Kg/Month	Cow	kgs	Kg/Month	dollars/ Month
3	0	0.006	55000	179634	1732.5	5500	0	180580	465	20000	4000	320
4	0.25	0.007833	86158.5	180470	2713.993	8615.85	45145	185416.7	467.9831	24623.25	4924.65	393.972
5	0.5	0.009667	109736.4	181230.6	3456.696	10973.64	91499.17	189201.3	470.696	28135.47	5627.095	450.1676
6	0.75	0.0115	127609.9	181916.8	4019.713	12760.99	138799.5	192177.1	473.1415	30810.39	6162.078	492.9662
7	1	0.013333	141186.6	182529.3	4447.379	14118.66	186843.8	194526.7	475.3225	32853.33	6570.667	525.6533

Fig. 10.6: Endogenous variables in the dairy waste model (set 2).

A	X	Y	Z	AA	AB	AC	AD	AE	AF
Time	(41) raw wastes=	(43) revenue earned=	(44) Revenues= INTEG (	(46) selling fertilizer =	(47) selling raw waste=	(49) total waste produced =	(50) waste collected =	(53) waste draining=	(54) Waste Drained Out= INTEG (
Month	kgs/Month	dollars/ Month	dollars	Kg/Month	kgs/Month	kgs/Month	kgs/Month	kgs/Month	kgs
0	38493	2052.5	0	49500	16000	427700	256620	171080	0
0.25	38672.14	3108.025	513.125	77542.65	19698.6	429690.5	257814.3	171876.2	42770
0.5	38835.14	3906.97	1290.131	98762.74	22508.38	431501.5	258900.9	172600.6	85739.05
0.75	38982.16	4512.82	2266.874	114848.9	24648.31	433135.1	259881.1	173254.1	128889.2
1	39113.42	4973.2	3395.079	127068	26282.67	434593.5	260756.1	173837.4	172202.7

Fig. 10.7: Endogenous variables in the dairy waste model (set 3).

Figure 10.8 displays the input parameters used in the model.

AG	AH	AI
PARAMETER	VALUE	UNITS
(31) INITIAL TIME =	0	Month
(48) TIME STEP =	0.25	Month
(02) AVERAGE CALVE WASTE=	140	Kg/Cow/Month
(03) AVERAGE COW WASTE=	840	kgs/(Cow*Month)
(04) AVERAGE TIME TO MATURE=	18	Month
(07) BIOGAS COLLECTION RATE=	0.7	liters/liters/Month
(09) BIOGAS CONVERSION RATE=	40	liters/Kg
(10) BIOGAS PRICE=	0.003	dollars/liter
(21) FERTILIZER PRICE=	0.035	dollars/Kg
(23) FERTILIZER SELLING RATE=	0.9	Kg/Kg/Month
(26) INITIAL BIOGAS=	0	liters
(27) INITIAL CALVES=	265	Cows
(28) INITIAL COWS=	465	Cow
(29) INITIAL FERTILIZER=	55000	kgs
(30) INITIAL RAW WASTES DUMPS=	20000	kgs
(35) PROPORTION OF DAIRY WASTE USE FOR BIOGAS=	0.15	fraction
(36) PROPORTION OF DAIRY WASTE USE FOR FERTILIZER=	0.7	fraction
(40) RAW WASTE SELLING RATE=	0.8	Kg/Kg/Month
(42) RAW WASTES PRICE=	0.02	dollars/Kg
(51) WASTE COLLECTION DRY SEASON=	0.6	fraction
(52) WASTE COLLECTION RAINY SEASON=	0.5	fraction

Fig. 10.8: Parameters for baseline run of the model in the interface worksheet.

Figure 10.9 shows the initial lookup table for birthing and culling behaviour.

AJ	AK	AL
Time,	(15) birthing behavior	(19) culling behavior
Month	Cows/Cow/Month	Cows/Cow/Month
0	0.05	0.05
6	0.05	0.05
12	0.05	0.05
18	0.05	0.05
24	0.05	0.05
30	0.05	0.05
36	0.05	0.05

Fig. 10.9: Lookup table for birthing and culling rates.

10.7 Calibration

Next, we calibrate the model by adjusting the values in the lookup table to find the best fit with the actual time-series data for calves and mature cows. Figure 10.10 shows how we set up squared-error minimization to do this.

Figure 10.11 illustrates the lookup table results of minimizing the total sum of squared errors.

Figures 10.12 and 10.13 illustrate the model's alignment with the time-series data for calves and mature cows after minimizing the total squared error.

	A	B	C	D	E	F	G	H	I	J
1	Date	Actual Calves	Model Calves	SE	SSE	Actual Mature Cows	Model Mature Cows	SSE	SSE	TSSE
2	1/1/2018	265	265	0	694436.7	465	465	0	348461.7	1042898
3	2/1/2018	272.5	273.5278	1.056327		457	456.4722	0.278549		
4	3/1/2018	246.5	281.1554	1200.997		474	448.8446	632.7942		
5	4/1/2018	240	287.9779	2301.878		492	442.0221	2497.789		
6	5/1/2018	243	294.0802	2609.189		488	435.9198	2712.349		
7	6/1/2018	237.5	299.5384	3848.766		477	430.4616	2165.825		
8	7/1/2018	257.5	304.4205	2201.531		476	425.5795	2542.224		
9	8/1/2018	262.5	308.7872	2142.505		463	421.2128	1746.17		
10	9/1/2018	266	312.693	2180.236		456	417.307	1497.148		
11	10/1/2018	298.5	316.1865	312.8128		428	413.8135	201.2572		
12	11/1/2018	341	319.3113	470.4009		506	410.6887	9084.239		
13	12/1/2018	358	322.1062	1288.365		488	407.8938	6417.002		

Fig. 10.10: Calibration setup showing the first 12 months: squared error minimization.

AJ	AK	AL	AM
Time,	(15) birthing behavior	(19) culling behavior	
Month	Cows/Cow/Month	Cows/Cow/Month	TSE
0	0.00	0.01	17506.77
6	0.07	0.05	
12	0.08	0.00	
18	0.09	0.08	
24	0.06	0.07	
30	0.04	0.04	
36	0.02	0.02	

Fig. 10.11: Optimized lookup table values after calibration.

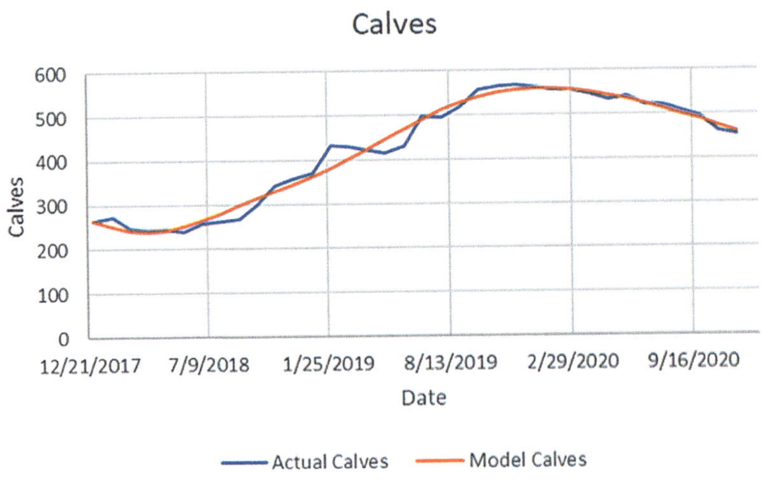

Fig. 10.12: Calibration result: modelled calves versus historical data.

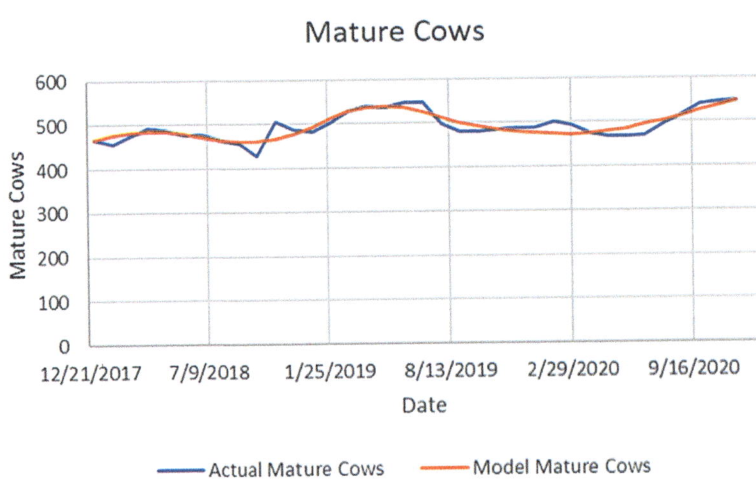

Fig. 10.13: Calibration result: modelled mature cows versus historical data.

10.8 Base Run Analysis

Waste revenue depends on waste collection, which is not entirely based on the number of cows and calves. The rainy season will impact the farm's ability to collect waste. Figure 10.14 illustrates the results of the baseline run, highlighting how the rainy season affects farmers' ability to collect dairy waste and, in turn, impacts their revenue.

Fig. 10.14: Base run results showing the impact of the rainy season.

10.9 Policy Runs and Sensitivity Analysis

To explore the potential benefits of improved dairy waste management, we conducted a series of policy scenarios that gradually enhance waste collection and expand biogas production capacity. These simulations reflect realistic, step-by-step changes that could be introduced over time through policy support rather than sudden, large-scale shifts. Table 10.1 outlines the setup for these runs.

Tab. 10.1: Scenario input parameters for policy phases.

Parameter	Baseline	Phase 1	Phase 2	Phase 3	Phase 4	Phase 5
Waste collection, dry season	0.2	0.4	0.6	0.75	0.85	0.95
Waste collection, rainy season	0.17	0.3	0.5	0.6	0.7	0.8
Proportion of waste to biogas	0.05	0.1	0.15	0.2	0.25	0.3
Proportion of waste to fertilizer	0.8	0.75	0.7	0.65	0.6	0.55
Biogas collection rate	0.5	0.6	0.7	0.8	0.9	0.95
Fertilizer selling rate	1.0	0.95	0.9	0.85	0.8	0.75
Raw dung selling rate	0.9	0.85	0.8	0.75	0.7	0.65

We defined six phases, each with gradual changes across key parameters, to implement the phased transition. Waste collection rates increase gradually, rising from 20% to 95% during the dry season and from 17% to 80% during the rainy season by phase 5. The share of collected waste used for biogas production increases from 5% to 30%, while the portion used for fertilizer decreases from 80% to 55%. This shift reflects a strategic move towards energy recovery. At the same time, biogas collection efficiency improved from 50% to 95%, which aligns with the infrastructure upgrades.

We also factored in market conditions. As more waste is collected and processed, the selling rates for raw dung and fertilizer gradually fall, with raw dung dropping from 0.9 to 0.65 and fertilizer from 1.0 to 0.75. This simulates a saturation effect in local markets, underscoring the need to diversify or expand their use.

To manage the scenario analysis, we used a dedicated worksheet called *"Scenarios,"* where parameter values for each policy phase are organized in a structured table (see Tab. 10.1). These values are displayed in columns N to S in Fig. 10.15. To run a specific scenario, we copy and paste its values into column U, which is linked to the Interface worksheet for simulation.

M	N	O	P	Q	R	S		T	U	V
Parameter	Baseline	Phase 1	Phase 2	Phase 3	Phase 4	Phase 5		SCENARIO PARAMETERS	VALUE	UNITS
Waste Collection Dry Season	0.2	0.4	0.6	0.75	0.85	0.95	(51)	WASTE COLLECTION DRY SEASON=	0.2	Units: fraction
Waste Collection Rainy Season	0.17	0.3	0.5	0.6	0.7	0.8	(52)	WASTE COLLECTION RAINY SEASON=	0.17	Units: fraction
Proportion of Waste to Biogas	0.05	0.1	0.15	0.2	0.25	0.3	(35)	PROPORTION OF DAIRY WASTE USE FOR BIOGAS=	0.05	Units: fraction
Proportion of Waste to Fertilizer	0.8	0.75	0.7	0.65	0.6	0.55	(36)	PROPORTION OF DAIRY WASTE USE FOR FERTILIZER=	0.8	Units: fraction
Biogas Collection Rate	0.5	0.6	0.7	0.8	0.9	0.95	(07)	BIOGAS COLLECTION RATE=	0.5	Units: 1/Month
Fertilizer Selling Rate	1	0.95	0.9	0.85	0.8	0.75	(23)	FERTILIZER SELLING RATE=	1	Units: 1/Month
Raw Dung Selling Rate	0.9	0.85	0.8	0.75	0.7	0.65	(40)	RAW WASTE SELLING RATE=	0.9	Units: 1/Month

Fig. 10.15: Scenario parameter table in the scenarios worksheet.

Columns A and B of the Scenarios worksheet display the simulation results directly linked to the Model worksheet (see Fig. 10.16).

B3 fx =Model!Y3

	A	B	C	D	E	F	G	H	I	J	K
1	Time	(43) revenue earned=			Time	Baseline	Phase 1	Phase 2	Phase 3	Phase 4	Phase 5
2	Month	dollars/Month			Month						
3	0	$2,285			0	$2,285	$2,169	$2,053	$1,936	$1,820	$1,704
4	0.25	$2,370			0.25	$2,370	$2,802	$3,108	$3,183	$3,083	$2,943
5	0.5	$2,437			0.5	$2,437	$3,282	$3,906	$4,126	$4,037	$3,878
6	0.75	$2,489			0.75	$2,489	$3,646	$4,510	$4,838	$4,758	$4,586
7	1	$2,530			1	$2,530	$3,923	$4,968	$5,379	$5,305	$5,122
8	1.25	$2,563			1.25	$2,563	$4,133	$5,315	$5,788	$5,720	$5,529
9	1.5	$2,589			1.5	$2,589	$4,294	$5,580	$6,100	$6,035	$5,838
10	1.75	$2,610			1.75	$2,610	$4,418	$5,782	$6,338	$6,275	$6,073
11	2	$2,627			2	$2,627	$4,512	$5,936	$6,519	$6,458	$6,253

Fig. 10.16: Simulation results setup for scenario comparison.

For each scenario, we copy the simulation results and paste them into the designated columns using Paste Special > Values. We also update the column label in row 1 to reflect the scenario name. For example, the baseline results from column B were copied and pasted into column F. This process is repeated for each scenario, filling columns G through K before plotting the results, as shown in Fig. 10.17.

Figure 10.17 shows a steady increase in monthly waste revenue across the different policy phases. As waste collection improves and more waste is directed towards

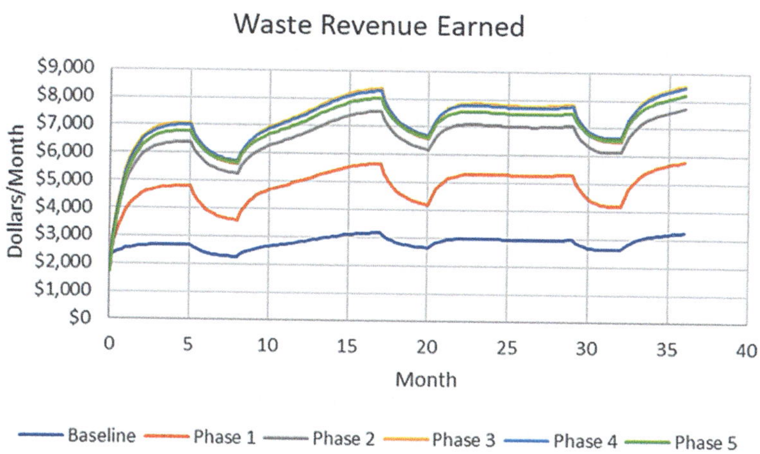

Fig. 10.17: Monthly waste revenue by scenario phase.

biogas production, revenue climbs from about $2,500 per month in the baseline scenario to nearly $8,500 in the most advanced phase. Phase 1 shows a noticeable improvement, reaching around $4,500 per month, while phases 2 through 5 see the most significant gains, all generating more than $6,000 per month.

One surprising result stands out: phase 5, despite having the highest waste collection and processing rates, generates slightly less revenue than phase 3 (see Fig. 10.18). At first glance, this doesn't make sense; you'd expect more waste processed to mean more income. However, the model suggests a more complex picture. This drop could be due to diminishing returns, local market saturation, or nonlinear effects between the amount of waste collected, the amount of product generated, and the amount that can be sold.

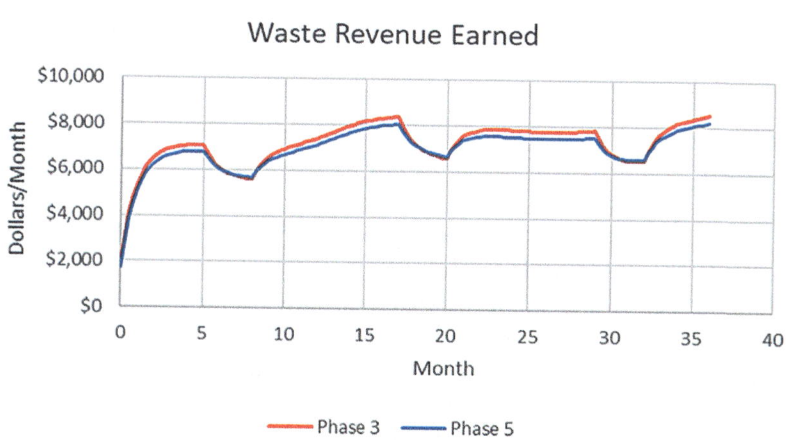

Fig. 10.18: Monthly waste revenue phases 3 and 5.

This highlights an important point: More isn't always better. Simply pushing for maximum output won't guarantee higher profits if the market can't absorb the extra supply or system dynamics introduce bottlenecks elsewhere.

Still, the overall trend is clear. A phased approach to policy that gradually improves collection, expands biogas production, and adapts to market constraints can yield strong financial results. The key is matching infrastructure investments with innovative waste management and diversified product end uses.

10.10 Policy Insights

This case study shows that a phased approach to dairy waste management can deliver substantial economic and environmental benefits. Gradually ramping up waste collection and shifting more processing towards biogas leads to higher monthly revenue, improved resource utilization, and reduced dependence on traditional disposal methods. The model clarifies that even when infrastructure upgrades are implemented over time, investments in collection and anaerobic digestion can yield significant returns and support the transition towards a circular bioeconomy.

However, the analysis also flags a critical caution. In phase 5, the most aggressive scenario, revenue levels off or even dips slightly. This may seem unexpected, but it highlights a fundamental issue: pushing the system too far can lead to diminishing returns. This can happen when product supply outpaces market demand or operational inefficiencies arise at higher volumes.

The key takeaway is that bigger isn't always better. Waste processing capacity must match actual demand for outputs such as fertilizer and biogas. For policy to be effective, it should be flexible, based on market feedback, and paced to accommodate investments, while offering a mix of end-use options. In short, a phased, data-driven strategy (rather than a one-size-fits-all solution) is the most reliable path to sustainable dairy waste management.

10.11 Conclusion

Building the system dynamics model in Excel was one of the most valuable parts of this case study. While Vensim helped structure the model in the early stages, Excel enabled calibration to real-world data. It facilitated the easy testing of phased policy scenarios by directly linking parameters to the interface.

One of the greatest strengths of system dynamics modelling is its ability to uncover counterintuitive results; outcomes that don't align with initial expectations but emerge from the system's internal structure. In this case study, for example, the drop in revenue during the most aggressive policy phase might initially seem surprising. But the model helps explain why it happens, revealing how feedback loops, time delays, and market constraints interact in ways that aren't always obvious. These insights are exactly why system dynamics is so valuable for complex decision-making; it helps policymakers and practitioners avoid unintended consequences by making the underlying system behaviour more transparent.

Using Excel brought several key advantages. It made the model more accessible and easier to understand, especially for stakeholders unfamiliar with specialized simulation tools. Since Excel is already widely used in agricultural management and policy settings, it was a practical choice for exploring system behaviour, adjusting assumptions, and running sensitivity tests in a user-friendly way.

Ultimately, the Excel version helped turn system dynamics from a theoretical tool into a practical one. Combining solid modelling with a familiar platform supports data-driven decisions that can enhance the environmental and economic performance of dairy waste management.

10.12 Discussion Questions

- What stakeholder risks arise if we present policy scenarios without first calibrating to herd time series? What's the minimum acceptable fit evidence?
- Which loop(s) dominate in each regime: rapid herd growth versus stabilization versus revenue scale-up? And how does that inform policy phasing?
- Why are lookup tables appropriate for birthing/culling here, and what governance (bounds, smoothness) should constrain them during SSE minimization?
- How do rainy-season constraints propagate to revenue outcomes, and what operating policies hedge that risk?
- Phase 5 underperforms Phases 3 and 4 in terms of revenue. What structural mechanisms (price erosion, saturation, and non-linear yields) could explain this, and what tests would you run next?
- When expanding biogas, what's the right pace of capacity deployment relative to collection and market absorption? Cite chapter insights.

10.13 Exercises

10.13.1 Structure read-across: Vensim → Excel
Task. Sketch the herd–waste–revenue stock/flow on paper, then list the Excel sheets you need (Model, Parameters, Lookups, and Interface).
Deliverable. One slide (diagram).

10.13.2 Lookup-based calibration

Task. Build lookup tables for birthing/culling. Create actual versus model and SE columns for calves and cows; compute total SSE and adjust lookup values to reduce error (manual pass or Solver).
Deliverable. Screenshot of the first 15 rows and SSE cell(s).

10.13.3 Scenario worksheet

Task. Recreate the Scenarios sheet with parameter blocks for baseline and phases 1–5 (collection, treatment shares, efficiencies, and selling rates). Set up copy → paste-values into a live "Current Scenario" column feeding the model.
Deliverable. Scenarios sheet screenshot and brief runbook (three to five bullets).

10.13.4 Rainy-season stress

Task. Introduce a rainy-season collection modifier. Plot monthly revenue by phase.
Deliverable. Chart and two-line interpretation of seasonality impact.

10.13.5 Counterintuitive outcome replication

Task. Reproduce the phase 5 < phase 3/4 revenue outcome. Run a one-factor sensitivity on selling rates and biogas share to test a saturation hypothesis.
Deliverable. Small table (parameter → change in revenue) and three-sentence root-cause note.

10.13.6 Portfolio policy design

Task. Propose a three-stage rollout (parameters, target outcomes, risks, and metrics). Ensure capacity adds are matched to demand signals.
Deliverable. One-page policy brief (bulleted).

10.13.7 Executive one-pager

Task. Draft 150–200 words: problem, method (Excel SD and calibration), key results, "why phase 5 dips," and your governance recommendation.
Deliverable. Text for a board pack.

Chapter 11
The Syrian Refugee Crisis

11.1 Learning Objectives

- Frame a humanitarian displacement problem as a stock-flow system with reinforcing and balancing loops.
- Translate your Vensim conceptual model into a maintainable Excel implementation (parameters, endogenous variables, and interface).
- Build lookup functions to represent humanitarian displacement policy/behavioural nonlinearity.
- Prepare humanitarian displacement reference modes and define an Excel sum of squared error (SSE) objective across multiple series.
- Calibrate with Solver under realism constraints and interpret actual versus model charts for fit quality and structural adequacy.
- Run a humanitarian displacement baseline and identify counterintuitive dynamics by tracing loop dominance.
- Design and analyse policy simulations to quantify their impacts.
- Communicate a stakeholder-ready brief: problem framing, data sources, fit evidence, scenario deltas, operational risks, and subsequent actions.

11.2 Introduction

The Syrian refugee crisis is one of the most challenging and heartbreaking humanitarian disasters in recent memory. Since civil unrest broke out in 2011, more than 13 million Syrians, over half the country's pre-war population, had been forced to leave their homes. Many fled to nearby countries, such as Turkey, Lebanon, and Jordan, placing a massive strain on local resources and infrastructure. Even with significant efforts from the UN and various non-governmental organizations, the sheer scale and complexity of the crisis have pushed traditional policy responses to their limits.

What makes this situation especially challenging is its unpredictability and complexity. Refugee flows don't follow a neat pattern. They're shaped by everything from outbreaks of violence and shifting perceptions of safety to international aid, local policies, and global politics. It's a dynamic, constantly changing system with feedback loops and time delays that standard analysis tools can't handle.

That's where system dynamics comes in [42]. It's a better fit for understanding systems like this, where everything affects everything else. In this chapter, we walk through a system dynamics model of the Syrian refugee crisis, built in Excel. The model tracks how people move through three main stages: staying in Syria, becoming refugees, or im-

https://doi.org/10.1515/9783111541389-013

migrating elsewhere. It also includes sub-models for conflict levels, refugee flows, and policy responses, such as how immigration caps or peacekeeping missions might evolve.

Initially developed in Vensim and rebuilt in Excel, the model shows how familiar tools can simulate real-world, high-stake crises. It also provides a means to explore "what if" scenarios and test various interventions. For policymakers, humanitarian workers, and analysts, this model can be a powerful tool for making more informed and thoughtful decisions amid ongoing chaos.

11.3 Problem Definition

The Syrian refugee crisis didn't happen overnight; it's the result of a long, brutal civil war that started with protests in 2011 and spiralled into a full-blown conflict involving multiple factions and foreign powers. The fighting has destroyed homes, wiped out infrastructure, and left millions of people with no choice but to flee. Many ended up in neighbouring countries or further abroad, often risking everything to find safety.

The problem is that most host countries weren't ready for this kind of mass displacement. Systems already under pressure, such as housing, employment, education, and healthcare, are now being stretched to their limits. Aid organizations have stepped in, but the number of people needing help is growing faster than the resources available to support them.

What makes this even more challenging is how everything is connected. Conflict causes people to flee, straining host countries. That can lead to political backlash, tighter immigration policies, or reduced aid. On the other hand, peacekeeping efforts, repatriation initiatives, or global resettlement programmes can help calm things down if they're rolled out quickly and at the correct scale.

System dynamics is particularly effective in making sense of complex systems, where feedback loops and time delays can create unexpected consequences. It helps us examine how violence, displacement, the growth of refugee camps, and policy choices interact. Instead of just reacting year to year, this approach allows us to explore long-term outcomes, 30 years down the line, based on the decisions we make today.

This kind of modelling offers a clearer view of the bigger picture for policymakers, aid workers, and researchers trying to make sense of the chaos. It's not just about tracking numbers; it's about understanding the cause-and-effect relationships that shape the future.

11.4 Reference Mode

To build and test the model, we first needed to understand how the Syrian conflict and refugee crisis have evolved. That meant identifying reference modes, basically, time-series patterns that show how key parts of the system have behaved in the past. These patterns help us set expectations for how things might evolve.

One of the most valuable indicators we examined was the number of battles over time. Battles are a direct indication of the intensity of the conflict and a significant factor in people's decisions to flee. More fighting usually means more people leaving. Tracking the battle trend provided a good starting point for shaping the conflict part of the model.

Figure 11.1 shows this clearly. Battle numbers spiked in the early years of the war, particularly around 2013–2014. That's when things escalated from isolated protests into a messy, multi-front war involving rebel groups, the Syrian regime, and outside countries. After that peak, battle frequency started to drop as the Syrian government regained control of the territory. Scattered violence continued in various areas, even as the major battles subsided. Overall, the data show a sharp rise, a short plateau, and then a slow decline, precisely the kind of multi-phase pattern we need to calibrate the conflict dynamics in the model.

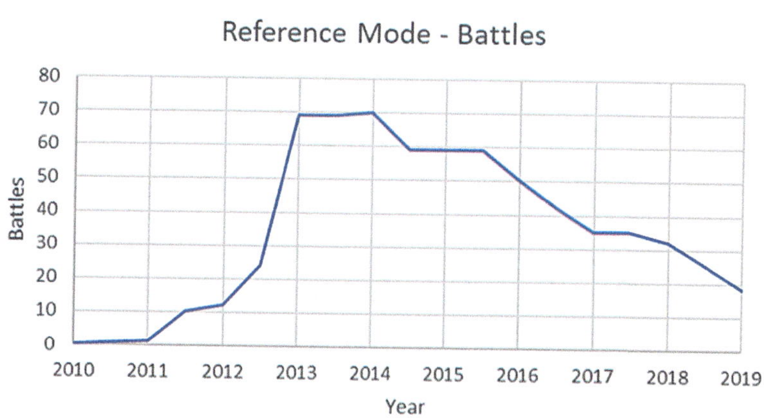

Fig. 11.1: Battle reference mode over time.

Next, Fig. 11.2 shows how Syria's population changed during the same period. The population fell by millions, reflecting the scale of the crisis. The curve shows a steady exponential decline, which we used to guide the handling of population loss in the model.

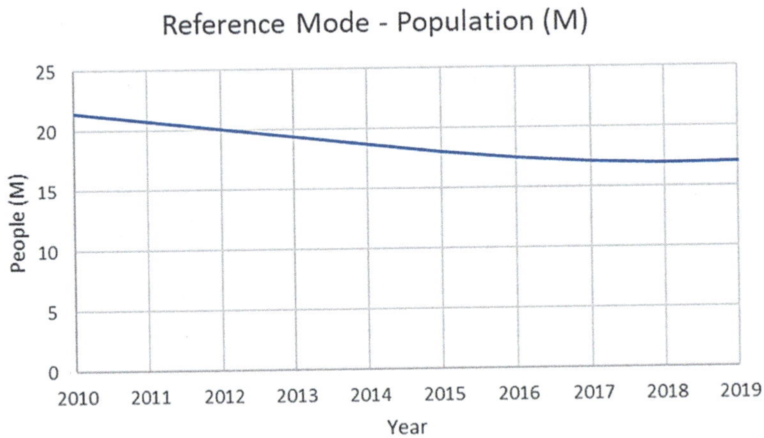

Fig. 11.2: Decline of the Syrian population over time.

Figure 11.3 tracks deaths tied to both the protests and the broader conflict. This data shows an S-curve with fast, exponential growth in the beginning, then levelling off as the conflict matured, slowing the pace of fatalities. This pattern helps us understand the lifecycle of violence in a long-term conflict.

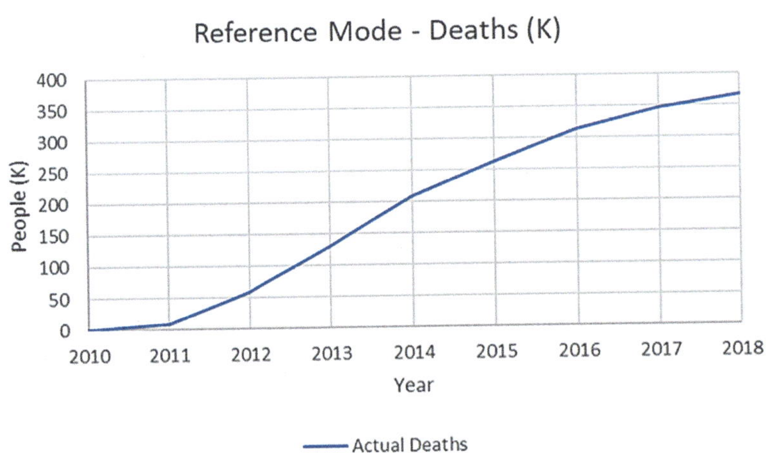

Fig. 11.3: Deaths during protests and battles in Syria.

Lastly, Fig. 11.4 shows the total number of refugees created by the war. This also follows an S-shaped curve: a surge in the early years, followed by slower growth as many people fled and borders tightened. This trend helps shape how we model refugee flows over time.

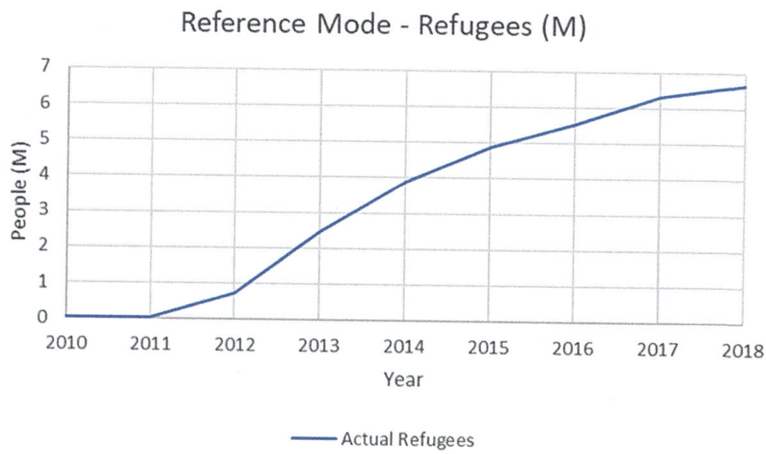

Fig. 11.4: Number of refugees from the Syrian civil war.

By grounding the model in these reference modes, using real data rather than just theory, we ensure it reflects how the crisis unfolded. Matching these patterns isn't just a nice bonus; it's critical. If the model can't mirror past behaviour, it can't be trusted to forecast future outcomes or test policy scenarios meaningfully.

11.5 Dynamic Hypothesis

At the heart of any system dynamics model is a set of cause-and-effect relationships that explain how the system behaves over time. We map these out using a causal loop diagram, which helps visualize the feedback loops that reinforce trends and that balance things out. We created a high-level conceptual map of the Syrian refugee crisis that captures the primary forces driving conflict, displacement, and potential paths to stability.

Figure 11.5 lays it all out. This diagram features two reinforcing loops and seven balancing loops, illustrating how various parts of the system interact with one another.

Let's break them down:

- R1 – Population growth: This is a classic reinforcing loop. More people mean more births, which in turn lead to even more people.
- B1 – Refugee departure: As the population increases, more people leave, resulting in a decrease in the population. This is a balancing loop that helps stabilize population levels.
- B2 – Refugee growth: As more people leave, the refugee population increases. However, as the number of refugees grows, the rate of new departures slows, maybe because fewer people are left to leave.
- B3 – Immigration: As refugee numbers rise, more immigrants enter host countries, reducing the number of refugees waiting to be resettled over time.

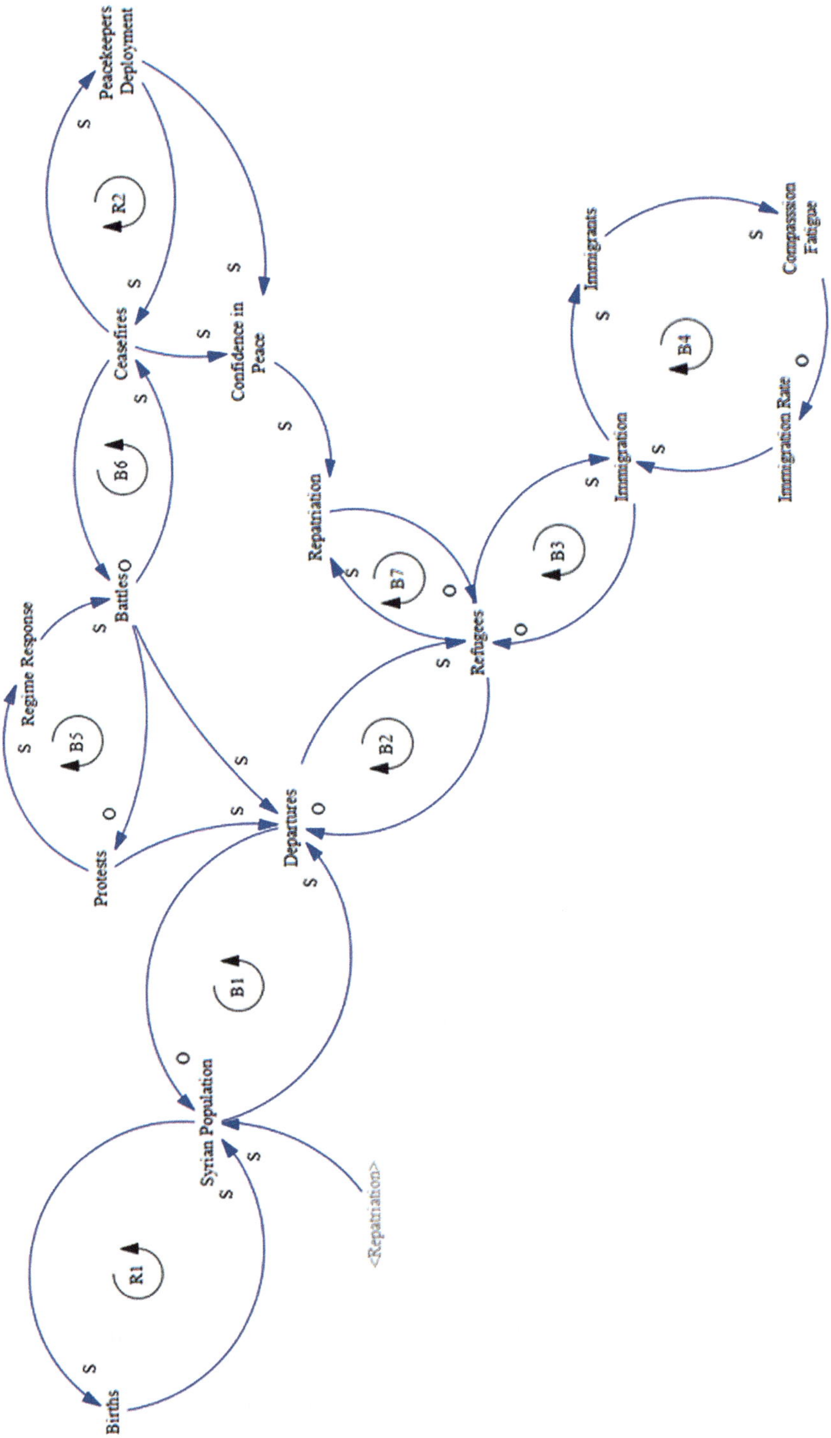

Fig. 11.5: Causal loop diagram of conflict and refugee dynamics.

- B4 – Compassion fatigue: This one's more social-political. An increase in immigrants can lead to public fatigue in host countries, which puts pressure on governments to reduce immigration rates, thus slowing the intake.
- B5 – Protest response: More protests spark stronger crackdowns by the regime, often leading to more battles. Eventually, this suppresses protests, a classic example of balancing feedback.
- B6 – Battle reduction: As battles increase, so does the pressure for ceasefires. More ceasefires lead to fewer battles, calming things down.
- R2 – Peacekeeping: Here's another reinforcing loop that pushes in a positive direction. More ceasefires can trigger additional peacekeeper deployments, which in turn lead to further ceasefires and build confidence in stability. That, in turn, supports efforts to repatriate.
- B7 – Repatriation: The refugee count drops when more refugees return to Syria. However, as the refugee population shrinks, so does the pace of repatriation. This self-correcting loop also increases Syria's population again.

These loops form the backbone of the model. They demonstrate how everything, from violence and movement to immigration policy, public opinion, peacekeeping, and repatriation, is tightly interconnected. Because some loops push the system forward while others pull it back, the model captures the push-and-pull dynamics that shape how the crisis evolves.

11.6 Model Formulation

To simulate the progression of the Syrian refugee crisis over time, we developed a system dynamics model centred on the key stocks and flows that drive conflict, displacement, and immigration. As in earlier chapters, we started by creating the model in Vensim to map out the structure, then moved everything into Excel so we could run scenarios, tweak parameters, and test different policy ideas.

11.6.1 The Vensim Model

We began by creating the initial model in Vensim to visualize the overall dynamics, how protests, battles, refugee flows, and immigration outcomes interrelate. The model is divided into two views, each displaying a distinct aspect of the system.

Figure 11.6 focusses on the relationship between protests, battles, ceasefires, and peacekeepers. In this setup, protests tend to spread; they're contagious. But protests also trigger regime crackdowns, which often escalate into battles. These battles suppress the protests, creating a balancing effect. Peacekeepers can be deployed if the

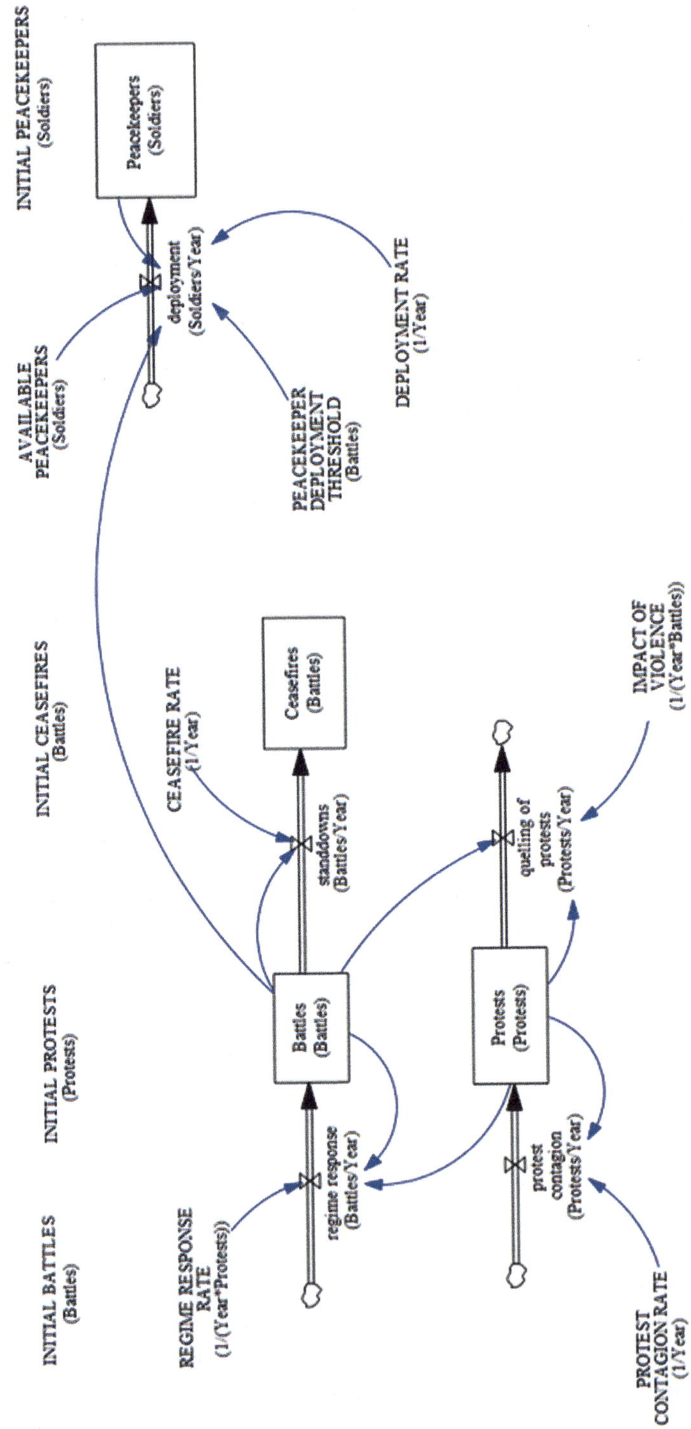

Fig. 11.6: Vensim model view showing protests, battles, ceasefires, and peacekeepers.

conflict subsides and combat numbers decrease. These peacekeepers can help establish safe zones and build trust in the possibility of peace.

Figure 11.7 shifts to the refugee flow side of things. The Syrian population grows through net births, but it also shrinks due to deaths from protests and battles. However, the most significant population change comes from people fleeing the country, which we model as net departures driven by unrest. Some who leave might return later if enough ceasefires hold and peacekeepers are on the ground.

Once people flee, they usually end up in refugee camps. The number of people in camps can increase due to new arrivals and births, or decrease when host countries accept immigrants. That immigration rate isn't constant; it can slow down as host nations experience compassion fatigue, where public support for accepting refugees begins to wear thin.

These two parts of the Vensim model lay the foundation for our Excel version, enabling us to visualize how conflict and displacement evolve and how different policies might impact the outcomes.

11.6.2 The Excel Model

While Vensim is excellent for building and simulating models, this book focusses on making system dynamics more accessible, primarily by leveraging tools people already know, such as Excel. We translated the complete Vensim model step by step into an Excel spreadsheet, following a similar approach to that used in Chapter 9.

Figure 11.8 illustrates the setup of the parameters. We moved all the model parameters into a dedicated column, making them easy to find and update when running different scenarios.

The columns in Figs. 11.9–11.11 show endogenous variables in alphabetical order.

To handle two complex relationships in the model, we added two small lookup tables, shown in Fig. 11.12. One lookup table adjusts the immigration rate based on compassion fatigue (using the ratio of immigrants to a threshold), and the other changes repatriation levels based on the effectiveness of peacekeeper deployment relative to the number of ceasefires.

We also built the interface and scenario worksheets to make everything easier to interact with. These are directly linked to the model sheet and allow users to tweak parameters, such as the intensity of the conflict, the timing of peacekeepers' deployment, or the number of immigrants a country is willing to accept. The best part? The results update instantly in the linked charts, showing how different policy choices shape refugee outcomes.

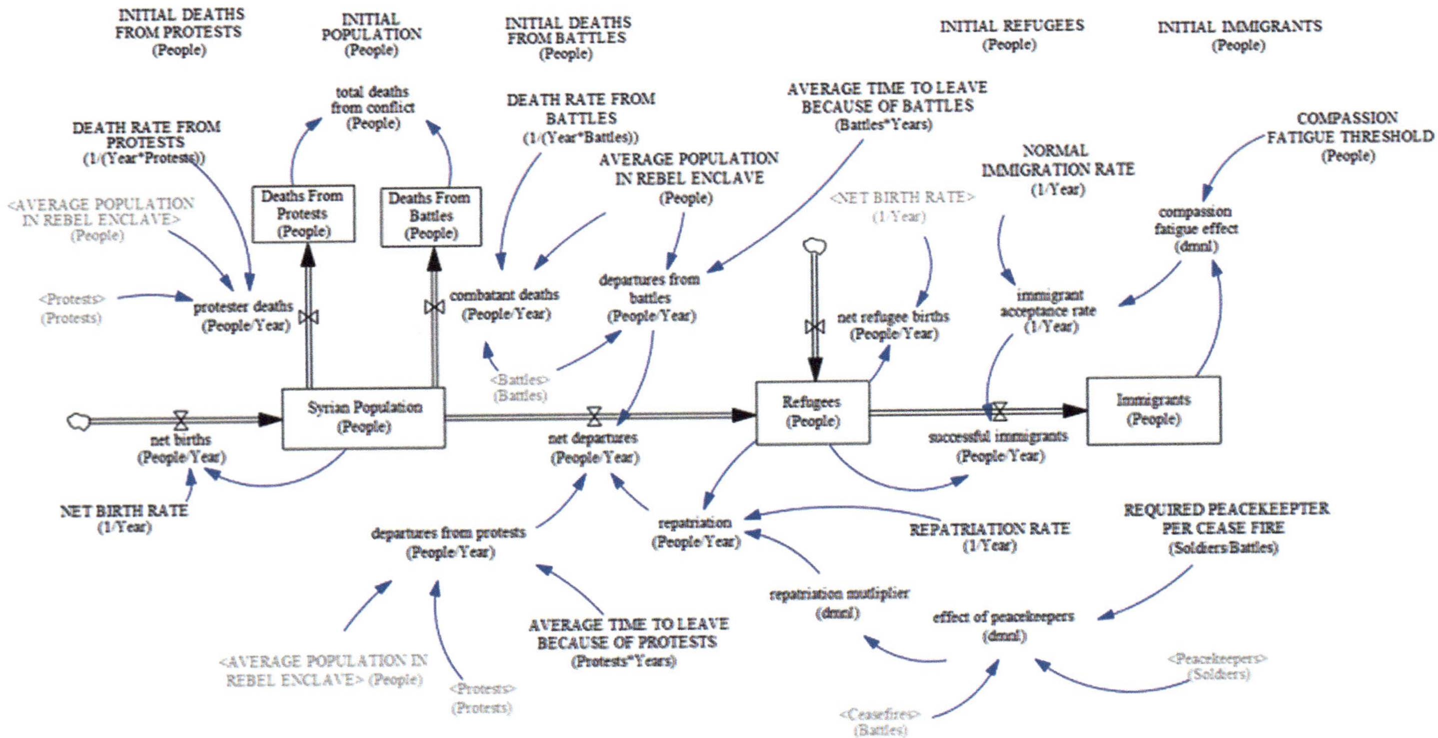

Fig. 11.7: Vensim model view of refugee movements and camp dynamics.

	A	B	C
1	PARAMETER	VALUE	UNITS
2	(38) INITIAL TIME =	2010	Units: Year
3	(65) TIME STEP =	0.125	Units: Year
4	(05) AVAILABLE PEACEKEEPERS=	30000	Units: Soldiers
5	(06) AVERAGE POPULATION IN REBEL ENCLAVE=	65000	Units: People
6	(07) AVERAGE TIME TO LEAVE BECAUSE OF BATTLES=	3.28	Units: Battles*Years
7	(08) AVERAGE TIME TO LEAVE BECAUSE OF PROTESTS=	35.8	Units: Protests*Years
8	(10) CEASEFIRE RATE=	0.195822	Units: 1/Year
9	(14) COMPASSION FATIGUE THRESHOLD=	2000000	Units: People
10	(15) DEATH RATE FROM BATTLES=	0.0133	Units: People/(People*Battles)/Year
11	(16) DEATH RATE FROM PROTESTS=	0.00161	Units: People/(People*Protests)/Year
12	(23) DEPLOYMENT RATE=	4	Units: Soldiers/Soldiers/Year
13	(28) IMPACT OF VIOLENCE=	0.069244	Units: Protests/(Protests*Battles)/Year

Fig. 11.8: Model parameters organized in the Excel interface.

	A	B	C	D	E	F	G	H	I	J	K	L
1	Time	(09) Battles= INTEG (	(11) Ceasefires= INTEG (	(12) combatant deaths=	(13) compassion fatigue effect = WITH LOOKUP (	(17) Deaths From Battles= INTEG (	(18) Deaths From Protests= INTEG (	(20) departures from battles=	(21) departures from protests=	(22) deployment=	(24) effect of peacekeepers = WITH LOOKUP (	(26) immigrant acceptance rate=
2		Units: Battles	Units: Battles	Units: People/Year	Units: dmnl	Units: People	Units: People	Units: People/Year	Units: People/Year	Units: Soldiers/Year	Units: dmnl	Units: 1/Year
3	2010	1	0.0001	864.5	1	0	0	19817.07	200149.1	4E-05	0.000666667	0.02
4	2010.125	1.044365	0.024578	902.8537	1	108.0625	1442.024	20696.26	223740.7	6E-05	4.06872E-06	0.02
5	2010.25	1.099173	0.050142	950.2353	1	220.9192	3054.02	21782.4	250027.2	9E-05	2.99153E-06	0.02
6	2010.375	1.166796	0.077047	1008.695	1	339.6986	4855.403	23122.48	279283.4	0.000135	2.9203E-06	0.02
7	2010.5	1.25032	0.105607	1080.901	1	465.7855	6867.57	24777.68	311799.4	0.000202	3.1958E-06	0.02

Fig. 11.9: Endogenous variables in the Syrian refugee model (set 1).

	A	M	N	O	P	Q	R	S	T	U	V	W
1	Time	(27) Immigrants= INTEG (	(40) net births=	(41) net departures=	(42) net refugee births=	(46) Peacekeepers= INTEG (	(48) protest contagion=	(50) protester deaths=	(51) Protests= INTEG (	(52) quelling of protests=	(54) Refugees= INTEG (	(55) regime response =
2		Units: People	Units: People/Year	Units: People/Year	Units: People/Year	Units: Soldiers	Units: Protests/Year	Units: People/Year	Units: Protests	Units: Protests/Year	Units: People	Units: Battles/Year
3	2010	-	515740	219966.1	2.656686	0	111.5815	11536.19	110.2359	7.633133	110	0.550744
4	2010.125	0	516593.7	244436.8	2218.965	0	124.7337	12895.97	123.2295	8.911415	92,073	0.642974
5	2010.25	230	517372	271809.3	4506.021	0	139.3882	14411.07	137.7073	10.481	186,972	0.756222
6	2010.375	698	518065.4	302405.4	6872.165	0	155.6983	16097.33	153.8207	12.42765	285,152	0.896677
7	2010.5	1,411	518663.6	336576.4	9326.653	0	173.8257	17971.49	171.7295	14.86776	386,998	1.072735

Fig. 11.10: Endogenous variables in the Syrian refugee model (set 2).

	A	X	Y	Z	AA	AB	AC
1	Time	(57) repatriation=	(58) repatriation mutliplier=	(62) standdowns=	(63) successful immigrants=	(64) Syrian Population= INTEG (	(66) total deaths from conflict=
2		Units: People/Year	Units: dmnl	Units: Battles/Year	Units: People/Year	Units: People	Units: People
3	2010	0.036745	0.000667	0.195822	2.204719	21,400,000	0
4	2010.125	0.18731	4.07E-06	0.20451	1841.464	21,435,422	1550.086
5	2010.25	0.279666	2.99E-06	0.215243	3739.437	21,467,716	3274.939
6	2010.375	0.416365	2.92E-06	0.228484	5703.041	21,496,492	5195.102
7	2010.5	0.618384	3.2E-06	0.24484	7739.961	21,521,311	7333.355

Fig. 11.11: Endogenous variables in the Syrian refugee model (set 3).

AG	AH	AI	AJ
Immigrants/COMPASSION FATIGUE THRESHOLD	(13) compassion fatigue effect = WITH LOOKUP (	(Peacekeepers/Ceasefires) /REQUIRED PEACEKEEPTER PER CEASE FIRE,	(24) effect of peacekeepers = WITH LOOKUP (
Units: dmnl	Units: dmnl	Units: dmnl	Units: dmnl
0	1	0	0
1	1	1	1
2	0.02	2	1

Fig. 11.12: Lookup tables for immigration and repatriation effects.

11.7 Calibration

Once the whole model was built in Excel, the next step was to ensure that its behaviour matched what happened in the real world. This process, called calibration, involved adjusting the model so that its outputs matched the historical data from the reference modes we examined earlier in Section 11.3.

To do this, we set up a squared error minimization process in Excel. We created two columns for each key variable (population, battles, refugees, and deaths), one for the actual historical data and one for the model's simulated values. Then, we calculated the squared error for each year by taking the difference between the actual values and the predicted values and squaring it. Adding up all those yearly errors gave us a total error score, a single number that told us how far off the model was (see Fig. 11.13).

	A	B	C	D	E	F	G	H	I	J	K	L	M	N	O	P	Q	R	S	T	U
1	Time	Actual Population	Model Population	SE	SSE	Time	Actual Battles	Model Battles	SE	SSE	Time	Actual Refugees	Model Refugees	SE	SSE	Time	Actual Deaths	Model Deaths	SE	SSE	TSSE
2																					
3	2010	21.4	21.4	0.00E+00	1.05E+00	2010	0	1	1.00E+00	5.51E+02	2010	0.0184	0.0185	1.00E-08	7.32E-01	2010	0	0	0.00E+00	1.14E+03	1.69E+03
4	2015	18	18.65632	4.31E-01		2011	1	4.030776	9.19E+00		2011	0.0199	0.5222013	2.52E-01		2011	7.8	32.03509	5.87E+02		
5	2016	17.5	17.70567	4.23E-02		2011.5	10	8.449532	2.40E+00		2012	0.729	1.1093009	1.45E-01		2012	57.1	71.25139	2.00E+02		
6	2017	17.1	17.03448	4.29E-03		2012	12	17.55397	3.08E+01		2013	2.47	2.087356	1.46E-01		2013	130.6	124.8852	3.27E+01		
7	2018	16.9	16.58677	9.81E-02		2012.5	24	33.83024	9.66E+01		2014	3.89	3.575394	9.90E-02		2014	206.6	193.4043	1.74E+02		
8	2019	17	16.31122	4.74E-01		2013	69	54.91607	1.98E+02		2015	4.87	4.9079408	1.44E-03		2015	261.8	256.9735	2.33E+01		
9						2013.5	69	70.43137	2.05E+00		2016	5.52	5.8011231	7.90E-02		2016	311.6	307.3022	1.85E+01		
10						2014	70	74.23055	1.79E+01		2017	6.31	6.3161427	3.77E-05		2017	345	345.7288	5.31E-01		
11						2014.5	59	70.26232	1.27E+02		2018	6.65	6.5534426	9.32E-03		2018	364.8	374.838	1.01E+02		
12						2015	59	63.44485	1.98E+01												
13						2015.5	59	56.15942	8.07E+00												
14						2016	50	49.24717	5.67E-01												
15						2016.5	42	42.99844	9.97E-01												
16						2017	35	37.46342	6.07E+00												
17						2017.5	35	32.60477	5.74E+00												
18						2018	32	28.3586	1.33E+01												
19						2019	18	21.43232	1.18E+01												

Fig. 11.13: Squared error calculation columns in Excel.

Next, we used Excel's Solver tool to minimize the total error. The Solver adjusted the key model parameters to find the best fit between the simulated and actual results. We linked the total error to a specific cell in the interface worksheet, allowing us to track it easily during calibration (see Fig. 11.14).

The Solver then fine-tuned the model by adjusting all parameters except the initial values, which we kept locked in based on real starting points (see Fig. 11.15).

	A	B	C	D
1	PARAMETER	VALUE	UNITS	TSSE
2	(38) INITIAL TIME =	2010	Units: Year	6.08E+02
3	(65) TIME STEP =	0.125	Units: Year	
4	(05) AVAILABLE PEACEKEEPERS=	30000	Units: Soldiers	
5	(06) AVERAGE POPULATION IN REBEL ENCLAVE=	65000	Units: People	
6	(07) AVERAGE TIME TO LEAVE BECAUSE OF BATTLES=	3.28	Units: Battles*Years	
7	(08) AVERAGE TIME TO LEAVE BECAUSE OF PROTESTS=	35.8	Units: Protests*Years	
8	(10) CEASEFIRE RATE=	0.195822	Units: 1/Year	
9	(14) COMPASSION FATIGUE THRESHOLD=	2000000	Units: People	
10	(15) DEATH RATE FROM BATTLES=	0.0133	Units: People/(People*Battles)/Year	
11	(16) DEATH RATE FROM PROTESTS=	0.00161	Units: People/(People*Protests)/Year	
12	(23) DEPLOYMENT RATE=	4	Units: Soldiers/Soldiers/Year	
13	(28) IMPACT OF VIOLENCE=	0.069244	Units: Protests/(Protests*Battles)/Year	
14	(29) INITIAL BATTLES=	1	Units: Battles	
15	(30) INITIAL CEASEFIRES=	0.0001	Units: Battles	
16	(31) INITIAL DEATHS FROM BATTLES=	0	Units: People	
17	(32) INITIAL DEATHS FROM PROTESTS=	0	Units: People	
18	(33) INITIAL IMMIGRANTS=	0	Units: People	
19	(34) INITIAL PEACEKEEPERS=	0.00001	Units: Soldiers	
20	(35) INITIAL POPULATION=	21400000	Units: People	
21	(36) INITIAL PROTESTS=	110.2359	Units: Protests	
22	(37) INITIAL REFUGEES=	18500	Units: People	
23	(39) NET BIRTH RATE=	0.0241	Units: People/People/Year	
24	(43) NORMAL IMMIGRATION RATE=	0.0713	Units: People/People/Year	
25	(45) PEACEKEEPER DEPLOYMENT THRESHOLD=	10	Units: Battles	
26	(49) PROTEST CONTAGION RATE=	1.012206	Units: Protests/Protests/Year	
27	(56) REGIME RESPONSE RATE=	0.004996	Units: Battles/(Protests*Battles)/Year	
28	(59) REPATRIATION RATE=	0	Units: People/People/Year	
29	(60) REQUIRED PEACEKEEPTER PER CEASE FIRE=	150	Units: Soldiers/Battles	

Fig. 11.14: The sum of squared errors linked to the interface worksheet.

The process worked well. After calibration, the model's output closely followed the historical data patterns across all significant variables:

- Figure 11.16 compares actual battle frequency with simulated battle frequency over time.
- Figure 11.17 illustrates the accuracy of the simulated population in matching the actual population decline.
- Figure 11.18 shows the fit for the refugee population.
- Figure 11.19 shows the trend line for total deaths during the conflict.

This strong alignment between the model and reality gave us confidence that the structure and assumptions were sound, setting us up for reliable policy testing in the following stages.

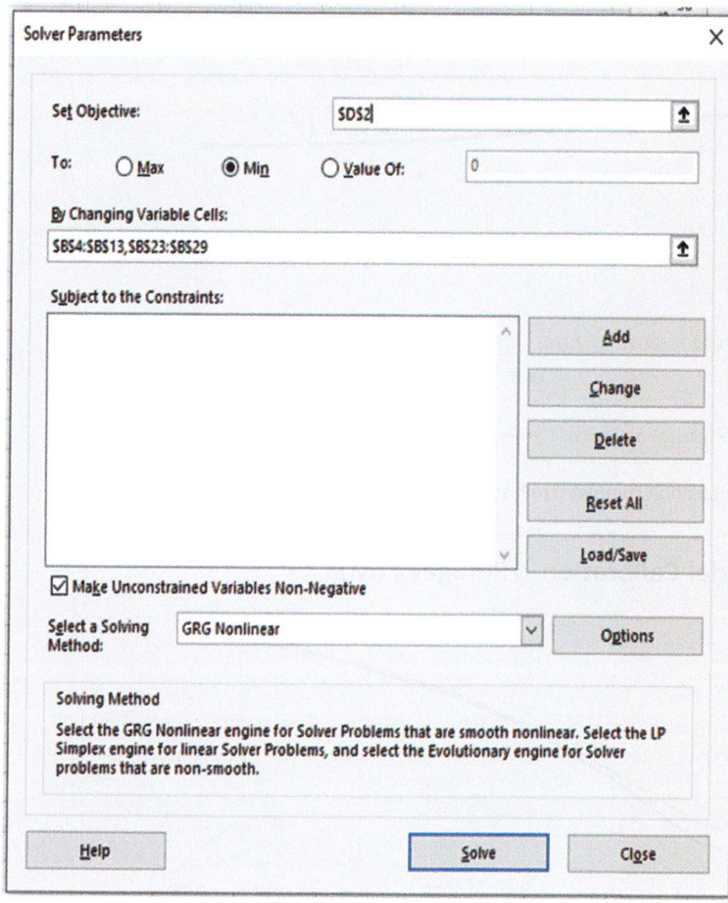

Fig. 11.15: Solver configuration to minimize the squared error.

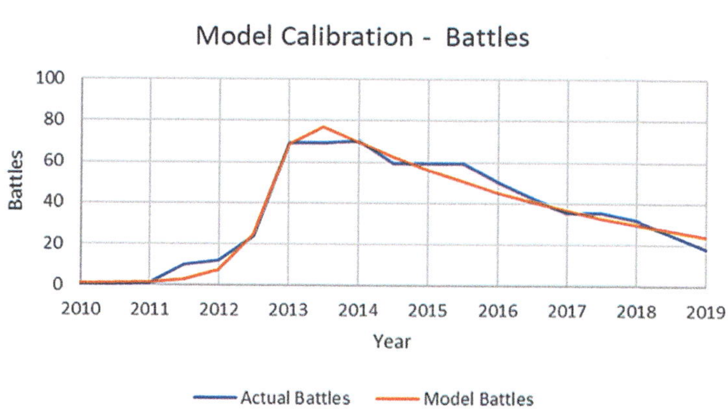

Fig. 11.16: Simulated battles compared to the historical reference mode.

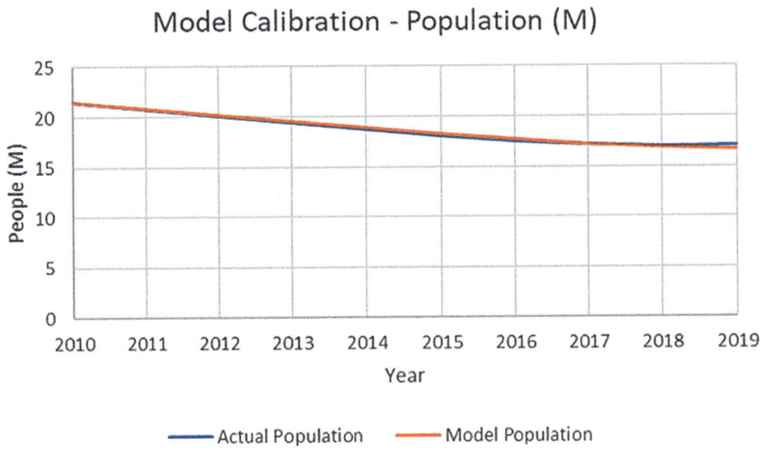

Fig. 11.17: Simulated population compared to historical data.

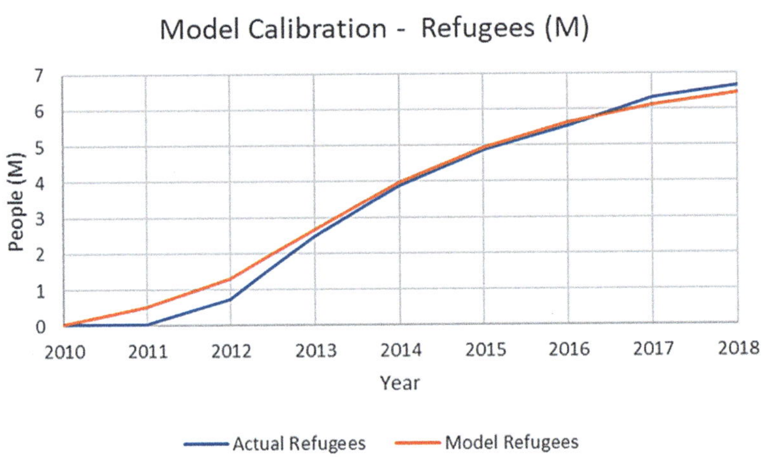

Fig. 11.18: Simulated refugee levels versus actual data.

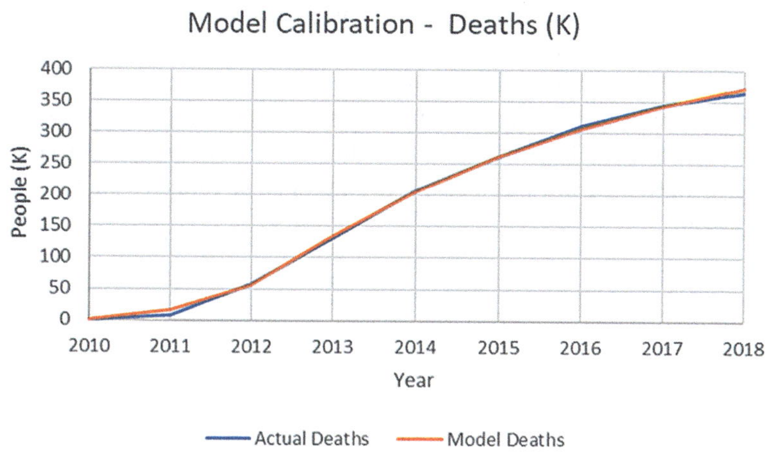

Fig. 11.19: Simulated death counts versus historical figures.

11.8 Baseline Run

With the model calibrated, we ran a baseline simulation from 2010 through 2040 using the fitted parameters and default policy settings. This run represents a "business-as-usual" scenario, no significant policy changes, just the system playing out as it's currently structured.

We began by examining how the conflict unfolds. Figure 11.20 shows the projected number of battles per year, extending beyond the historical data into the future. The model suggests that fighting peaked around 2014, which aligns with the actual events. After that, the number of battles gradually declines. This drop stems from

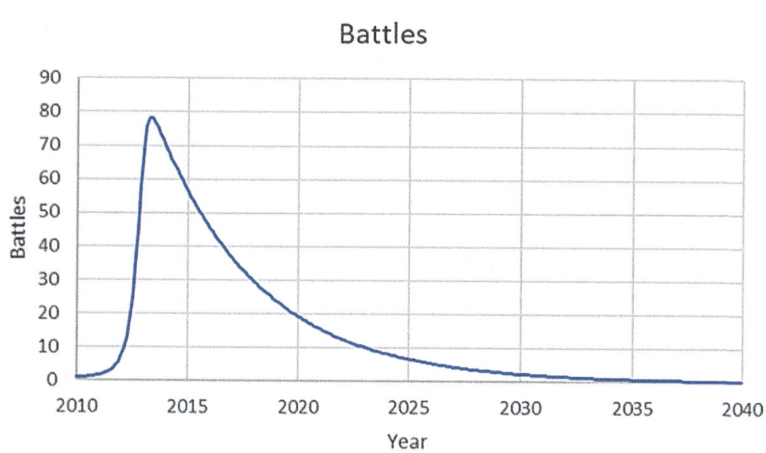

Fig. 11.20: Forecast of battles per year through 2040.

the model's logic: as ceasefires begin to hold, even occasionally, the conditions for ongoing, large-scale conflict slowly deteriorate.

Now, here's where things get interesting – and a bit unexpected.

Figure 11.21 shows the projected number of refugees, and at first glance, it looks like the historical S-curve trend is continuing. But after 2020, something surprising happened: Instead of flattening out like before, the number of refugees started to grow exponentially again.

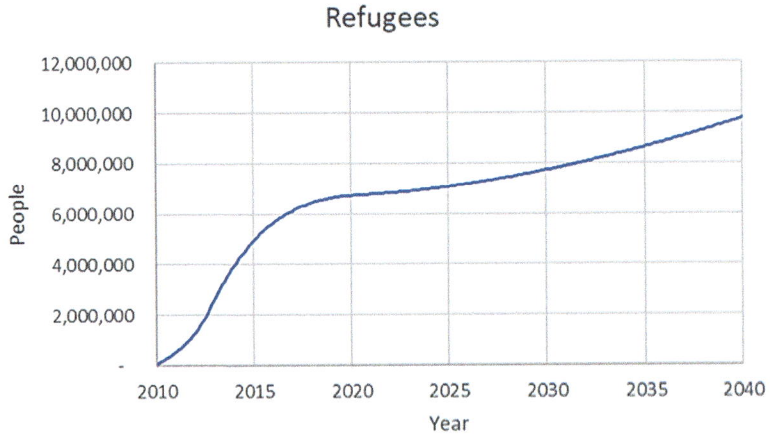

Fig. 11.21: Projected number of refugees from 2020 to 2040.

This result is counter-intuitive. You might expect the curve to level off permanently, but the model shows a second surge. Why? The answer lies in what's happening with immigration.

Figure 11.22 shows that host countries stop accepting many refugees after a certain point. This is due to compassion fatigue, which occurs when nations reach a breaking point because of a lack of capacity or political resistance. As immigration slows and eventually stalls, the refugees who might've otherwise been resettled stay in camps or informal settlements. The outflow clogs up, and the refugee population builds up again, this time with no clear release valve.

So, even though battles are declining, the number of displaced people continues to rise – not because more are fleeing, but because fewer can exit the system. This unexpected feedback loop highlights the importance of immigration policy and global support in preventing the crisis from spiralling.

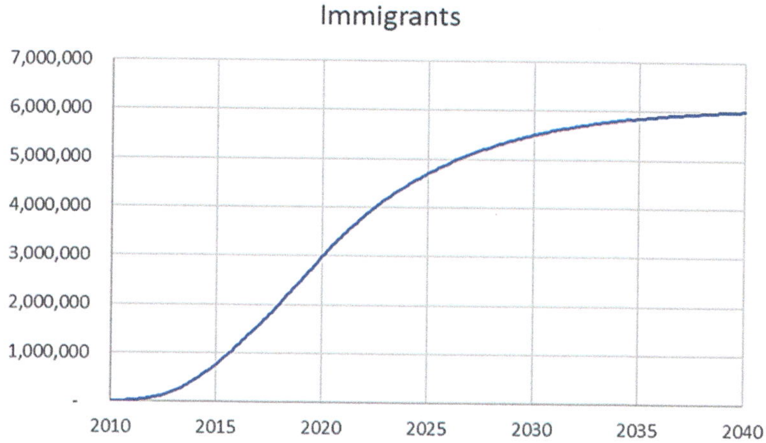

Fig. 11.22: Immigration limit due to compassion fatigue.

11.9 Policy Runs and Sensitivity Analysis

Using the model, we ran two key scenarios to see how different policy choices might change the future. One examined the consequences of immigration restrictions due to growing compassion fatigue. The other explored a more hopeful future where refugees return to Syria, thanks to more substantial peacekeeping efforts and a return to stability.

We used Excel's parameter tables to set up each scenario and tracked the results using time-series charts, making it easy to see how the outcomes shift depending on our assumptions.

11.9.1 Compassion Fatigue Scenario

In this scenario, we examined the consequences of host countries withdrawing immigration as they approach a limit, whether political, social, or logistical. To model this, we used a "compassion fatigue" function that gradually reduces the immigration rate once a certain number of accepted refugees has been reached.

We implemented this in Excel using a lookup table. The function only occurs after the number of immigrants exceeds a defined threshold. At that point, the regular immigration rate is multiplied by a decreasing factor, simulating the growing public and political pressure to slow down or stop new arrivals.

Figure 11.23 shows the number of refugees over time under three different thresholds. The baseline case used a threshold of 3 million immigrants. We also tested 6 million, which gave some short-term relief, and 9 million, which helped flatten the

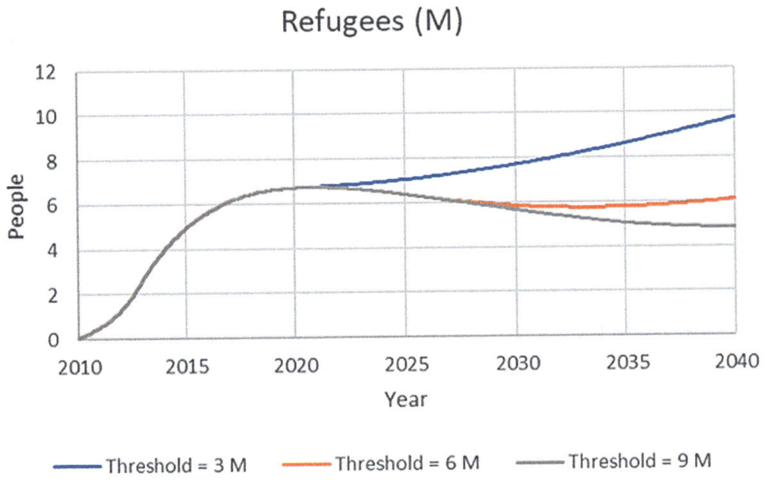

Fig. 11.23: Effect of compassion fatigue thresholds on refugee numbers.

curve but didn't solve the problem. Even with the highest threshold, there will still be 5 million refugees stuck in camps by 2040.

The takeaway is clear: immigration alone isn't enough to resolve the crisis. It can temporarily ease the pressure, but the refugee population continues to grow without addressing the root causes.

11.9.2 Repatriation Scenario

In this scenario, we examined what could happen if the violence in Syria decreases to a level where ceasefires can be sustained and peacekeepers can be deployed. As stability improves, refugees return home only when there's enough confidence that the peace will last.

We modelled this using a "confidence in peace" multiplier that boosts the repatriation rate as more peacekeepers are deployed and ceasefires take effect. In the baseline scenario, the repatriation rate was very low, at just 0.001 people/people/year, and peacekeepers would only be deployed if the number of battles dropped below 10. But at that low rate, hardly any refugees returned, even when the conflict slowed.

So, we examined what would happen if we increased the repatriation rate. Figure 11.24 displays the results for rates of 0.1, 0.2, and 0.3. As expected, increasing the rate makes a big difference. The higher the rate, the more the refugee population drops over time. This suggests that, when supported by absolute stability and strong peacekeeping, repatriation could be a more effective long-term solution than relying solely on immigration.

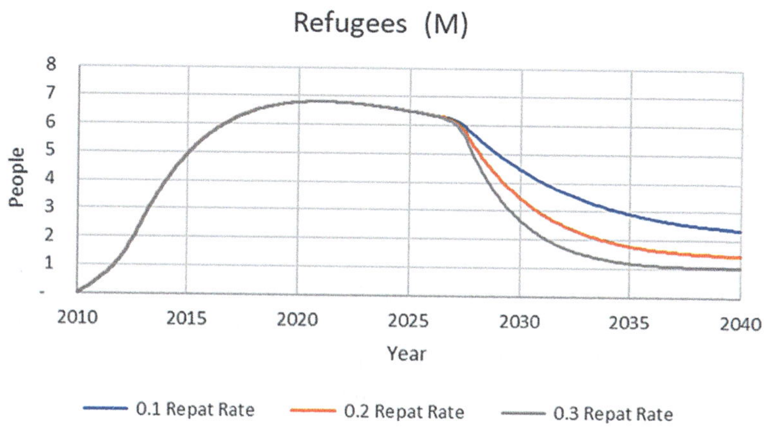

Fig. 11.24: Impact of varying repatriation rates on refugees.

Another key parameter in the model is the peacekeeper deployment threshold, the number of ongoing battles at which peacekeepers are allowed to enter Syria. In the baseline scenario, this threshold is set to 10. Figure 11.25 illustrates the effects of adjusting the repatriation rate to 5, 10, and 15, using a rate of 0.2 people per person per year.

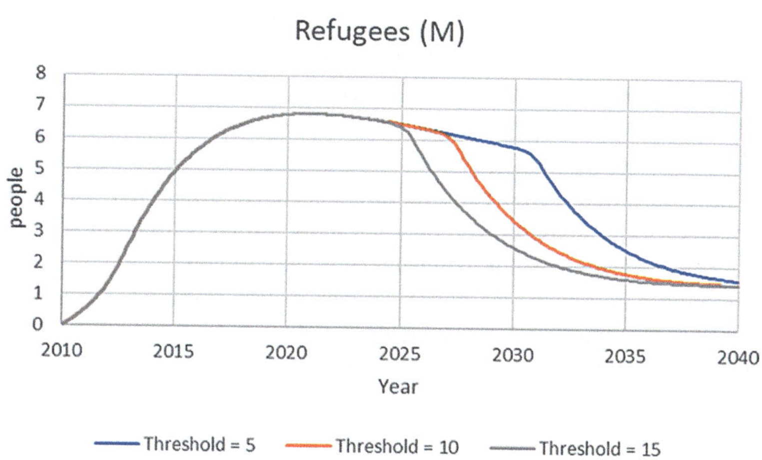

Fig. 11.25: Impact of peacekeeper deployment thresholds on repatriation.

The results are clear: Lowering the threshold allows peacekeepers to deploy sooner, which speeds up the start of the repatriation process. In other words, if peacekeepers are sent in earlier, while the conflict is still simmering but no longer full-blown, it gives refugees more confidence to return home sooner.

These policy runs make one thing clear: immigration alone won't solve the Syrian refugee crisis. As compassion fatigue sets in, host countries are less willing or able to take in more refugees. Repatriation, however, can have a profound impact, although it's not a silver bullet. Refugees must be willing to return, depending on whether they believe it's safe. If peacekeepers are deployed and stability begins to take hold, that confidence can grow, making returning a real option for many.

11.10 Conclusion and Recommendations

The Syrian refugee crisis is a systems problem shaped by feedback loops, time delays, and nonlinear effects. Modelling it in Excel with system dynamics helps capture that complexity and shows how today's policy choices shape tomorrow's outcomes. The baseline simulations made one thing clear: if there's no serious intervention, the crisis will continue to worsen, even if the fighting slows down. While the historical data suggested the refugee numbers were levelling off, the model showed that the trend wouldn't last. Without action, the situation becomes unsustainable.

Among the scenarios we tested, immigration provided short-term relief but didn't offer a long-term solution. Displacement continues, and host countries eventually push back due to compassion fatigue. Repatriation, on the other hand, proved more promising. It highlighted the crucial role that early peacekeeper deployment can play, restoring order and giving refugees the confidence to return.

There are three key takeaways for policymakers: don't depend on immigration to resolve the crisis in the long term; invest early in peacekeeping and conflict resolution; and create safe, credible pathways for people to return home.

Using Excel Solver, we calibrated the model to match real-world data on population and conflict, which added credibility to the results. A significant benefit of Excel is its ease of adjusting parameters and running quick scenario tests. That makes it useful for decision-makers and analysts who may not have formal training in system dynamics but still need powerful tools for exploring complex problems.

Ultimately, this model demonstrates how feedback-driven thinking, combined with a widely accessible tool like Excel, can provide insight into humanitarian crises and inform the development of more thoughtful, more humane policy responses.

11.11 Discussion questions

- Which feedback loops most plausibly drive refugee stock growth in the baseline once open conflict subsides?
- What minimum evidence of fit should be shown (and to which variables) before presenting forward scenarios?
- Where are lookups preferable to single time-constant goal-gap adjustments, and what guard-rails (bounds/monotonicity) should apply?

- If the model fits the population well but struggles with refugee rates, is that a parameter problem or a structural gap? What probes would you run?
- How would you defend immigration-threshold assumptions to governance, given political and Rule of 72 sensitivity analysis?
- Under what conditions does repatriation dominate as the release valve, and what indicators signal readiness?
- What constitutes a credible sensitivity plan so leadership doesn't over-index on a single scenario?

11.12 Exercises

11.12.1 Structure mapping: Vensim → Excel
Task. List the model's stocks/flows and map each to Excel worksheets: parameters, model, interface, and scenarios.
Deliverable. One slide or page with the mapping plus a simple causal sketch.

11.12.2 Lookup implementation
Task. Build two lookups: (A) Immigration rate multiplier versus cumulative immigrants (compassion fatigue); (B) Repatriation rate multiplier versus peacekeeper/ceasefire confidence. Use linear interpolation with anchored ranges.
Deliverable. Screenshot of lookup tables and the interpolation formulas.

11.12.3 Calibration scaffold
Task. Create actual, model, error, squared error columns for battles, population, refugees, deaths, and compute per-series and total SSE.
Deliverable. First 15 rows and a small summary table of SSE by series and total.

11.12.4 Solver configuration
Task. Use Solver to minimize total SSE by varying selected parameters under realism bounds.
Deliverable. Solver dialogue screenshot and before/after SSE.

11.12.5 Baseline run analysis
Task. Run the baseline. Produce a three-chart pack: battles, refugees, population (actual vs. model through history, then forecast).
Deliverable. Charts and a 120-word diagnosis of any refugee resurgence despite falling conflict, citing the release valve logic.

11.12.6 Immigration threshold scenario
Task. Create three immigration thresholds (e.g. low/medium/high). Re-run and compare the refugee stock by horizon.
Deliverable. Overlay chart and two-sentence takeaway on "thresholds relieve pressure but don't resolve stock growth."

11.12.7 Repatriation and peacekeeper triggers
Task. Hold immigration at baseline; vary repatriation rate (three levels) and peacekeeper deployment trigger (earlier/on-time/later).
Deliverable. 2 × 3 table of peak refugees and time-to-reduce by X%; three-sentence recommendation.

11.12.8 Robustness sweep
Task. ± 10% one-at-a-time sensitivity on calibrated parameters most tied to refugees (lookup points, adjustment times). Report the % change in the number of refugees.
Deliverable. Mini tornado table (parameter → % change of refugees).

11.12.9 Executive brief
Task. Draft 150–200 words covering purpose, fit evidence, key baseline risk, scenario impacts, and concrete next steps (e.g. refine lookups; extend data; test alternate structures).
Deliverable. One paragraph suitable for a steering committee pack.

Chapter 12
Diabetes in India

12.1 Learning Objectives

- Explain why this case moves from Vensim to Excel and how that enables broader stakeholder use of a dynamic model.
- Summarize the problem context and explain why linear projections are insufficient compared to feedback/delay structures.
- Use reference modes to set calibration targets and evaluate trajectory/shape rather than a pointwise fit.
- Interpret the dynamic hypothesis: reinforcing/balancing loops and five policy levers.
- Translate the structure to Excel, implement third-order policy delays, and expose a simple interface for scenarios.
- Build a calibration worksheet (actual vs. model; sum of squared error (SSE)) and confirm a credible historical match.
- Run policy scenarios and diagnose counterintuitive effects.
- Configure Solver for a constrained policy mix optimization and interpret the chapter's benchmark result.

12.2 Introduction

This chapter is another case study about using Excel to build and run a slightly more complex system dynamics model than in the previous chapters. We start by using the specialized software Vensim, then we move everything into Excel. Hence, it's easier for more people, especially public health folks and policymakers, to explore and test ideas.

The topic we're modelling is type 2 diabetes in India, but the real point is how Excel can simulate a complex system over time [43]. The model tracks how people move through different health stages, from being at risk, to developing diabetes (diagnosed or not), to treatment, and eventually to diabetes-related deaths. It also includes how the healthcare system responds, such as screening, treatment rates, and prevention efforts.

By setting this up in Excel, we can utilize it with real-world data, run what-if scenarios through 2045, and examine how different strategies might impact the future. This chapter describes how the Excel model was adapted from a model initially developed in Vensim, its operation, how to adjust assumptions, and how to interpret the results, all utilizing tools that most people already have on their computers.

https://doi.org/10.1515/9783111541389-014

12.3 Problem Definition

The diabetes crisis in India isn't just about numbers but system-level gaps. People move through different stages of the disease, but the health system struggles to keep up. Many go undiagnosed for years, especially in rural areas, where access is limited and treatment costs can be a barrier. Even when people are diagnosed, they require lifelong care, which adds to the strain on already overburdened services such as clinics, labs, and hospitals.

There's also a disconnect in how health programmes are run. Awareness campaigns often fail to connect with screening or treatment efforts, resulting in short-lived results. Because diabetes is a lifelong condition, prevention is crucial, but hard to track or reward since the benefits show up years later.

This is where the system dynamics model comes in. We can identify the real pressure points by simulating how people transition between health states – from being at risk to being diagnosed – and how the healthcare system responds to these transitions. It helps us understand how different strategies play out over time and how investing in one area (like prevention or screening) affects others (like long-term care or mortality).

Linear projections using statistical regression can't capture this kind of complexity. However, a dynamic model can illustrate feedback loops, delay times, and reinforced or dampened trends, enabling policymakers to test ideas before implementing them in the real world.

12.4 Reference Mode

We utilized two key reference mode graphs, based on historical and projected data, to ground the model in reality. The first shows India's population growth over time, providing the demographic backdrop for understanding the diabetes burden (Fig. 12.1). The second figure shows the increase in the number of people with diabetes over the past two decades, projecting a linear trend through 2045 (Fig. 12.2).

Together, these graphs set expectations for how the model should behave. The diabetes curve exhibits a sharp upward trend beginning in the early 2000s, reflecting both the actual increase in cases and advancements in diagnosis. This trend is expected to continue, highlighting the growing challenge ahead. The population graph adds context; more people mean more at-risk individuals, but the diabetes rate is rising faster than population growth alone would explain.

These patterns are the foundation for model calibration. We're not trying to match every data point exactly, but we aim to capture the overall shapes, turning points, and trajectories. If the model can reflect these dynamics, we can trust it more when using it to test future policies.

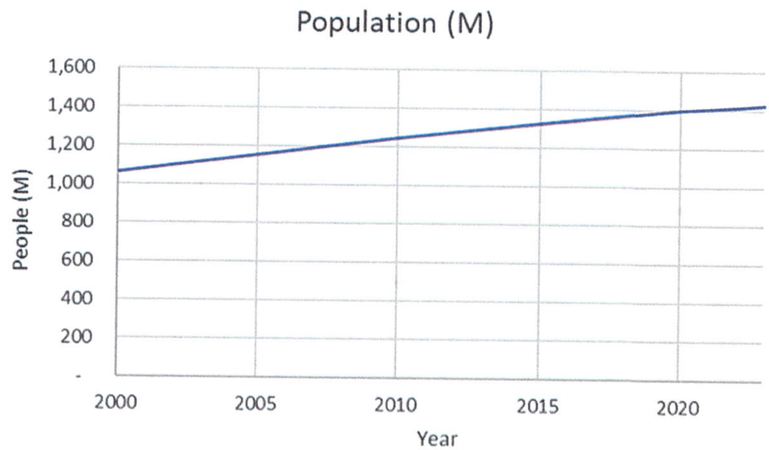

Fig. 12.1: India's population growth from 2000 to 2023.

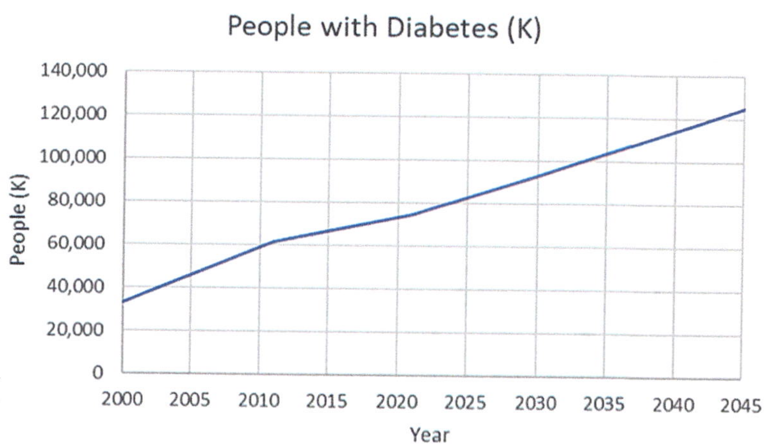

Fig. 12.2: Historical and projected increase in diabetes cases in India from 2000 to 2045.

12.5 Dynamic Hypothesis

Figure 12.3 shows a causal loop diagram (CLD) of the diabetes situation in India. It provides a broad overview of how various factors contribute to or hinder the problem. The diagram features five reinforcing loops, all of which are related to population growth. Seven balancing loops act as counterweights, trying to stabilize the population.

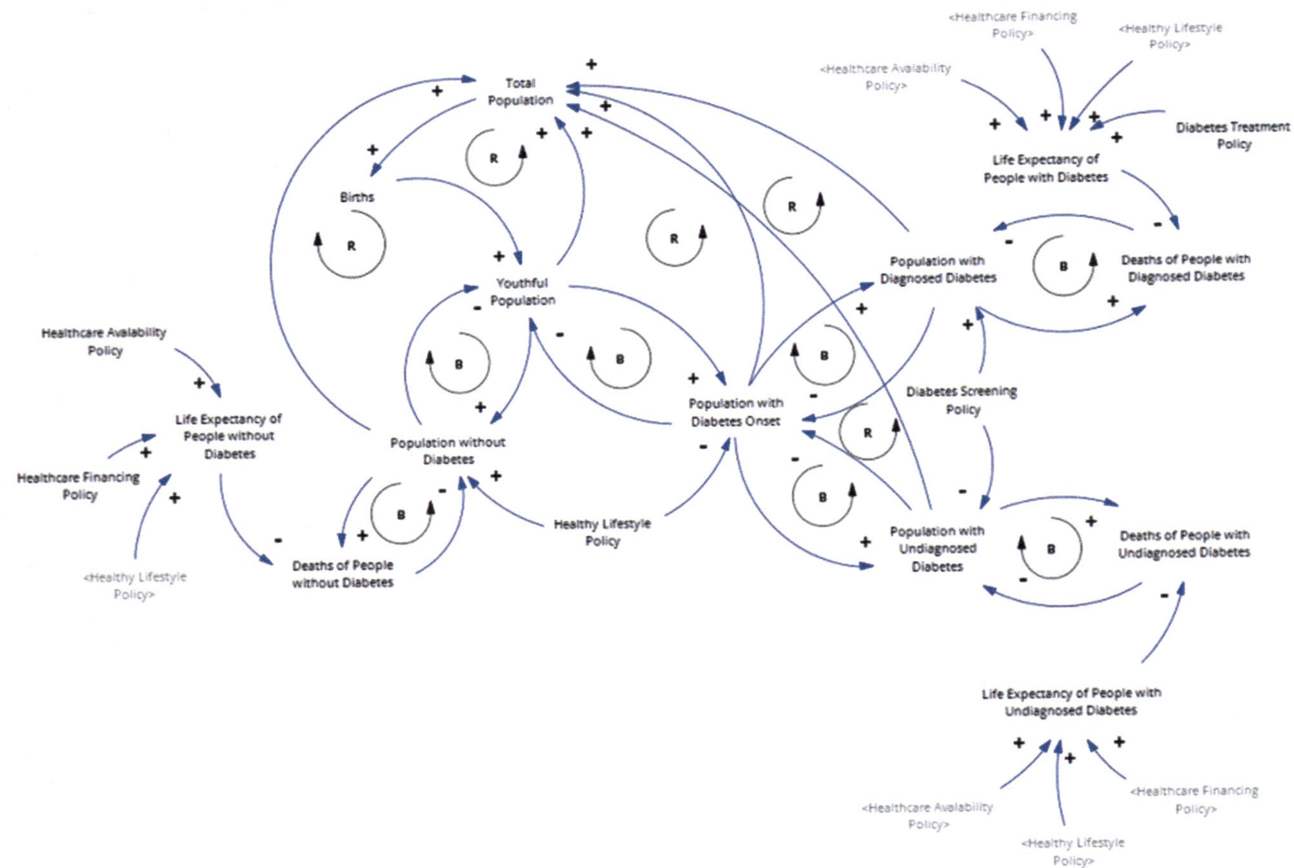

Fig. 12.3: Causal loop diagram of diabetes dynamics in India, showing key feedback loops and policy levers.

The diagram also highlights five external levers that influence this system:

- Diabetes screening increases the number of people diagnosed (by reducing the undiagnosed group), making it easier to manage the condition earlier.
- A healthy lifestyle policy aims to prevent diabetes by promoting habits that reduce the incidence of new cases and supporting individuals who do not have diabetes.
- Diabetes treatment policy, which helps people with diabetes live longer, affects population size and the long-term burden of the disease.
- Healthcare availability improves overall life expectancy, not just for those with diabetes but for the entire population.
- Healthcare financing, similar to availability, boosts access and quality of care across the board, supporting longer, healthier lives.

Overall, the diagram connects all these moving parts, disease dynamics, policies, and population trends, showing how everything feeds back into itself. Some parts push the problem forward, while others pull it back.

12.6 Model Formulation

To analyse the dynamics of diabetes in India, we developed a system dynamics model that captures the key stocks and flows influencing the prevalence of the disease, including population, health transitions, diagnosis rates, treatment access, and prevention efforts. We initially built the model in Vensim to map out the system structure, then transferred it to Excel for calibration, simulation, and policy testing.

12.6.1 The Vensim Model

The Vensim model provides a high-level view of how people transition between health states: from healthy to prediabetic, to diabetic, both diagnosed and undiagnosed, and eventually to outcomes such as treatment, complications, or death. Figure 12.4 illustrates these flows, highlighting how lifestyle risk factors, screening rates, and access to healthcare impact state transitions.

Figure 12.5 illustrates the life expectancy calculations for individuals in three different states: those without diabetes, those with undiagnosed diabetes, and those with diagnosed diabetes. We take a weighted average of these values to estimate the overall average life expectancy of the entire population.

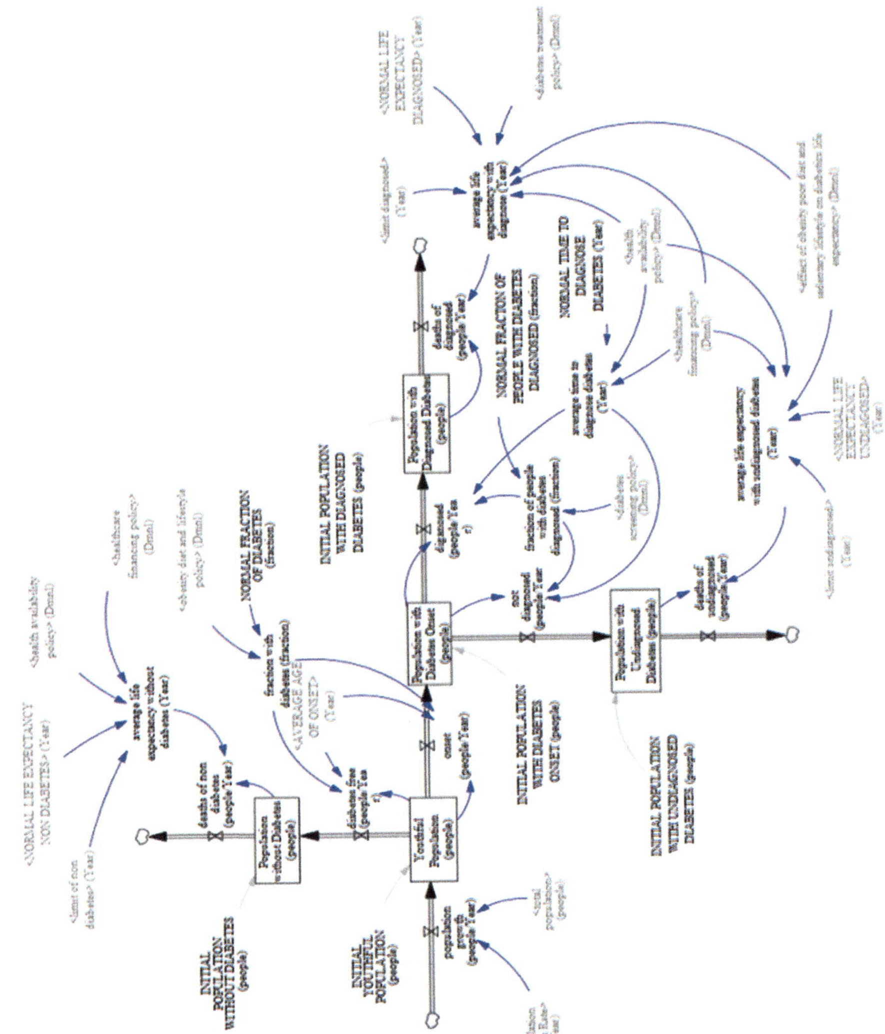

Fig. 12.4: Stock and flow diagram of transitions between diabetes health states in the Vensim model.

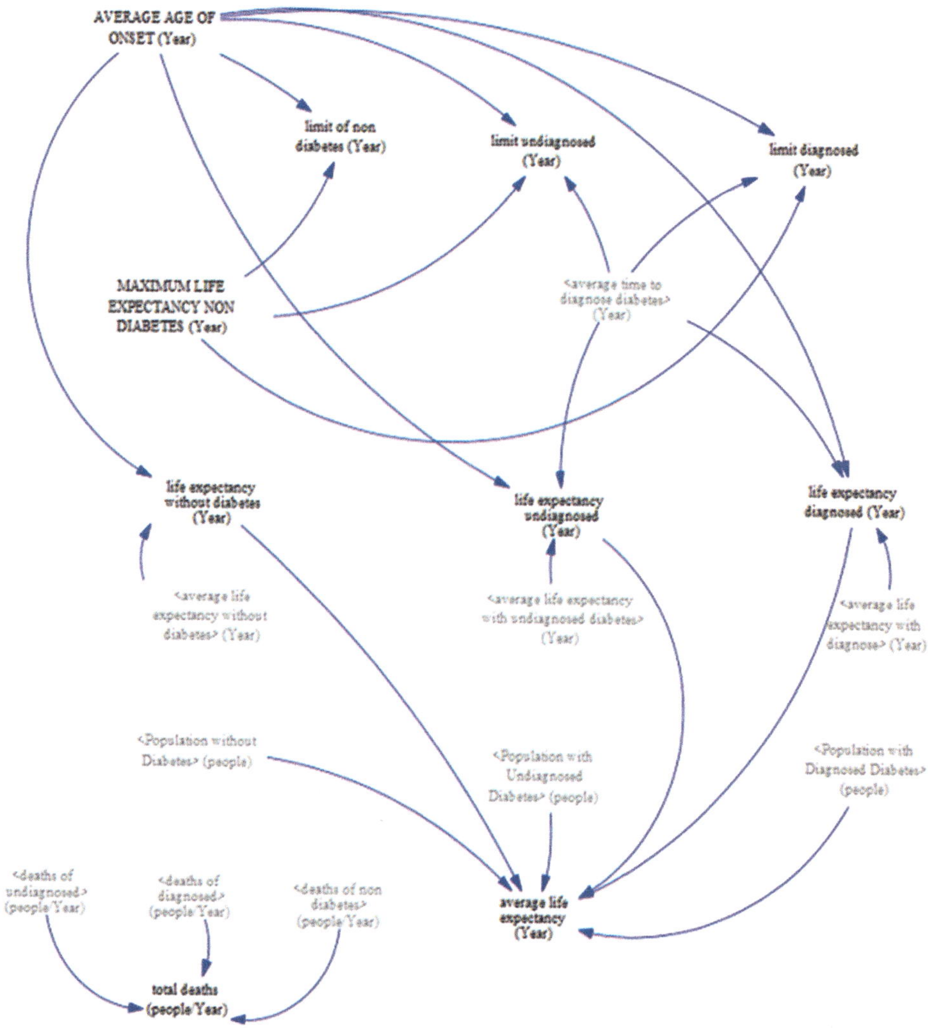

Fig. 12.5: Life expectancy calculation based on diabetes health state and policy variables.

One of this model's features is identifying policies that can be employed to improve the situation. These policies are illustrated in Fig. 12.6, which includes diabetes screening, diabetes treatment, healthcare availability, healthcare financing, and lifestyle improvements. We assume each of these policies can affect various parts of the system. However, even though we presume the policies will be implemented in 2023, it will take many years to see results. So, we have modelled them as a third-order delay.

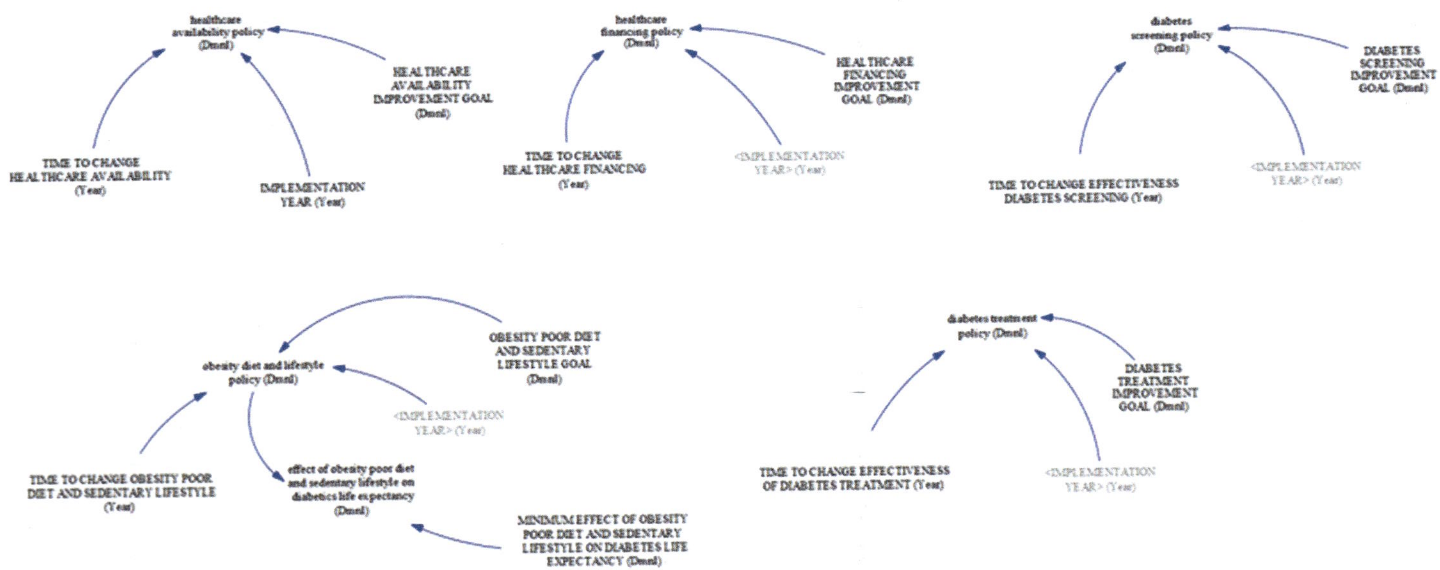

Fig. 12.6: Third-order policy delay functions for diabetes-related interventions.

12.6.2 The Excel Model

To make the model accessible for broader use, especially in policy settings, we converted it into an Excel version using the same approach outlined in Chapter 9.

The model runs from 2000 to 2045, with each row representing 0.25 years. Figures 12.7–12.9 show the endogenous variables: stocks, flows, and auxiliaries.

	A	B	C	D	E	F	G	H	I	J	K	L
1	Time	average life expectan cy	(03) average life expectan cy with diagnose =	(04) average life expectan cy with undiagno sed diabetes =	(05) average life expectan cy without diabetes =	(06) average time to diagnose diabetes =	(07) change in populati on growth rate=	(08) deaths of diagnose d=	(09) deaths of non diabetes =	(10) deaths of undiagno sed=	(11) diabetes free=	(13) diabetes screenin g policy=
2		Units: Year	Units: Year	Units: Year	Units: Year	Units: Year	Units: 1/Year/Y ear	Units: people/Y ear	Units: people/Y ear	Units: people/Y ear	Units: people/Y ear	Units: Dmnl
3	2000	73.82043	24	14	40	6	-0.00169	1361433	10202400	12388643	3124485	1
4	2000.25	73.82931	24	14	40	6	-0.00167	1403046	10158163	12284319	3205033	1
5	2000.5	73.83902	24	14	40	6	-0.00165	1443034	10114706	12179363	3284629	1
6	2000.75	73.84949	24	14	40	6	-0.00163	1481493	10072018	12073949	3363280	1
7	2001	73.86066	24	14	40	6	-0.00161	1518513	10030088	11968244	3440991	1

Fig. 12.7: Endogenous variables in the Indian diabetes model (set 1).

	A	M	N	O	P	Q	R	S	T	U	V	W	X	Y	Z
1	Time	(15) diabetes treatmen t policy=	(16) diganose d=	(17) effect of obesity poor diet and sedentar y lifestyle on diabetics life expectan cy	(19) fraction of people with diabetes diagnose d=	(20) fraction with diabetes =	(22) health availabili ty policy=	(24) healthcar e financing policy=	(33) life expectan cy diagnose d=	(34) life expectan cy undiagno sed=	(35) life expectan cy without diabetes =	(36) limit diagnose d=	(37) limit of non diabetes =	(38) limit undiagno sed=	(48) not diagnose d=
2		Units: Dmnl	Units: people/Y ear	Units: Dmnl	Units: fraction	Units: fraction	Units: Dmnl	Units: Dmnl	Units: Year	Units: Year	Units: Year	Units: Year	Units: Year	Units: Year	Units: people/Y ear
3	2000	1	5356253	1	0.45	0.65	1	1	70	60	80	44	50	44	6546531
4	2000.25	1	5241874	1	0.45	0.65	1	1	70	60	80	44	50	44	6406735
5	2000.5	1	5135067	1	0.45	0.65	1	1	70	60	80	44	50	44	6276193
6	2000.75	1	5035481	1	0.45	0.65	1	1	70	60	80	44	50	44	6154477
7	2001	1	4942784	1	0.45	0.65	1	1	70	60	80	44	50	44	6041180

Fig. 12.8: Endogenous variables in the Indian diabetes model (set 2).

	A	AA	AB	AC	AD	AE	AF	AG	AH	AI	AJ	AK
1	Time	(49) obesity diet and lifestyle policy=	(51) onset=	(52) population growth=	(53) Population Growth Rate= INTEG (	Population with Diabetes Onset	Population with Diagnosed Diabetes	Population with Undiagnosed Diabetes	(57) Population without Diabetes = INTEG (	(66) total deaths=	(67) total population=	(68) Youthful Population= INTEG (
2		Units: Dmnl	Units: people/Year	Units: people/Year	Units: 1/Year				Units: people	Units: people/Year	Units: people	Units: people
3	2000	1	5802615	45748993	0.043875	7.14E+07	3.27E+07	1.73E+08	4.08E+08	23952476	1.04E+09	3.57E+08
4	2000.25	1	5952204	45544218	0.04345154	6.99E+07	33673105	1.72E+08	4.06E+08	23845528	1.05E+09	3.66E+08
5	2000.5	1	6100026	45339353	0.04303337	6.85E+07	34632812	1.71E+08	4.05E+08	23737102	1.05E+09	3.75E+08
6	2000.75	1	6246092	45134458	0.04262043	6.71E+07	35555820	1.69E+08	4.03E+08	23627459	1.06E+09	3.84E+08
7	2001	1	6390413	44929593	0.04221265	6.59E+07	36444317	1.68E+08	4.01E+08	23516846	1.06E+09	3.93E+08

Fig. 12.9: Endogenous variables in the Indian diabetes model (set 3).

	A	B	C	D	E	F	G	H	I	J	K	L
1	Time	policy implementation	desired policy value	first order change	First Order Policy Value	second order change	Second Order Policy Value	third order change	(13) diabetes screening policy=	PARAMETERS	VALUE	UNITS
2		Units: Dmnl	Units: Dmnl	Units: Dmnl/Year	Units: Dmnl	Units: Dmnl/Year	Units: Dmnl	Units: Dmnl/Year	Units: Dmnl	INITIAL TIME	2000	YEAR
3	2000	1	1	0	1	0	1	0	1	TIME STEP	0.25	YEAR
4	2000.25	1	1	0	1	0	1	0	1	INITIAL POLICY VALUE	1	POLICY UNITS
5	2000.5	1	1	0	1	0	1	0	1	(12) DIABETES SCREENING IMPROVEMENT GOAL=	0.1	Units: Dmnl
6	2000.75	1	1	0	1	0	1	0	1	(25) IMPLEMENTATION YEAR=	2023	Units: Year
7	2001	1	1	0	1	0	1	0	1	(60) TIME TO CHANGE EFFECTIVENESS DIABETES SCREENING=	5	Units: Year

Fig. 12.10: Third-order delay implementation worksheet in Excel.

We also developed a worksheet for the third-order delays in the policy implementation (Fig. 12.10). We linked the third-order delay values to the model worksheet in the appropriate policy column.

Lastly, we built an interactive interface worksheet connected to the Model sheet. This allows users to test different policy interventions, such as increasing diabetes screening coverage, scaling lifestyle intervention programmes, or subsidizing healthcare (Fig. 12.11). Adjusting these levers updates the results in real-time through linked charts, making it easier for policymakers and researchers to assess the trade-offs and long-term impacts of their decisions.

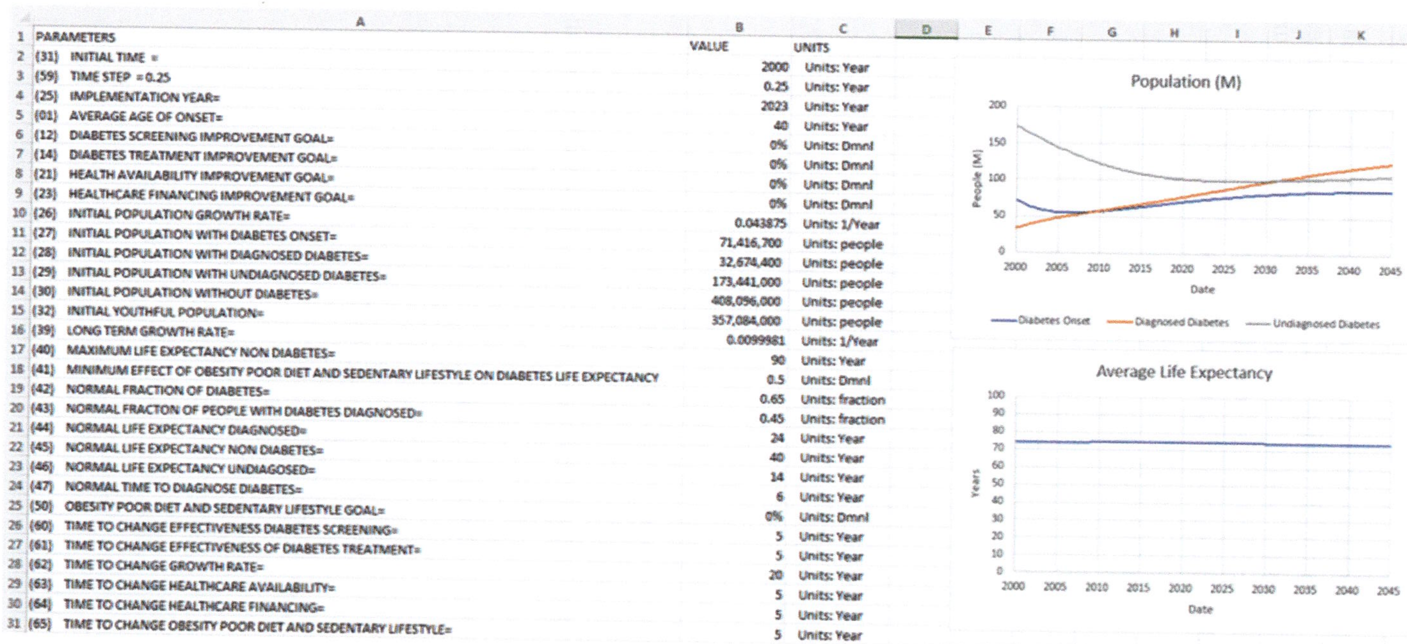

	A	B	C
1	PARAMETERS	VALUE	UNITS
2	(31) INITIAL TIME =	2000	Units: Year
3	(59) TIME STEP = 0.25	0.25	Units: Year
4	(25) IMPLEMENTATION YEAR=	2023	Units: Year
5	(01) AVERAGE AGE OF ONSET=	40	Units: Year
6	(12) DIABETES SCREENING IMPROVEMENT GOAL=	0%	Units: Dmnl
7	(14) DIABETES TREATMENT IMPROVEMENT GOAL=	0%	Units: Dmnl
8	(21) HEALTH AVAILABILITY IMPROVEMENT GOAL=	0%	Units: Dmnl
9	(23) HEALTHCARE FINANCING IMPROVEMENT GOAL=	0%	Units: Dmnl
10	(26) INITIAL POPULATION GROWTH RATE=	0.043875	Units: 1/Year
11	(27) INITIAL POPULATION WITH DIABETES ONSET=	71,416,700	Units: people
12	(28) INITIAL POPULATION WITH DIAGNOSED DIABETES=	32,674,400	Units: people
13	(29) INITIAL POPULATION WITH UNDIAGNOSED DIABETES=	173,441,000	Units: people
14	(30) INITIAL POPULATION WITHOUT DIABETES=	408,096,000	Units: people
15	(32) INITIAL YOUTHFUL POPULATION=	357,084,000	Units: people
16	(39) LONG TERM GROWTH RATE=	0.0099981	Units: 1/Year
17	(40) MAXIMUM LIFE EXPECTANCY NON DIABETES=	90	Units: Year
18	(41) MINIMUM EFFECT OF OBESITY POOR DIET AND SEDENTARY LIFESTYLE ON DIABETES LIFE EXPECTANCY	0.5	Units: Dmnl
19	(42) NORMAL FRACTION OF DIABETES=	0.65	Units: fraction
20	(43) NORMAL FRACTON OF PEOPLE WITH DIABETES DIAGNOSED=	0.45	Units: fraction
21	(44) NORMAL LIFE EXPECTANCY DIAGNOSED=	24	Units: Year
22	(45) NORMAL LIFE EXPECTANCY NON DIABETES=	40	Units: Year
23	(46) NORMAL LIFE EXPECTANCY UNDIAGOSED=	14	Units: Year
24	(47) NORMAL TIME TO DIAGNOSE DIABETES=	6	Units: Year
25	(50) OBESITY POOR DIET AND SEDENTARY LIFESTYLE GOAL=	0%	Units: Dmnl
26	(60) TIME TO CHANGE EFFECTIVENESS DIABETES SCREENING=	5	Units: Year
27	(61) TIME TO CHANGE EFFECTIVENESS OF DIABETES TREATMENT=	5	Units: Year
28	(62) TIME TO CHANGE GROWTH RATE=	20	Units: Year
29	(63) TIME TO CHANGE HEALTHCARE AVAILABILITY=	5	Units: Year
30	(64) TIME TO CHANGE HEALTHCARE FINANCING=	5	Units: Year
31	(65) TIME TO CHANGE OBESITY POOR DIET AND SEDENTARY LIFESTYLE=	5	Units: Year

Fig. 12.11: Interactive worksheet for simulating diabetes policy effects in Excel.

12.7 Calibration

Once the Excel-based simulation engine was constructed, the next step was calibration, ensuring the model could reasonably replicate historical data. Calibration serves two purposes: it validates the model's structure and aligns the simulated behaviour with known real-world patterns, increasing confidence in its predictive power.

Figure 12.12 aligns with the population and simulated values from 2000 to 2023.

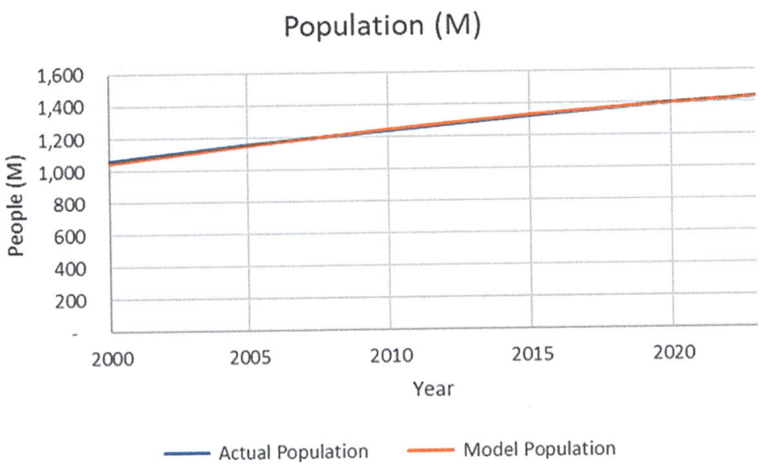

Fig. 12.12: Calibration results comparing simulated vs actual population data.

Figure 12.13 illustrates the alignment between historical and projected values for individuals with diabetes.

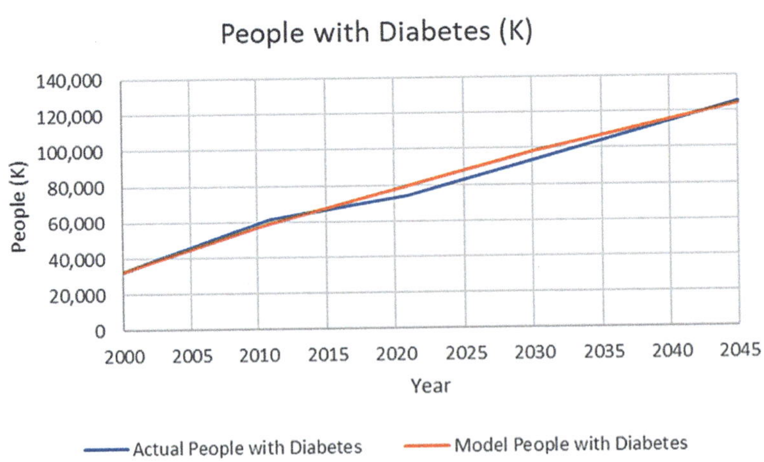

Fig. 12.13: Simulated vs. actual diabetes prevalence calibration results.

With the model calibrated to historical data, we explored its baseline projections and simulated the effects of various health policy interventions, as discussed in the following sections.

12.8 Baseline Run

The baseline scenario, shown in Fig. 12.14, projects the future trajectory of diabetes in India to 2045, assuming that current health policies, risk factors, screening programmes, and treatment capacity remain unchanged. This "status quo" case is a reference point for evaluating alternative interventions in subsequent sections.

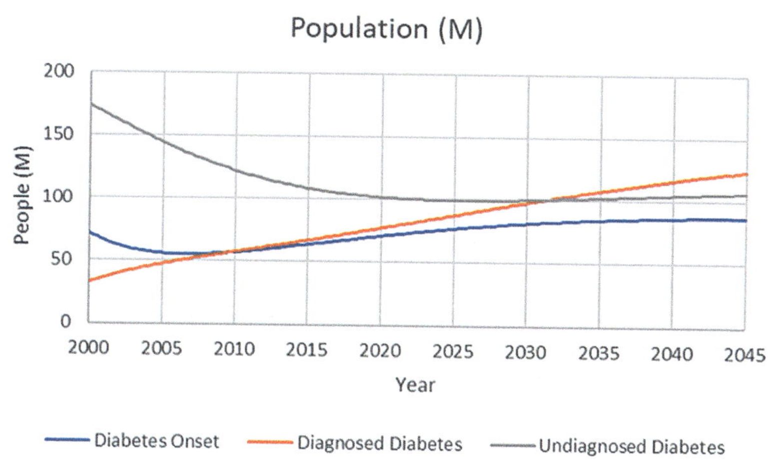

Fig. 12.14: Baseline model projection of diabetes prevalence in India to 2045.

12.9 Policy Scenarios

With this model, we can examine five options. We will look at them one at a time and together.

12.9.1 Enhanced Screening Programme

The first policy assumes we can increase diabetes screening by 50% over 20 years, starting in 2023. Figure 12.15 shows the results we can compare to the baseline run. Increased screening has led to many more people being diagnosed and many fewer people remaining undiagnosed.

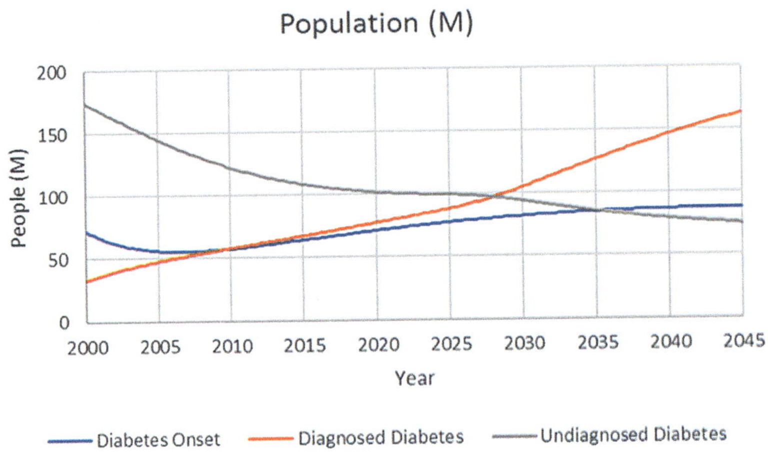

Fig. 12.15: Effect of enhanced diabetes screening policy through 2045.

12.9.2 Prevention Campaigns and Lifestyle Programmes

The second policy involves initiatives aimed at preventing diabetes through targeted diet and lifestyle modifications. Figure 12.16 shows the results. This policy substantially decreases the number of people with diabetes onset. However, counterintuitively, it moves these people into the population with diabetes. It doesn't reduce the number of people with diabetes, while it increases the number of people with undiagnosed diabetes. This should be investigated further.

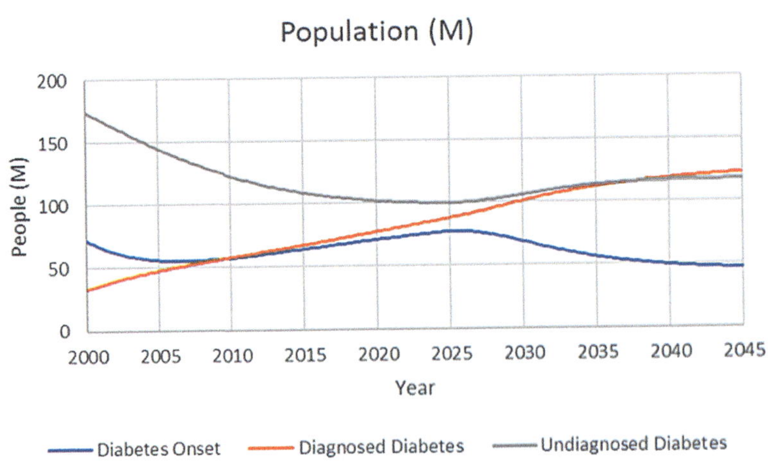

Fig. 12.16: Results of prevention campaigns and lifestyle programmes.

12.9.3 Expanded Treatment Infrastructure

We will consider expanded treatment infrastructure, which only affects people with diagnosed diabetes (see Fig. 12.17). Although generally beneficial, this population lives longer, which increases the total number of people in the population.

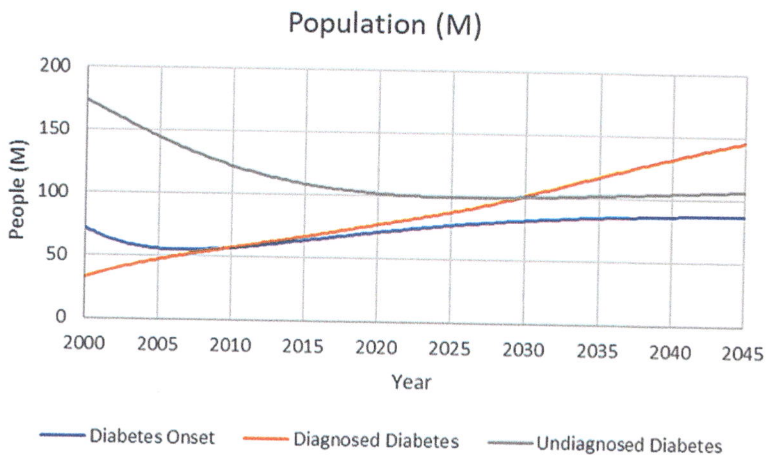

Fig. 12.17: Projected results of expanded diabetes treatment access.

12.9.4 Healthcare Availability

When healthcare availability is increased, it helps everyone live longer. This results in fewer people developing diabetes, more people being diagnosed with diabetes than in the baseline case, and, counterintuitively, many more people with undiagnosed diabetes (see Fig. 12.18). This should be investigated further.

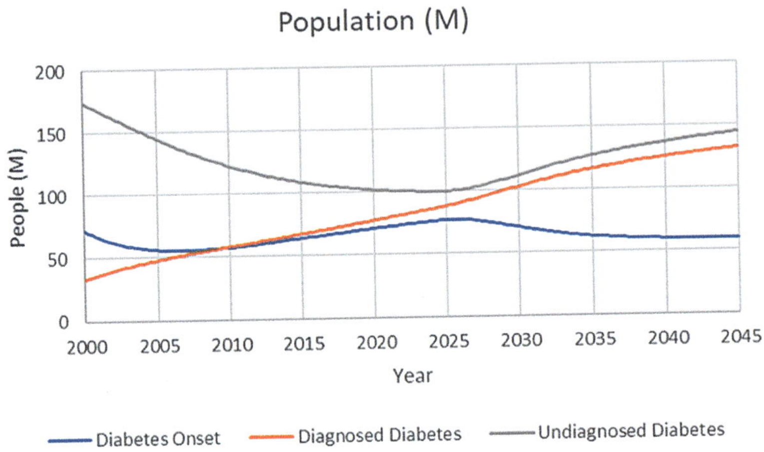

Fig. 12.18: Results of improvements in healthcare availability.

12.9.5 Healthcare Financing

When healthcare financing is improved, this has a similar effect to healthcare availability. It will help people live longer in general and reduce the number of people with diabetes onset, resulting in high numbers of people with undiagnosed diabetes and, counterintuitively, even higher numbers of people diagnosed with diabetes (see Fig. 12.19). This should be investigated further.

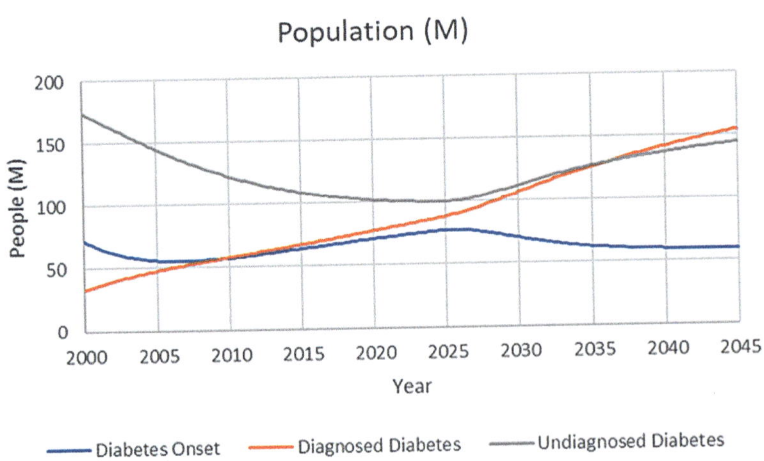

Fig. 12.19: Impact of better healthcare financing on population and diabetes outcomes.

12.9.6 Policy Optimization

Finally, we can use the Solver to conduct a constrained optimization to find the best mix of policies. We assumed that we could increase the effectiveness of each policy by 50% at an equal cost. We can optimize the distribution of policy improvements to maximize the average life expectancy of the total population in 2045.

First, we will examine the improvement in life expectancy compared to the baseline case, where no investment is made in these policies. Then, we will consider the results when we concentrate all our effort on each policy separately. Table 12.1 shows the results. The model predicts that life expectancy can be increased from 73.9 years in the baseline case to 84.7 years in 2045, with effort shared equally between financing and lifestyle policies.

Tab. 12.1: Optimization results for five diabetes policies show gains in life expectancy by 2045.

Screening (%)	Treatment (%)	Availability (%)	Financing (%)	Lifestyle (%)	Life expectancy (2045)
0	0	0	0	0	73.9
50	0	0	0	0	74.4
0	50	0	0	0	76.8
0	0	50	0	0	79.6
0	0	0	50	0	82.0
0	0	0	0	50	80.8
10	10	10	10	10	81.2
0	0	0	25	25	84.7

12.10 Discussion

With this model, we have seen some fascinating counterintuitive results. Many of the policies, although well-intentioned, seemed to exacerbate the problems. For example, although several policies reduced the number of people with diabetes onset, they created more people with diabetes and, more disturbingly, more people with undiagnosed diabetes. The policies led to longer life expectancies. Although there are side effects associated with each of these policies, the overall outcome of increased life expectancy for the population is positive.

12.11 Conclusion

This chapter shows what you can do with a system dynamics model built entirely in Excel. Moving the model out of Vensim and into a spreadsheet made it easier for more people to explore a complex, multifaceted public health issue, such as diabetes in India, without requiring specialized software or coding skills.

The model explains how people transition between health states and how different policies, such as improved screening, increased treatment, or enhanced prevention, unfold over time. The Excel version lets you tweak assumptions, run scenarios, and see how one change ripples through the system.

The simulations clearly demonstrate that fixing one part of the system doesn't resolve the entire problem. Screening finds more cases, but that creates pressure on care services. Treatment keeps people alive, but it doesn't slow down the number of new diagnoses. Prevention helps, but it also increases the number of people who are living with the disease without knowing it. It's a balancing act, and Excel helps make that complexity visible.

That's the real value here. A model like this helps policymakers and health planners identify the unintended consequences of good intentions before implementing real-world programmes. It's not just about figuring out what works, but also about spotting what might backfire.

With Excel, the barrier to entry is low. Anyone with a basic understanding of spreadsheets can start experimenting, testing, and planning. That hands-on, systems thinking is needed to tackle something as challenging as diabetes, not just in India but anywhere.

12.12 Discussion Questions

- Which reference-mode features must the model reproduce before any forward scenarios are briefed to health leadership, and why?
- Where do policy levers create beneficial but counterintuitive side effects (e.g. longer life ⇒ larger diagnosed/undiagnosed stocks), and how would you communicate the trade-off?
- What justifies modelling policy implementation as a third-order delay rather than a single time constant? Cite structural or empirical reasons.
- What should be included on an interface sheet versus what should be hidden on model sheets to keep the workbook audit-ready and usable?
- For this chapter's calibration scope, which variables deserve series-level SSE and which can be inspected visually only? Defend your cut.
- The optimization elevates 2045 life expectancy with a targeted policy mix. What constraints (bounds/floors/ceilings) are mandatory to avoid nonsense solutions?

12.13 Exercises

12.13.1 Structure and levers
Task. Sketch the stock/flow for healthy → prediabetic → diabetic (diagnosed/undiagnosed) with deaths; list the five levers and the expected sign of impact.
Deliverable. One slide (diagram and lever table).

12.13.2 Third-order delay sheet
Task. Create a policy delay worksheet and wire a third-order delay that feeds the Model sheet; run with a time step of 0.25.
Deliverable. Screenshot of formulas for one row; note dt.

12.13.3 Interface wiring
Task. Build an interface tab with inputs for screening, lifestyle, treatment, availability, and financing. Link charts to model outputs.
Deliverable. Interface screenshot.

12.13.4 Calibration scaffold
Task. Add actual/model/SE for population and diabetes prevalence; compute per-series SSE and total SSE (2000–2023).
Deliverable. First 12 rows and SSE cells.

12.13.5 Baseline run
Task. Run the status quo to 2045; export charts for population and diabetes.
Deliverable. Two charts and a two sentence read out.

12.13.6 Screening scenario
Task. Increase screening by 50% over 20 years from 2023; compare diagnosed cases to undiagnosed cases at baseline.
Deliverable. Overlay a chart and two bullets.

12.13.7 Lifestyle and availability paradox
Task. Run diet and lifestyle, and healthcare availability policies separately; explain why undiagnosed conditions can increase even as onset falls or life expectancy rises.
Deliverable. Short diagnostic note (≤120 words).

12.13.8 Policy-mix optimization
Task. Set a Solver model to allocate improvements (bounded at ≤50%) to maximize 2045 life expectancy.
Deliverable. Solver dialogue and before/after 2045 life expectancy; two-line rationale.

Chapter 13
Hiring and Promoting Minorities in a Legal Aid Organization

13.1 Learning Objectives

- Frame a talent pipeline as a stock-flow system across the gates of recruitment, hiring, promotion, and exits.
- Translate a Vensim pipeline model into a maintainable Excel implementation (parameters, model, interface), preserving units, naming, and auditability.
- Build a multi-series calibration spreadsheet (actual vs. model vs. squared error) for minority/majority attorneys and supervisors, and compute total SSE.
- Configure Solver to minimize sum of squared error (SSE) subject to realism constraints.
- Diagnose baseline dynamics to 2050 and attribute them to loop dominance and promotion delays.
- Design and run policy experiments for (a) targeted outreach, (b) mentorship for promotion, and (c) upstream qualifications, each with phased delays.
- Optimize a combined policy mix to achieve governance targets with credible investment levels.
- Produce a stakeholder-ready brief that includes problem framing, data sources, fit evidence, scenario deltas, risks, guard-rails, and an annual refresh plan.

13.2 Introduction

Legal-aid organizations exist to give marginalized communities a fair shot in court. Yet many of the offices doing that work don't look like the clients they serve. People of colour make up a large share of the client base but a much smaller slice of staff attorneys, and an even thinner slice of supervisors. The gap isn't just about optics; it shapes which cases get priority, how clients feel represented, and whether rookie lawyers of colour decide to stay or move on.

Closing that gap turns out to be a systems problem, not just a recruiting problem. Each career stage (application, hiring, onboarding, case assignments, mentorship, performance reviews, promotion) acts like a gate. Small biases at any one gate, when repeated year after year, create a bottleneck that starves the leadership pipeline. Traditional metrics (headcounts and year-over-year diversity snapshots) can't reveal where the real choke points sit or how one policy tweak might ripple through the whole talent flow.

https://doi.org/10.1515/9783111541389-015

That's where system dynamics earns its keep [44]. We first map the staffing pipeline in Vensim, tracing the stock-and-flow of candidates from law school outreach to supervisory roles. We convert the Vensim model into Excel. That step, used in every chapter of this book, removes the barrier to entry. Anyone with a spreadsheet can now run "what-if" tests to see what happens if we invest in earlier outreach. How many years until the talent pipeline fills? Which lever delivers the fastest, most durable gains? Because the math is stored in Excel, staff can tweak assumptions, stress-test scenarios, and share results without specialized software or coding skills.

In short, this chapter demonstrates how a system dynamics lens, combined with a tool that everyone already has, transforms diversity goals from vague commitments into clear, testable strategies. By surfacing the hidden feedback loops that create today's leadership gaps, the model helps legal-aid organizations chart a path to teams and leaders that reflect the communities they defend.

13.3 Problem Definition

Legal-aid non-profits serve communities where half or more of the clients are people of colour, yet the internal numbers tell a different story. In 2013, only 31% of staff attorneys and 29% of supervisors identified as members of minority groups. That gap is more than a statistic; it shapes client trust, case outcomes, and whether talented lawyers of colour see a future inside the organization.

The board has committed to closing that gap within a generation: by 2050, at least 50% of attorneys *and* supervisors should come from the same minority groups that make up the client base. Hitting that mark requires more than better recruiting brochures. What matters is the entire talent pipeline, from law-school outreach and entry-level hiring to mentorship, performance reviews, and promotion windows. Minor leaks at any point compound over decades, starving leadership roles of diverse candidates and reinforcing the very imbalance the organization hopes to fix.

13.4 Reference Mode

Before we can test policies, we need a clear understanding of how representation has evolved. Following the format used for the previous chapters, we plot two short but telling time series.

Figure 13.1 shows the fraction of minority attorneys from 2013 to 2019. The curve starts at 31% in 2013, nudges up to roughly 33% by 2015, then gradually increases to 39% by 2017 before levelling off through 2019. The gentle rise, followed by a plateau, suggests that early recruitment efforts gained traction but stalled without more substantial support for retention.

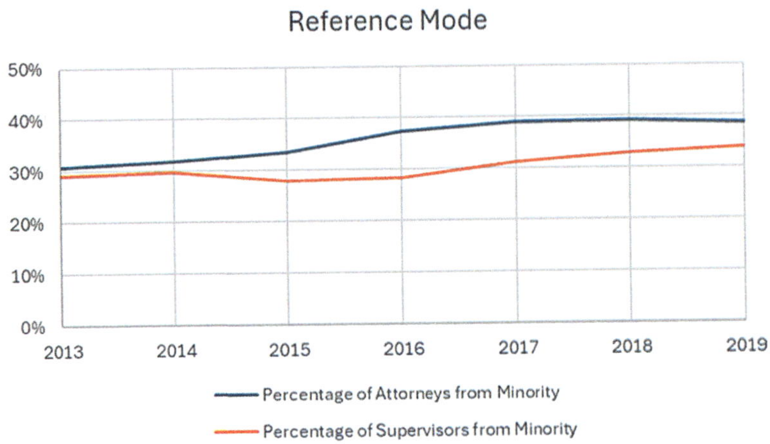

Fig. 13.1: Reference modes for diversity in a legal aid organization.

Figure 13.1 also shows the fraction of minority supervisors from 2013 to 2019. This series begins at a lower level, at 29% in 2013. It dips slightly in 2015 and 2016 (a "worse-before-better" blip typical when seasoned supervisors retire) and recovers to 31% by 2017. A modest uptick in internal promotions lifts the line to 34% in 2019.

Taken together, the two figures show a closing of the gap between client diversity (≈ 50% minorities) and both staff tiers. More critical for modelling, they reveal four key behavioural cues we must replicate: slow linear gains; a mid-decade dip in supervisor progress that coincides with the attorney increases, which is evidence of feedback between the two pipelines; persistent lag in supervisory diversity, signalling promotion delays, not just hiring gaps; and an unclear natural convergence towards 50%, if left alone, the system may drift towards a lower than 50% equilibrium.

These reference modes serve as the calibration targets for our Vensim-built model and its subsequent Excel conversion. Suppose the simulated curves can reproduce the shallow rise-and-stall pattern through 2019. In that case, we can trust them to explore what mix of hiring, mentorship, and accelerated promotion is needed to hit the 50% goal by 2050.

13.5 Dynamic Hypothesis

The model is built around a set of reinforcing and balancing feedback loops that capture how representation evolves through workforce flows (see Fig. 13.2). At the heart of the structure are two organizational levels (minority attorneys and minority supervisors). The model simulates how people are hired and promoted in the system over time.

One of the key reinforcing loops stems from the idea that minority representation among attorneys can influence the attractiveness of the organization to prospective mi-

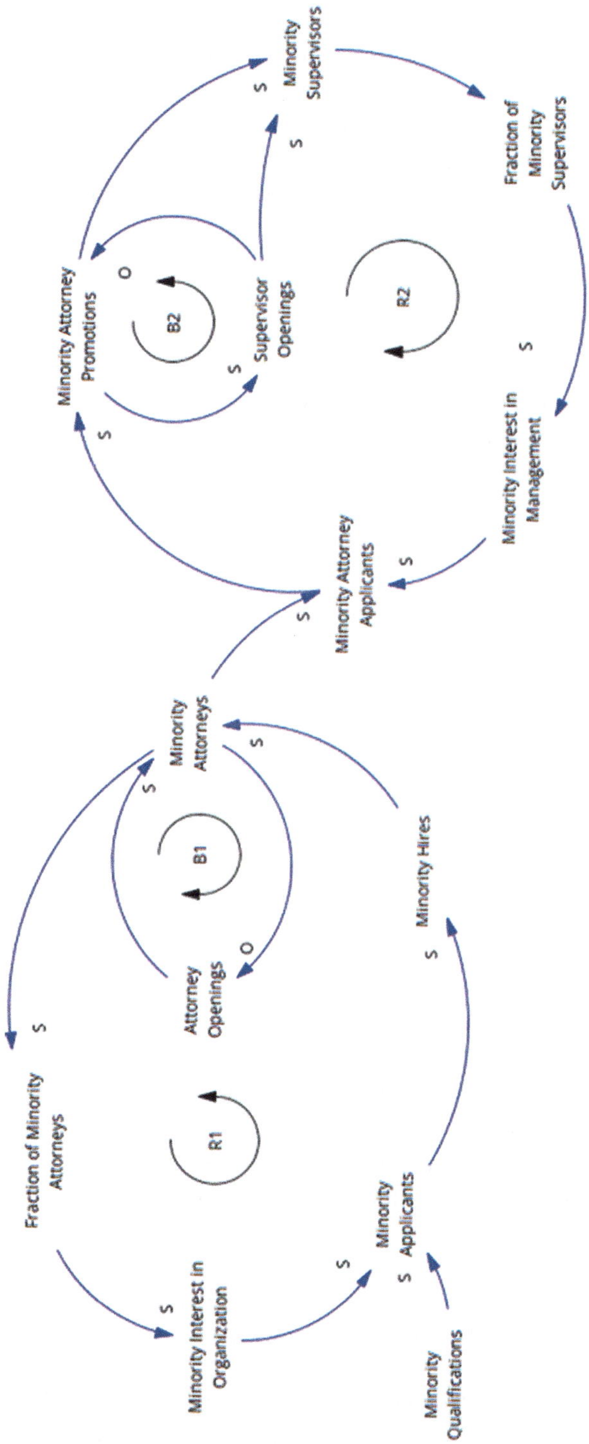

Fig. 13.2: Causal loop diagram of the legal aid representativeness problem.

nority applicants (R1). As more minority individuals are hired, the visibility of representation improves. This, in turn, increases the interest of qualified minority candidates in applying to the organization. Higher interest rates lead to a larger pool of qualified minority applicants at the entry level, which supports future gains in representativeness.

A similar reinforcing feedback loop is involved with minority supervisors. Increasing the number of minority supervisors improves perceived inclusiveness, which in turn attracts more minority attorney applicants, resulting in higher numbers of minority promotions into leadership roles (R2).

At the same time, workforce transitions are governed by balancing loops. For instance, when there are limited vacancies at the attorney and supervisor levels, hiring and promoting rates decline, slowing the advancement of representativeness (B1 and B2). Similarly, exits, whether voluntary or due to retirement, create opportunities for new hires, thereby regulating the pace of flow through the system.

The interaction between these reinforcing and balancing dynamics determines whether minority representation among managers increases steadily, plateaus, or reverses. The model enables users to examine how hiring ratios, promotion probabilities, and exit rates influence these trajectories. It also illustrates how long it can take for policy changes to have visible effects, especially when initial representation levels are low, and the pathway to leadership involves delays.

By conceptualizing this feedback explicitly, the model provides a rigorous framework for understanding why progress can be slow and what kinds of interventions may accelerate change. These structural insights guide the formulation of the stock-and-flow model described in the next section and inform the policy experiments explored later in this chapter.

13.6 Model Formulation

13.6.1 The Vensim Model

We developed a flexible and straightforward Vensim model that illustrates how individuals progress through an organization over time. It tracks who's on staff, who gets hired, who earns a promotion, and who leaves. The model maintains separate stocks for the majority and minority employees at every level, from entry-level roles to management. Flows connect the stocks. They capture hiring, promotions, retirements, and resignations (see Fig. 13.3).

Several levers on the model control the rate at which diversity improves. First, positions can only be filled if they are open. The model accounts for whether the organization is expanding or contracting based on its current positions and desired future positions, using a goal-gap model.

The model accounts for what share of the broader talent market is qualified for an entry-level job. If only a small slice of the minority population meets the qualifica-

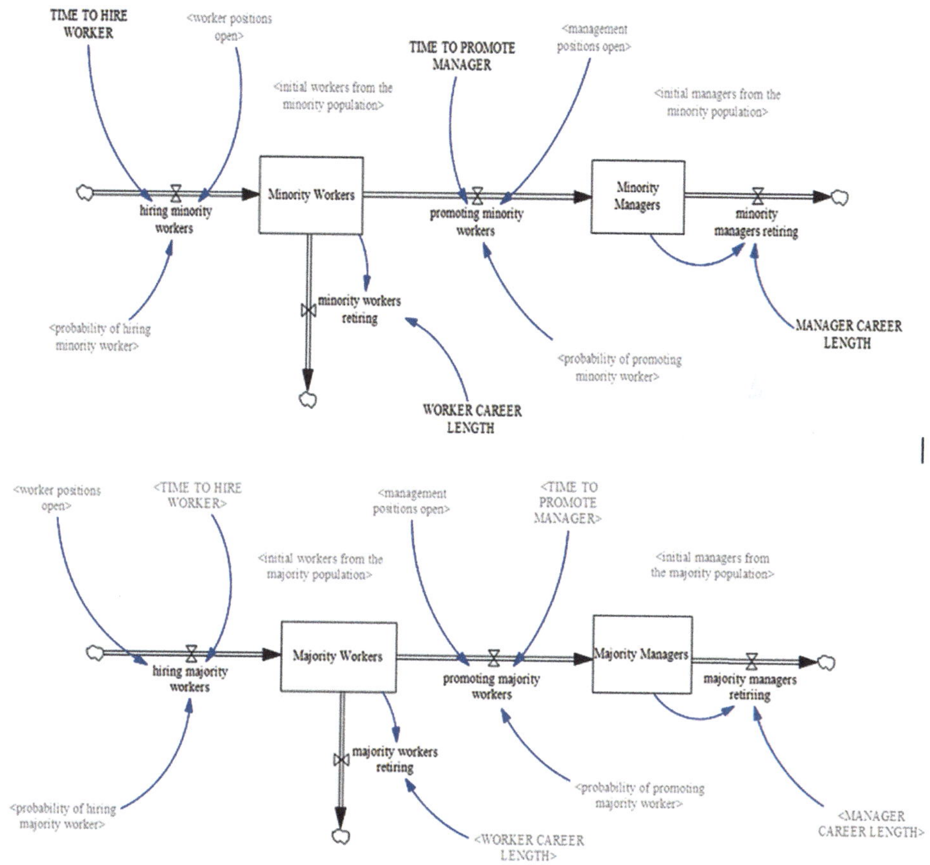

Fig. 13.3: Vensim stock and flow diagram of hiring and promoting employees.

tions, even strong pro-diversity hiring rules will not increase representativeness. Of those who qualify, the model accounts for how many even want to apply. Interest can rise or fall in response to factors such as compensation, workplace culture, or the visibility of minority leaders (see Fig. 13.4).

The probability of hiring a minority applicant or promoting a minority attorney to a supervisory position is based on the fraction of minority applicants and the hiring and promotion strategies employed by management (Fig. 13.5). In the legal aid organization, we assume that hiring and promotion strategy are unbiased; therefore, the probability of hiring and promotion is solely based on the fraction of applicants and attorneys who are from minority groups. This fraction can be influenced by the current representativeness of the organization, which will affect interest from both minority and majority populations.

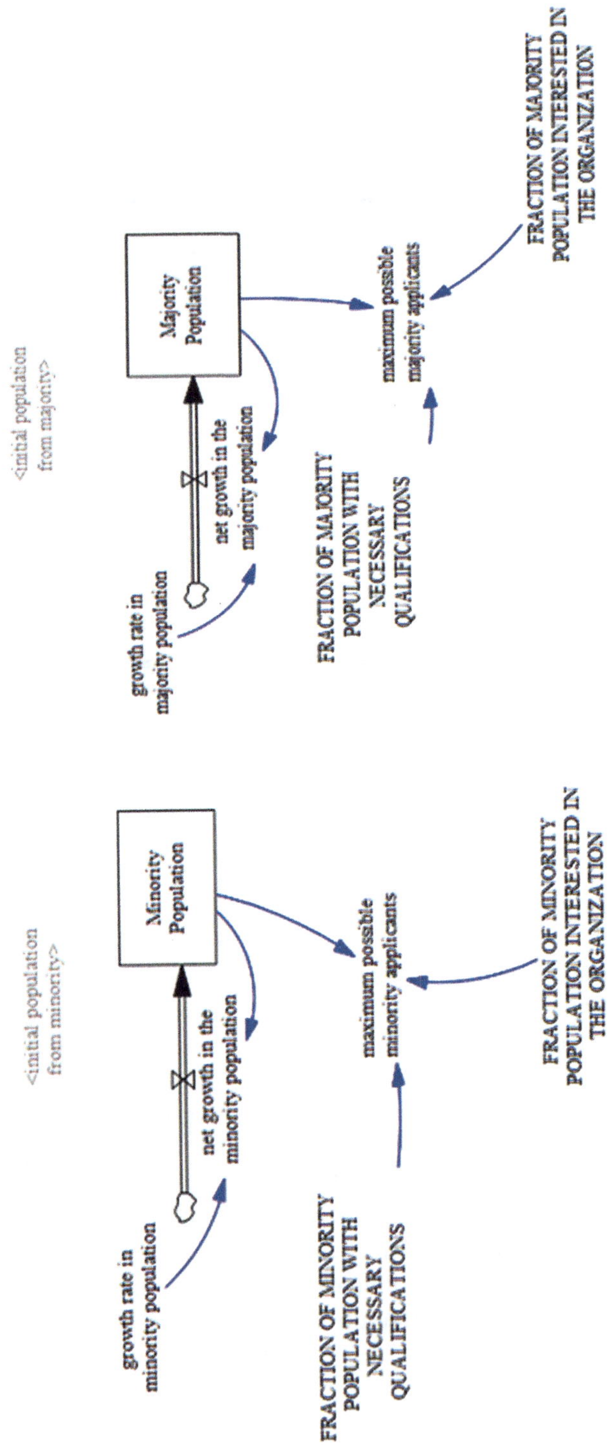

Fig. 13.4: Vensim diagram of qualifications and interest in populations outside the organization.

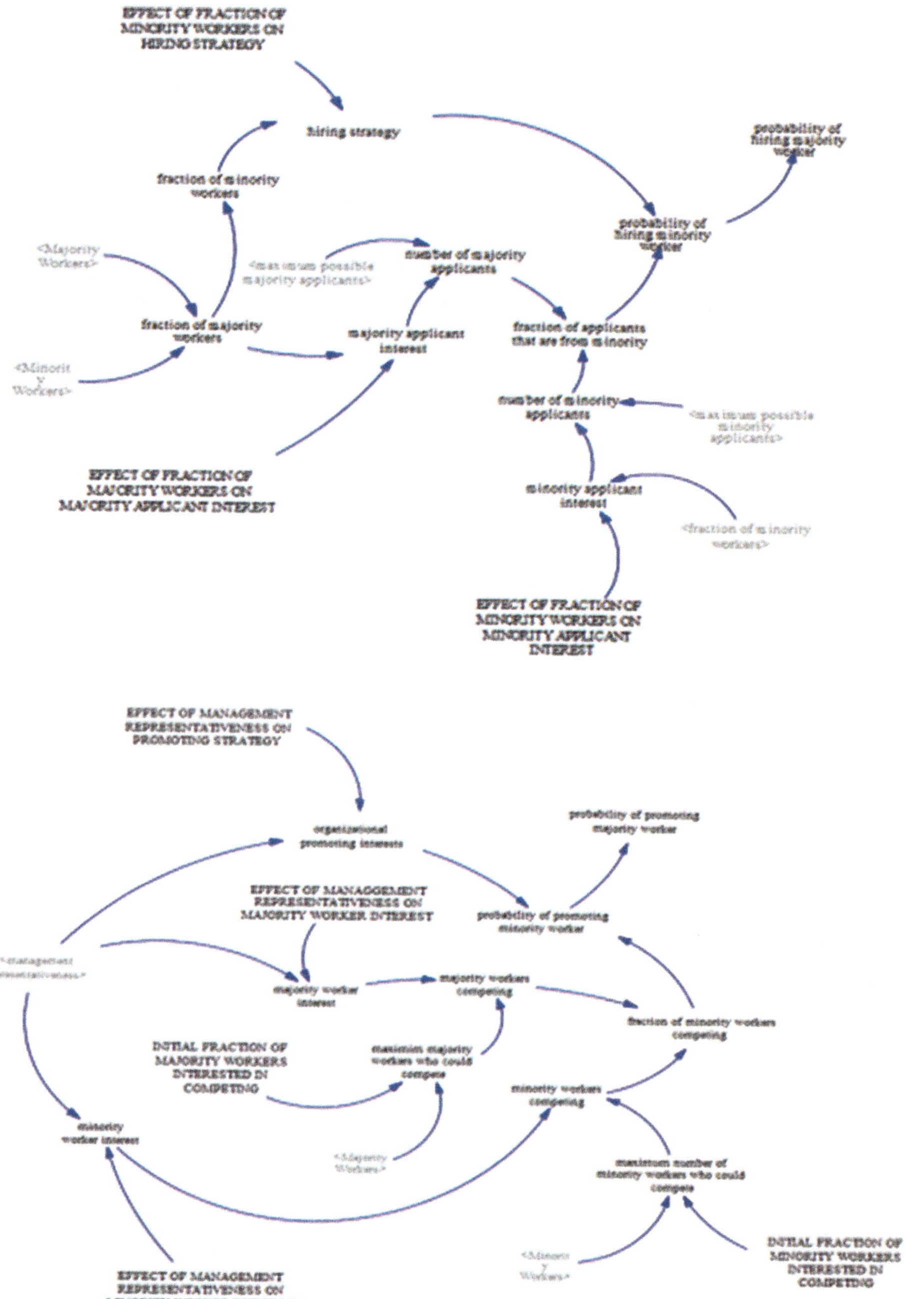

Fig. 13.5: Model of representativeness' influence on hiring and promoting decisions.

13.6.2 The Excel Model

Just as we did in the previous chapters, we took the model built in Vensim and rebuilt it in Excel, so anyone with a basic spreadsheet programme can run it. The first step was to copy the Vensim equations into a new worksheet, so we had the whole logic in front of us. Next, we transposed those equations into a single horizontal line on the model sheet, aligning them from left to right so you can scroll across and view the entire set at a glance. We extracted all constants (initial values, growth rates, and multipliers) and placed them in a separate column, allowing you to adjust assumptions without needing to dig through formulas. We then linked the parameters in the model worksheet to the cells in the interface worksheet. Figures 13.6 and 13.7 show the parameters in the interface worksheet.

	A	B	C	D
1	PARAMETER	VALUE	UNITS	TSSE
2	(37) INITIAL TIME = 2015	2013	Units: Year	10,950
3	(80) TIME STEP = 0.125	0.125	Units: Year [0,?]	
4	(03) DESIRED NUMBER OF MANAGERS=	377	Units: people	
5	(04) DESIRED NUMBER OF WORKERS=	1609	Units: people	
6	(14) FRACTION OF MAJORITY POPULATION INTERESTED IN THE ORGANIZATION=	5%	Units: fraction	
7	(15) FRACTION OF MAJORITY POPULATION WITH NECESSARY QUALIFICATIONS=	1%	Units: fraction	
8	(18) FRACTION OF MINORITY POPULATION INTERESTED IN THE ORGANIZATION=	57%	Units: fraction	
9	(19) FRACTION OF MINORITY POPULATION WITH NECESSARY QUALIFICATIONS=	0%	Units: fraction	
10	(26) INITIAL FRACTION OF MAJORITY WORKERS INTERESTED IN COMPETING=	100%	Units: fraction	
11	(27) INITIAL FRACTION OF MINORITY WORKERS INTERESTED IN COMPETING=	85%	Units: fraction	
12	(28) INITIAL FRACTION OF POPULATION FROM THE MINORITY=	25%	Units: fraction	
13	(31) INITIAL MANAGERS=	225	Units: people	
14	(32) INITIAL MINORITY MANAGERS=	65	Units: people	
15	(33) INITIAL MINORITY WORKERS=	250	Units: people	
16	(34) INITIAL POPULATION=	1.95E+07	Units: people	
17	(38) INITIAL WORKERS=	800	Units: people	
18	(40) MAJORITY GROWTH RATE=	0.0017	Units: 1/Year	
19	(51) MANAGER CAREER LENGTH=	5	Units: Year	
20	(58) MINORITY GROWTH RATE=	0.0113	Units: 1/Year	

Fig. 13.6: The parameters of the hiring and promoting model (set 1).

	A	B	C
1	PARAMETER	VALUE	UNITS
21	(81) TIME TO CHANGE MANAGER POSITIONS=	1.4	Units: Year
22	(82) TIME TO CHANGE WORKER POSITIONS=	1.9	Units: Year
23	(83) TIME TO HIRE WORKER=	0.5	Units: Year
24	(84) TIME TO PROMOTE MANAGER=	0.5	Units: Year
25	(86) WORKER CAREER LENGTH=	10	Units: Year

Fig. 13.7: The parameters of the hiring and promoting model (set 2).

The model is one of the larger ones in the book, featuring numerous moving parts that interact with each other. Figures 13.8–13.12 show all of the endogenous variables in the model (stocks, flows, and auxiliaries). In each figure, you can see the variable names in alphabetical order and the units for the variable. Also, the results of the first few time-step calculations are shown. This can help debug the Excel conversion.

Taken together, these figures present the entire set of calculations laid out in a familiar grid-based Excel interface.

	A	B	C	D	E	F	G	H	I	J	K	L	M
1	Time	(01) change in manager positions=	(02) change in worker positions=	(12) fraction of applicants that are from minority=	(13) fraction of majority managers =	(16) fraction of majority workers=	Fraction of minority supervisors	Fraction of minority attorneys	(21) fraction of minority workers competing=	(22) fraction of organization on minority=	(23) fraction of population from minority=	(24) hiring majority workers=	(25) hiring minority workers=
2	Year	Units: people/Year	Units: people/Year	Units: fraction	Units: fraction	Units: fraction			Units: fraction	Units: fraction	Units: fraction	Units: people/Year	Units: people/Year
7	2013.5	74.80148	321.2285	0.394164	0.711804	0.678743	0.288196	0.321257	0.287549	0.314093	0.2509	210.0964	136.6915
8	2013.625	68.07041	300.3657	0.394317	0.711837	0.674506	0.288163	0.325494	0.291532	0.317404	0.251126	232.6483	151.4605
9	2013.75	61.94504	280.8578	0.394471	0.71166	0.670189	0.28834	0.329811	0.295596	0.32083	0.251351	247.7226	161.3783
10	2013.875	56.37087	262.6169	0.394626	0.711278	0.665982	0.288722	0.334018	0.299562	0.324228	0.251577	256.9863	167.5221
11	2014	51.2983	245.5607	0.394783	0.710715	0.661994	0.289285	0.338006	0.303326	0.327507	0.251803	261.8018	170.7734

Fig. 13.8: Endogenous variables in the organizational diversity model (set 1).

	A	N	O	P	Q	R	S	T	U	V	W	X	Y
1	Time	(29) initial majority managers =	(30) initial majority workers=	(35) initial population from majority=	(36) initial population from minority=	(39) majority applicant interest=	(41) Majority Managers = INTEG (	(42) majority managers retiring=	(43) Majority Population= INTEG (	(44) majority worker interest=	(45) Majority Workers= INTEG (	(46) majority workers competing=	(47) majority workers retiring=
2	Year	Units: people	Units: people	Units: people	Units: people	Units: fraction	Units: people	Units: people/Year	Units: people	Units: fraction	Units: people	Units: people	Units: people/Year
7	2013.5	160	550	1.46E+07	4.88E+06	0.5	160.8971	32.17943	14637435	0.5	554.6113	277.3057	55.46113
8	2013.625	160	550	1.46E+07	4.88E+06	0.5	165.1686	33.03373	14640546	0.5	565.6468	282.8234	56.56468
9	2013.75	160	550	1.46E+07	4.88E+06	0.5	169.8821	33.97641	14643657	0.5	578.8146	289.4073	57.88146
10	2013.875	160	550	1.46E+07	4.88E+06	0.5	174.7489	34.94978	14646769	0.5	593.4309	296.7154	59.34309
11	2014	160	550	1.46E+07	4.88E+06	0.5	179.578	35.9156	14649881	0.5	608.9384	304.4692	60.89384

Fig. 13.9: Endogenous variables in the organizational diversity model (set 2).

	A	Z	AA	AB	AC	AD	AE	AF	AG	AH	AI	AJ	AK
1	Time	(48) management positions filled=	(49) management positions open=	(50) management representativeness =	(52) Manager Positions = INTEG (	(53) maximim majority workers who could compete=	(54) maximum number of minority workers who could compete=	(55) maximum possible majority applicants =	(56) maximum possible minority applicants =	(57) minority applicant interest=	(59) Minority Managers = INTEG (	(60) minority managers retiring=	(61) Minority Population= INTEG (
2	Year	Units: people	Units: people	Units: fraction	Units: people	Units: people	Units: people	Units: people	Units: people	Units: fraction	Units: people	Units: people/Year	Units: people
7	2013.5	226.0413	46.56561	1.148647	272.6069	554.6113	223.8441	5050.713	3286.06	0.5	65.14418	13.02884	4902602
8	2013.625	232.0317	49.92542	1.147486	281.9571	565.6468	232.7616	5036.631	3278.987	0.5	66.86305	13.37261	4909527
9	2013.75	238.7123	51.75366	1.147157	290.4659	578.8146	242.8936	5019.975	3270.25	0.5	68.83018	13.76604	4916462
10	2013.875	245.6829	52.52618	1.147647	298.209	593.4309	253.7975	5001.718	3260.478	0.5	70.93397	14.18679	4923406
11	2014	252.6723	52.58307	1.148855	305.2554	608.9384	265.127	4982.608	3250.157	0.5	73.09434	14.61887	4930361

Fig. 13.10: Endogenous variables in the organizational diversity model (set 3).

	A	AL	AM	AN	AO	AP	AQ	AR	AS	AT	AU	AV	AW
1	Time	(62) minority worker interest=	(63) Minority Workers= INTEG (	(64) minority workers competin g=	(65) minority workers retiring=	(66) net growth in the majority population =	(67) net growth in the minority population =	(68) number of majority applicants =	(69) number of minority applicants =	(70) organizati onal hiring interests=	(71) organizati onal promoting interests=	(72) overall represent ativeness =	(73) probabilit y of hiring majority worker=
2	Year	Units: fraction	Units: people	Units: people	Units: people/Y ear	Units: people/Y ear	Units: people/Y ear	Units: people	Units: people	Units: fraction	Units: fraction	Units: fraction	Units: fraction
7	2013.5	0.5	262.5043	111.9221	26.25043	2.49E+04	5.54E+04	2525.356	1643.03	0.5	0.5	1.251864	0.605836
8	2013.625	0.5	272.962	116.3808	27.2962	2.49E+04	5.55E+04	2518.316	1639.494	0.5	0.5	1.263922	0.605683
9	2013.75	0.5	284.8438	121.4468	28.48438	2.49E+04	5.56E+04	2509.988	1635.125	0.5	0.5	1.276422	0.605529
10	2013.875	0.5	297.631	126.8988	29.7631	2.49E+04	5.56E+04	2500.859	1630.239	0.5	0.5	1.288784	0.605374
11	2014	0.5	310.9172	132.5635	31.09172	2.49E+04	5.57E+04	2491.304	1625.079	0.5	0.5	1.30065	0.605217

Fig. 13.11: Endogenous variables in the organizational diversity model (set 4).

	A	AX	AY	AZ	BA	BB	BC	BD	BE	BF	BG
1	Time	(74) probabilit y of hiring minority worker=	(75) probabilit y of promoting majority worker=	(76) probabilit y of promoting minority worker=	(77) promoting majority workers=	(78) promoting minority workers=	(85) Total Employee s=	(87) Worker Positions = INTEG (	(88) worker positions filled=	(89) worker positions open=	(90) worker represent ativeness =
2	Year	Units: fraction	Units: fraction	Units: fraction	Units: people/Y ear	Units: people/Y ear	Units: people	Units: people	Units: people	Units: people	Units: fraction
7	2013.5	0.394164	0.712451	0.287549	66.35142	26.77979	1043.157	990.5096	817.1156	173.394	1.280418
8	2013.625	0.394317	0.708468	0.291532	70.74113	29.10972	1070.64	1030.663	838.6088	192.0544	1.296139
9	2013.75	0.394471	0.704404	0.295596	72.91098	30.59634	1102.371	1068.209	863.6584	204.5505	1.31215
10	2013.875	0.394626	0.700438	0.299562	73.58266	31.46971	1136.745	1103.316	891.0619	212.2542	1.327698
11	2014	0.394783	0.696674	0.303326	73.26649	31.89965	1172.528	1136.143	919.8556	216.2876	1.342346

Fig. 13.12: Endogenous variables in the organizational diversity model (set 5).

13.7 Calibration

Calibrating a system dynamics model is the step that turns a conceptual map into a decision-ready tool. By tuning parameters until the model's simulated outputs line up with historical data, you ground every feedback loop and delay in real-world behaviour. This reduces guesswork, exposes structural weaknesses, and builds confidence that the model's future projections reflect the system you're trying to understand, not just the assumptions inside your head.

We began calibration with four historical time series: the annual number of minority and majority attorneys and the yearly number of minority and majority supervisors. For every year in each series, the workbook displays: (1) the actual value, (2) the model's estimate, and (3) the squared error (i.e. the difference between the two values, squared so large misses count more). A total squared error cell tallies the inaccuracy penalty across all four time-series (see Fig. 13.13). Using Excel's Solver add-in, we allowed the programme to vary the key parameters until the total squared error reached its lowest possible value, yielding a statistically tight fit without requiring manual tuning.

	A	B	C	D	E	F	G	H	I	J	K	L	M	N	O	P	Q	R
1	Year	Actual Minority Supervisors	Model Minority Supervisors	SE	SSE	Actual Minority Attorneys	Model Minority Attorneys	SE	SSE	Actual Majority Supervisors	Model Majority Supervisors	SE	SSE	Actual Majority Attorneys	Model Majority Attorneys	SE	SSE	TSSE
2	2013	66	65	1	265	249	250	1	2,784	160	160	0	718	558	550	64	7,182	10,950
3	2014	78	73	24		287	311	572		184	180	20		614	609	26		
4	2015	82	88	40		381	410	870		212	209	8		760	729	975		
5	2016	88	98	97		493	479	198		222	223	1		824	809	224		
6	2017	113	104	87		533	522	125		250	229	458		835	855	388		
7	2018	106	107	2		526	549	528		217	230	171		820	879	3,489		
8	2019	114	110	14		589	567	490		222	230	61		936	891	2,016		

Fig. 13.13: The time series data, model estimates, and squared error.

Once Solver settled on the optimal parameters, we plotted the model's output against the historical points (Figs. 13.14 and 13.15). In both graphs, the orange line represents the simulated values while the blue line shows the actual data. The model line closely hovers over the data. Minor deviations remain because no model is perfect; however, the visual overlap confirms what the minimized error statistic already indicated: the calibrated model tracks real-world trends well enough to serve as a dependable base for scenario testing and future projections.

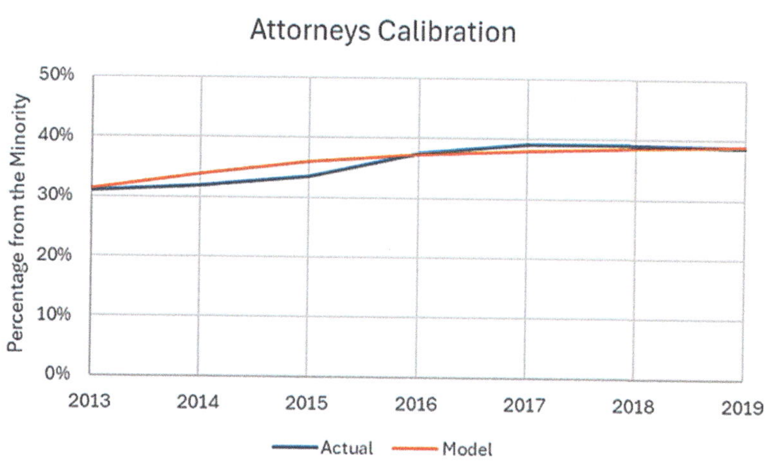

Fig. 13.14: Model fit of historical data on the fraction of minority attorneys.

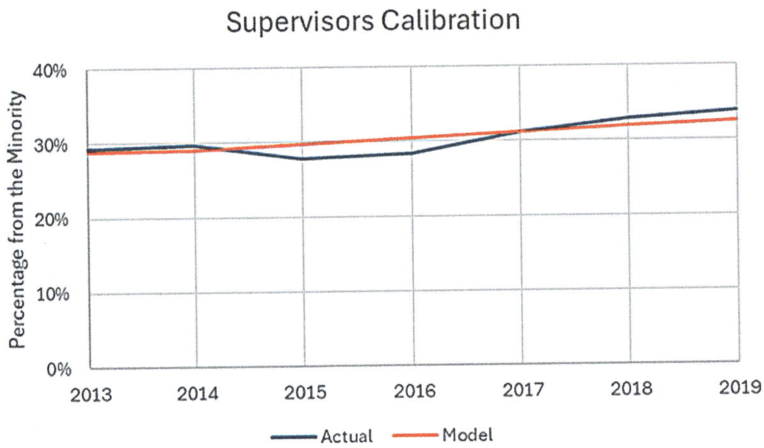

Fig. 13.15: Model fit of historical data on the fraction of minority supervisors.

13.8 Baseline Case

In the baseline case (Fig. 13.16), the model projects only a gradual shift in workforce composition. Over the next 25 years, the percentage of minority attorneys and supervisors is expected to increase, albeit at a modest pace; by 2050, minorities are projected to account for approximately 45% of attorneys and 42% of supervisors. Although these gains outpace the historical trend, they still fall short of the 50% benchmark set to mirror the firm's client base, signalling that passive growth alone will not close the representation gap.

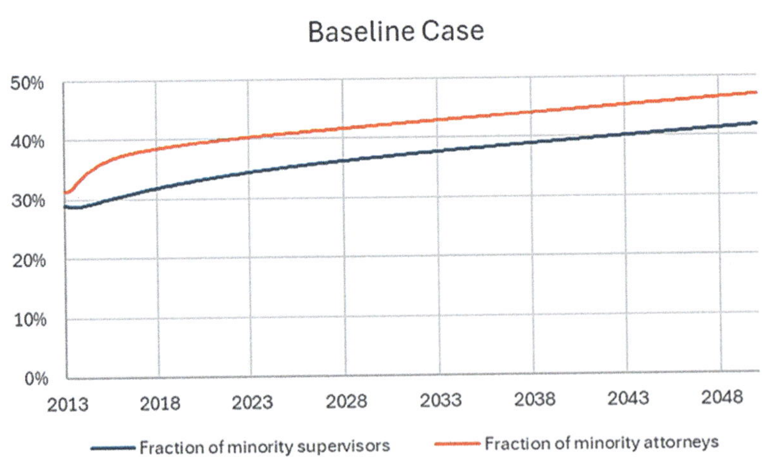

Fig. 13.16: The baseline case with no policy interventions.

13.9 Policy Runs

With the baseline case showing that passive trends alone can't reach the 50% representation target, we now shift to policy runs (model experiments that test proactive levers the firm can pull). Three interventions are on the table, each targeting a different bottleneck in the talent pipeline. Targeted outreach broadens the top of the funnel by sparking organizational interest among minority law students and lateral candidates. Mentorship for promotion pairs minority attorneys with senior sponsors to raise promotion aspirations and success rates. Long-term qualifications enhancement invests in scholarships, internships, and specialized training to expand the pool of highly qualified minority applicants in the years to come. After testing each policy individually, we combine all three to see whether their reinforcing impacts can close the representation gap faster, more reliably, and at a lower cumulative cost than any single initiative on its own.

All policies are assumed to launch in 2025, but none flip a switch overnight. Outreach campaigns require cycles of recruitment, mentorship relationships take time to bear fruit, and qualification programmes must move cohorts through school and early careers. To capture this reality, the model phases in each intervention over several years, allowing its effects to compound gradually before reaching full strength. Figure 13.17 shows the policy section of the interface worksheet. The value column shows the implementation date, improvement values, and improvement delays. The final value column displays the values in 2050, 25 years after the initial improvement. Notice that the management interest is 100% in 2050, which implies that all minority workers are interested in promotion. Therefore, the improvement value cannot exceed 17%.

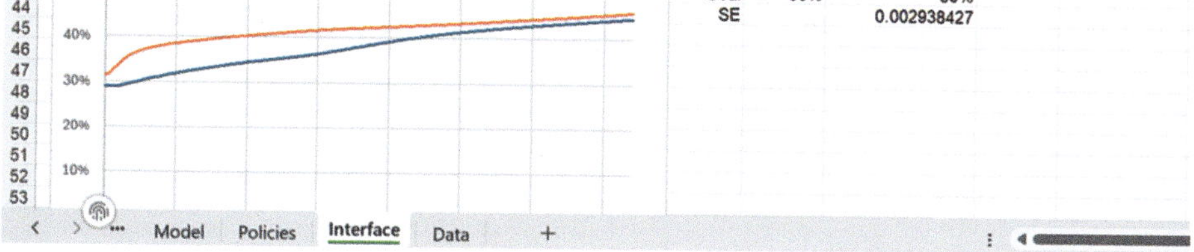

Fig. 13.17: Policy section of the interface worksheet.

Figure 13.18 shows the policies worksheet for the management interest improvement section, and you can see we modelled the improvement as a third-order delay.

	Y	Z	AA	AB	AC	AD	AE	AF	AG	AH	AI	AJ
1	Time	policy implementation	desired policy value	first order change	First Order Policy Value	second order change	Second Order Policy Value	third order change	Management Interest Improvement	PARAMETERS	VALUE	UNITS
2	2013	1	1	0	1	0	1	0	100%	INITIAL TIME	2013	YEAR
3	2013.1	1	1	0	1	0	1	0	100%	TIME STEP	0.125	YEAR
4	2013.3	1	1	0	1	0	1	0	100%	INITIAL POLICY VALUE	1	POLICY UNITS
5	2013.4	1	1	0	1	0	1	0	100%	POLICY IMPROVEMENT	0.17	POLICY UNITS
6	2013.5	1	1	0	1	0	1	0	100%	POLICY IMPLEMENTATION DATE	2025	YEAR
7	2013.6	1	1	0	1	0	1	0	100%	TOTAL DELAY TIME	5	YEAR

Fig. 13.18: Policy worksheet showing the model for the third-order delay.

13.9.1 Organizational Interest

In this scenario, we test a single lever: increasing outreach to spotlight the organization's mission and career path for minority law school graduates. We assume the campaign kicks off in 2025 and requires two years to gain traction, enough time for new brochures, campus visits, and alums ambassadors to start shifting perceptions. Using Solver to achieve the 50% supervisor benchmark by 2050, the model indicates that we must increase the interest level of minority applicants by approximately 43% above its baseline value with a two-year implementation delay (see Fig. 13.19). Figure 13.20 charts the result: the sharper inflow of diverse talent initially fills the attorney pool, and as those hires advance, it lifts supervisor representation to the 50% target just before the mid-century mark.

Fig. 13.19: Organizational interest improvement implementation.

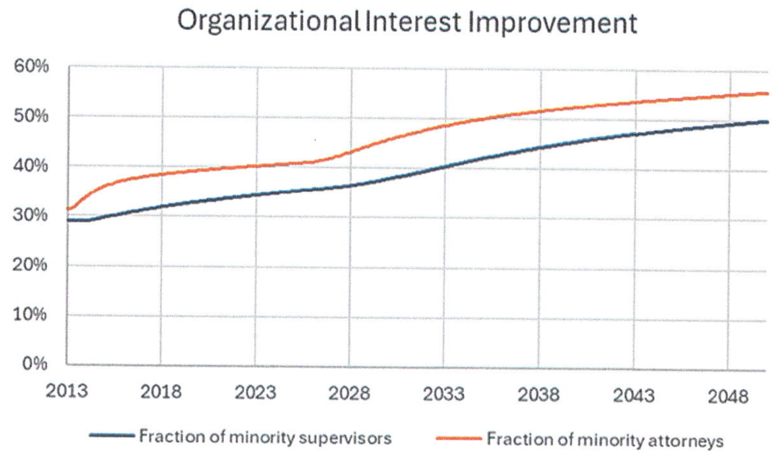

Fig. 13.20: The results of a targeted outreach programme.

13.9.2 Management Interest

The mentorship programme focusses on the middle of the pipeline, pairing minority attorneys with senior sponsors to spark a genuine interest in pursuing management tracks and to facilitate a smoother promotion process. Launched in 2025 and phased over five years, the initiative maximizes the interest level as much as the model allows (see Fig. 13.21), essentially saturating the effect of mentoring on career aspirations. Even at this level, however, the structural bottlenecks remain. As a result, the share of minority supervisors climbs but plateaus at roughly 45% by 2050, five points

Fig. 13.21: Management interest improvement implementation limit.

short of the 50% benchmark (see Fig. 13.22). The run underscores that boosting ambition alone can't close the gap; without more diverse talent entering the pipeline earlier, the mentorship lift reaches a hard limit.

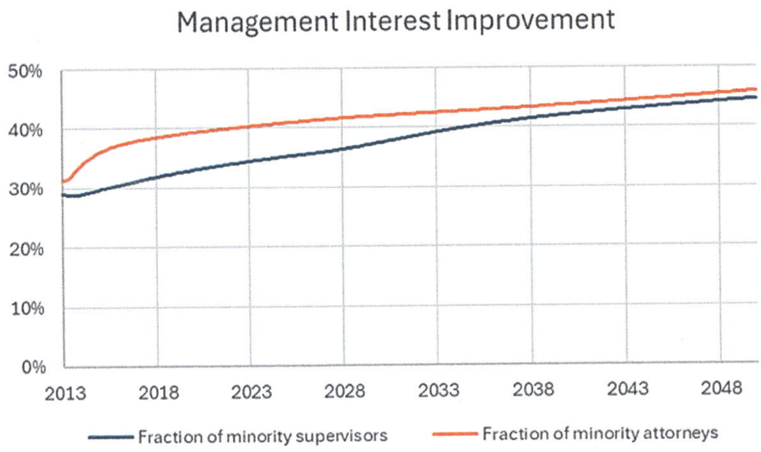

Fig. 13.22: Results of the mentorship programme.

13.9.3 Pipeline Development

The third experiment shifts the focus far upstream by expanding the pool of highly qualified minority candidates, funding scholarships, internships, bar-prep stipends, and early-career fellowships that nurture talent within the organization for years to come. Launched in 2025, the programme assumes a gradual build-out: cohorts must complete law school, pass the bar, and gain early experience before they can be hired, allowing the full impact to unfold gradually. Even after 25 years, the programme has not yet reached its improvement goal (see Fig. 13.23). Model sweeps indicate that the 50% supervisor target is technically achievable with this lever alone (see Fig. 13.24), but only if the pipeline of qualified minority applicants more than doubles (an increase of approximately 109% above today's baseline). While that jump borders on unrealistic in the short term, a sustained, well-funded effort over two decades could plausibly achieve it, illustrating both the power and the long-term potential of deep pipeline investments.

13.9.4 Combined Policy

When all three levers are pulled together, the model shows that a modest push on each front can reach the 50% minority-supervisor benchmark by 2050 without resorting to extreme spending. The optimized mix calls for a 22% boost in applicant interest

Fig. 13.23: Qualifications improvement implementation was not completed.

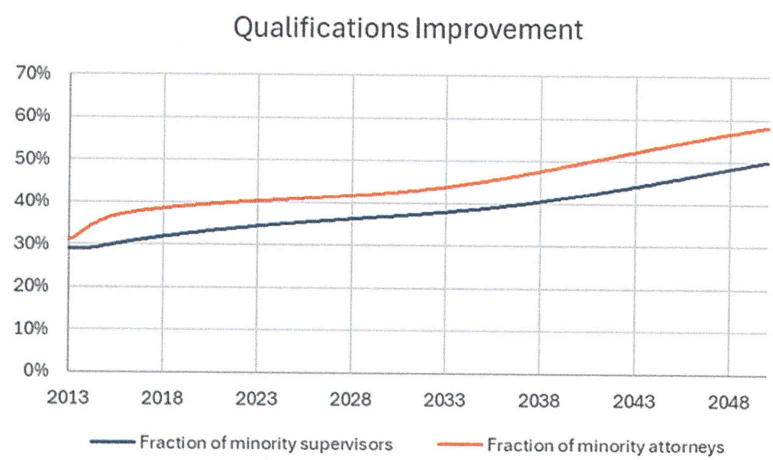

Fig. 13.24: Results of the qualifications enhancement programme.

via targeted outreach, phased in over just 2 years; a 17% rise in management ambition through mentorship, spread over five years to reflect relationship-building; and a 9% expansion of the qualifications pipeline, ramped up gradually over 20 years as new scholarship and training cohorts work their way into the hiring pool. The combined effect widens the entry funnel, accelerates promotions, and steadily feeds more qualified candidates into senior roles, allowing the supervisors' fraction to meet the 50% threshold on schedule while keeping each intervention at a realistic scale.

The integrated strategy does more than meet the headline goal for supervisors; it closes the gap between the representativeness of attorneys and supervisors. Under the combined policy mix, minority attorneys are projected to reach 52% by 2050, while supervisors are expected to reach the 50% mark (Fig. 13.25). That ensures that the minority attorneys are not overpopulated in the organization.

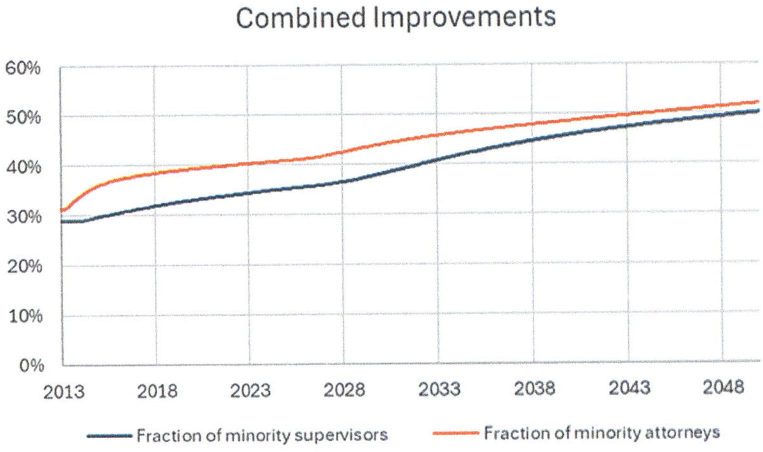

Fig. 13.25: Results of a combination of policies.

13.10 Conclusion

Re-casting the hiring and promotion model from Vensim into Excel turned a specialized simulation into a practical planning tool. Because every stock, flow, and feedback loop now lives in transparent spreadsheet formulas, staff can watch results update in real time, no licenses, coding, or steep learning curves required. That same accessibility powered earlier case studies, where Excel allowed frontline users to move quickly from "What does the model say?" to "What can we try next?"

Excel's Solver add-in was the bridge from plausibility to precision. By minimizing the total SSEs, Solver calibrated the model so that its simulated history closely followed the real time-series curves. The same approach validated models in previous chapters, giving decision-makers confidence that the structure, delays, and feedback loops accurately reflected reality before policies were tested.

Once calibrated, the spreadsheet became a sandbox for strategy. Policy runs allow users to stress-test outreach, mentorship, and pipeline investments (individually and in combination) using the Solver to identify the least-cost mix that still delivers 50% minority supervisors by 2050, with a built-in attorney cushion. Because the policy levers, ramp-up times, and optimization targets all reside in plain cells, the workbook can evolve alongside new data, shifting budgets, or revised equity goals without requiring a rebuild of the model from scratch.

In short, Excel and Solver did more than crunch numbers; they made system dynamics participatory. By lowering technical barriers, they enable legal-aid leaders to explore feedback-driven insights on their screens, transforming diversity commitments into data-driven roadmaps that can be monitored, adjusted, and most importantly, kept on track.

13.11 Discussion Questions

- Where are the bottlenecks, and how would you evidence each before proposing policy?
- What parameter bounds and structural constraints are mandatory in Solver to prevent implausible diversity or capacity outcomes?
- Under what conditions are lookup tables preferable to single time-constant adjustments, and how will you govern them?
- Why do leadership tiers lag staff tiers, and how does that inform expectations for time-to-impact and interim performance indicators?
- What are the failure modes of single-lever strategies, and what early indicators would you track for each?
- What is the minimum fit evidence you require before briefing forward scenarios to the board?
- Which governance mechanisms mitigate operational risks associated with the plan?
- How will you communicate trade-offs without over-promising?

13.12 Exercises

13.12.1 Pipeline CLD
Task. Draft a causal loop diagram linking applicant interest, hiring, mentoring, promotion, vacancies, exits, and representation at two levels (attorneys, supervisors).
Deliverable. One slide with labelled loops (R/B) and a 2-sentence narrative.

13.12.2 Excel model scaffold
Task. Create parameters, model, and interface sheets. Add columns for time, minority/majority attorneys and supervisors, hires, promotions, and exits. Initialize with start-year values and Euler updates.
Deliverable. Screenshot of the first 12 rows and the parameter block.

13.12.3 Calibration to history
Task. Add actual/model/error/squared error for four series (minority/majority attorneys, minority/majority supervisors). Compute per-series and total SSE.
Deliverable. SSE table and two overlay charts (actual vs. model).

13.12.4 Solver configuration

Task. Minimize total SSE by varying a small set of parameters within specified bounds.
Deliverable. Solver dialogue screenshot; before/after SSE; two-line rationale for bounds.

13.12.5 Baseline read-out

Task. Run the baseline to 2050. Produce a three-chart pack (attorney share, supervisor share, and vacancy rate) and a 120-word analysis of lag/plateau behaviour.
Deliverable. Charts and narrative.

13.12.6 Single-policy runs

Task. Implement three policies with phased ramps: (A) targeted outreach, (B) mentorship for promotion, and (C) qualifications.
Deliverable. Policy inputs table, three charts (one per policy), and a three-bullet comparison.

13.12.7 Combined policy optimization

Task. Use Solver to find a moderate mix of policies that meets the supervisor diversity target by 2050 while minimizing a simple cost proxy (e.g. weighted sum of improvements).
Deliverable. Inputs, Solver setup, outcome versus target, and a three-sentence executive takeaway.

13.12.8 Robustness and governance

Task. ±10% one-at-a-time sensitivity on calibrated parameters linked to supervisor outcomes. Propose annual checkpoint metrics and triggers.
Deliverable. Mini tornado table and a half-page governance note.

13.12.9 Board brief

Task. Draft 150–200 words covering problem framing, historical fit evidence, baseline risk, scenario deltas, and the integrated roadmap (what launches when, expected milestones).
Deliverable. One paragraph suitable for a board pack.

Chapter 14
Enhancing the Success Rate of Women-of-Colour Entrepreneurs

14.1 Learning Objectives

- Explain the entrepreneurial challenges faced by women of colour (WoC) in the United States, including systemic barriers, financial constraints, and network access issues.
- Describe the purpose and value of a system dynamics model for analysing the entrepreneurial pipeline, with a focus on tracking individuals through multiple business cycles.
- Interpret reference mode graphs to identify participation trends, persistence gaps, and critical attrition points in the WoC entrepreneurial journey.
- Differentiate between reinforcing and balancing feedback loops in the dynamic hypothesis and explain their impact on long-term system behaviour.
- Outline the process of translating a Vensim model into Excel, including modular worksheet design (model, data, parameters, policies, and scenarios) and the rationale for using Excel as a delivery platform.
- Apply model calibration concepts, including constrained optimization and total sum of squared error minimization, to align model outputs with historical data.
- Analyse baseline and policy scenario results to assess the potential impact of targeted interventions on WoC entrepreneurial outcomes.
- Recommend policy or programmatic actions based on model findings, considering both intended benefits and possible unintended consequences.

14.2 Introduction

Starting your own business is one of the most effective ways to create jobs, generate wealth, and foster new ideas in the United States. Yet, who gets to tap that power is still shaped by deep-rooted inequities. WoC run approximately half of all women-owned small businesses, but they often face greater hurdles than their white or male counterparts. Finding investors takes longer, personal savings stretch thinner, and insider networks (frequently the quickest route to mentors, suppliers, or early customers) are harder to break into. Those extra obstacles translate into higher startup failure rates and slower growth, even when WoC entrepreneurs bring the same grit, talent, and innovative spark to the table.

This chapter tackles those disparities head-on by introducing a simulation model that maps the typical entrepreneurial journey of WoC in the US economy [45]. Think

https://doi.org/10.1515/9783111541389-016

of it as a flight simulator, but for business ownership. The model, first crafted in the system dynamics software Vensim and later rebuilt in Excel, traces a founder from the moment they spot an opportunity, through the launch and scaling of their venture, to one of three outcomes: a thriving enterprise, a graceful exit, or an unfortunate shutdown. Crucially, it continues to track the person even after a setback or a successful sale to see whether they re-enter the game, armed with the lessons learned.

Why build such a model? Because it lets us run "what-if" experiments that are impossible or too expensive to try in real life, it is invaluable. Where along the pipeline does targeted support deliver the most value? Early-stage funding, management training, or post-failure re-entry programmes? How do economic shocks hit WoC-owned firms compared with others? The Great Recession of 2008 and the COVID-19 crisis offer two stark test cases. And, most importantly, which policy levers move the needle for long-term, widespread impact?

Choosing Excel as the primary platform matters. Vensim excels at drawing feedback loops and causal diagrams, whereas Excel is nearly universally used for similar purposes. Programme managers at a local non-profit, staffers in a city's small-business office, or analysts inside a community bank can all download a workbook, tweak a few cells, and watch the outcomes shift, with no special licenses and no steep learning curve. That democratization means more voices can test ideas, challenge assumptions, and fine-tune interventions before scarce dollars are spent in the real world.

The rest of this chapter walks through the nuts and bolts. We outline how each feedback loop was translated into equations, and then show how the model was calibrated using publicly available data and validated against historical trends. We present a baseline scenario that reflects "business as usual," highlight the pressure points where WoC founders most commonly encounter challenges, and explore a set of policy simulations that illuminate high-leverage solutions. Finally, we distill those findings into practical recommendations: concrete steps investors, educators, policymakers, and community organizations can take to help WoC-owned businesses not only survive but flourish, even when the broader economy hits a rough patch.

By combining straightforward storytelling with hands-on analytics, this chapter aims to provide readers with both a sharper understanding of the problem and a set of tools they can apply immediately.

14.3 Problem Definition

WoC are launching new companies at a faster rate than almost any other group in the United States. But once those businesses open their doors, staying open is the hard part. Many face steep odds: loans are harder to get, cash reserves are thinner, and trusted mentors or networks can be scarce. As a result, too many promising ventures stall or shut down before they can grow.

The real issue isn't getting more WoC to try entrepreneurship; it's helping them stick with it and succeed over the long haul. Standard policies often focus solely on the business itself, treating closure as the end of the story. Our approach is different: we track the entrepreneur. Whether her first effort thrives, fizzles, or leads her to start over, we follow her journey to see how experience, setbacks, and support shape the next step.

Big shocks make things worse. During the 2008 financial crisis, for example, many women-owned firms in retail and services lost sales overnight and had to wait longer for relief funds to arrive. Setbacks like that highlight the fragility of support systems for marginalized founders.

14.4 Reference Mode

We analysed data from the US Bureau of Labour Statistics on self-employment and small business ownership among WoC to ground the model in observed trends. Figures 14.1–14.3 illustrate the number of WoC businesses in their first year, during their early life, from 2 to 5 years of operation, and in a more mature stage, from 6 to 10 years of operation, spanning the period from 1994 to 2019.

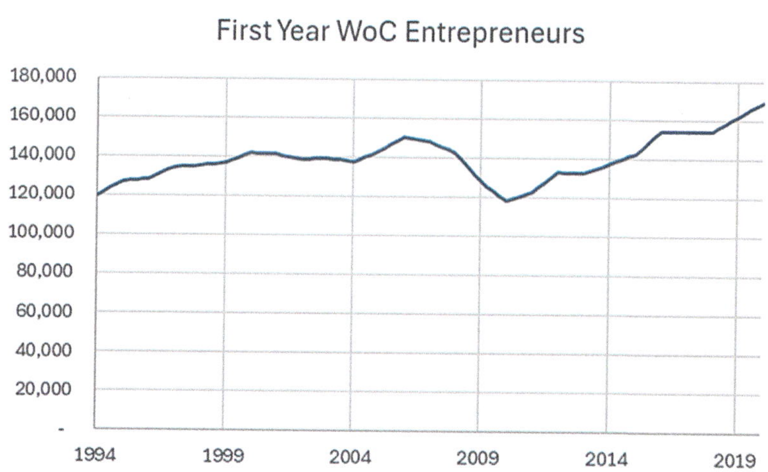

Fig. 14.1: WoC entrepreneurs in their first year of business.

What do these three graphs tell us?

Figure 14.1 shows that more WoC entrepreneurs are stepping up. US Bureau of Labour Statistics data show a clear upward line: every year, over 120,000 more WoC choose self-employment. In other words, interest and entry are booming. But notice the sharp but temporary decline around the 2008 financial crisis.

Figure 14.2 shows that staying open is the hard part. It tracks how many of those new firms remain in business. At a rate of over 120,000 new businesses starting

Fig. 14.2: WoC entrepreneurs with businesses in their early stages of operation.

Fig. 14.3: WoC entrepreneurs with businesses at a more mature stage.

each year, as shown in Fig. 14.1, in a perfect world, more than 120,000 * 4 = 480,000 would survive 2–5 years. However, only between 350,000 and 400,000 survive beyond the first few years. In short, participation is high, but persistence is fragile.

Figure 14.3 illustrates the decline in the number of WoC businesses during their sixth to tenth year of operation. At a rate of over 400,000/4 = 100,000 WoC businesses moving to the six to ten-year population, as shown in Fig. 14.2, ideally, more than 100,000 * 5 = 500,000 would survive. However, only between 250,000 and 300,000 survive beyond the first five years. This mid-life drop highlights a second "valley of death," when WoC-owned firms have outgrown startup resources but still lack the steady cash flow and scale needed to weather setbacks.

These three patterns form the backbone of our "reference mode," the yardstick we use to test whether the simulation behaves realistically. Our model must accurately reproduce the shape of the pipeline, including the surge of newcomers, the steep attrition curve in the first few years, followed by a more gradual decline over time, with significant sensitivity to macroeconomic factors. Matching that flow gives us confidence that any policy experiments we run later will rest on a realistic picture of how WoC businesses start, stall, and restart in the real world.

Most importantly, the graphs shift the conversation from "Why do individual firms fail?" to "What system conditions keep WoC founders in a start-stop cycle – and how can we break it?" Answering that bigger question is where the proper leverage for change lies.

14.5 Dynamic Hypothesis

There are eight reinforcing loops and six balancing loops in the dynamic hypothesis (see Fig. 14.4). The core balancing loops in the model represent entrepreneurial momentum. As more WoC successfully start (B1), the more WoCs sustain businesses and draw from the previous phase of operations (B2, B3, and B4). The more WoC entrepreneurs retire, the fewer are available to retire (B5 and B6).

Finally, the model differentiates between two distinct outcomes for those exiting entrepreneurship: discontinuation and successful exit. Discontinuation represents involuntary exits due to business failure or personal constraints, while successful exits reflect women who achieve their goals and may choose to exit on their terms. These WoC entrepreneurs may re-enter the system by starting a new business. These represent the reinforcing loops (R1–R8), as more WoC entrepreneurs exit, more are available to re-enter.

Together, these feedback loops represent a dynamic system with competing pressures. On one hand, we see mechanisms that can foster a resilient base of WoC entrepreneurs over time. On the other hand, structural and economic forces counteract this growth, leading to prolonged periods of stagnation or reversal. This dynamic hypothesis guides the stock-and-flow formulation of the model and provides the structure necessary to test interventions, particularly those aimed at reducing discontinuation and improving re-entry.

14.6 Model Formulation

14.6.1 The Vensim Model

The original Vensim model captures the entrepreneurial journey of WoC as a set of interrelated population stocks and flows (see Fig. 14.5). The stocks represent different stages of entrepreneurial activity, including aspiring entrepreneurs, active entrepreneurs (1 year, 2–5 years, 6–10 years, and greater than 10 years), discontinued entrepre-

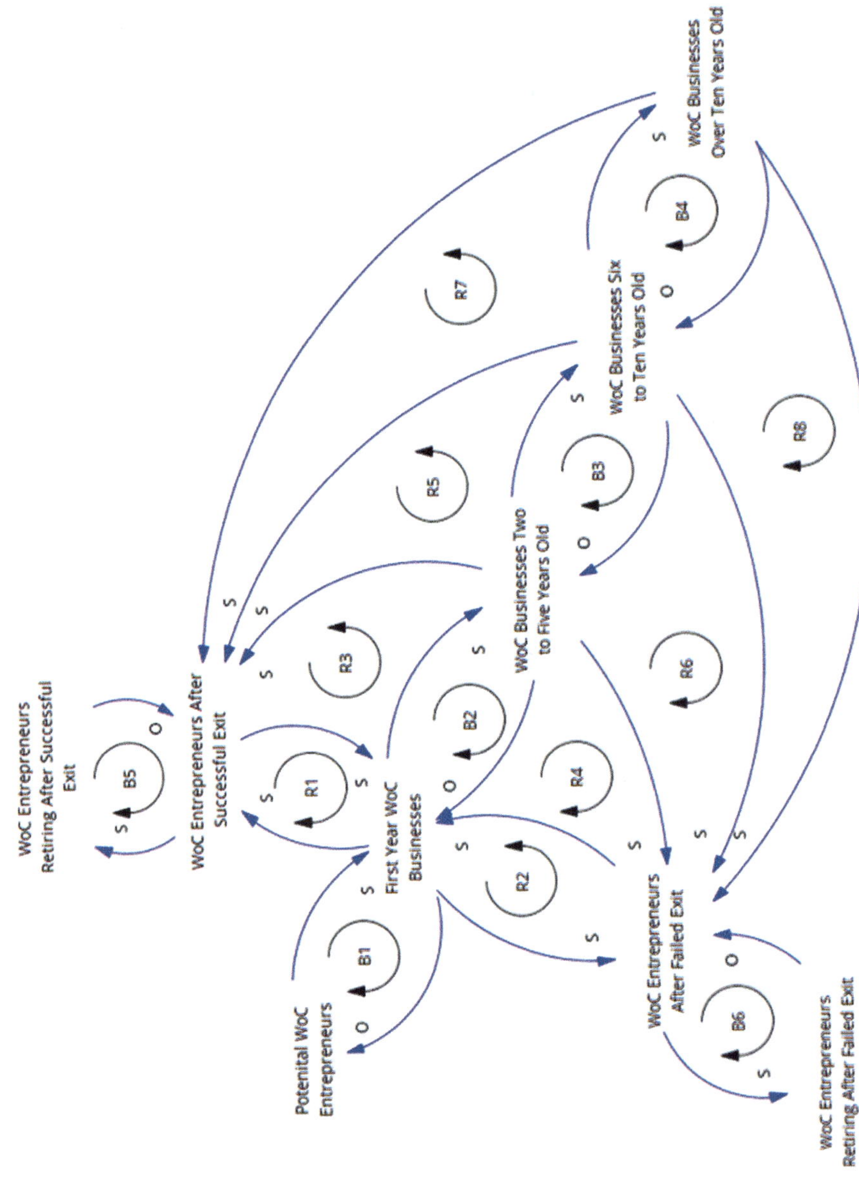

Fig. 14.4: Dynamic hypothesis for the WoC entrepreneurs' journey.

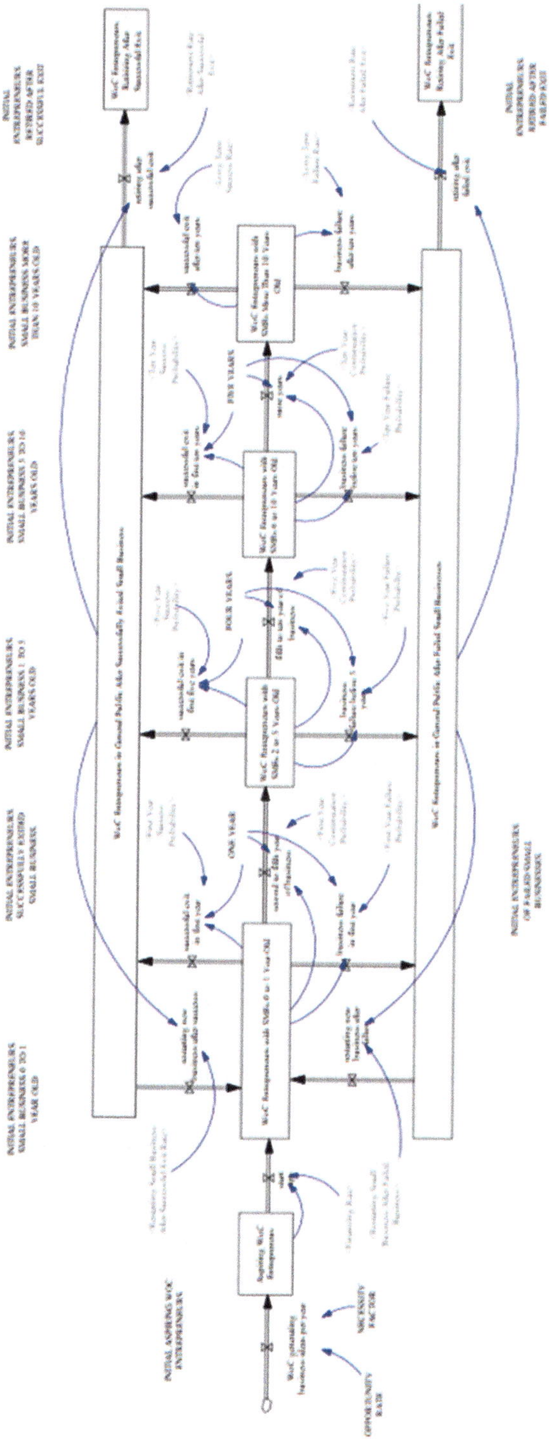

Fig. 14.5: Stock-and-flow diagram of WoC entrepreneurs' journey.

neurs (following both successful and failed exits), and retired entrepreneurs (following both successful and failed exits).

Probabilistic rates govern the flows between these states, including entry into entrepreneurship, discontinuation, re-entry after discontinuation, and transition to a successful exit. Key drivers such as exogenous shocks (e.g. economic downturns) influence the magnitude and direction of these flows.

We model each rate of change using a first-order delay. Figure 14.6 illustrates an example goal-gap model for the startup rate, where the gap between the current rate and the desired rate is closed over time as the rate is adjusted.

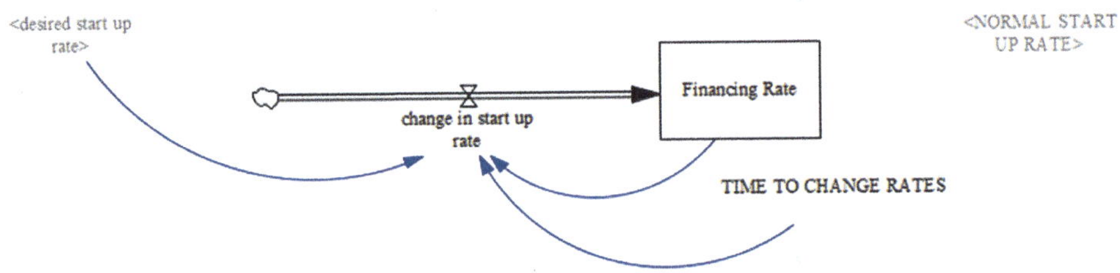

Fig. 14.6: Example of a time-varying rate.

The desired rate takes on three values: a normal rate, a rate during the financial crisis, and a rate after the COVID crisis, allowing policies to be applied using a multiplier (Fig. 14.7). The multipliers can increase the success rates by up to twice the normal value and decrease the failure rate by half the normal value. The multiplier can be used to optimize where effort should be expended to improve the long-term results.

14.6.2 The Excel Model

The Vensim model clearly illustrates the core feedback structures in the dynamic hypothesis, particularly the reinforcing loop of entrepreneurial experience, leading to higher re-entry and resilience, and the balancing loop of high failure rates reducing system participation. However, to make the model more accessible to a broader audience, including practitioners and policy analysts, the structure was fully translated into Excel.

The Excel implementation replicates all the elements of the Vensim logic while offering a more intuitive and modifiable interface. The steps in converting the Vensim model to the Excel model spreadsheet were the same as in the earlier chapters. The workbook was then divided into separate Worksheets to make the model modular. The workbook is organized into five main worksheets: model, data, parameters, policies, and scenarios.

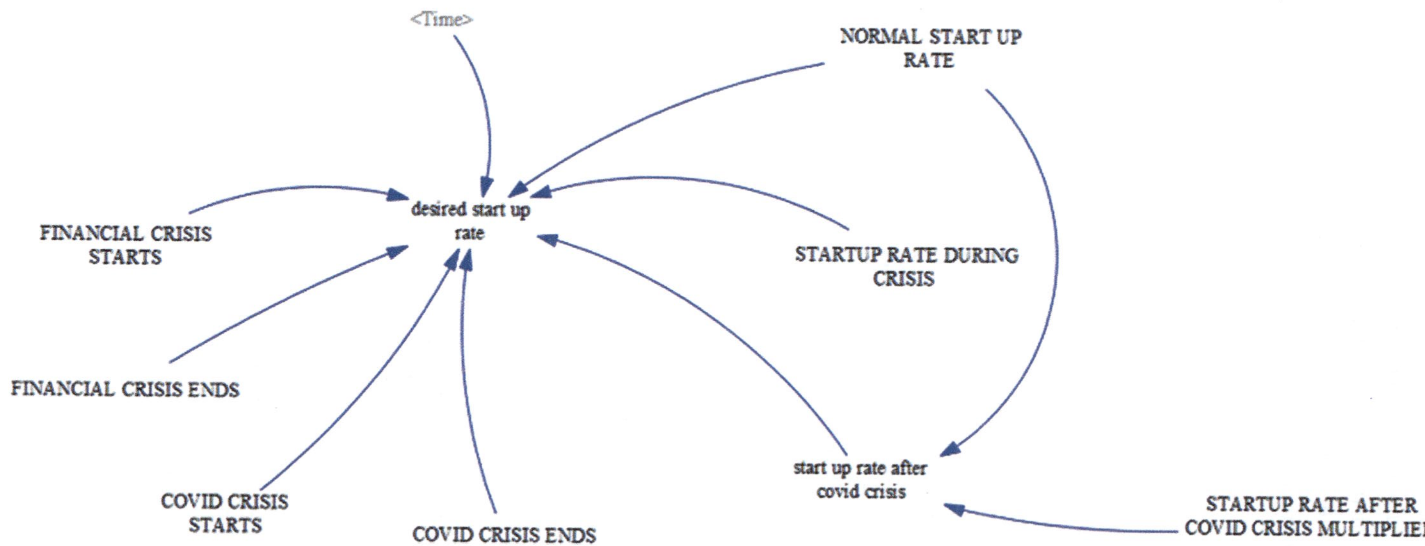

Fig. 14.7: Calculation of an example of the desired rate during and after a crisis.

The parameters worksheet contains all the constant values used in the simulation. Figures 14.8–14.10 display all the model parameters linked to the model worksheet. Cell D2 displays the total SSE, which is derived from the data worksheet. A constrained optimization process using the Excel Solver is employed to determine the parameters that yield the minimum total SSE.

	A	B	C	D
1	PARAMETER	VALUE	UNITS	TSSE
2	(067) INITIAL TIME = 1994	1994	Units: year	6.41E+09
3	(134) TIME STEP = 0.03125	0.25	Units: year [0,?]	
4	(019) COVID ENDS=	2023	Units: year	
5	(020) COVID STARTS=	2020	Units: year	
6	(036) FINANCIAL CRISIS ENDS=	2010	Units: year	
7	(037) FINANCIAL CRISIS STARTS=	2007	Units: year	
8	(042) FIRST YEAR FAILURE RATE DURING CRISIS=	42.2%	Units: Dmnl	
9	(046) FIRST YEAR SUCCESS RATE DURING CRISIS=	2.5%	Units: Dmnl	
10	(051) FIVE YEAR FAILURE RATE DURING CRISIS=	27.0%	Units: Dmnl	
11	(055) FIVE YEAR SUCCESS RATE DURING CRISIS=	2.5%	Units: Dmnl	
12	(056) FIVE YEARS=	5	Units: years	
13	(057) FOUR YEARS=	4	Units: years	
14	(058) INITIAL ASPIRING WOC ENTREPRENEURS=	119,578	Units: people	
15	(059) INITIAL ENTREPRENEURS OF FAILED SMALL BUSINESSES=	569,952	Units: people	
16	(060) INITIAL ENTREPRENEURS RETIRED AFTER FAILED EXIT=	-	Units: people	
17	(061) INITIAL ENTREPRENEURS RETIRED AFTER SUCCESSFUL EXIT=	-	Units: people	
18	(062) INITIAL ENTREPRENEURS SMALL BUSINESS 0 TO 1 YEAR OLD=	119,578	Units: people	
19	(063) INITIAL ENTREPRENEURS SMALL BUSINESS 2 TO 5 YEARS OLD=	331,939	Units: people	
20	(064) INITIAL ENTREPRENEURS SMALL BUSINESS 6 TO 10 YEARS OLD=	266,363	Units: people	
21	(065) INITIAL ENTREPRENEURS SMALL BUSINESS MORE THAN 10 YEARS OLD=	5,699,520	Units: people	
22	(066) INITIAL ENTREPRENEURS SUCCESSFULLY EXITED SMALL BUSINESS=	56,995	Units: people	

Data | Vensim | Model | Parameters | Policies | Scenarios

Fig. 14.8: Parameters of the WoC entrepreneur model (set 1).

	A	B	C
1	PARAMETER	VALUE	UNITS
22	(066) INITIAL ENTREPRENEURS SUCCESSFULLY EXITED SMALL BUSINESS=	56,995	Units: people
23	(071) LONG TERM FAILURE RATE DURING CRISIS=	15.1%	Units: 1/year
24	(075) LONG TERM SUCCESS RATE DURING CRISIS=	2.5%	Units: 1/year
25	(077) NECESSITY FACTOR=	29.6%	Units: Dmnl
26	(078) NORMAL FIRST YEAR FAILURE RATE=	30.2%	Units: Dmnl
27	(079) NORMAL FIRST YEAR SUCCESS RATE=	2.5%	Units: Dmnl
28	(080) NORMAL FIVE YEAR FAILURE RATE=	33.8%	Units: Dmnl
29	(081) NORMAL FIVE YEAR SUCCESS RATE=	2.5%	Units: Dmnl
30	(082) NORMAL LONG TERM FAILURE RATE=	5.5%	Units: 1/year
31	(083) NORMAL LONG TERM SUCCESS RATE=	2.5%	Units: 1/year
32	(084) NORMAL RESTARTING SMALL BUSINESS AFTER FAILED EXIT RATE=	14.1%	Units: 1/year
33	(085) NORMAL RESTARTING SMALL BUSINESS AFTER SUCCESSFUL EXIT RATE=	45.5%	Units: 1/year
34	(088) NORMAL RETIRING WOC ENTREPRENEUR AFTER FAILED EXIT RATE=	84.9%	Units: 1/year
35	(089) NORMAL RETIRING WOC ENTREPRENEUR AFTER SUCCESSFUL EXIT RATE=	51.1%	Units: 1/year
36	(090) NORMAL START UP RATE=	3.9%	Units: 1/year
37	(091) NORMAL TEN YEAR FAILURE RATE=	48.7%	Units: Dmnl
38	(092) NORMAL TEN YEAR SUCCESS RATE=	2.5%	Units: Dmnl
39	(093) ONE YEAR=	1	Units: year
40	(094) OPPORTUNITY RATE=	658,526	Units: people/year
41	(100) RESTARTING SMALL BUSINESS AFTER FAILED EXIT RATE DURING CRISIS=	13.3%	Units: 1/year
42	(104) RESTARTING SMALL BUSINESS AFTER SUCCESSFUL EXIT RATE DURING CRISIS=	30.6%	Units: 1/year

Data | Vensim | Model | Parameters | Policies | Scenarios

Fig. 14.9: Parameters of the WoC entrepreneur model (set 2).

	A	B	C
1	PARAMETER	VALUE	UNITS
43	(111) RETIRING WOC ENTREPRENEUR AFTER FAILED EXIT RATE DURING CRISIS=	85.7%	Units: 1/year
44	(114) RETIRING WOC ENTREPRENEUR AFTER SUCCESSFUL EXIT RATE DURING CRISIS=	48.3%	Units: 1/year
45	(120) STARTUP RATE DURING CRISIS=	1.5%	Units: 1/year
46	(129) TEN YEAR FAILURE RATE DURING CRISIS=	65.7%	Units: Dmnl
47	(133) TEN YEAR SUCCESS RATE DURING CRISIS=	2.5%	Units: Dmnl
48	(135) TIME TO CHANGE RATES=	2	Units: years

Fig. 14.10: Parameters of the WoC entrepreneur model (set 3).

Figures 14.11–14.17 show all of the endogenous variables (stocks, flows, and auxiliaries) in the model. These variables are displayed in alphabetical order.

	A	B	C	D	E	F	G	H	I	J	K	L	M
1	Time	(001) Aspiring WoC Entrepreneus= INTEG (	(002) business failure after ten years=	(003) business failure before 5 years=	(004) business failure before ten years=	(005) business failure in first year=	(006) change in first year failure rate=	(007) change in first year success rate=	(008) change in five year failure rate=	(009) change in five year success rate=	(010) change in long term failure rate=	(011) change in long term success rate=	(012) change in restarting business after successful exit rate=
2	Units: year	Units: people	Units: people/year	Units: people/year	Units: people/year	Units: people/year	Units: Dmnl/year	Units: Dmnl/year	Units: Dmnl/year	Units: Dmnl/year	Units: 1/year	Units: 1/year	Units: 1/year
3	1994	119578	313001	28055	25948.5	36143.3	0	0	0	0	0	0	0
4	1994.25	167094	307105	28055	25948.5	35473	0	0	0	0	0	0	0
5	1994.5	214148	301326	28055	25948.5	35489	0	0	0	0	0	0	0
6	1994.75	260745	295662	28055	25948.5	35888.3	0	0	0	0	0	0	0
7	1995	306888	290112	28055	25948.5	36477.7	0	0	0	0	0	0	0

Fig. 14.11: Endogenous variables of the WoC entrepreneur model (set 1).

	A	N	O	P	Q	R	S	T	U	V	W	X	Y	Z
1	Time	(013) change in restarting small business after failed business=	(014) change in retirement rate after failed exit=	(015) change in retirement rate after successful exit=	(016) change in start up rate=	(017) change in ten year failure rate=	(018) change in ten year success rate=	(021) desired first year failure rate=	(022) desired first year success rate=	(023) desired five year failure rate=	(024) desired five year success rate=	(025) desired long term failure rate=	(026) desired long term success rate=	(027) desired restarting small business after failed exit rate=
2	Units: year	Units: 1/year	Units: 1/year	Units: 1/year	Units: 1/year	Units: Dmnl/year	Units: Dmnl/year	Units: Dmnl	Units: Dmnl	Units: Dmnl	Units: Dmnl	Units: 1/year	Units: 1/year	Units: 1/year
3	1994	0	0	0	0	0	0	0.30226	0.025	0.33807	0.025	0.054917	0.025	0.140555
4	1994.25	0	0	0	0	0	0	0.30226	0.025	0.33807	0.025	0.054917	0.025	0.140555
5	1994.5	0	0	0	0	0	0	0.30226	0.025	0.33807	0.025	0.054917	0.025	0.140555
6	1994.75	0	0	0	0	0	0	0.30226	0.025	0.33807	0.025	0.054917	0.025	0.140555
7	1995	0	0	0	0	0	0	0.30226	0.025	0.33807	0.025	0.054917	0.025	0.140555

Fig. 14.12: Endogenous variables of the WoC entrepreneur model (set 2).

A portion of the data worksheet is shown in Fig. 14.18, illustrating the actual time series of WoC entrepreneurs in their first year of business, which served as the reference mode. Then, this time series is compared to the time series model estimates, including the squared error between the data and the model time series, as well as the sum of the squared errors for the entire time series. This is used for the calibration graphs.

	A	AA	AB	AC	AD	AE	AF	AG	AH	AI	AJ	AK	AL	AM
1	Time	(028) desired restarting small business after successful exit rate=	(029) desired retiring WoC entrepreneur after failed exit rate=	(030) desired retiring WoC entrepreneur after successful exit rate=	(031) desired start up rate=	(032) desired ten year failure rate=	(033) desired ten year success rate=	(034) fifth to ten year of business=	(038) Financing Rate= INTEG (	(039) First Year Continuation Probability=	(040) First Year Failure Probability= INTEG (	(044) first year failure rate after covid crisis=	(043) First Year Success Probability= INTEG (	(044) first year success rate after covid crisis=
2	Units: year	Units: 1/year	Units: 1/year	Units: 1/year	Units: 1/year	Units: Dmnl	Units: Dmnl	Units: people/year	Units: 1/year	Units: Dmnl	Units: Dmnl	Units: Dmnl	Units: Dmnl	Units: Dmnl
3	1994	0.45524167	0.84945	0.51104856	0.0389	0.48709	0.025	52855.22	0.0389	0.67274	0.30226	0.2341986	0.025	0.025
4	1994.25	0.45524167	0.84945	0.51104856	0.0389	0.48709	0.025	52855.22	0.0389	0.67274	0.30226	0.2341986	0.025	0.025
5	1994.5	0.45524167	0.84945	0.51104856	0.0389	0.48709	0.025	52855.22	0.0389	0.67274	0.30226	0.2341986	0.025	0.025
6	1994.75	0.45524167	0.84945	0.51104856	0.0389	0.48709	0.025	52855.22	0.0389	0.67274	0.30226	0.2341986	0.025	0.025
7	1995	0.45524167	0.84945	0.51104856	0.0389	0.48709	0.025	52855.22	0.0389	0.67274	0.30226	0.2341986	0.025	0.025

Fig. 14.13: Endogenous variables of the WoC entrepreneur model (set 3).

	A	AN	AO	AP	Formula Bar	AR	AS	AT	AU	AV	AW	AX	AY	AZ
1	Time	(047) Five Year Continuation Probability=	(048) Five Year Failure Probability= INTEG (	(049) five year failure rate after covid crisis=	(052) Five Year Success Probability = INTEG (	(053) five year success rate after covid crisis=	(069) Long Term Failure Rate= INTEG (	(070) long term failure rate after covid crisis=	(072) Long Term Success Rate= INTEG (	(073) long term success rate after covid crisis=	(076) more years=	(095) restarting new business after failure=	(096) restarting new business after success=	(097) Restarting Small Business After Failed Business= INTEG (
2	Units: year	Units: Dmnl	Units: Dmnl	Units: Dmnl	Units: Dmnl	Units: Dmnl	Units: 1/year	Units: 1/year	Units: 1/year	Units: 1/year	Units: people/year	Units: people/year	Units: people/year	Units: 1/year
3	1994	0.636926	0.33807	0.28978953	0.025	0.025	0.054917	0.05491713	0.025	0.025	25992.2	80109.6	25946.6	0.140555
4	1994.25	0.636926	0.33807	0.28978953	0.025	0.025	0.054917	0.05491713	0.025	0.025	25992.2	74448.6	36623.1	0.140555
5	1994.5	0.636926	0.33807	0.28978953	0.025	0.025	0.054917	0.05491713	0.025	0.025	25992.2	69957.9	44408.7	0.140555
6	1994.75	0.636926	0.33807	0.28978953	0.025	0.025	0.054917	0.05491713	0.025	0.025	25992.2	66376.2	50014.3	0.140555
7	1995	0.636926	0.33807	0.28978953	0.025	0.025	0.054917	0.05491713	0.025	0.025	25992.2	63496	53976	0.140555

Fig. 14.14: Endogenous variables of the WoC entrepreneur model (set 4).

	A	BA	BB	BC	BD	BE	BF	BG	BH	BI	BJ	BK	BL	BM
1	Time	(098) restarting small business after failed exit rate after covid crisis=	(101) Restarting Small Business After Successful Exit Rate= INTEG (	(102) restarting small business after successful exit rate after covid crisis	(105) Retirement Rate After Failed Exit= INTEG (	(106) Retirement Rate After Successful Exit= INTEG (	(107) retiring after failed exit=	(108) retiring after successful exit=	(109) retiring WoC entrepreneur after failed exit rate after covid crisis=	(112) retiring WoC entrepreneur after successful exit rate after covid crisis	(116) second to fifth year of business =	(117) start up rate after covid crisis=	(118) start ups=	(121) successful exit after ten years=
2	Units: year	Units: 1/year	Units: 1/year	Units: 1/year	Units: 1/year	Units: 1/year	Units: people/year	Units: people/year	Units: 1/year	Units: 1/year	Units: people/year	Units: 1/year	Units: people/year	Units: people/year
3	1994	0.140555	0.45524167	0.455242	0.849445	0.51105	484142.883	29127.3	0.8037321	0.51104856	80445.3	0.03890362	4652.02	142488
4	1994.25	0.140555	0.45524167	0.455242	0.849445	0.51105	449930.542	41112.7	0.8037321	0.51104856	78953.5	0.03890362	6500.57	139803.64
5	1994.5	0.140555	0.45524167	0.455242	0.849445	0.51105	422791.194	49852.7	0.8037321	0.51104856	78989.1	0.03890362	8331.15	137172.92
6	1994.75	0.140555	0.45524167	0.455242	0.849445	0.51105	401145.024	56145.4	0.8037321	0.51104856	79877.9	0.03890362	10143.9	134594.75
7	1995	0.140555	0.45524167	0.455242	0.849445	0.51105	383738.388	60592.8	0.8037321	0.51104856	81189.7	0.03890362	11939.1	132068.1

Fig. 14.15: Endogenous variables of the WoC entrepreneur model (set 5).

	A	BN	BO	BP	BQ	BR	BS	BT	BU	BV	BW	BX	BY	BZ
1	Time	(122) successful exit in first five years=	(123) successful exit in first ten years=	(124) successful exit in first year=	(125) Ten Year Continuation Probability=	(126) Ten Year Failure Probability = INTEG (	(127) ten year failure rate after covid crisis=	(130) Ten Year Success Probability = INTEG (	(131) ten year success rate after covid crisis=	(136) total WoC entrepreneurs =	(137) WoC Entrepreneurs in General Public After Failed Small Businesses= INTEG	(138) WoC Entrepreneurs in General Public After Successfully Exited Small Business = INTEG (	(139) WoC Entrepreneurs Retiring After Failed Exit= INTEG (	(140) WoC Entrepreneurs Retiring After Successful Exit= INTEG (
2	Units: year	Units: people/year	Units: people/year	Units: people/year	Units: Dmnl	Units: Dmnl	Units: Dmnl	Units: Dmnl	Units: Dmnl	Units: people	Units: people	Units: people	Units: people	Units: people
3	1994	2074.622	1331.813	2989.44975	0.48791014	0.48709	0.441501	0.025	0.025	717,880	569,952	56,995	-	-
4	1994.25	2074.622	1331.813	2934.01361	0.48791014	0.48709	0.441501	0.025	0.025	715,663	529,676	80,448	121,036	7,282
5	1994.5	2074.622	1331.813	2935.33713	0.48791014	0.48709	0.441501	0.025	0.025	715,715	497,726	97,550	233,518	17,560
6	1994.75	2074.622	1331.813	2968.36405	0.48791014	0.48709	0.441501	0.025	0.025	717,037	472,244	109,863	339,216	30,023
7	1995	2074.622	1331.813	3017.11291	0.48791014	0.48709	0.441501	0.025	0.025	718,986	451,752	118,566	439,502	44,060

Fig. 14.16: Endogenous variables of the WoC entrepreneur model (set 6).

	A	CA	CB	CC	CD	CE	CF
1	Time	(141) WoC Entrepreneurs with SMEs 0 to 1 Year Old= INTEG (	(142) WoC Entrepreneurs with SMEs 2 to 5 Years Old= INTEG (	(143) WoC Entrepreneurs with SMEs 6 to 10 Years Old= INTEG (	(144) WoC Entrepreneurs with SMEs More Than 10 Years Old= INTEG (	(145) WoC generating business ideas per year=	(146) first year failure rate after covid crisis=
2	Units: year	Units: people	Units: people	Units: people	Units: people	Units: people/year	Units: Dmnl
3	1994	119,578	331,939	266,363	5,699,520	194,717	0.2341986
4	1994.25	117,361	331,939	266,363	5,592,146	194,717	0.2341986
5	1994.5	117,413	331,939	266,363	5,486,917	194,717	0.2341986
6	1994.75	118,735	331,939	266,363	5,383,790	194,717	0.2341986
7	1995	120,685	331,939	266,363	5,282,724	194,717	0.2341986

Fig. 14.17: Endogenous variables of the WoC entrepreneur model (set 7).

	A	B	C	D	E	F
1	Year	Actual First Year	Actual First Year	Model First Year	SE	SSE
2	1994	569,419	119,578	119,578	6.99E-15	1.34E+09
3	1994.25	578,168	121,415	117,361	1.64E+07	
4	1994.5	586,917	123,253	117,413	3.41E+07	
5	1994.75	595,666	125,090	118,735	4.04E+07	
6	1995	604,415	126,927	120,685	3.90E+07	
7	1995.25	605,721	127,201	122,866	1.88E+07	
8	1995.5	607,027	127,476	125,042	5.92E+06	
9	1995.75	608,332	127,750	127,079	4.50E+05	
10	1996	609,638	128,024	128,910	7.85E+05	
11	1996.25	617,007	129,571	130,510	8.81E+05	
12	1996.5	624,376	131,119	131,879	5.78E+05	
13	1996.75	631,745	132,666	133,032	1.33E+05	
14	1997	639,114	134,214	133,988	5.09E+04	

Fig. 14.18: A portion of the data worksheet of the WoC entrepreneur model.

The policies worksheet can be used to adjust the multipliers linked to the model worksheet (see Fig. 14.19) and experiment with the effort expended at various times in the WoC entrepreneurs' journey to improve long-term results. We can see four performance measures on rows 17–21: WoC entrepreneurs in business in 2050, retired WoC entrepreneurs after a failed exit in 2050, retired WoC entrepreneurs after a successful exit in 2050, and a combination of these three measures (ongoing – failed exit + successful exit). In this worksheet, we can also conduct a constrained optimization. The constrained values are shown in Fig. 14.19 as minimum and maximum limits in columns D–G.

	A	B	C	D	E	F	G
1	Policy	Value	Units	Constraint Parameter	Minimum	2030 Value	Maximum
2	Reduce First Year Failure Fraction	0%	Units: Dmnl	First Year Continuation Fraction	1%	67%	99%
3	Increase First Year Success Fraction	0%	Units: Dmnl	Five Year Continuation Fraction	1%	64%	99%
4	Reduce Five Year Failure Fraction	0%	Units: Dmnl	Long Term Continuation Rate	1%	92%	99%
5	Increase Five Year Success Fraction	0%	Units: Dmnl	Failed Exit Continuation Rate	1%	1%	99%
6	Reduce Long Term Failure Rate	0%	Units: Dmnl	Successful Exit Continuation Rate	1%	3%	99%
7	Increase Long Term Success Rate	0%	Units: Dmnl	Startup Rate	1%	4%	99%
8	Increase Restarting After Failed Exit	0%	Units: Dmnl	Ten Year Continuation Rate	1%	49%	99%
9	Increase Restarting After Successfule Exit	0%	Units: Dmnl				
10	Reduce Retiring After Failed Exit	0%	Units: Dmnl				
11	Reduce Retiring After Successful Exit	0%	Units: Dmnl				
12	Increase Start Up Rate	0%	Units: Dmnl				
13	Reduce Ten Year Failure Fraction	0%	Units: Dmnl				
14	Increase Ten Year Success Fraction	0%	Units: Dmnl				
15	Effort	0%	Units: Dmnl	Effort Constraint		0%	100%
16							
17	Resutls with Policies Applied	2050 Values					
18	Total WoC Entrepreneurs in Business in 2050	1,211,709	Units: people				
19	WoC Enterpreneurs Retired After Failed Exit in 2050	10,235,878	Units: people				
20	WoC Entrepreneurs Retired After Successful Exit in 2050	1,325,256	Units: people				
21	In Business + Retired After Successful Exit - Retired After Failed Exit in 2050	(7,698,914)	Units: people				

Fig. 14.19: The policy worksheet of the WoC entrepreneur model.

The policy worksheet also includes three graphs illustrating the trend in the number of WoC entrepreneurs in business, the cumulative number of WoC entrepreneurs who have retired after a successful exit, and the cumulative number of WoC entrepreneurs who have retired after a failed exit.

The scenarios worksheet is a tool for comparing the results of different policies.

14.7 Calibration

The model was calibrated to reflect real-world dynamics using publicly available data, minimizing the total SSEs between the model and the data through constrained optimization with the Excel Solver. The calibration results are presented in Figs. 14.20–14.22.

Ultimately, the calibration process ensured that the model behaved in line with historical data. It established a credible baseline against which policy interventions, such as improving re-entry rates or reducing discontinuation, could be compared in the following sections.

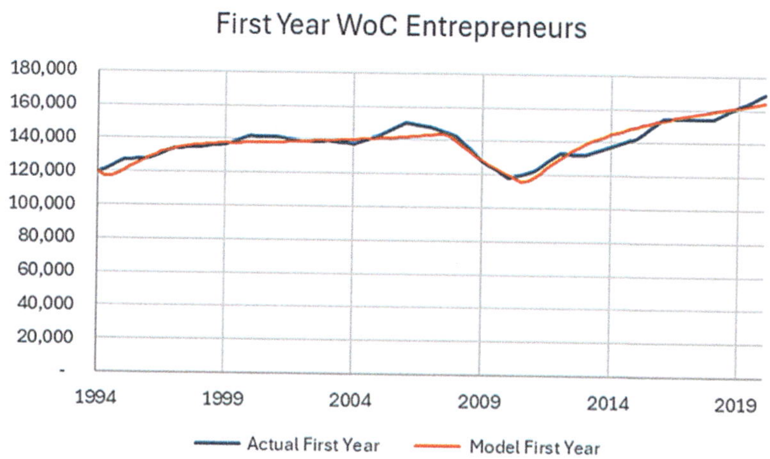

Fig. 14.20: Calibration of WoC entrepreneurs in their first year of business.

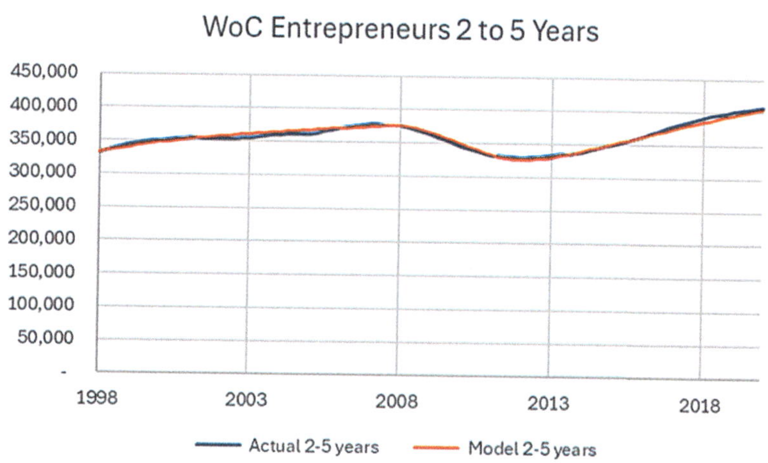

Fig. 14.21: Calibration of WoC entrepreneurs in the early life of their businesses.

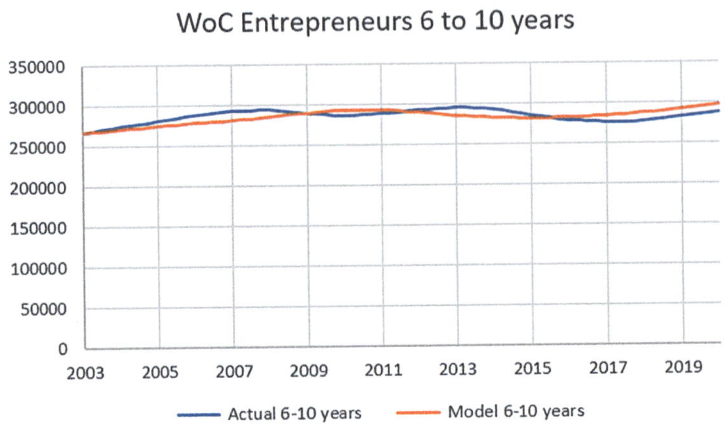

Fig. 14.22: Calibration of WoC entrepreneurs in a more mature stage of business.

14.8 Baseline Run

The baseline scenario simulates the progression of WoC entrepreneurs through the business lifecycle over a multi-decade period using calibrated parameters that reflect current conditions. Entry, discontinuation, re-entry, and successful exit rates vary over time without additional interventions, but with the application of external macroeconomic shocks. This scenario represents a "status quo" view of the system: what the future might look like if historical patterns and systemic barriers remain unchanged.

Figure 14.23 illustrates that while the number of active WoC entrepreneurs increases steadily over time, significant fluctuations occur due to the financial crisis in 2008 and the COVID-19 crisis in 2020.

Fig. 14.23: WoC entrepreneurs with ongoing businesses.

Figure 14.24 shows the WoC entrepreneurs who have retired after a failed exit, and Fig. 14.25 shows the WoC entrepreneurs who have retired after a successful exit. We can see that the number of retirees after a failed exit is eight times higher than the number of retirees after successful exits.

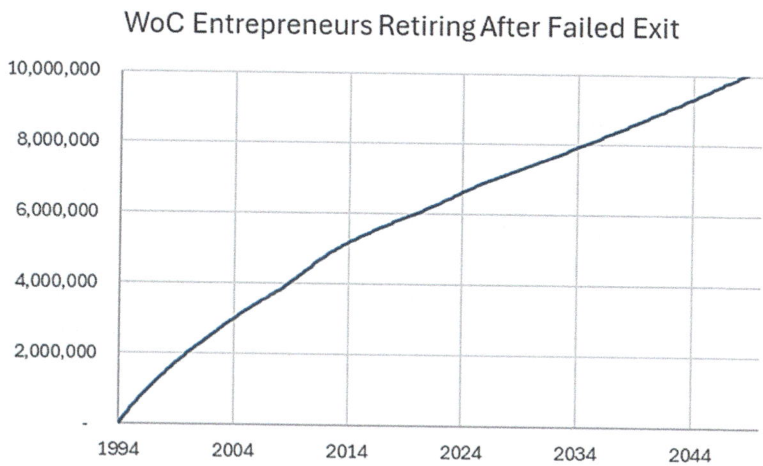

Fig. 14.24: Cumulative WoC entrepreneurs who have retired after a failed exit.

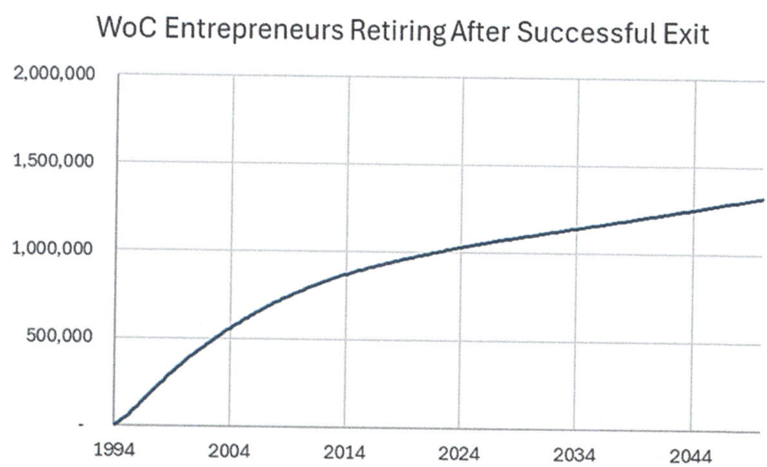

Fig. 14.25: Cumulative WoC entrepreneurs who have retired after a successful exit.

This behaviour establishes the benchmark against which all subsequent policy scenarios are evaluated. It highlights the potential and limitations of current pathways, reinforcing the importance of modelling interventions that target leverage points within the entrepreneurial system.

14.9 Policy Runs

Building on the baseline scenario, a series of policy interventions was simulated to assess their potential to improve outcomes for WoC entrepreneurs. These interventions were guided by the model's structure and focussed on key leverage points identified in the dynamic hypothesis: increasing entry rates, improving persistence, and strengthening re-entry. The objective was to explore how changes in these policies could shift long-term system behaviour and use the model to identify combinations of policies with the highest potential impact. We again used a constrained optimization approach to maximize or minimize the four performance measures in 2050. Table 14.1 shows the results.

Tab. 14.1: Results of various policy scenarios to support WoC entrepreneurs.

Policy	Baseline	Maximize ongoing	Minimize failed	Maximize success	Maximize overall
Reduce first-year failure fraction	0%	35%	37%	0%	50%
Increase first-year success fraction	0%	0%	0%	0%	0%
Reduce 5-year failure fraction	0%	2%	22%	0%	26%
Increase 5-year success fraction	0%	0%	0%	0%	0%
Reduce long-term failure rate	0%	0%	6%	0%	0%
Increase long-term success rate	0%	0%	0%	55%	0%
Increase restarting after failed exit	0%	0%	0%	0%	0%
Increase restarting after successful exit	0%	0%	0%	0%	0%
Reduce retiring after failed exit	0%	0%	8%	0%	8%
Reduce retiring after successful exit	0%	0%	0%	0%	0%
Increase startup rate	0%	63%	0%	29%	0%
Reduce 10-year failure fraction	0%	0%	27%	16%	16%
Increase 10-year success fraction	0%	0%	0%	0%	0%
Total effort	0%	100%	100%	100%	100%
Results in 2050 with policies applied					
Total WoC entrepreneurs (K)	1,212	1,481	1,331	1,319	1,354
WoC entrepreneurs retired after failed exit (K)	10,236	10,632	9,948	10,458	9,955
WoC entrepreneurs retired after successful exit (K)	1,325	1,366	1,353	1,391	1,349
Relative change from baseline					
Total WoC entrepreneurs		22%	10%	9%	12%
WoC entrepreneurs retired after failed exit		4%	−3%	2%	−3%
WoC entrepreneurs retired after successful exit		3%	2%	5%	2%

14.9.1 Maximizing the WoC Entrepreneurs with Ongoing Businesses

This policy resulted in a 22% increase in the number of WoC entrepreneurs with ongoing companies and a 3% increase in retirees after successful exits. In comparison, it increased the number of retirees after failed exits by 4%. Therefore, this policy has mixed results.

14.9.2 Minimizing the WoC Entrepreneurs Retired After Failed Exit

This policy resulted in a 3% decrease in the number of retirees after failed exits, a 10% increase in the number of WoC entrepreneurs with ongoing businesses, and a 2% increase in the number of retirees after successful exits. Therefore, this policy has positive results in all three dimensions.

14.9.3 Maximizing the WoC Entrepreneurs Retired After Successful Exit

This policy resulted in a 5% increase in the number of retirees after successful exit, a 9% increase in WoC entrepreneurs with ongoing businesses, and a 2% increase in the number of retirees after failed exit. Therefore, this policy has mixed results.

14.9.4 Maximizing the Combined Performance Measure

This policy resulted in a 12% increase in WoC entrepreneurs with ongoing businesses, a 3% decrease in the number of retirees after failed exit, and a 2% increase in the number of retirees after successful exit. Therefore, this policy produces the best results.

14.10 Conclusion and Recommendations

This chapter delivered a working system dynamics model of the entrepreneurship pipeline for WoC. It implemented it end-to-end in Excel to make it deployable by non-specialists. The structure tracks how founders transition between a small set of clearly defined states over time: operating businesses and retirement, whether after a successful or failed exit. Flows capture entry, discontinuation, and re-entry, with time-varying rates that respond to macroeconomic shocks and policy changes. We used simple first-order "goal-gap" adjustments for rates, so the model can represent temporary crises and gradual recoveries without over-engineering the math. The model was calibrated to observed time series, so the baseline reproduces historical behaviour before any "what-if" policies are tested.

Excel is the right delivery vehicle for this model. The workbook represents a logical architecture (model, data, parameters, policies, and scenarios), allowing users to view inputs, assumptions, and results without needing to navigate a specialized tool. The model sheet simulates stocks and flows using formula-based methods. The data sheet holds historical series and side-by-side model time series fit charts. The parameters sheet consolidates constants and Solver settings. The policies sheet exposes business-facing levers. The scenarios sheet records runs and a small KPI pack for decision comparisons. Because Excel is ubiquitous, stakeholders can open the file, audit it line by line, recalibrate with Solver, and run scenarios immediately. That combination of a transparent structure, traceable assumptions, and no new software to learn turns a robust system dynamics model into an operational decision-making tool.

14.11 Discussion Questions

- What are the key systemic barriers that contribute to higher failure rates among WoC entrepreneurs, and how do these barriers manifest in the simulation model?
- Why does the chapter argue for tracking entrepreneurs rather than businesses, and how does this perspective change the types of policy interventions considered?
- Looking at the reference mode, why is there a "second valley of death" for businesses in years 6–10, and what types of policies could address it?
- How do reinforcing and balancing feedback loops interact to shape the overall trajectory of WoC entrepreneurship in the model?
- In what ways does the Excel implementation of the model enhance accessibility and increase the potential for stakeholder engagement compared to the original Vensim version?
- How does calibration improve the credibility of the model, and what risks exist if calibration is poorly executed?
- Based on the policy run results, which intervention appears most effective overall, and what trade-offs must be considered when selecting it?
- How might macroeconomic shocks like the 2008 financial crisis or COVID-19 affect the dynamics of WoC entrepreneurship differently than other groups?

14.12 Exercises

14.12.1 Attrition hot-spot analysis

Task. Using the baseline scenario outputs, identify the stages with the highest attrition rate. Quantify the delta between entrants and successful exits at each stage.

Deliverable. A table showing, per stage, entrants, successful exits, and the computed differences, plus a one- to two-paragraph summary of where attrition is highest.

14.12.2 Reference mode comparison

Task. Compare Figs. 14.1–14.3; synthesize what the trends imply about entry, persistence, and long-term survival for WoC entrepreneurs.
Deliverable. A concise (200–300 words) narrative linking the three figures to entry dynamics, persistence, and survival.

14.12.3 Feedback loop write-ups

Task. From Fig. 14.4, select one reinforcing loop and one balancing loop; explain how each shapes behaviour over time.
Deliverable. Two one-paragraph explanations (one per loop), each naming the loop and describing its effect on system trajectories.

14.12.4 Policy portfolio evaluation

Task. Using Tab. 14.1, determine which policy yields the strongest combined performance on ongoing businesses, reduced failed exits, and increased successful exits; justify the selection.
Deliverable. A 300-word memo that states the recommended policy, decision criteria, comparative evidence, and risks/assumptions.

14.12.5 Excel policy intervention trial

Task. In the policies worksheet, adjust policy multipliers to define a proposed intervention. Document parameter changes, run the model, and compare the outcomes to the baseline.
Deliverable. Change log (before/after values), result screenshots (key outputs), and a 150- to 200-word summary of impacts versus baseline.

14.12.6 Single-parameter recalibration

Task. Using the parameters and data worksheets, recalibrate one rate (e.g. the 5-year failure fraction) to improve the fit; then compute the change in total SSE.
Deliverable. Parameter value before/after, SSE before/after, and a 3- to 5-sentence note on fit improvement and side-effects.

14.12.7 ±10% sensitivity probe

Task. Choose a key parameter (e.g. re-entry rate after failed exit) and vary it by ±10%; quantify effects on ongoing entrepreneurs in 2050.
Deliverable. A three-row table (−10%, baseline, +10%) with 2050 ongoing counts, plus a two- to three-sentence interpretation.

14.12.8 First-year failure mitigation design
Task. Propose a real-world programme/policy to reduce the first-year failure fraction for WoC entrepreneurs; specify how to represent it in the model (which parameter(s) change and by how much).
Deliverable. A 200- to 250-word design brief describing the intervention, modelled parameter adjustments, and expected qualitative effects.

Chapter 15
Modelling the Sustainability of Canada's Oil Sands

15.1 Learning Objectives

- Explain the trade-offs between economic growth, environmental integrity, and social well-being in Canada's oil sands sector.
- Interpret how system dynamics models capture reinforcing and balancing feedback loops in resource-based industries.
- Assess the strengths of translating a Vensim model into Excel for accessibility, transparency, and experimentation.
- Evaluate calibration methods and understand their role in aligning models with real-world data.
- Analyse baseline projections and policy scenarios to understand the long-term sustainability implications of reinvestment strategies.
- Critically appraise counterintuitive policy outcomes.

15.2 Introduction

Unconventional energy resources such as the Canadian oil sands present a complex trade-off between economic growth, environmental degradation, and social impact. While oil sands development contributes significantly to employment, government revenues, and national energy security, it poses substantial risks regarding land disruption, water usage, greenhouse gas (GHG) emissions, and impacts on Indigenous communities. Balancing these competing objectives is crucial to determining whether oil sands development can be sustainable.

This chapter introduces a system dynamics model of the Canadian oil sands sector originally developed in Vensim and later implemented in Excel [46]. The model captures the interrelationships between economic profitability, environmental emissions, social well-being, and oil extraction dynamics. By translating the model into Excel, we enable broader access and allow stakeholders – especially policymakers, educators, and analysts – to experiment with scenarios and understand the long-term consequences of various policy paths.

We walk through each stage of the modelling process, including the problem definition, dynamic hypothesis, model structure, calibration, base run projections, and policy experiments. The emphasis is on making the Excel implementation intuitive and transparent, allowing users to adjust assumptions, visualize system behaviour, and assess the sustainability of oil sands development under different economic and regulatory conditions.

https://doi.org/10.1515/9783111541389-017

15.3 Problem Definition

The Canadian oil sands are one of the world's most extensive unconventional energy resources, located primarily in Alberta. Their development has delivered substantial economic benefits, including increased employment, enhanced government revenues, and improved energy security. At the same time, oil sands projects incur significant environmental and social costs, including GHG emissions, excessive water consumption, land disturbance, and long-term impacts on Indigenous communities and their traditional ways of life. Balancing these competing outcomes is central to the debate over whether the sector can be sustainable.

Extraction from oil sands differs fundamentally from conventional oil. Mining and in situ drilling methods require far greater inputs of energy and water, making production more carbon-intensive and more vulnerable to fluctuations in global oil prices. When prices fall, projects quickly become uneconomical, while tighter environmental regulations or carbon pricing further raise costs. This interplay between profitability and sustainability creates inherent tensions that evolve across different timescales: financial returns are realized quickly, while environmental degradation and social disruption accumulate over years or decades.

These dynamics make consistent policy design difficult. Short-term incentives to maximize economic growth often undermine long-term environmental and social objectives, producing unintended consequences. For example, raising environmental standards may improve sustainability in the long run, but it may also discourage short-term investment and employment. Conversely, subsidies to stimulate output may boost growth but accelerate ecological decline.

15.4 Reference Mode

To validate and ground the model in real-world behaviour, we examined historical data provided by Canada's Energy Regulator (CER), which tracks annual oil sands production, GHG emissions, and key economic indicators. This dataset spans over a decade and captures significant fluctuations in output and environmental impact, making it an ideal benchmark for developing reference modes.

Oil extraction in the Canadian oil sands is carried out using two methods: mining and drilling. Mining is typically used when the oil sands are located near the surface. In this process, large shovels and trucks are employed to excavate the sand, which is then processed to separate the bitumen from the sand, clay, and water. Drilling, by contrast, is used when the deposits are buried too deeply for surface mining to be feasible. This method involves in situ techniques, most commonly Steam-Assisted Gravity Drainage (SAGD), where steam is injected underground to heat the bitumen, making it fluid enough to be pumped to the surface. Together, mining and drilling enable the extraction of bitumen from Canada's vast oil sands reserves, though each method presents distinct technical challenges, costs, and environmental considerations.

Oil production from oil sands increased steadily from 2005 to 2019, driven by strong global oil demand and sustained investment in extraction infrastructure (see Figs. 15.1 and 15.2). Production peaked in 2018 before declining in 2019, primarily due to the decline in international oil prices and the economic impact of the COVID-19 pandemic. This trend provides a necessary behavioural signature for replicating the model, a reinforcing growth pattern interrupted by external shocks and market saturation.

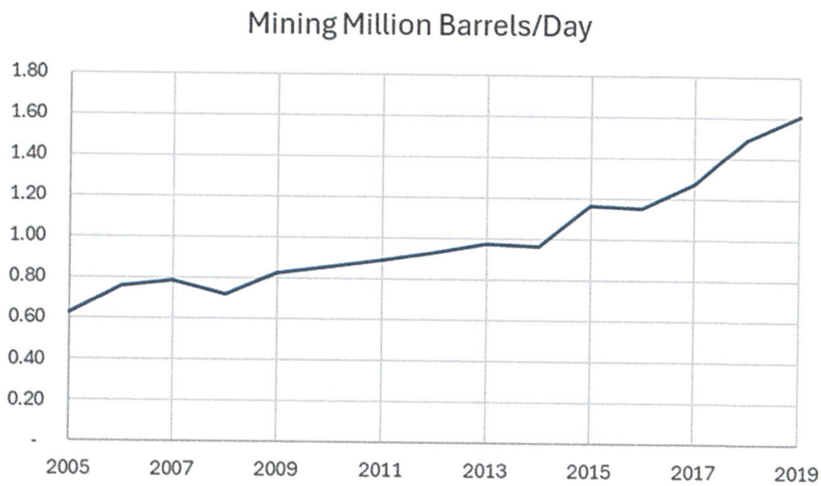

Fig. 15.1: Reference mode of oil extraction by mining.

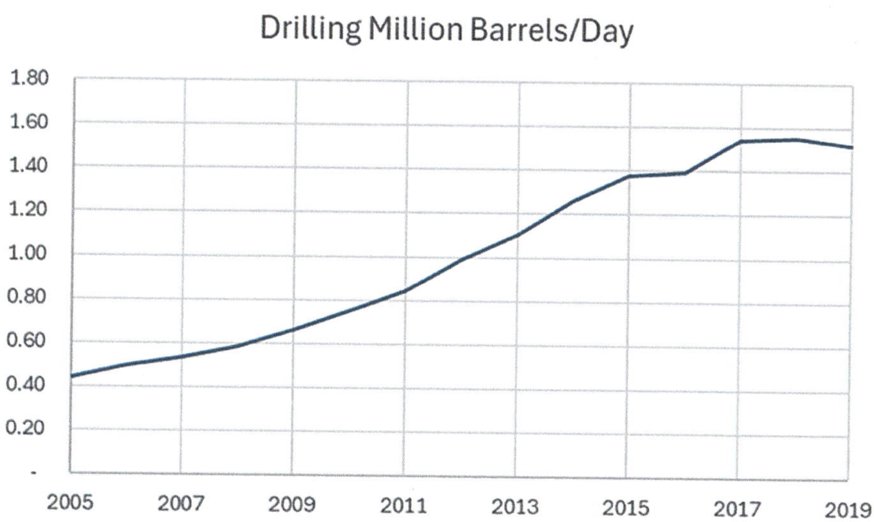

Fig. 15.2: Reference mode of oil extraction by drilling.

Simultaneously, data on emissions per barrel show a more gradual trend (see Figs. 15.3 and 15.4). While overall GHG emissions rose with production volumes, emissions intensity (i.e. emissions per barrel of oil) began to level off due to the adoption of more efficient technologies and operational improvements. This shift illustrates how environmental performance can, to a limited extent, decouple from raw output growth. However, total emissions continued to grow because reductions in intensity were outpaced by rising production.

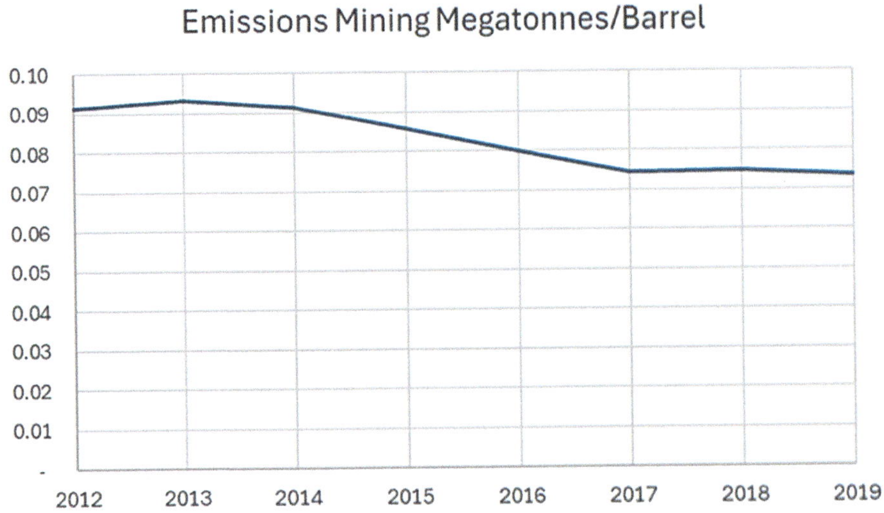

Fig. 15.3: Reference mode of emissions per barrel from mining.

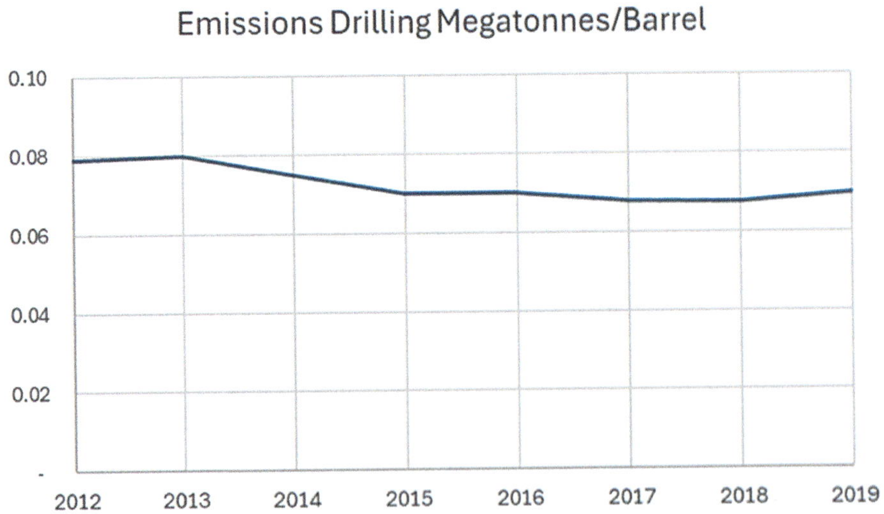

Fig. 15.4: Reference mode of emissions per barrel from drilling.

Together, these time-series trends form the model's reference modes. They define the expected system behaviour under "business-as-usual" conditions and help structure the dynamic hypothesis and stock-and-flow logic.

These reference modes serve two key roles in the modelling process: they act as calibration targets during model validation and as visual baselines against which future policy scenarios are compared. If the model cannot replicate these historical patterns, its ability to simulate future dynamics credibly is compromised.

The model gains credibility and relevance by starting with well-documented empirical trends and embedding them into the system structure. The CER data helps ensure the simulation is theoretically sound and reflective of real-world dynamics in Canada's unconventional oil sector.

15.5 Dynamic Hypothesis

The behaviour observed in oil sands development (i.e. fluctuating output, growing emissions, and social pressure) suggests a system shaped by multiple interacting feedback loops. These loops reinforce growth or act as balancing forces that constrain expansion in response to environmental, social, or economic conditions. Figure 15.5 shows four balanced feedback loops and one reinforcing feedback loop in the oil sands causal loop diagram.

Reinforcing loop R1 (profit-driven expansion): When oil prices rise above production costs, producers experience higher profits. These profits enable further investment in labour and capital, which increases the extraction rate. This, in turn, boosts total oil output and, if prices remain favourable, generates even more profit. This positive feedback drives the industry's growth phase.

Balancing loop B1 (productivity reinvestment): As productivity reinvestment increases, profit decreases, and productivity reinvestment decreases. Balancing loop B2 (social service reinvestment): As social services reinvestment increases, profit decreases, and social services reinvestment decreases. Balancing loop B3 (reinvestment in emissions reduction): As emissions reduction reinvestment increases, profit decreases, and emissions reduction reinvestment decreases.

Balancing loop B4 (production costs): Higher profits support reinvestment in capital and labour, leading to more capital and labour. This, in turn, results in increased depreciation and wages, leading to greater costs and lower profits.

Profits increase economic well-being, social services enhance social well-being, and reduced emissions improve environmental well-being. Ultimately, all of these factors collectively impact overall well-being.

This dynamic hypothesis sets the stage for building and implementing the complete stock-and-flow model. It ensures that the system structure reflects both the reinforcing forces that drive industry growth and the balancing mechanisms that shape its long-term sustainability.

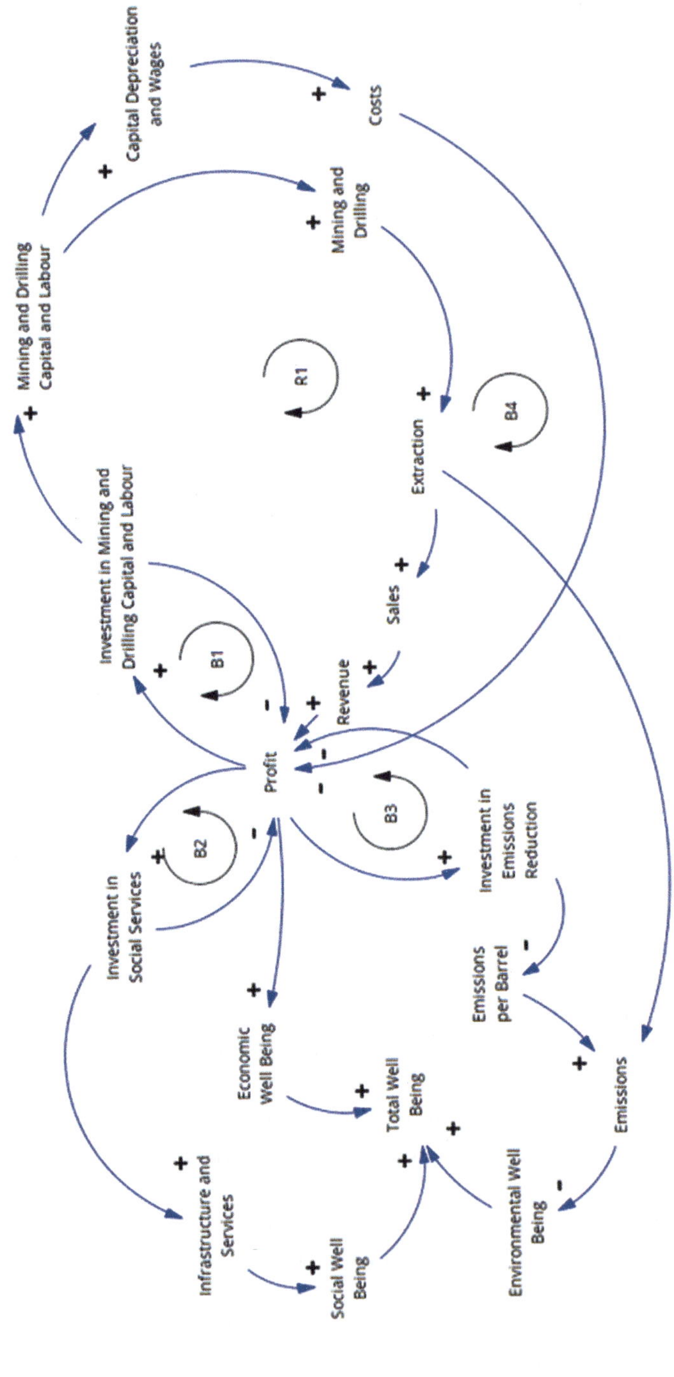

Fig. 15.5: Causal loop diagram of the Canadian oil sands model.

15.6 Model Formulation

15.6.1 Vensim Model Formulation

The Vensim model of the Canadian oil sands includes stock-and-flow structures for oil reserves with extraction by mining and drilling (Fig. 15.6), active workforce (Fig. 15.7), oil production capital (Fig. 15.8), social services and infrastructure (Fig. 15.9), accumulated emissions (Fig. 15.10) and key economic indicators (Fig. 15.11).

We will not dwell on the Vensim model here. Our purpose is to demonstrate how this reasonably large model can be converted to Excel and how the specialized features available in Excel can be utilized for calibration and policy analysis.

15.6.2 The Excel Model Formulation

We used the same process to convert the model to Excel as shown in the earlier chapters. The Excel version of the model was structured into multiple worksheets to enhance clarity and usability. We separated the workbook into four worksheets: data, model, calibration, and policies.

All parameters, including emissions factors, base productivity levels, and fiscal multipliers, were centralized in a calibration sheet, along with the total sum of squared error (see Figs. 15.12–15.14).

The calibration worksheet also contains comparison graphs of the time-series data and model estimates for oil extraction by drilling and mining from 2005 to 2019, as well as for emissions per barrel from 2012 to 2019. These will be discussed in the calibration section below.

The simulation itself was built in a worksheet titled model, where each endogenous variable was assigned a column, and each row represented the values over the years from 2005 to 2050 (see Figs. 15.15–15.19).

There are also two columns computed using lookup tables in the model worksheet. One represents a simple model of the price elasticity of demand, and the other represents historical data of the price of a barrel of oil (see Fig. 15.20).

Figures 15.21 and 15.22 show the lookup tables.

There is also a worksheet entitled data, which contains the time Series data for oil extraction using drilling and mining from 2005 to 2019 (see Fig. 15.23) and emissions per barrel from drilling and mining from 2011 to 2018 (see Fig. 15.24).

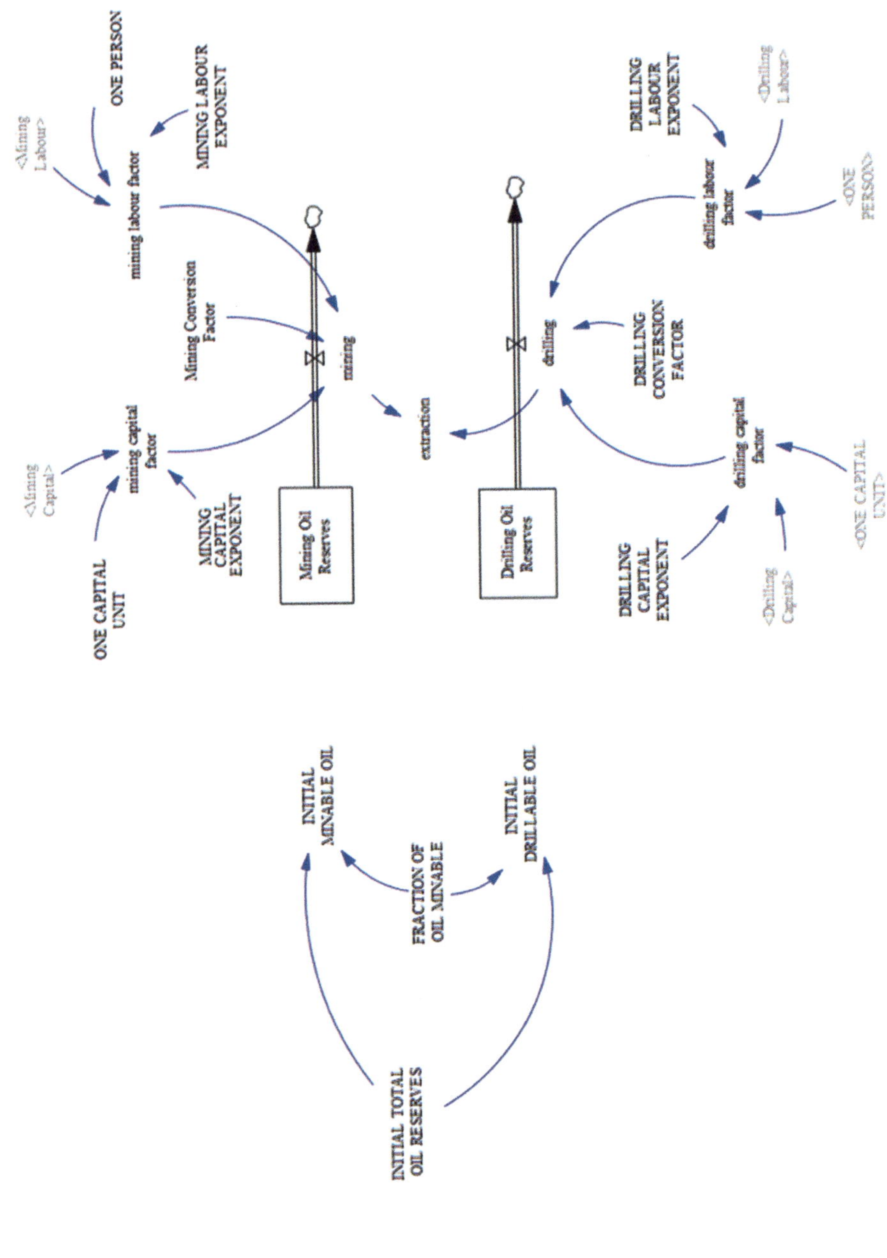

Fig. 15.6: Vensim model of oil extraction by mining and drilling.

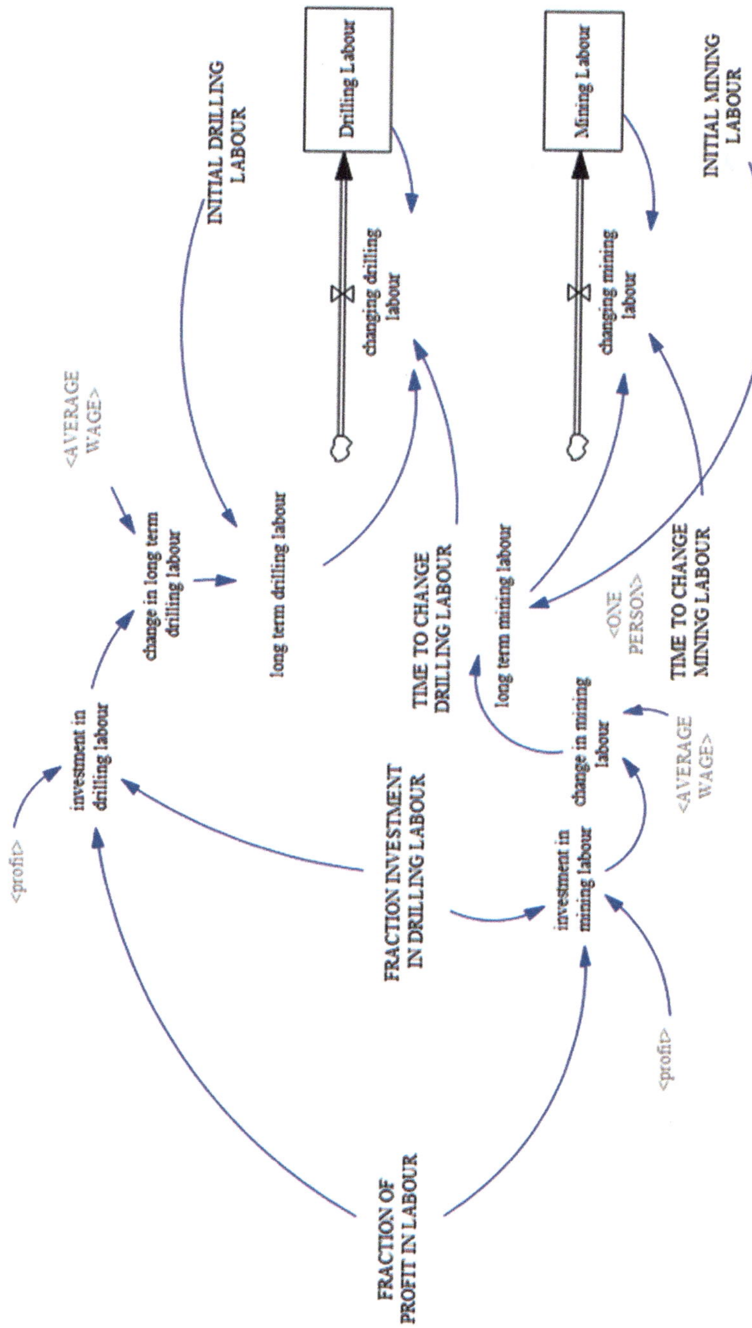

Fig. 15.7: Vensim model of labour.

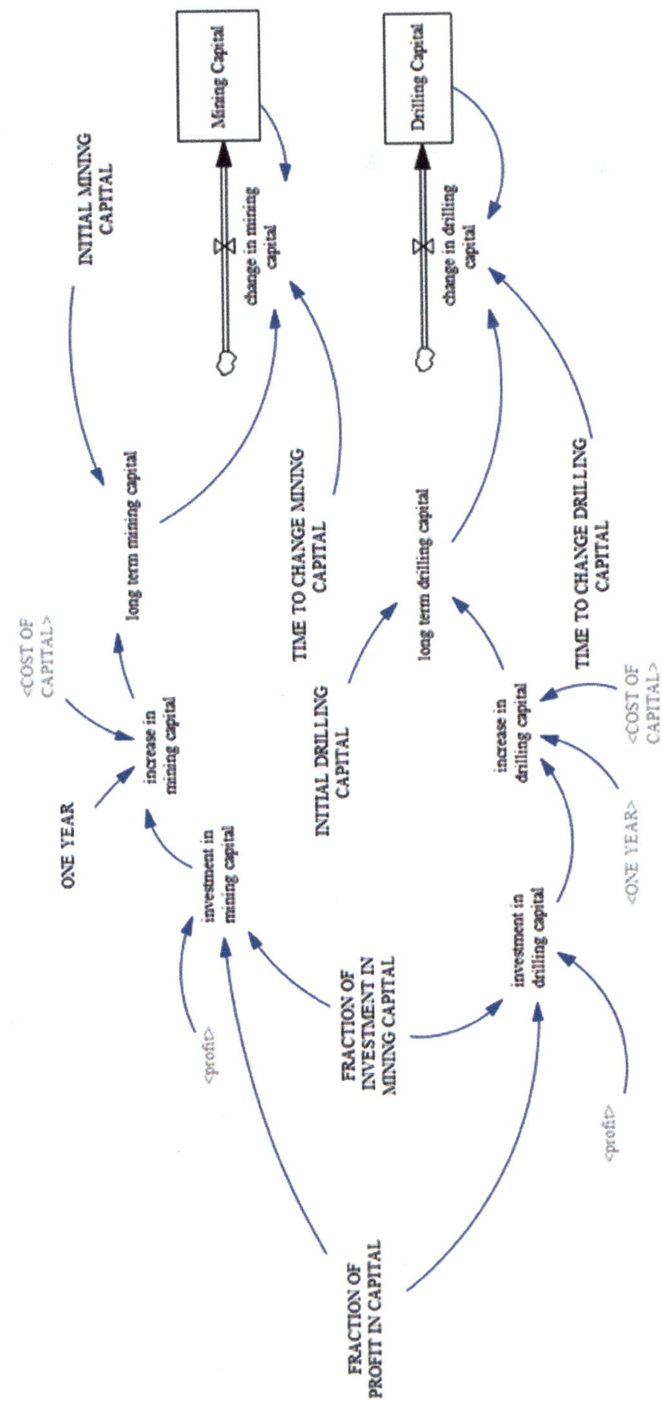

Fig. 15.8: Vensim model of capital.

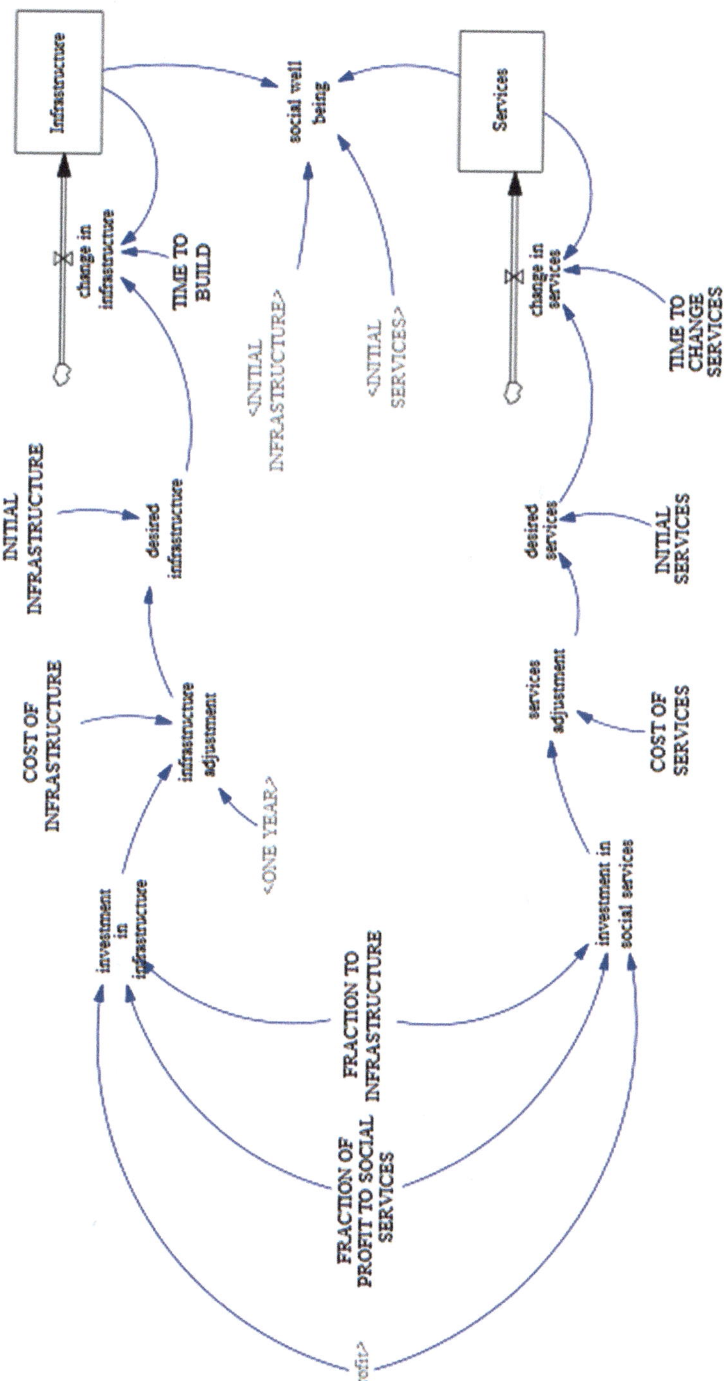

Fig. 15.9: Vensim model of social well-being.

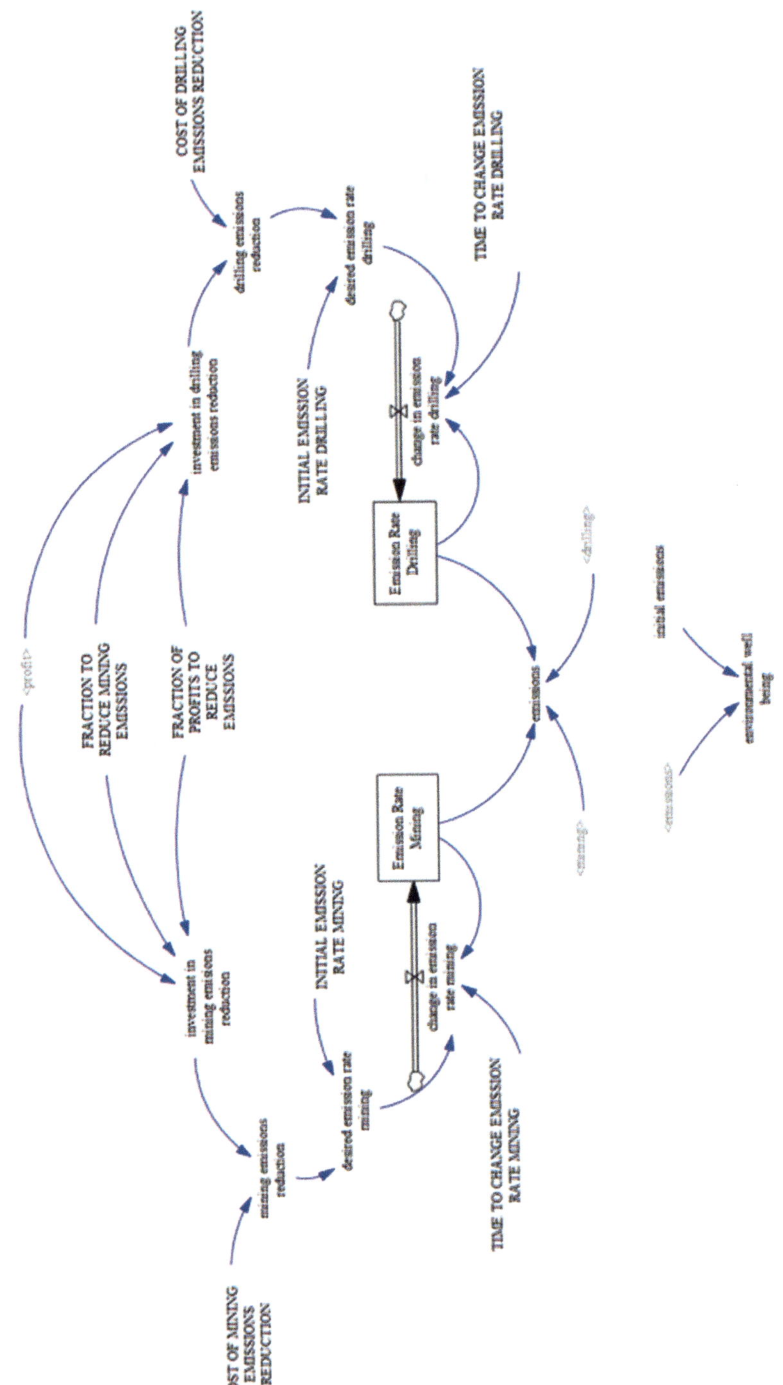

Fig. 15.10: Vensim model of environmental well-being.

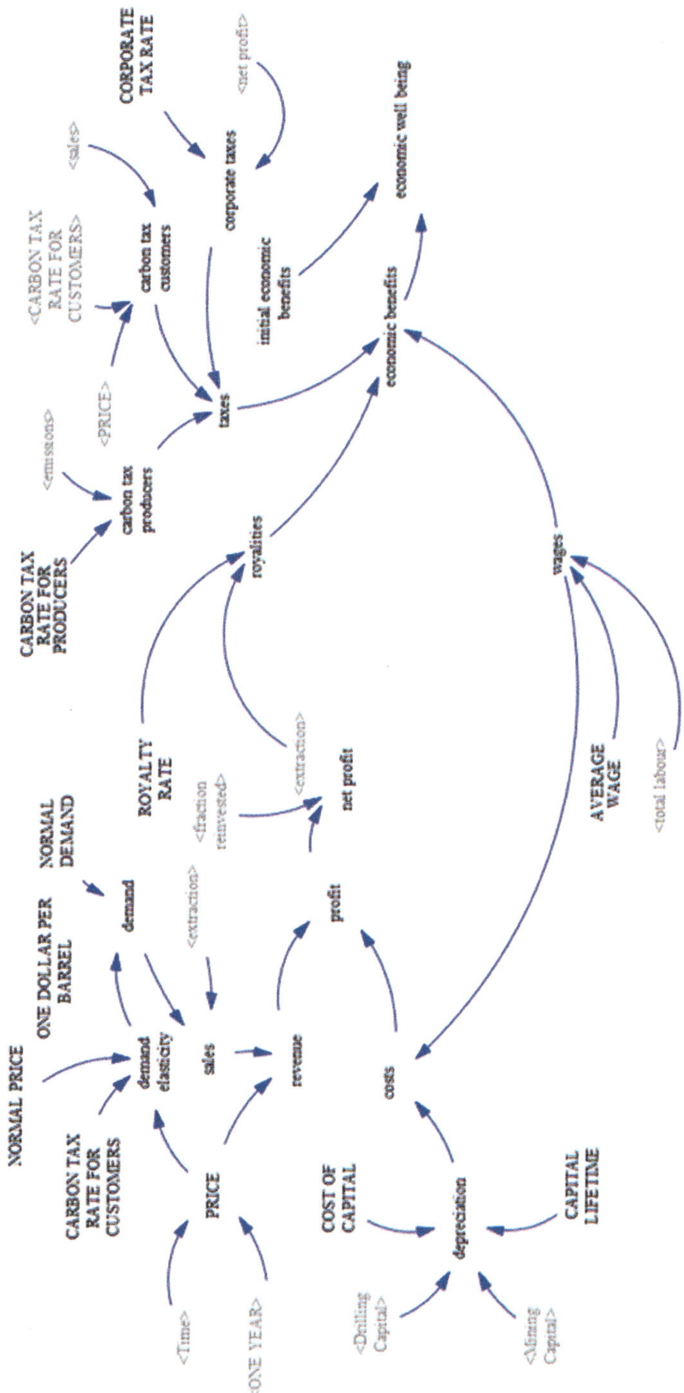

Fig. 15.11: Vensim model of economic well-being.

	A	B	C	D
1	PARAMETER	VALUE	UNITS	TSSE
2	(076) INITIAL TIME =	2005	Units: year	0.12
3	(121) TIME STEP =	0.25	Units: year [0,?]	
4	(001) AVERAGE WAGE=	$338,909	Units: dollars/person/year	
5	(002) CAPITAL LIFETIME=	25	Units: year	
6	(005) CARBON TAX RATE FOR CUSTOMERS=	24%	Units: dmnl	
7	(006) CARBON TAX RATE FOR PRODUCERS=	0.2%	Units: dollars/kg	
8	(017) CORPORATE TAX RATE=	10%	Units: dmnl	
9	(019) COST OF CAPITAL=	$42,016	Units: dollars/capital units	
10	(020) COST OF DRILLING EMISSIONS REDUCTION=	10	Units: (dollars/year)/(kg/barrels)	
11	(021) COST OF INFRASTRUCTURE=	1000000	Units: dollars/buildings	
12	(022) COST OF MINING EMISSIONS REDUCTION=	10	Units: barrels*dollars/(year*kg)	
13	(023) COST OF SERVICES=	1000000	Units: dollars/service units	
14	(034) DRILLING CAPITAL EXPONENT=	1.18	Units: dmnl	
15	(036) DRILLING CONVERSION FACTOR=	1,740	Units: barrels/year	
16	(039) DRILLING LABOUR EXPONENT=	-0.18	Units: dmnl	
17	(050) FRACTION INVESTMENT IN DRILLING LABOUR=	0%	Units: dmnl	
18	(051) FRACTION OF INVESTMENT IN MINING CAPITAL=	47%	Units: dmnl	
19	(052) FRACTION OF OIL MINABLE=	20%	Units: fraction	

< > Data | Vensim Model | Model | Calibration | Policies | +

Fig. 15.12: Calibrated parameters in the Canadian oil sands model (set 1).

	A	B	C
1	PARAMETER	VALUE	UNITS
20	(053) FRACTION OF PROFIT IN CAPITAL=	79%	Units: dmnl
21	(054) FRACTION OF PROFIT IN LABOUR=	20%	Units: dmnl
22	(055) FRACTION OF PROFIT TO SOCIAL SERVICES=	0%	Units: dmnl
23	(056) FRACTION OF PROFITS TO REDUCE EMISSIONS=	0%	Units: dmnl
24	(058) FRACTION TO INFRASTRUCTURE=	50%	Units: dmnl
25	(059) FRACTION TO REDUCE MINING EMISSIONS=	50%	Units: dmnl
26	(065) INITIAL DRILLING CAPITAL=	79,765	Units: capital units
27	(066) INITIAL DRILLING LABOUR=	27,197	Units: people
28	(068) INITIAL EMISSION RATE DRILLING=	91	Units: kg/barrels
29	(069) INITIAL EMISSION RATE MINING=	120	Units: kg/barrels
30	(071) INITIAL INFRASTRUCTURE=	100	Units: buildings
31	(073) INITIAL MINING CAPITAL=	36,460	Units: capital units
32	(074) INITIAL MINING LABOUR=	13,246	Units: people
33	(075) INITIAL SERVICES=	1,000	Units: service units/year
34	(077) INITIAL TOTAL OIL RESERVES=	1.694E+11	Units: barrels
35	(093) MINING CAPITAL EXPONENT=	1.30	Units: dmnl
36	(095) MINING CONVERSION FACTOR=	5,030	Units: barrels/year
37	(098) MINING LABOUR EXPONENT=	-0.30	Units: dmnl

< > Data | Vensim Model | Model | Calibration | Policies | +

Fig. 15.13: Calibrated parameters in the Canadian oil sands model (set 2).

	A		B	C
1	PARAMETER		VALUE	UNITS
38	(102)	NORMAL DEMAND=	710,875,962	Units: barrels/year
39	(103)	NORMAL PRICE=	68	Units: dollars/barrels
40	(104)	ONE CAPITAL UNIT=	1	Units: capital units
41	(105)	ONE DOLLAR PER BARREL=	1	Units: dollars/barrels
42	(106)	ONE PERSON=	1	Units: people
43	(107)	ONE YEAR=	1	Units: year
44	(113)	ROYALTY RATE=	2%	Units: dollars/barrels
45	(122)	TIME TO BUILD=	2	Units: year
46	(123)	TIME TO CHANGE DRILLING CAPITAL=	15	Units: years
47	(124)	TIME TO CHANGE DRILLING LABOUR=	40	Units: years
48	(125)	TIME TO CHANGE EMISSION RATE DRILLING=	41	Units: years
49	(126)	TIME TO CHANGE EMISSION RATE MINING=	25	Units: years
50	(127)	TIME TO CHANGE MINING CAPITAL=	63	Units: years
51	(128)	TIME TO CHANGE MINING LABOUR=	4	Units: years
52	(129)	TIME TO CHANGE SERVICES=	10	Units: years

Fig. 15.14: Calibrated parameters in the Canadian oil sands model (set 3).

	A	B	C	D	E	F	G	H	I	J	K	L	M	N	O	P	Q	R
1	Time	(003) carbon tax customers=	(004) carbon tax producers=	(007) change in drilling capital=	(008) change in emission rate drilling=	(009) change in emission rate mining=	(010) change in infrastructure=	(011) change in long term drilling labour=	(012) change in mining capital=	(013) change in mining labour=	(014) change in services=	(015) changing drilling labour=	(016) changing mining labour=	(018) corporate taxes=	(024) costs=	(025) demand=	(027) depreciation=	(028) desired emission rate drilling=
2	Units: year	Units: dollars/year	Units: dollars/year	Units: capital units/year	Units: (kg/barrels)/year	Units: (kg/barrels)/year	Units: buildings/year	Units: people	Units: capital units/year	Units: people	Units: service units/year/year	Units: people/year	Units: people/year	Units: dollars/year	Units: dollars/year	Units: barrels/year	Units: dollars/year	Units: kg/barrels
3	2005	3.75E+09	1.02E+08	1045.019	-2.23551	-4.72641	0.00027	0	217.3863	918.7544	5.36E-05	0	204.3891	1249634	1.39E+10	1.39E+09	196596851	0
4	2005.25	4.12E+09	1.01E+08	2016.421	-2.2218	-4.67998	0.000491	0	422.2124	1788.087	0.000103	0	386.4164	2432048	1.39E+10	1.25E+09	197130697	0
5	2005.5	4.49E+09	1.01E+08	2988.653	-2.20818	-4.634	0.000689	0	629.7603	2672.373	0.000152	0	561.6466	3634800	1.4E+10	1.12E+09	198161947	0
6	2005.75	4.87E+09	1.01E+08	3968.39	-2.19464	-4.58848	0.000869	0	841.4102	3577.492	0.000201	0	731.7658	4865887	1.4E+10	9.81E+08	199692103	0
7	2006	5.27E+09	1E+08	4962.506	-2.18118	-4.5434	0.001034	0	1058.602	4509.598	0.000251	0	898.4273	6133681	1.41E+10	8.44E+08	201726073	0

Fig. 15.15: Endogenous variables in the Canadian oil sands model (set 1).

	A	S	T	U	V	W	X	Y	Z	AA	AB	AC	AD	AE	AF	AG	AH
1	Time	(029) desired emission rate mining=	(030) desired infrastructure=	(031) desired services=	(032) drilling=	(033) Drilling Capital= INTEG (	(035) drilling capital factor=	(037) drilling emissions reduction=	(038) Drilling Labour= INTEG (	(040) drilling labour factor=	(041) Drilling Oil Reserves = INTEG (	(042) economic benefits=	(043) economic well being=	(044) Emission Rate Drilling= INTEG (	(045) Emission Rate Mining= INTEG (	(046) emissions=	(047) environmental well being=
2	Units: year	Units: kg/barrels	Units: buildings	Units: service units/year	Units: barrels/year	Units: capital units	Units: dmnl	Units: kg/barrels	Units: people	Units: dmnl	Units: barrels	Units: dollars/year	Units: dmnl	Units: kg/barrels	Units: kg/barrels	Units: kg/year	Units: dmnl
3	2005	0	1.00E+02	1000.434	167887176	79764.75	587672.783	1004.034	27197.13	0.16419397	1.36E+11	1.76E+10	1	91.14233	120.2777	4.52E+10	1
4	2005.25	0	1.00E+02	1000.435	168534543	80026.01	589938.829	1954.06	27197.13	0.16419397	1.35E+11	1.8E+10	1.021543	90.58345	119.0961	4.49E+10	1.006813
5	2005.5	0	1.00E+02	1000.435	169784730	80530.11	594314.984	2920.427	27197.13	0.16419397	1.35E+11	1.84E+10	1.044546	90.028	117.9261	4.47E+10	1.011903
6	2005.75	0	1.00E+02	1000.436	171640249	81277.28	600810.05	3909.56	27197.13	0.16419397	1.35E+11	1.88E+10	1.069104	89.47596	116.7676	4.45E+10	1.015203
7	2006	0	1.00E+02	1000.436	174108706	82269.37	609450.646	4928.185	27197.13	0.16419397	1.35E+11	1.92E+10	1.095332	88.9273	115.6205	4.45E+10	1.016652

Fig. 15.16: Endogenous variables in the Canadian oil sands model (set 2).

	A	AI	AJ	AK	AL	AM	AN	AO	AP	AQ	AR	AS	AT	AU	AV	AW	AX
1	Time	(048) extraction=	(057) fraction reinvested=	(060) increase in drilling capital=	(061) increase in mining capital=	(062) infrastructure= INTEG (	(063) infrastructure adjustment=	(064) INITIAL DRILLABLE OIL=	(067) initial economic benefits=	(070) initial emissions=	(072) INITIAL MINABLE OIL=	(078) initial workforce=	(053) FRACTION OF PROFIT IN CAPITAL=	(051) FRACTION OF INVESTMENT IN MINING CAPITAL=	(079) investment in drilling capital=	(056) FRACTION OF PROFITS TO REDUCE EMISSIONS=	(059) FRACTION TO REDUCE MINING EMISSIONS=
2	Units: year	Units: barrels/year	Units: dmnl	Units: capital units	Units: capital units	Units: buildings	Units: buildings	Units: barrels	Units: dollars/year	Units: kg/year	Units: barrels	Units: people	Units: dmnl	Units: dmnl	Units: dollars/year	Units: dmnl	Units: dmnl
3	2005	4.17E+08	0.991968	15687.22	13635.5	99.98457	5.39E-04	1.36E+11	1.76E+10	4.52E+10	3.39E+10	40443.61	0.79183081	0.465015	6.59E+08	1.2892E-05	0.49947209
4	2005.25	4.17E+08	0.991968	30530.59	26537.51	99.98464	1.05E-03	1.36E+11	1.76E+10	4.52E+10	3.39E+10	40443.61	0.79183081	0.465015	1.28E+09	1.2892E-05	0.49947209
5	2005.5	4.19E+08	0.991968	45629.28	39661.45	99.98476	1.57E-03	1.36E+11	1.76E+10	4.52E+10	3.39E+10	40443.61	0.79183081	0.465015	1.92E+09	1.2892E-05	0.49947209
6	2005.75	4.21E+08	0.991968	61083.68	53094.57	99.98493	2.10E-03	1.36E+11	1.76E+10	4.52E+10	3.39E+10	40443.61	0.79183081	0.465015	2.57E+09	1.2892E-05	0.49947209
7	2006	4.25E+08	0.991968	76998.87	66928.22	99.98515	2.65E-03	1.36E+11	1.76E+10	4.52E+10	3.39E+10	40443.61	0.79183081	0.465015	3.24E+09	1.2892E-05	0.49947209

Fig. 15.17: Endogenous variables in the Canadian oil sands model (set 3).

	A	AY	AZ	BA	BB	BC	BD	BE	BF	BG	BH	BI	BJ	BK	BL	BM	BN	BO
1	Time	(080) investment in drilling emissions reduction=	(054) FRACTION OF PROFIT IN LABOUR=	(050) FRACTION INVESTMENT IN DRILLING LABOUR=	(081) investment in drilling labour=	(055) FRACTION OF PROFIT TO SOCIAL SERVICES=	(058) FRACTION TO INFRASTRUCTURE=	(082) investment in infrastructure=	(083) investment in mining capital=	(084) investment in mining emisions reduction=	(085) investment in mining labour=	(086) investment in social services=	(087) long term drilling capital=	(088) long term drilling labour=	(089) long term mining capital=	(090) long term mining labour=	(091) mining=	(092) Mining Capital= INTEG (
2	Units: year	Units: dollars/year	Units: dmnl	Units: dmnl	Units: dollars/year	Units: dmnl	Units: dmnl	Units: dollars/year	Units: dollars/year	Units: dollars/year	Units: dollars/year	Units: dollars/year	Units: capital units	Units: people	Units: capital units	Units: people	Units: barrels/year	Units: capital units
3	2005	1.00E+04	0.20012406	0	0.00E+00	6.9285E-07	0.5	5.39E+02	5.73E+08	1.00E+04	3.11E+08	5.39E+02	95451.97	27197.13	50095.62	14165.23	2.49E+08	36460.12
4	2005.25	1.95E+04	0.20012406	0	0.00E+00	6.9285E-07	0.5	1.05E+03	1.11E+09	1.95E+04	6.06E+08	1.05E+03	110295.3	27197.13	62997.63	15034.56	2.49E+08	36514.47
5	2005.5	2.92E+04	0.20012406	0	0.00E+00	6.9285E-07	0.5	1.57E+03	1.67E+09	2.91E+04	9.06E+08	1.57E+03	125394	27197.13	76121.57	15918.85	2.49E+08	36620.02
6	2005.75	3.91E+04	0.20012406	0	0.00E+00	6.9285E-07	0.5	2.10E+03	2.23E+09	3.90E+04	1.21E+09	2.10E+03	140848.4	27197.13	89554.69	16823.97	2.50E+08	36777.46
7	2006	4.93E+04	0.20012406	0	0.00E+00	6.9285E-07	0.5	2.65E+03	2.81E+09	4.92E+04	1.53E+09	2.65E+03	156763.6	27197.13	103388.3	17756.07	2.51E+08	36967.81

Fig. 15.18: Endogenous variables in the Canadian oil sands model (set 4).

	A	BP	BQ	BR	BS	BT	BU	BV	BW	BX	BY	BZ	CA	CB	CC	CD	CE	CF
1	Time	(094) mining capital factor=	(096) mining emissions reduction=	(097) Mining Labour= INTEG (	(099) mining labour factor=	(100) Mining Oil Reserves= INTEG (	(101) net profit=	(108) overall well being=	(110) profit=	(111) revenue=	(112) royalities=	(114) sales=	(116) Services= INTEG (	(117) services adjustment=	(119) social well being=	(120) taxes=	(130) total labour=	(132) wages=
2	Units: year	Units: dmnl	Units: kg/barrels	Units: people	Units: dmnl	Units: barrels	Units: dollars/year	Units: dmnl	Units: dollars/year	Units: dollars/year	Units: dollars/year	Units: barrels/year	Units: service units/year	Units: service units/year	Units: dmnl	Units: dollars/year	Units: people	Units: dollars/year
3	2005	858786.2	1001.917	13246.48	5.76E-02	3.39E+10	12496341	1	1.56E+09	1.55E+10	8330876.54	4.17E+08	1000.434	0.000539	1	3.86E+09	40443.61	1.3707E+10
4	2005.25	860451.6	1949.938	13297.57	5.75E-02	3.38E+10	24320477	1.009452	3.03E+09	1.69E+10	8347701.86	4.17E+08	1000.434	0.00104901	1	4.22E+09	40494.7	1.3724E+10
5	2005.5	863688.5	2914.266	13394.18	5.74E-02	3.38E+10	36348000	1.018817	4.53E+09	1.85E+10	8380563.5	4.19E+08	1000.434	0.00156779	1.000001	4.59E+09	40591.31	1.3757E+10
6	2005.75	868521.7	3901.313	13534.59	5.72E-02	3.37E+10	48658875	1.028103	6.06E+09	2.01E+10	8429870.89	4.21E+08	1000.434	0.0020988	1.000002	4.97E+09	40731.72	1.3804E+10
7	2006	874988.9	4917.789	13717.53	5.70E-02	3.36E+10	61336814	1.037329	7.64E+09	2.17E+10	8496161.34	4.25E+08	1000.434	0.00264563	1.000003	5.37E+09	40914.66	1.3866E+10

Fig. 15.19: Endogenous variables in the Canadian oil sands model (set 5).

	A	CG	CH	CI
1	Time	(PRICE+PRICE*CARBON TAX RATE FOR CUSTOMERS)/NORMAL PRICE,	DEMAND ELASTICITY	PRICE
2	Units: year	Units: dmnl	Units: dmnl	Units: dollars/barrels
3	2005	0.68096055	1.95711835	37.1130769
4	2005.25	0.74509126	1.76472621	40.6082692
5	2005.5	0.80922198	1.57233407	44.1034615
6	2005.75	0.87335269	1.37994193	47.5986538
7	2006	0.9374834	1.1875498	51.0938462

Fig. 15.20: Endogenous variables calculated using lookup tables.

CQ	CR	CS	CT
(PRICE+PRICE*CARBON TAX RATE FOR CUSTOMERS)/NORMAL PRICE,	(026) demand elasticity = WITH LOOKUP (	Time/ONE YEAR,	(109) PRICE = WITH LOOKUP (
Units: dmnl	Units: dmnl	Units: dmnl	Units: dollars/barrels
0	4	2005	37.1131
1	1	2006	51.0938
4	0.2	2007	58.8515
		2008	68.1346
		2009	89.6638
		2010	57.5877

Fig. 15.21: Lookup tables in the Canadian oil sands model (set 1).

CS	CT
Time/ONE YEAR,	(109) PRICE = WITH LOOKUP (
2011	75.4915
2012	95.9462
2013	95.5105
2014	84.2792
2015	42.9785
2016	39.1227
2017	49.0515
2018	60.4777
2019	55.6485
2020	37.3762

Fig. 15.22: Lookup tables in the Canadian oil sands model (set 2).

	A	B	C	D	E	F	G	H	I
1	Year	Actual Min	Model Min	SE		Actual Dril	Model [	SE	
2					SSE				SSE
3	2005	0.63	0.68	0.00	0.10	0.44	0.46	0.00	0.02
4	2006	0.76	0.69	0.01		0.49	0.48	0.00	
5	2007	0.78	0.70	0.01		0.54	0.52	0.00	
6	2008	0.72	0.73	0.00		0.58	0.58	0.00	
7	2009	0.83	0.77	0.00		0.66	0.67	0.00	
8	2010	0.86	0.83	0.00		0.75	0.79	0.00	
9	2011	0.89	0.88	0.00		0.85	0.87	0.00	
10	2012	0.93	0.95	0.00		0.99	1.01	0.00	
11	2013	0.98	1.04	0.00		1.11	1.16	0.00	
12	2014	0.96	1.12	0.03		1.26	1.29	0.00	
13	2015	1.16	1.19	0.00		1.38	1.37	0.00	
14	2016	1.15	1.26	0.01		1.40	1.41	0.00	
15	2017	1.28	1.32	0.00		1.55	1.47	0.01	
16	2018	1.49	1.39	0.01		1.55	1.52	0.00	
17	2019	1.61	1.45	0.02		1.52	1.56	0.00	

Fig. 15.23: Time-series data and model values for actual and model oil extraction.

	A	J	K	L	M	N	O	P	Q	R	S	T
1	Year		Actual Emissions Rate Drilling	Model Emission Rate Drilling	SE			Actual Emissions Rate Mining	Model Emissions Rate Mining	SE		
2						SSE					SSE	TSSE
3	2005					0.00					0.00	0.12
4	2006											
5	2007											
6	2008											
7	2009											
8	2010											
9	2011	0.079	0.788	0.786	0.00		0.091	0.912	0.949	0.00		
10	2012	0.080	0.798	0.767	0.00		0.093	0.931	0.912	0.00		
11	2013	0.075	0.747	0.749	0.00		0.091	0.913	0.877	0.00		
12	2014	0.070	0.701	0.730	0.00		0.086	0.858	0.843	0.00		
13	2015	0.070	0.698	0.713	0.00		0.080	0.801	0.810	0.00		
14	2016	0.068	0.677	0.695	0.00		0.074	0.744	0.779	0.00		
15	2017	0.068	0.676	0.678	0.00		0.075	0.748	0.749	0.00		
16	2018	0.070	0.696	0.662	0.00		0.073	0.735	0.720	0.00		

Fig. 15.24: Time-series data and model values for actual and model emissions rate.

15.7 Calibration

Model calibration was conducted to ensure that simulated outputs align with observed historical data for oil sands production and emissions. The calibration process utilized time-series data from CER, covering oil extraction, mining, and drilling (2005–2019), as well as emissions per barrel (2011–2018). The model parameters were adjusted using the Excel Solver to minimize the sum of squared errors between the model's outputs and the empirical data.

Figures 15.25 and 15.26 show the calibration results for oil extraction by mining and drilling, respectively. The simulated trajectories closely follow the observed pro-

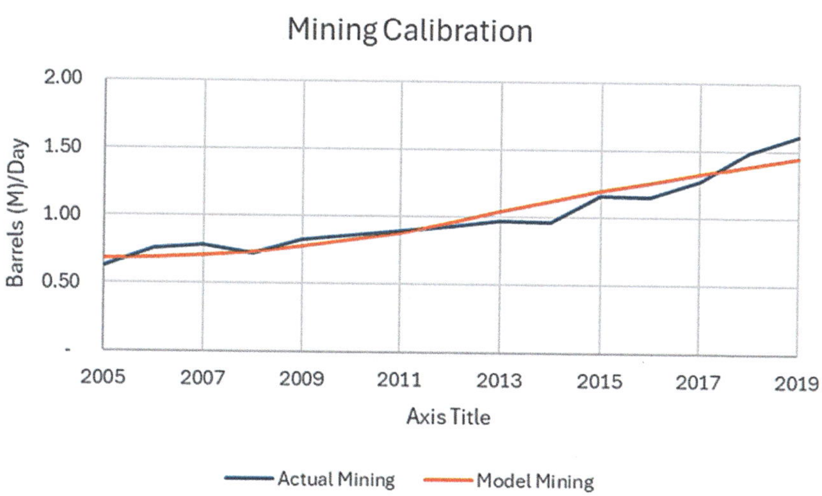

Fig. 15.25: Graphic representation of the match for oil extraction by mining.

duction patterns, capturing the steady growth in output. The fit demonstrates the model's ability to replicate the reinforcing feedback loop.

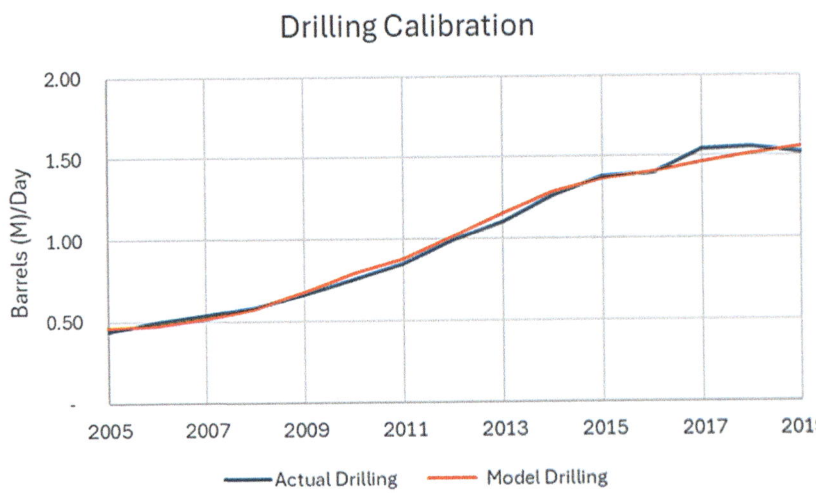

Fig. 15.26: Graphic representation of the match for oil extraction by drilling.

The calibration of emissions intensity is illustrated in Figs. 15.27 and 15.28. The model replicates the gradual decline in emissions per barrel, reflecting the adoption of more efficient extraction and upgraded technologies. Although overall emissions rose due to increased production volumes, the decreasing intensity trend was captured by adjusting technology adoption parameters and reinvestment fractions. This provides

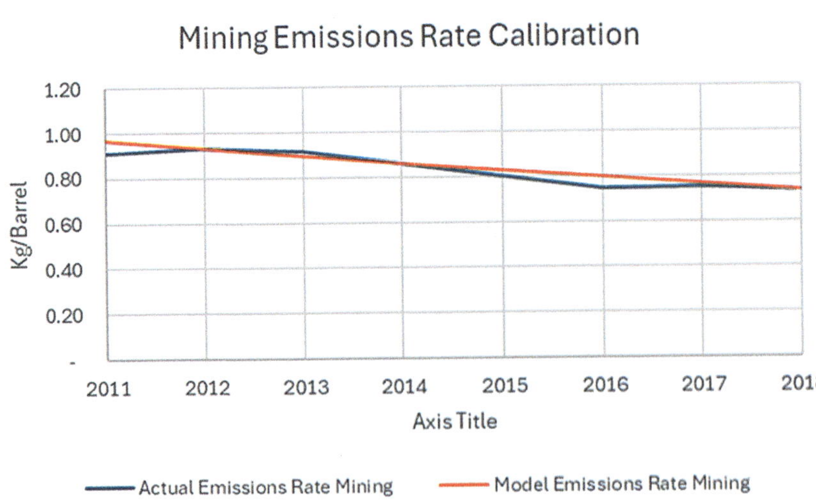

Fig. 15.27: Graphic representation of the match for the mining emissions rate.

confidence that the model structure correctly reflects the decoupling of environmental intensity from production growth.

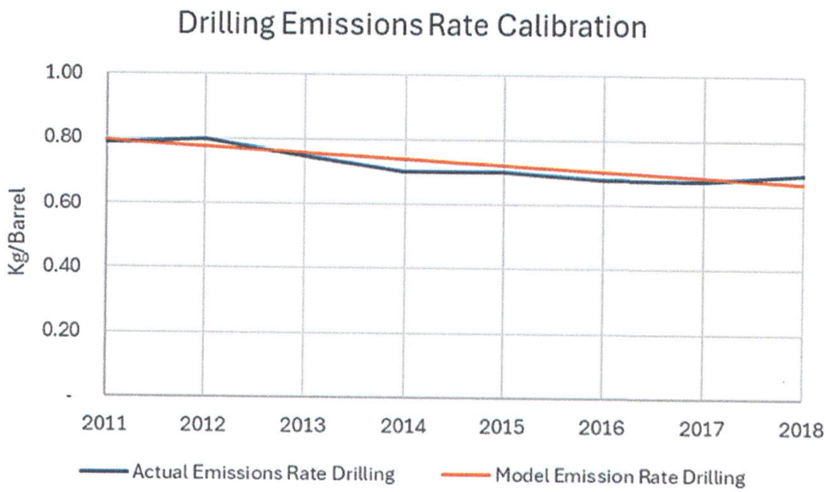

Fig. 15.28: Graphic representation of the match for the drilling emissions rate.

Overall, the calibration exercise confirms that the model can reproduce key historical dynamics of Canada's oil sands sector across both economic and environmental dimensions. The close alignment between simulated and actual data provides a solid foundation for the baseline projections and policy experiments discussed in the following sections.

15.8 Baseline Run

The baseline run represents the "business-as-usual" trajectory of the Canadian oil sands sector, assuming no significant policy changes beyond those already in place by 2019. Model parameters were fixed at their calibrated values, and the simulation was extended through 2050 to explore long-term dynamics under current extraction, reinvestment, and regulatory patterns.

Figure 15.30 illustrates the results of well-being across economic, social, and environmental dimensions. Financial well-being is expected to continue rising over the next 15 years, but it is projected to plateau around 2030. However, this expansion comes at the cost of environmental degradation. Environmental well-being is below 1.0 for the complete period. However, there is a "worse-before-better" pattern, as increasing profits are reinvested in emission reduction. Social well-being remains stagnant due to a lack of investment in social services.

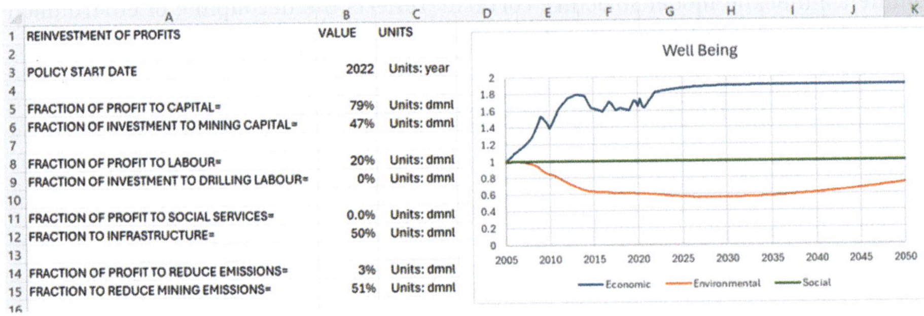

Fig. 15.30: The policy worksheet showing baseline well-being results.

In sum, the baseline run provides a critical reference point for evaluating alternative policy interventions. By demonstrating how the system operates under current conditions, it highlights the trade-offs between profitability, environmental integrity, and social outcomes that must be addressed for oil sands development to achieve sustainability.

15.9 Policy Runs

Policy runs were conducted to assess how alternative reinvestment strategies affect economic, social, and environmental outcomes in the Canadian oil sands sector. Each scenario diverts a portion of profits from the baseline allocation and channels them into labour, capital, social services, or emissions reduction. Results are compared against the baseline results in 2050 to evaluate trade-offs and identify leverage points for sustainability.

15.9.1 Shift Reinvestment from Labour to Capital

In this scenario, 10% of profits were redirected from labour to capital investment. As shown in Fig. 15.31, the policy boosts productivity by accelerating capital accumulation, but the gains are offset by rising depreciation and operating costs. Economic well-being declines by 9%, while environmental well-being decreases by 15%. The results highlight that prioritizing capital over labour intensifies extraction pressures and worsens ecological impacts, leading to a less sustainable outcome overall.

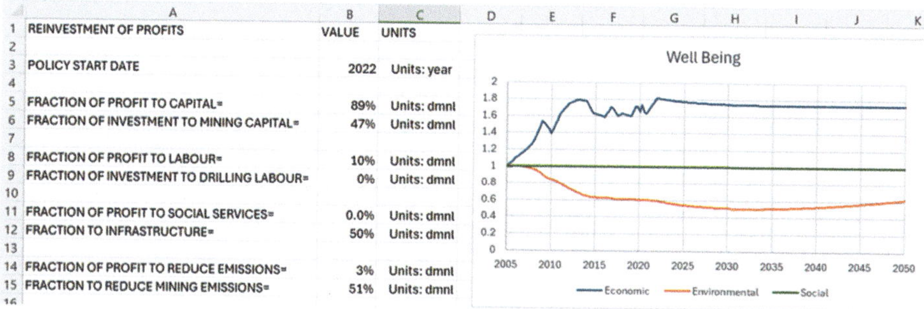

Fig. 15.31: Results with 10% of profits diverted from labour to capital.

15.9.2 Shift Reinvestment from Capital to Labour

Redirecting 10% of profits from capital investment to labour, illustrated in Fig. 15.32, yields opposite effects. Economic well-being increases by 7% and environmental well-being improves by 14%. The stronger role of labour moderates capital-driven expansion, easing environmental stress while supporting steady output. This suggests that enhancing workforce participation provides a more balanced path between economic growth and ecological integrity.

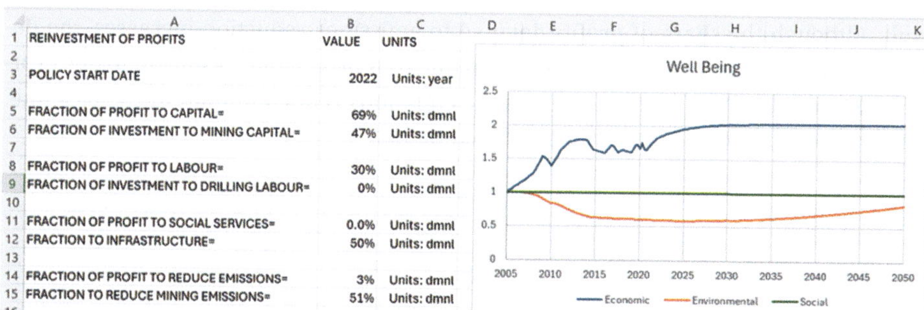

Fig. 15.32: Results with 10% of profits diverted from capital to labour.

15.9.3 Reinvestment in Social Services

Figure 15.33 shows the effects of diverting 0.1% of profits from both labour and capital to social services. Social well-being increases by 18%, reflecting improvements in public health, education, and community support. The impact on economic and environmental outcomes is minimal, suggesting that even modest investments in social services can yield substantial social benefits without compromising production or exacerbating emis-

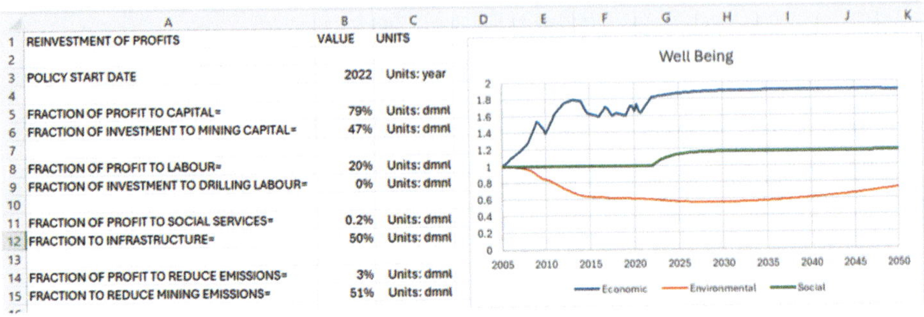

Fig. 15.33: Results with 0.1% of profits diverted from capital and labour to social services.

sions. This scenario underscores the potential of targeted reinvestment in social infrastructure to address long-standing equity concerns.

15.9.4 Reinvestment in Emissions Reduction

In the final scenario, 5% of profits were reallocated from labour and capital to emissions reduction measures. Figure 15.34 demonstrates that economic well-being declines slightly (−4%) due to reduced reinvestment in productive assets, while environmental well-being also declines modestly (−2.7%). This is a highly counterintuitive result. Although the share of profits devoted to emissions reduction increases, the decrease in earnings from redirecting investment from production results in lower profits. Consequently, there are fewer funds for emissions reduction than in the baseline, ultimately leading to less environmental well-being.

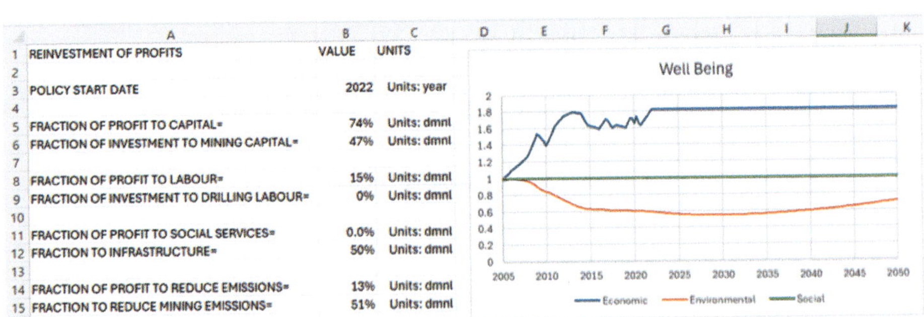

Fig. 15.34: Results with 5% of profits diverted from capital and labour to emissions reduction.

15.9.5 Summary of Policy Results

Across all scenarios, the model reveals clear trade-offs between profitability, environmental sustainability, and social well-being. Reinvestment in labour and social services delivers the most balanced outcomes, while capital-focused strategies exacerbate ecological risks. Emissions reduction policies counterintuitively result in environmental losses because they reduce profits that could be reinvested. Together, these policy runs underscore the complexity involved in reallocating resources away from pure profit maximization and toward broader social and ecological objectives.

15.10 Conclusion

This chapter has demonstrated how system dynamics can be used to explore the sustainability of Canada's oil sands by examining the trade-offs between economic profitability, environmental integrity, and social well-being. The model shows that under baseline conditions, financial performance improves in the short to medium term. Environmental and social outcomes remain weak, highlighting the structural imbalance in the sector's development path. Policy experiments further revealed that shifts in reinvestment strategies produce significant trade-offs: capital-focused growth undermines sustainability, while reinvestment in labour and social services yields more balanced outcomes.

One of the most interesting and counterintuitive results arises from the scenario that diverts 5% of profits reinvestment from capital and labour to emissions reduction. Intuitively, one might expect this policy to improve environmental well-being; however, the model shows a decline instead. The explanation lies in the profit dynamics: by reducing reinvestment in production, overall profitability falls, leaving fewer total funds available for emissions-reduction measures than in the baseline. As a result, despite the higher share of profits allocated to environmental mitigation, the absolute level of investment remains lower, resulting in worse environmental outcomes. This result underscores the importance of understanding feedback structures; well-intentioned policies can fail or even backfire if they inadvertently weaken the very resource base that sustains their implementation.

A central contribution of this work lies in the translation of a large-scale Vensim model into Excel. The Excel-based approach delivers three distinct advantages. First, it lowers the barrier to entry, making advanced system dynamics models accessible to policymakers, students, and practitioners who may not be familiar with specialized simulation software. Second, Excel provides transparency; assumptions, parameters, and results are visible and modifiable in a familiar environment, fostering experimentation and learning. Third, the integration of calibration tools, lookup tables, and policy experiments within Excel enables rapid scenario testing and sensitivity analysis, eliminating the need for advanced technical training.

The ability to embed the model in Excel ensures that the discussion of sustainability is not limited to experts but can be broadened to include a wider community of decision-makers and stakeholders. This accessibility is crucial in a sector where the social, environmental, and economic stakes are deeply interconnected and widely debated.

In conclusion, while no model can predict the future of Canada's oil sands with certainty, this Excel-based system dynamics framework provides a robust tool for exploring alternative pathways and their implications. It demonstrates that sustainability requires deliberate choices about reinvestment priorities and highlights how transparent, accessible modelling can support more informed policy dialogue. Future work should extend this framework to include regulatory shifts, Indigenous perspectives, and global energy transitions, ensuring that the model continues to provide relevant insights in a rapidly changing world.

15.11 Discussion Questions

- What are the main economic, social, and environmental trade-offs associated with oil sands development, and how does system dynamics help us explore them?
- How do reinforcing and balancing feedback loops influence the long-term sustainability of the oil sands sector?
- Why is calibration essential in system dynamics modelling, and how does the Excel implementation facilitate this process?
- The chapter highlights a counterintuitive result: diverting profits to emissions reduction lowers environmental well-being. Why does this occur, and what does it reveal about policy design?
- From a policymaker's perspective, how might the accessibility of Excel-based models influence stakeholder engagement and decision-making?
- What role should Indigenous perspectives and global energy transitions play in future modelling of the oil sands sector?

15.12 Exercises

15.12.1 Model interpretation
Task: Using the causal loop diagram (Fig. 15.5), enumerate all feedback loops, classify each as reinforcing or balancing, and explain each loop's contribution to sector-level sustainability challenges.
Deliverable: One-page loop inventory (table) with: loop ID, variable list/order, R/B classification, concise narrative on sustainability impact; plus, a marked-up causal loop diagram (CLD) image with loop labels.

15.12.2 Excel exploration

Task: Build a minimal stock-and-flow model in Excel (e.g. reserves → production) with explicit formulas and a time base; run a baseline and vary a single parameter (e.g. extraction rate) to observe behaviour over time.

Deliverable: Excel workbook with separate tabs for: parameters, equations, simulation, and charts. Include a scatter chart comparing baseline versus experiment and a five- to seven-sentence interpretation.

15.12.3 Calibration practice

Task: Import a small dataset (e.g. emissions per barrel, 2011–2018) and calibrate relevant parameters using Excel Solver to minimize SSE (or another stated objective).

Deliverable: Calibration report (half page) listing: calibrated parameter values, objective metric, constraints, Solver settings; overlay chart (historical vs. simulated) and a short goodness-of-fit assessment.

15.12.4 Policy simulation

Task: Implement a baseline scenario, then simulate one policy (e.g. divert 10% of profits from capital to labour). Track economic, social, and environmental indicators and compare outcomes.

Deliverable: Two charts (baseline vs. policy) and a 200- to 300-word policy memo summarizing directional changes, trade-offs, and a clear recommendation.

15.12.5 Counterintuitive dynamics

Task: Analyse the emissions-reduction reinvestment case to explain why observed outcomes contradict intuition; propose an alternative policy that produces genuine environmental improvement.

Deliverable: Short essay (300–400 words) with causal reasoning tied to feedback structure and a bullet list of the proposed policy's expected loop effects.

15.12.6 Critical reflection

Task: Evaluate whether Excel-based system dynamics models are "good enough" for real-world energy policy relative to Vensim; specify where Excel's transparency is a net benefit vs. a liability.

Deliverable: One-page comparative brief with criteria (modelling capability, calibration, sensitivity, transparency, auditability, scalability), a use-case matrix (Excel vs. system dynamics tools), and a bottom-line recommendation.

Chapter 16
Conclusion

16.1 Learning Objectives

- Consolidate your understanding of system dynamics modelling and simulation in Excel by reflecting on the whole sequence of modelling steps and their integration into managerial decision-making.
- Explain the advantages of using Excel for developing and testing system dynamics models, particularly for exploring dynamic complexity in business contexts.
- Critically evaluate the policy insights that emerge from model-based experimentation, including counterintuitive results that challenge traditional managerial thinking.
- Extend the skills acquired in this course to real-world business problems, demonstrating the transferability of system dynamics methods across sectors and decision environments.

16.2 Introduction

This book has taken you on a journey through the principles and applications of system dynamics modelling and simulation, using Excel as both the medium of instruction and the modelling environment. The intention has been to make the powerful insights of system dynamics accessible to those who may not have prior experience with quantitative modelling, but who are accustomed to using Excel as a core analytical tool in their studies and professional careers. What began in Chapter 1 with a simple introduction to the logic of feedback has evolved into a structured methodology for addressing complex managerial and policy issues. This concluding chapter draws the threads together, revisiting the significant themes of the book and highlighting the enduring lessons that we should take from them as we apply system dynamics in practice.

16.3 Part 1: Building the Foundations

Chapters 1 through 8 provided the conceptual and practical foundations of system dynamics. The discussion began with the recognition that many of the most pressing problems in management and policy are dynamic, interconnected, and counterintuitive in nature. Traditional tools of analysis, while effective for static problems, often fall short when feedback processes, delays, and nonlinearities shape outcomes. System dynamics offers a disciplined approach to understanding such complexity. Through the use of

https://doi.org/10.1515/9783111541389-018

causal loop diagrams, we learned how to map reinforcing and balancing feedback structures, seeing how small changes can amplify over time or how corrective actions can stabilize systems. These visual tools provided an essential first step, helping us to think dynamically rather than statically.

The transition from conceptual diagrams to stock-and-flow models in Excel marked a critical step in the learning process. By translating causal hypotheses into formal structures, we could simulate system behaviour and compare results with observed patterns. Chapters on model formulation emphasized that the goal is not to replicate reality in exhaustive detail but to capture the essential dynamics that drive behaviour. We learned to distinguish between levels (stocks) and rates (flows), as well as auxiliary variables, appreciating how accumulation and delay generate dynamic complexity. Working in Excel reinforced the idea that one does not need specialized software to begin building meaningful models. Instead, Excel serves as an accessible platform where formulas, charts, and simulations can be combined to produce valuable insights.

Throughout this first part, by specifying expected patterns of behaviour and articulating causal explanations, we developed the discipline of aligning models with both data and theory. This process instilled the lesson that modelling is as much about communication as computation. A well-structured reference mode provides a narrative that stakeholders can engage with, critique, and refine. In this way, the early chapters not only built technical competence but also laid the foundations for collaborative problem-solving.

16.4 Part 2: Expanding into Application

Chapters 9 through 15 deepened and broadened the learning, moving from foundation-building to application. Here, we engaged with calibration, baseline development, and policy design. The discussion of calibration emphasized that models gain credibility not simply by being plausible but by demonstrating consistency with both historical data and reasonable assumptions about underlying processes. Excel's optimization and Solver tools enabled us to fit model parameters to observed data, thereby bridging the gap between conceptual structures and empirical evidence. This process also taught the humility required in modelling: calibration is not a mechanical exercise but an iterative dialogue between model, data, and judgment.

The development of baseline cases highlighted the importance of establishing a reference scenario before exploring policy interventions. By constructing a baseline, we learned to assess whether the model reproduces historical trends and whether it provides a credible projection of future behaviour under current assumptions. This step underscored that policy analysis without a baseline is meaningless. Without understanding where the system is heading without interventions, one cannot evaluate the impact of proposed strategies.

The exploration of policy results showcased one of the most potent aspects of system dynamics: its ability to reveal counterintuitive outcomes. We observed how well-intentioned interventions can backfire, how delays in perception and action can exacerbate problems, and how reallocating resources can lead to trade-offs among competing objectives. In particular, the diversion of profit reinvestment from capital and labour to emissions reduction provided a vivid example of how pursuing sustainability goals can alter growth trajectories in ways that managers may not anticipate. By simulating such scenarios in Excel, we experienced first hand the power of modelling to challenge intuition and sharpen strategic thinking.

Scenario design rounded out the advanced topics, showing that uncertainty is not an obstacle to modelling but a central feature to be embraced. By testing how outcomes vary under different assumptions, managers can identify robust strategies that perform well across a range of futures rather than optimizing for a single forecast. This principle is especially valuable in turbulent environments, where adaptability and resilience are as important as efficiency.

16.5 Lessons for Management Practice

Taken together, the two parts of this book illustrate a comprehensive workflow for system dynamics modelling, from problem definition to hypothesis building, model construction, calibration, validation, and policy design. But beyond the technical steps, several enduring lessons stand out.

First, system dynamics cultivates a mindset that is indispensable for modern managers. It trains us to seek feedback, anticipate potential delays, and consider unintended consequences. These habits are not confined to modelling exercises; they extend into everyday management practice, from supply chain decisions to marketing strategies to organizational design.

Second, Excel-based modelling demonstrates that system dynamics is not restricted to specialists or advanced software users. By leveraging a familiar tool, this book has shown that we can engage directly in model building, rather than outsourcing the task to technical experts. This accessibility democratizes modelling, enabling managers to test ideas, communicate insights, and participate actively in analytical discussions.

Third, the iterative nature of modelling emphasizes that learning is continuous. Models are never final; they are evolving representations that improve as more data, experience, and stakeholder input are incorporated. For managers, this means that modelling should not be seen as a one-off project but as an ongoing practice of organizational learning.

Ultimately, system dynamics underscores the strategic importance of long-term thinking. In a world where quarterly results often dominate managerial attention, system dynamics encourages leaders to look beyond the immediate horizon, considering sustainability, resilience, and the systemic impact of their decisions. By cultivating this perspective, managers are better equipped to navigate complexity and lead organizations toward enduring success.

16.6 Looking Ahead

While this book concludes here, the journey of system dynamics continues. The models presented in Part 1 were deliberately simplified to serve as learning tools; however, the methods were scalable to larger, more detailed applications, as shown in Part 2. Specialized software packages exist, but the fundamental principles remain the same: system dynamics in Excel can be highly effective in many ways. For us, the challenge is to carry forward the mindset cultivated in these chapters: to think dynamically, to act systemically, and to lead responsibly.

In closing, system dynamics offers more than a set of techniques; it offers a way of seeing the world. Excel provides the means to put that vision into practice in a manner that is accessible, transparent, and immediately applicable. Together, they form a powerful combination for managers who aspire to make better decisions in an increasingly complex and interconnected world. The hope is that this book has not only equipped you with skills but also inspired you to apply them: to question assumptions, to test strategies, and to embrace the discipline of learning from dynamic systems. In doing so, you will be better prepared to face the managerial challenges of today and tomorrow.

16.7 Discussion Questions

- Looking back across the entire book, which aspect of system dynamics modelling do you believe is most valuable for business leaders, and why?
- Several chapters highlighted counterintuitive policy results. How should managers prepare themselves to recognize and respond to such unexpected outcomes in practice?
- Excel is not traditionally considered a simulation tool, yet this book demonstrates its effectiveness. What are the trade-offs of using Excel compared to specialized system dynamics software?
- If you were to advise a management team on implementing system dynamics thinking, how would you explain the relevance of feedback loops, delays, and nonlinearity without overwhelming them?
- How can system dynamics models be used not only to solve immediate problems but also to foster a culture of long-term, systemic thinking in organizations?

16.8 Exercises

16.8.1 Integrative model build
Task: In Excel, build a compact end-to-end system dynamics model covering: problem definition, reference mode, dynamic hypothesis, model formulation, calibration, baseline, and one policy. Choose any domain (e.g. workforce planning, customer retention, sustainability).
Deliverable: Excel workbook with tabs: *Data, Structure (equations), Parameters, Baseline, Policy, Charts*. One side-by-side chart: baseline versus policy on key performance indicators. A 200- to 300-word lessons-learned note capturing scope, key feedback, fit quality, and decision takeaway.

16.8.2 Counterintuitive outcomes
Task: Take a prior chapter model and implement a policy that appears beneficial at first glance; run and evaluate whether results align with intuition. Diagnose using feedback loops and delays.
Deliverable: Updated Excel workbook (add *Policy Test* tab) with changed assumptions highlighted. Overlay chart(s) showing baseline versus policy over time. A 250- to 350-word explanation referencing specific loops/delays causing the observed behaviour, plus a one-sentence recommendation.

16.8.3 Managerial application
Task: Select a live management problem from your experience. Define objectives, stakeholders, performance indicators, and time horizon; outline how an Excel-based system dynamics model would structure the problem, test scenarios, and inform policy.
Deliverable: One-page executive summary for a management audience, including: problem statement, proposed model boundary, key stocks/flows, data needs, scenario set, evaluation criteria, and expected benefits. Slide (single page) with a simple CLD or stock-and-flow sketch plus a three-step action plan (build → test → decide).

References

[1] Forrester, J. W. Industrial Dynamics. Cambridge, Massachusetts, United States, MIT Press, 1961.
[2] Forrester, J. W. Urban Dynamics. Cambridge, Massachusetts, United States, MIT Press, 1969.
[3] Forrester, J. W. World Dynamics. Cambridge, Massachusetts, United States, Wright-Allen Press, 1971.
[4] Meadows, D. H., Meadows, D. L., Randers, J., Behrens, W. W. The Limits to Growth. Washington, D.C., United States, Potomac Associates, 1972.
[5] System Dynamics Society. (Accessed Sep. 10, 2024 at https://systemdynamics.org).
[6] System Dynamics Society. System Dynamics Society Conferences. (Accessed Sep. 10, 2024 at https://systemdynamics.org/conference/).
[7] Ventana Systems, Inc. Vensim. (Accessed Sep. 10, 2024 at https://www.vensim.com).
[8] isee systems, inc. Stella. (Accessed Sep. 10, 2024 at https://www.iseesystems.com).
[9] Powersim Software AS. Powersim. (Accessed Sep. 10, 2024 at https://www.powersim.com).
[10] Senge, P. M. The Fifth Discipline: The Art and Practice of the Learning Organization. New York, New York, United States, Doubleday/Currency, 1990.
[11] Sterman, J. D. Business Dynamics: Systems Thinking and Modeling for a Complex World. Boston, Massachusetts, United States, Irwin McGraw-Hill, 2000.
[12] Microsoft Corporation. Microsoft Excel. (Accessed Sep. 10, 2024 at https://www.microsoft.com/excel).
[13] Saltelli, A., Tarantola, S., Campolongo, F. Sensitivity analysis as an ingredient of modeling. Statistical Science, 2000, 15(4), 377–395.
[14] Homer, J. B., Hirsch, G. B. System dynamics modeling for public health: Background and opportunities. American Journal of Public Health, 2006, 96(3), 452–458.
[15] Ford, A. Modeling the Environment: An Introduction to System Dynamics Models of Environmental Systems. Washington, D.C., United States, Island Press, 1999.
[16] Cavana, R. Y., Dangerfield, B. C., Pavlov, O. V., Radzicki, M. J., Wheat, I. D. Feedback Economics: Economic Modeling with System Dynamics. Cham, Switzerland, Springer Nature, 2021.
[17] Vanderby, S., Carter, M. W. An evaluation of the applicability of system dynamics to patient flow modelling. Journal of the Operational Research Society, 2010, 61(11), 1572–1581.
[18] Wang, Y., Hu, B., Zhao, Y., Kuang, G., Zhao, Y., Liu, Q., Zhu, X. Applications of system dynamics models in chronic disease prevention: A systematic review. Preventing Chronic Disease, 2021, 18, 210175.
[19] Sterman, J. D., Booth Sweeney, L. Cloudy skies: Assessing public understanding of global warming. System Dynamics Review, 2002, 18(2), 207–240.
[20] Ford, A. System dynamics and the electric power industry. System Dynamics Review, 1996, 12(1), 57–85.
[21] Akkermans, H. A., Van Oorschot, K. E. Developing a balanced scorecard with system dynamics. Journal of the Operational Research Society, 2005, 56(8), 931–941.
[22] Shepherd, S. P. A review of system dynamics models applied in transportation. Transportmetrica B: Transport Dynamics, 2014, 2(2), 83–105.
[23] Groff, J. S. Dynamic systems modeling in educational system design and policy. New Approaches in Educational Research, 2013, 2(2), 72–81.
[24] AnyLogic Company. 2024. AnyLogic (Version 8.7.10). (Accessed Sep. 10, 2024 at https://www.any logic.com).
[25] Fortmann-Roe, S. Insight Maker (Version 5.0). (Accessed Sep. 10, 2024 at https://insightmaker.com).
[26] Callaham, J. There are now 1.2 billion Office users and 60 million Office 365 commercial customers. Windows Central. Nov. 19, 2018. (Accessed Sep. 10, 2024 at https://www.windowscentral.com/there-are-now-12-billion-office-users-60-million-office-365-commercial-customers).
[27] Butcher, J. C. Numerical Methods for Ordinary Differential Equations. Chichester, West Sussex, England, John Wiley & Sons, 2008.

https://doi.org/10.1515/9783111541389-019

[28] Richmond, B. (1994). Systems thinking/system dynamics: Let's just get on with it. System Dynamics Review, 10(2–3), 135–157.

[29] Ventana Systems. (n.d.). "Vensim® PLE Plus". (Accessed May 13, 2024 at https://vensim.com/vensim-ple-plus/).

[30] Kirkwood, C. (n.d.). "Vensim® PLE Quick Reference and Tutorial". Arizona State University, (Accessed May 13, 2024, at https://www.public.asu.edu/~kirkwood/sysdyn/VenPLE.pdf).

[31] Ventana Systems. (2017). "Building A Simple Vensim Model". (Accessed May 13, 2024, at https://www.youtube.com/watch?v=0JsI9ZYPS54).

[32] Hougton, J. "Vensim Tutorials". 2019. (Accessed May 13, 2024, at https://www.youtube.com/playlist?list=PLjztUIYQYXduYTpNtDwfbe6G4DXAbiB).

[33] Technology for Teachers and Students. (2022). "Excel for Beginners – The Complete Course". (Accessed May 13, 2024, at https://www.youtube.com/watch?v=wbJcJCkBcMg).

[34] DCP Web Designer. (n.d.). "Libre Office 7 Calc Spreadsheets Beginners Tutorial". (Accessed May 13, 2024, at https://www.youtube.com/watch?v=bgO40-CjYNY).

[35] Coupler.io Academy. "Google Sheets Tutorial for Beginners". (n.d.) (Accessed May 13, 2024, at https://www.youtube.com/watch?v=FIkZ1sPmKNw).

[36] Our World in Data (2026), Population Growth, (Accessed January 24, 2026, at https://ourworldindata.org/population-growth).

[37] US Treasury, Fiscal Data. (Accessed October 18, 2025, at https://fiscaldata.treasury.gov/datasets/historical-debt-outstanding/historical-debt-outstanding).

[38] United Nations, Department of Economic and Social Affairs, Population Division. (2024). World Population Prospects 2024: Data Sources. (UN DESA/POP/2024). (Accessed November 23, 2024, at https://population.un.org/wpp/Download/Standard/MostUsed/).

[39] Homer, J. Best practices in system dynamics modeling, revisited: A practitioner's view. System Dynamics Review, 2019, 35(2), 177–181.

[40] Mishra, V., Koul, S., Taylor, I. W. The Carbon Footprint of Large Language Models: The Case of ChatGPT. In: Presented at the 2025 International System Dynamics Conference. Boston, USA, August 4–8, 2025.

[41] Shamsuddoha, M., Koul, S., Taylor, I. W. Eco-efficient dairy waste treatment: Validating a sustainable system dynamics framework. Operations Research Forum, 2024, 5(12).

[42] Taylor, I. W. Using System Dynamics to Examine Alternative Futures for the Syrian Refugee Crisis. In: Leclair, P. (ed) Refugee Crisis: Global Perspectives, Challenges and Issues. 2020, Nova Science Publishers, Hauppauge, New York, United States, 2020.

[43] Mishra, V., Koul, S., Taylor, I. W. Digital Twin for Diabetes Management Using System Dynamics Simulation – The Case of India. In: Singh, J.P., Singh, M.P., Singh, A.K., Mukhopadhyay, S., Mandal, J.K., Dutta, P. (eds) Computational Intelligence in Communications and Business Analytics. CICBA 2024. Communications in Computer and Information Science, vol 2366. Springer, Cham. Switzerland, 2025.

[44] Taylor, I., Isbrandt, S., Rich, E., Vogel, M. A model to assist leaders increase diversity in their organizations. Presented at the 2021 International System Dynamics Conference, Virtually Chicago, USA, August 4–8, 2025. (Accessed November 3, 2025, at https://proceedings.systemdynamics.org/2021/papers/P1319.pdf).

[45] Koul, S., Taylor, I. W., Falebita, O. A., Ono, T., Chen, R., Vogel, M. T. Examining the success of women of colour-owned small and medium-sized enterprises in the United States: A system dynamics perspective. International Entrepreneurial Management Journal, 2022, 18, 1373–1401.

[46] Falebita, O. A., Koul, S., Taylor, I. W. Unconventional energy resources: A system dynamics evaluation of social, environmental and economic aspects. International Journal of Energy and Environmental Engineering, 2022, 13, 483–498.

Index

https://doi.org/10.1515/9783111541389-020

Printed and bound by CPI Group (UK) Ltd, Croydon, CR0 4YY
13/09/2026
14960853-0002